Averting Global War

Averting Global War

Regional Challenges, Overextension, and Options for American Strategy

Hall Gardner

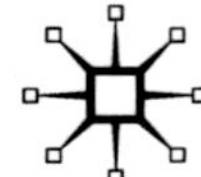

AVERTING GLOBAL WAR
Copyright © Hall Gardner, 2007.

First published in hardcover in 2007 by PALGRAVE MACMILLAN® in the United States—a division of St. Martin's Press LLC, 175 Fifth Avenue, New York, NY 10010.

Where this book is distributed in the UK, Europe and the rest of the world, this is by Palgrave Macmillan, a division of Macmillan Publishers Limited, registered in England, company number 785998, of Houndmills, Basingstoke, Hampshire RG21 6XS.

Palgrave Macmillan is the global academic imprint of the above companies and has companies and representatives throughout the world.

Palgrave® and Macmillan® are registered trademarks in the United States, the United Kingdom, Europe and other countries.

ISBN: 978-0-230-60086-7

Library of Congress Cataloging-in-Publication Data

Gardner, Hall.
  Averting global war : regional challenges, overextension, and options for American strategy / Hall Gardner.
    p. cm.
  Includes bibliographical references and index.
    ISBN 0-230-60085-9 (hardcover : alk. paper)—ISBN 0-230-60086-7 (pbk. : alk. paper)
  1. War—Prevention—International cooperation. 2. Conflict management—Case studies. 3. Geopolitics. I. Title.

JZ6387.G37 2007
355'.033073—dc22   2007018466

A catalogue record of the book is available from the British Library.

Design by Scribe Inc.

First PALGRAVE MACMILLAN paperback edition: May 2010

Transferred to Digital Printing in 2010.

Printed in the United States of America.

For my family, once again

Upon the breaking and shivering of a great state and empire, you may be sure to have wars. . . . The great accessions and unions of kingdoms do likewise stir up wars; for when a state grows to an over-power, it is like a great flood, that will be sure to overflow. . . . When a warlike state grows soft and effeminate, they may be sure of a war. For commonly such states are grown rich in the time of their degenerating; and so the prey inviteth, and their decay in valor, encourageth a war.

—Francis Bacon (1561–1626), "Of Vicissitude of Things"

Contents

Preface

The purpose of *Averting Global War: Regional Challenges, Overexten-sion, and Options for American Strategy* is to develop a more concilia-tory U.S. strategy intended to resolve key international disputes and conflicts that have arisen since the September 11, 2001 attacks on the World Trade Center and Pentagon—or at least attempt to transform those disputes and conflicts in such a way that they not further "widen" or possibly draw major pow-ers into confrontation. The book argues that shifting post–cold war alliance and power relationships at the global, regional, and domestic levels; the introduction of revolutionary military technologies and strategies, including asymmetrical tactics of warfare; conflicting irredentist claims; the quest for guaranteed access to energy supplies and trade; and the protection of "vital" spheres of interest and security have all augmented the likelihood of even wider regional conflicts—if not a major power war—given the increasingly fractious nature of major and regional power rivalries coupled with significant acts of "terrorism."

The book accordingly examines both domestic U.S. and international debates and responses to a number of major international disputes, conflicts, and crises. It concludes by arguing that the next U.S. administration, whether Democratic or Republican, will need to work diligently to forge a truly multilateral strategy, along with both "democratic liberal" and "illiberal" major and regional powers, in the formation of cooperative and interlocking patchworks of "regional security communities" that are intended to stabilize—and then develop—volatile areas throughout the planet—if the very real possibility of major power war is to be averted in the not-so-distant future.

In attempting to identify differing species of foreign policy makers, I have out-lined an ornithology of hawks, doves, owls, eagles, ostriches, gulls, vultures, super hawks, and chicken hawks whose explicit meanings in reference to U.S. foreign policy are defined in Chapter 10. In the effort to prevent wider conflicts, I have urged American policy makers to adopt an "owlish" geostrategy, with the under-standing that owls as birds of prey represent realists, but they also symbolize fore-sight (in that they can look in all directions) in the Occidental tradition stemming from ancient Greece.

And yet, as we are increasingly confronted with multicultural perspectives in this era of "globalization," I subsequently learned that owls can represent birds of ill omen in Arabic and Persian cultures, whereas in ancient Egypt owls were considered more positively as guardians of the Afterworld. In Hebrew folklore, owls symbolize blindness and desolation. One can add that in China the owl is associated with lightning, noise (drums), and energy, implying excessive yang or male-oriented, perhaps military, activities. One could add different meanings for owls in Russia, India, Japan, and elsewhere, plus various organizations that have adopted the owl as an emblem. Even in American culture, screech owls, for example, can represent the demonic.

My point is that what is considered a wise, "owlish" strategy from the American and European perspective (although in Polish folklore owls are linked to sickness and death!) might not convey wisdom in some of the very countries that most concern this book. It could actually signify the exact opposite of what was intended, hence resulting in misunderstanding and suspicion, if not conflict! It is consequently only through engaged dialogue that that we can begin to understand the full meaning(s) of our conceptions, intent, and ultimate goals. It is only through dialogue and diplomacy that we can begin to reach compromise, or at least agree to disagree, without turning to violence to assert our preconceptions and interests. Let us accordingly hope that the owl of the future has enough foresight to break significantly with the past so as to take on new meanings, becoming the guardian of a global peace dedicated to full human development with a modicum of justice and in more conscientious interaction with the planet's natural environment.

A number of these chapters were based on papers or speeches delivered at various conferences but have been rewritten and integrated in such a way as to form a coherent whole. The first chapter, "Triptych of Terrorism," was based on my speech at the conference on "Transatlantic Security Dialogue," organized by the Istituto Affari Internazionali and held on February 28, 2006, in Brussels; my chapter on Russia and NATO was based in part on my presentation on the "wider" Black Sea region at the Cicero Foundation Conference, "The Coming Enlargement with Romania, Bulgaria and Croatia," held on October 13, 2006, in Paris, while my chapter on "The Three Dimensions of 'Montezuma's Revenge'" was based, in part, on my lecture on Central American migration in the United States, again at a Cicero Foundation conference, "Integrating Migrants in Europe," held in June 2005 in Paris. The original version of my chapter on North Korea was additionally published by the Cicero Foundation in June 2006. My concept of "regional security communities" was developed in my seminar discussion at the October 2006 World Political Forum in Bosco Marengo, Italy, while my chapter on the Iraqi crisis was based in part on my testimony, "American Policy toward the 'Greater Middle East' after the November 2006 U.S. Mid-Term Congressional Elections," which was delivered at the Assemblée Nationale for the Commission des affaires étrangères in Paris on February 7, 2007.

I would like to thank my editor, Toby Wahl, and the editorial staff at Palgrave for seeing this project through, plus my former student, Jung Woo Lee, for volunteering to work on the Index. The views expressed are, of course, my own responsibility.

Preface: 2010 Edition

Since first completing this book in September 2007, a number of events have pointed to the ongoing spread and intensification of conflicts throughout the world. Although scenarios involving major power warfare have generally been downplayed, the August 2008 Georgia-Russia conflict (predicted as a possibility in Chapters 2 and 10) did raise the specter of major power warfare—provoked accidentally on purpose. If the United States, the North Atlantic Treaty Organization (NATO), the European Union (EU), and Russia cannot soon develop and implement a new European security architecture, a future confrontation between Russia and NATO cannot be excluded. Such a clash could potentially be sparked as Moscow seeks to safeguard its "near abroad" and acts to check a "Baltic-Black Sea" alliance while an expanding NATO and EU seek to protect eastern European states against Russian pressures and to secure energy transit routes.

It is furthermore not impossible that the nuclear and ballistic missile programs of North Korea and Iran—each provoking spiraling "insecurity-security dialectics" that spread threat perceptions to states throughout each region—could potentially draw Russia or China into opposing sides against the United States if concerted efforts fail to prevent a potentially destabilizing arms race in both the so-called Greater Middle East and Northeast Asia (see Chapters 1, 3, 7, and 10). While China promised negotiations in March 2009 leading to a peace treaty based on the "one-China policy," Chinese-Taiwanese suspicions have remained high at the same time that domestic dissent within China has not abated. The precautionary measures taken by Beijing against potential protesters during the twentieth anniversary of the June 1989 Tiananmen Square crackdown have revealed the government's continuing fears of internal dissent and political opposition. At that time, in the spring of 1989, both Taiwan and the United States had been accused of abetting the prodemocracy movement that was regarded by Chinese hardliners as a threat to Communist Party rule. Communist Party hardliners then chose the path of repression, rather than that of engaged political reforms. The situation has not entirely improved: by the end of 2009, the Obama administration pressed for major arms sales to Taiwan to counter Chinese military capabilities—resulting in Chinese counterthreats (see Chapter 8).

As different regional conflict zones interlink and overlap in strategic terms, conflicts in Iraq, Afghanistan, and Pakistan and between the Israelis and the Palestinians continue to fuel the so-called global war on terrorism—with no clear end in sight. This appears true given the efforts of violent, largely decentralized pan-Islamist cells to destabilize a number of states while concurrently plotting against U.S. and European targets (if not targets in India, Russia, China, as well as Arab and Islamic countries). It is also clear that the December 2008 Israeli thrust into Gaza appeared almost inevitable given the failure of the Bush administration and the Quartet Group to make progress on Israeli-Palestinian peace negotiations and the inability of Hamas and Fatah to resolve their disputes. The situation in Afghanistan and Pakistan has deteriorated perhaps much more rapidly than this book first anticipated in 2007—with the real danger of a sociopolitical destabilization of nuclear Pakistan following U.S. and Pakistani military efforts to eradicate Taliban and Al-Qaeda elements in northwest Pakistan. President Obama's decision to withdraw forces "responsibly" from Iraq has been met with significant acts of terrorism intended to destabilize the present Iraqi government after U.S. troops leave. For its part, Tehran has reacted to Obama's promises of direct negotiations with mixed views, but the United States will need to assess the outcome of the chaotic June 2009 Iranian presidential elections before it can implement a coherent strategy. There is a real danger that domestic Iranian instability, combined with Israeli-Saudi-Iranian rivalry, could draw the Gulf states, as well as the United States, into conflict with Iran—if the United States, the UN Security Council, and Iran cannot find face-saving ways to resolve their differences and begin serious negotiations (see Chapters 3, 4, 5, 6, 10, and postscript). On the one hand, global financial and foreign policy crises have become increasingly problematic and destabilizing; on the other, the Obama administration will need to focus more attentively on U.S. domestic concerns and on America's own backyard—in that the drug wars along the U.S.-Mexican border have, for example, escalated since this book was written (see Chapter 9 and postscript).

President Obama will consequently need to tackle tough dilemmas in each region—for the most part through "owlish" multilateral and "dovish" concerted approaches. Yet, if multilateral and concerted efforts fail, the United States will still need to keep a number of unilateral options open. At the same time, however, it is not at all clear how unilateral "eagle-like" U.S. military actions can succeed in stabilizing a number of regions in turmoil *in the long term*. (For an ornithology of foreign policy birds, see the original preface and Chapter 10.) The global crisis will accordingly require profound diplomatic engagement on the part of the Obama administration in order to work in a concerted manner with both allies and former rivals—in order to stabilize and pacify zones of conflict with effective international development assistance and overlapping multilateral security supports that concurrently seek to address human rights violations and environmental concerns—while working to establish a modicum of justice through engaged dialogue and reconciliation.

Let us hope the Obama administration can pick the right combination of foreign policy birds (owls, doves, or eagles) out of its hat to avert an even greater catastrophe than the world is presently confronting—a crisis that is so profoundly shaking the confidence and legitimacy of the entire post–cold war, post–September 11 international and interstate system.

—Paris, February 2010

INTRODUCTION

"Crying Wolf" Once Again?

"Crying Wolf!" during the Cold War

Judging by the output of fiction with nuclear themes, coupled with movies, spy novels, folk music, poetry, and political analysis, the fear of nuclear war between the United States and Soviet Union (and China) pervaded much of the popular "underground" spirit during the cold war, particularly during the period from 1980 to 1989.[1] U.S. and European peace and "antinuclear" movements urged radical reductions in nuclear weapons—in the fear that the "arms race" would inevitably lead to conventional conflict, if not to nuclear war.

The largely unexpected end of the cold war in the 1986–1989 period consequently appeared to make the antinuclear and peace movements look like little boys and girls who "cried wolf!" far too many times. Although "doves" could argue that the end of the cold war was a consequence of unilateral concessions on the part of an enlightened Soviet leadership, "hawks" could argue that it was U.S. and NATO nuclear and conventional force *superiority* that had impelled Soviet withdrawal from Eastern Europe and the subsequent collapse of the Warsaw Pact.

Although the cold war conflicts protested by U.S. and European peace movements had decimated a number of societies in "peripheral" regions in Asia and Africa as well as in Central and Latin America, what became known as the "long cold war peace" did not bring with it a *direct* conventional or nuclear confrontation between the two superpowers (except for a few very dangerous historical moments involving nuclear "brinkmanship").[2] The cold war did, however, directly or indirectly cause as many as twenty to twenty five million deaths with the use of conventional weaponry in interstate conflict (or as much as seventy-six million deaths including intrastate "genocide" and "democide" in the period 1947–1987)[3]—and left hundreds of millions of landmines scattered throughout dozens of war-torn countries.[4]

The hopes raised by the peaceful razing of the Berlin Wall, which resulted in the "liberation" of Eastern Europe from Soviet controls, and the much trumpeted "victory" of the forces of "liberal democracy" over those of totalitarianism, however, did not set the stage for the peaceful settlement of disputes throughout the planet, nor did it result in a much anticipated "peace dividend" despite a considerable reduction in military expenditure during the administration of Bill Clinton.

While the Solidarity movement in Poland and the Velvet Revolution in Czechoslovakia helped to liberate much of Eastern Europe peacefully from Soviet controls, the collapse of indirect Soviet military pressures and influence over Yugoslavia worked to unleash secessionist movements that opposed the Communist regime established by Marshall Josip Broz Tito. Moreover, the Chinese leadership largely justified the June 1989 Tiananmen Square crackdown on pro-democracy activists as a means to prevent a Polish-style solidarity movement that it claimed would eventually result in China's disaggregation. Challenged by a democracy movement from within, the Chinese Communist leadership opted for a dual policy of repression and co-optation through appeals to nationalism and patriotism that has involved a general militarization in defense of "Socialist spiritual civilization" and for unification with Taiwan. (See Chapter 8.)

Contrary to the hopes raised at the end of the cold war, the largely unforeseen collapse of the Soviet Union in August 1991 has continued to send shock waves throughout the planet by opening up a wider zone of actual or potential conflict, plus terrorist and black market activities, in the Balkans, eastern Europe, the wider Black Sea region, the Caucasus, central Asia, as well as much of Africa and the Middle East more indirectly—followed by the rise of an unstable, and increasingly authoritarian, Russia. Here, for example, a particularly tense situation arose in the period from 1991 to 1994 when Ukraine (but also Belarus and Kazakhstan) threatened to hold onto large stockpiles of former Soviet nuclear weaponry—leading Moscow, in turn, to threaten preemptive action against Kiev in particular. Belarus, Kazakhstan, and Ukraine eventually returned all nuclear warheads to Russia for decommissioning by 1994, but only after being pressured by Moscow and financially assisted by Washington through a mix of multilateral *dissuasion* and *persuasion*. In effect, joint U.S.-Russian cooperation against the spread of weapons of mass destruction (WMD) coupled with multilateral security guarantees for Ukraine granted by the United States, Russia, China, the United Kingdom, and France represented an action that recognized and legitimized Russian primacy over ex-Soviet states but at the same time helped to establish a loose regional security community to guarantee Ukrainian security. (See Chapters 2 and 10.)

By contrast, however, while joint U.S.-Russian cooperation helped to prevent the spread of nuclear capabilities to former Soviet republics, the dual, almost simultaneous, explosion of nuclear "firecrackers" (as one Indian ambassador put it) by both India and Pakistan in 1998, was symbolic of the rise of a highly uneven polycentric global system. Both India and Pakistan were able to develop nuclear capabilities—despite U.S. pressures to check their further spread beyond those already possessed by the five permanent members (P-5) of the UN Security Council. Moreover, while the United States has continued to confront both North Korea and Iran over their potential nuclear weapons capability,

Washington ignored the actual (but undeclared) nuclear capability of Israel and reluctantly accepted the 1998 fait accompli of both India and Pakistan as nuclear weapons states, thus raising accusations of "double standards" by those states that seek a "self help" independent nuclear deterrent.

The collapse of the Soviet empire likewise led to a reassessment of U.S. and European global strategy—resulting in the so-called great NATO enlargement debate. On the one hand, U.S. opponents of NATO enlargement argued for engaging in a truly concerted and multilateral strategy with the new Russian Federation in the effort to implement an all-European system of security by expanding and strengthening the Partnership for Peace Initiative in the form of a "regional security community" that would be backed by NATO, EU, and Russian security guarantees.[5] On the other hand, supporters of NATO enlargement urged the United States to "seize the unipolar moment"[6] in a neo-Wilsonian and neoconservative crusade to "democratize" states throughout the world and to secure those "democratic" gains in eastern Europe in particular through NATO (and EU) enlargement—while concurrently acting to *preclude* the feared possibility of an eventual Russian resurgence.

Initially, the United States and NATO went "out of area" in dealing with the conflicts in Bosnia, largely in cooperation with Russia through multilateral contact group diplomacy, but then opted to turn against Russian interests following NATO intervention in the war "over" Kosovo in 1999 without a clear UN mandate. NATO concurrently took advantage of Russian political economic weakness to expand its membership into central Europe by NATO's fiftieth anniversary in 1999 and then deep into eastern Europe up to the Russian border by 2004. One of the major dilemmas discussed in this book is consequently whether the United States and NATO should continue to expand NATO membership as far as Ukraine and Georgia, or whether the United States, NATO, and the European Union should work to bring Russia and Ukraine into a "regional security community" that would involve greater U.S.-Russian cooperation through the NATO-Russia Council. (See Chapter 2.)

Post-September 11, 2001: "Crying Wolf" Once Again?

The horrific events of September 11, 2001 altered the triumphal mood of neo-Wilsonian and neoconservative "democratic internationalism" considerably. The "bolt from the blue sky" feared by nuclear strategists during the cold war came unexpectedly in non-nuclear form: Four passenger jets—four riders of a mini-apocalypse—evaded U.S. systems of deterrence and manipulated a nonmilitary commercial technology to destroy two major symbols of U.S. prestige and power, the World Trade Center and the Pentagon. The fourth plane was purportedly headed for a third symbolic target, the White House (or possibly for the Fort Detrick bio defense labs or else the Three Mile Island nuclear plant)—but, as is generally portrayed, was brought down by the brave rebellion of its passengers (although it might have been obliterated by a U.S. fighter jet).[7]

It can be added that overreaction to the mini-apocalypse of the September 11 attacks (which had been preceded by attacks on U.S. embassies in Kenya and

Tanzania, among other attacks by burgeoning pan-Islamist movements)—combined with doomsday fears of WMD in the hands of "rogue states"—permitted the administration of George W. Bush to obtain strong public and Congressional support for "preemptive" intervention in Iraq in 2003—without either UN or NATO backing as had been the case for U.S. intervention against al-Qaida and the Taliban in Afghanistan in 2001. It was thus in contemplating formerly "unthinkable" catastrophic scenarios that the Bush administration opted to act "preemptively" in the second Persian Gulf War in March 2003—but without a clear exit strategy and without truly thinking through the ultimate regional consequences and global ramifications. (See Chapters 1, 3, and 10.)

In effect, despite former secretary of defense Donald Rumsfeld's belated regrets for using the term (see Chapter 1), the United States has become fully engaged in a "global war on terror." The danger is that the two faceted nature of that "global war"—as a war against *both* antistate partisan groups willing to use extreme violence to achieve their goals *and* as a war against "rogue" states that seek to develop WMD or that in some other major way attempt to challenge U.S. interests and regional peace—could easily widen, risking U.S. hypertrophy, if not drawing in the major powers at cross purposes as well. In the aftermath of the attacks on September 11, 2001, the United States has expanded its military presence into the Black Sea, the Caucasus, central Asia, and into many areas that were once former Soviet spheres of influence and security. In response, Russia appears to be reasserting its regional predominance with respect to central Asia (in Uzbekistan, for example), the wider Black Sea region, and the Caucasus (by suppressing Chechen secession movements and pressuring Georgia in particular).

Moscow has additionally been threatening the possibility of a new arms rivalry in response to NATO enlargement and the potential deployment of BMDs in eastern Europe. It has likewise been seeking out a closer alliance with China in the formation of the Shanghai Cooperation Organization, and has engaged in major arms sales and military cooperation arrangements, which tacitly back China's irredentist claims to Taiwan. The major goals of Sino-Russian cooperation are to "contain" and influence central Asian states and to check both "Islamist" and "democratic" movements, while strengthening controls over the Russian far east—in addition to countering U.S. and Japanese political, economic, and military influence. (See Chapter 8.) While Moscow has thus far stomached NATO enlargement to its former red line, the Baltic states, it is not absolutely certain that it will accept NATO enlargement to the Ukraine or Georgia. Warnings that NATO enlargement into former Soviet and Russian spheres of influence and security could potentially provoke a Russian backlash, if not provoke wider regional wars, have largely been dismissed as "crying wolf!"— once again. (See Chapter 2.)

Crisis in U.S. Domestic and Foreign Policy

The resurgence of a number of regional powers (not to overlook numerous antistate partisan movements willing to engage in acts of "terrorism") that have begun to challenge U.S. interests—or else the interests of U.S. allies—illustrates the reality of a highly uneven polycentric world system in which states (and partisan movements willing to use extreme violence) possess very different power and force capabilities and differing degrees of political, economic, financial, socio-cultural, ideological, and media influence. At present, there is no countervailing power or group of powers that could possibly check U.S. global expansion. The United States can continue to play "divide and rule" for a period of time but at the risk of being dragged, either accidentally or intentionally (or else "accidentally on purpose"), into wider conflicts. Much like the "sound of one hand clapping," the United States is involved in a "monocontainment" of potentially rival states and antistate partisan movements, at the risk of *hypertrophy*.

Moreover, the September 11 attacks raised significant questions as to the weakness of U.S. domestic security precautions and resulted in the hasty formulation of the PATRIOT Act and the Homeland Security Organization. This fundamental restructuring and centralization of the domestic state security bureaucracies under an increasingly powerful federal government (linked to the military-industrial complex) could further undermine traditional "checks and balances" and permit "exceptional" measures that risk the violation of traditional U.S. freedoms and liberties. It could likewise permit executive military action overseas without strong congressional or judicial oversight and consequently continue to draw the United States into unnecessary conflicts and debacles. Here, for example, President George W. Bush, Jr., has maintained the position that he has the right as commander in chief to maintain troops in Iraq and confront Iran without congressional approval. (See Chapters 3 and 4.)

One of the principal theses of this book is that the goals of U.S. global strategy have been at odds with the dynamic nature of the global market forces and political economy. Despite U.S. military predominance, U.S. global strategy has proved ineffective, if not counterproductive, in a number of crucial areas. U.S. intervention in oil rich Iraq, for example, has not yet reaped the benefits of low cost high quality oil as expected by neoconservative supporters of that intervention. (See Chapters 3, 4, and 9). The general rise in world oil prices is, to a large extent, due to increased Chinese and Indian demand coupled with financial speculation and a lack of adequate refinery capability, not to overlook sociopolitical conflict within major oil producing countries, such as Nigeria and Iraq, which cut back on supply. The rise of world oil prices has nevertheless permitted major U.S. rivals and oil producers such as Russia, Iran, Saudi Arabia, and Venezuela to gain increasing political-economic influence in asserting their own interests or in countering those of the United States, while the major energy consumers (the United States, EU countries, China, India, and Japan) seek to secure guaranteed access to oil and other energy supplies in the long term, in addition to striving for greater political economic influence.

Although the roots of a future global war are not limited to energy and resource issues *alone*, potential conflict revolves among energy consumers in terms of rivalry to obtain *secure access* to energy supplies as inexpensively as possible as well as between energy producers and energy consumers that may be in competition over spheres of influence and security involving conflicting irredentist claims. This tension and rivalry puts greater political, economic, and military pressures on territories with energy reserves, as well as on land-based transport routes and sea lines of communication. Here, for example, China's burgeoning demand for energy has led it to scour the globe in search for guaranteed supplies of energy, which is in potential conflict with India, Japan, as well as the United States. China's burgeoning demand for energy accordingly puts increasing pressure on Taiwan in that Beijing wants to be in a position to control sea lines of communication, trade, and energy transport in Asia so as to guarantee its growing resource demand. As a consequence, China's claims to Taiwan continue to raise tensions with the United States and Japan, which seek to sustain their hegemonic control over those sea lines of communication. Concurrently, the U.S. addiction to cheap Chinese products, coupled with China's massive foreign exchange reserves and savings, has had the effect of weakening U.S. strategic and political economic leverage in engaging Beijing over issues affecting North Korea, Iran, and Taiwan, among other issues. (See Chapters 3, 6, 7, and 8.)

In addition, contrary to its intent, U.S. intervention in both Afghanistan and Iraq has tended to foster even greater terrorist activity by providing new causes for jihadist and Islamist movements. There has furthermore been a resurgence of the Taliban despite (or because of) U.S. and NATO intervention—in part due to the increase in revenues from poppy production in Afghanistan. (See Chapter 6.) Moreover, the U.S.-backed "war on drugs" in Latin America has had little to no effect on limiting the supply of drugs to the United States. One can additionally argue that the "war on drugs," combined with efforts to expel "illegal" immigrants from the United States, could further exacerbate political economic instability in Mexico and other Central American countries by significantly cutting back immigrant remittances to their families and thus causing greater unemployment and concurrently augmenting problems related to drug smuggling, criminality—if not recruits for terrorism. (See Chapter 9.)

A real danger exists that a number of regional wars, particularly those in the Middle East and Persian Gulf, but also the "frozen conflicts" of the Caucasus in the "wider" Black Sea region (in which Russia is directly involved), as well as conflicts over central, south, and east Asia (most crucially, North and South Korea and Taiwan) and throughout Africa, and possibly in the Balkans once again, can widen even further, drawing in regional actors—or even the major powers. The irony is that a number of the conflicts in "peripheral regions" such as those taking place in Africa may be extremely violent, but are unlikely to draw in the major powers into direct confrontations—unlike those disputes and conflicts, generally scattered throughout in Eurasia, which might not appear to be as violent, but that are considered "vital" from the perspective of major and regional powers in terms of geostrategic, political-economic, and sociocultural considerations. The dilemma then is how is to prevent major powers from ultimately intervening at cross-purposes against one another or in support of allies on opposing sides in any number of actual or potential disputes and conflicts. This can be accomplished by bringing the major and regional powers into common cause as guarantors of security and as peacekeepers in the formation of interlocking "regional security communities." (See Chapters 1 and 10.)

Here, however, the key question remains whether a number of state leaderships will attempt to obtain security "independence" by means of "self help" (through, for example, the unilateral development of WMD) or whether they will join confederal or multilateral "regional security communities" backed by the major military and political-economic powers. If the latter proves to be the case, then the question becomes whether these differing regional groupings can join together as cooperative, inclusive, and interlocking communities—or whether such regional associations will forge rival exclusive and antagonistic blocs or alliances—such as the increasingly possible formation of a U.S.-NATO-Japanese alliance versus a Russian-Chinese Eurasian alliance, for example. The key dilemma for the twenty-first century will thus be how to prevent the formation of antagonistic alliances by finding ways to construct interlocking "regional security communities" while engaging primarily in a strategy of *multilateral dissuasion* and *persuasion* against potential violent threats to peace. (See Chapter 10.)

Despite the gravity of the global crisis and the need for continued international cooperation, the question remains whether the United States will be willing to sustain and build international and multilateral commitments in the near future—and not return to a more traditional pre-World War II "isolationism." While the United States has tended to focus on tensions and conflicts in Eurasia and the "greater Middle East," major problems closer to the U.S. backyard have begun to draw U.S. attention. Ruled by its increasingly autocratic president, Hugo Chávez, Venezuela appears to be challenging traditional U.S. *hegemony* (defined as "imperialism with better manners") in South and Central America through his "Bolivarian Revolution" that seeks to forge a potentially exclusive regional bloc. Here, Venezuela's attempts to forge trade and arms deals with China, Russia, and Iran have attracted U.S. attention—given the Monroe Doctrine and the Roosevelt corollary's opposition to a foreign military presence. This once again raises the threat of a much wider regional conflict within the historical U.S. sphere of influence and security, particularly as the Venezuelan crisis is already linked to the ongoing "war on drugs" in Colombia and the United States and Venezuela have begun to compete for political-economic influence throughout much of Latin America. (See Chapter 9.)

Concurrently, increasing "illegal" immigration (largely from Mexico and Central America)—coupled with perceived growing disparities between the extreme wealthy and the middle and lower classes within the United States itself—has begun to exacerbate domestic U.S. socioeconomic tensions. These issues were raised in the Democrats' response to President Bush's 2007 State of the Union Address. The latter Democrats' response not only revealed the growing domestic opposition to the Iraq War but also indicated a deeper opposition to the growing gap in salary between chief executive officers (CEOs), the middle classes and labor, inadequate health care, the need to more rapidly develop alternative energy technologies and to focus attention on issues related to corruption and lobbying.[8] Class and ethnic tensions—given the dubious argument that Hispanic immigrants are somehow different in nature from previous European immigrants[9] —are likely to augment as the new wave of Latin (and Asian) immigrants seek permanent residence status, enfranchisement, and status as *political equals* within highly *inequitable* U.S. socioeconomic conditions and circumstances.

The major risk is that as class, ethnic, and factional disputes intensify in the United States itself in the coming years (sparked by both the immigration question and opposition to U.S. intervention overseas), it is very possible for the United States to move back into its more traditional pre-World War II position of isolationism in the effort to deal more effectively with its own domestic socioeconomic and hemispheric crises—thus ignoring burgeoning overseas conflicts, crimes against humanity, and real threats to world security. Yet even here, should U.S. policy once again flip-flop from a superhawkish (if not vulture-like) unilateral interventionism and back to an ostrich-like isolationism, the latter stance will not prevent the United States from eventually being sucked back into the maelstrom of overseas conflict. Much as the very different attacks on December 7, 1941 and September 11, 2001 drew the "Sleeping Giant" into global military engagement, the question this time—unlike the very different situation before U.S. involvement in World War II—is how to engage in both diplomatic and military terms without provoking yet another major-power war.

Chapter Outline

Averting Global War consequently seeks to examine the major post-September 11, 2001 regional disputes and conflicts throughout the world. Its purpose is to show how these conflicts influence both U.S. domestic and foreign policy in that they possess much wider ramifications given their interaction with shifting regional and global power and alliance configurations. Each chapter seeks to depict the multidimensional and interrelated geostrategic, military-technological, political economic, energy-ecological, sociocultural, and ideological aspects of interstate and intrastate rivalries in their global and regional contexts.

These major disputes and conflicts include: the ongoing "global war on terrorism"; NATO (and EU) enlargement to Russian borders and to the "wider Black Sea region"; the development of BMDs; U.S. intervention in Iraq; U.S. confrontation with Iran; the conflict between Israel and the Palestinians and intra-Palestinian feuding; the widening "zone of conflict" from Central Asia to sub-Saharan Africa; the global ramifications of North Korea's nuclear program and China's claims to Taiwan; Venezuela's "Bolivarian Revolution" and the "war on drugs" in Latin America, coupled with the domestic sociopolitical effects of Latin American immigration upon U.S. domestic policy. The book's ultimate goal is to articulate an U.S. strategy that is intended to manage, transform, or resolve, if at all possible, a number of these disputes and conflicts so as to prevent them from further "deepening" or "widening"—and to avert the real possibility of direct major power confrontation involving both covert and overt methods of warfare.

Chapter 1, Triptych of Terrorism, argues that there are three interrelated "temptations" in the context of the "global war on terror," which is defined as a war against *both* antistate partisan groups and "rogue states". These temptations, which need to be transcended if the "global war on terror" is ever to come to an end, include: the tendency to lump all "Islamist" groups together as the major threat to U.S. interests; the danger of overreaction to even horrific attacks; and the question of fighting the "global war on terrorism" with immoral means. While Washington has already fallen into the trap of *overreaction* as set by *al-Qaida*, the United States and Europe cannot assume that the major threat to world peace will necessarily come from differing pan-Islamist movements. The chapter introduces the concept of the post-September 11, 2001 "insecurity-security dialectic" and argues that neither "terrorist" movements nor "rogue states" can be fought by military means alone but will require a more clever "owlish" strategy involving multilateral dissuasion and persuasion.

Chapter 2, The Un-Coordinated NATO-EU "Double Enlargement": Toward the Isolation of Russia?, discusses the global and regional ramifications of potential BMD deployments in eastern Europe and of possible NATO and European Union (EU) enlargement to Ukraine and Georgia. It examines the role Turkey plays in the "wider Black Sea region," and the shifting nature of U.S.-NATO-Russian-EU-Turkish relationship. It argues that the United States, NATO, and Russia will need to strengthen decision-making processes within the NATO-Russia Council and bring both Russia and Ukraine into a new form of NATO membership in order to prevent the real possibility of conflict—which could be sparked by U.S.-NATO-Russian tensions over eastern Europe, Ukraine, and the "wider" Black Sea region, most pertinently, Georgia and the Caucasus.

Chapter 3, Iraq: Sinking Deeper into Mesopotamian Quicksand, examines the destabilizing domestic, regional, and international ramifications of the George W. Bush administration's essentially unilateral decision to intervene in Iraq in the effort to "preempt" Iraq's presumed WMD capabilities. The chapter focuses on the contemporary U.S. congressional debate as to whether or not to withdraw from Iraq, while pointing out the failure of U.S. intervention in Iraq to stabilize the country and to "democratize" the region in accord with the George W. Bush administration's "neoconservative" and neo-Wilsonian goals—not to overlook the political, financial, and human costs of a long-term "occupation." The chapter argues that the United States risks foreign policy paralysis if the Bush administration can not soon find a diplomatic resolution to the crisis as Democrats in Congress attempt to pressure the administration to change course—but as the imperial diarchy of President George W. Bush and Vice President Dick Cheney dig in their heels in backing a neoconservative and "faith based" foreign policy.

Chapter 4, Iran: Nuclear High Tension and Holocaust Polemics: "Cruise Missile Diplomacy" or a "New Diplomatic Offensive"?, takes a critical look at the massive buildup of U.S. military forces in the Persian Gulf and the "hawkish" U.S. efforts to negotiate from a "position of strength"—which is a situation that is complicated by U.S. efforts to extricate itself from Iraqi quicksand after its ill-conceived and ill-executed intervention. Iran's quest for ballistic missile capability has begun to fuel a spiraling "insecurity-security dialectic" if the United States deploys BMD systems in the Caucasus and eastern Europe in response to Iranian capabilities, which in turn affect Moscow's geopolitical, defense, and nuclear strategy (as argued in Chapter 2). The chapter likewise examines Iran's nuclear enrichment program and seeks options to ameliorate tensions and dispel mutual suspicions. It argues for a step-by-step face-saving process of negotiation of all outstanding disputes that could possibly lead to *regime recognition* and security guarantees for Iran—but without ruling out *regime reform*—if direct military confrontation is to be averted.

Chapter 5, Israel and Palestinian Fratricide: Beyond the "Two State Solution"?, discusses the question of the Israeli-built security barrier as it afflicts the ongoing Israeli-Palestinian conflict and examines intra-Palestinian discord and appropriate steps to deal with Hamas following the latter's seizure of Gaza in June 2007. The chapter argues for the formation of a new form of loose Palestinian confederation linked indirectly to Jordan, Egypt, and Israel as well—as part of a much larger Mediterranean union led by the European Union and Turkey. It additionally proposes the formation of a NATO-EU-Russian "regional security community" under a UN mandate that protects both Israel and Palestinians from acts of terror and counterterror, as well as from WMD, as threatened by Iran or other states in the region. It is argued that finding a resolution to the Palestinian question is key to winding down the "global war on terrorism."

Chapter 6, An Ever-widening Zone of Conflict, Terrorism, and Black Market Activities: From Central Asia to Sub-Saharan Africa, traces how efforts to crack the Soviet empire and its alliances through support for religious ideology not only opened up a wider region of conflict involving both state-supported and antistate terrorism and a zone of black market activities (involving drug smuggling, organized crime, and human trafficking) in central Asia, but did so indirectly within the Middle East and Africa as well. The United States subsequently expanded its military presence into central Asia, as well as in north and sub-Saharan Africa, as these regions have become increasingly interconnected with pan-Islamist partisan movements of the "greater" Middle East. Concurrently, U.S., EU, Russian, Indian, and Chinese rivalry for control or access to oil and energy resources has greatly exacerbated the chances for wider regional conflicts. The possibility of cooperation over central Asia between NATO, the EU, Russia, and China is discussed, as are the formation of "regional security communities" for African countries.

Chapter 7, North Korea: Beyond "Backdoor" Multilateralism, examines North Korea's threat to develop nuclear weapons and ballistic missiles and outlines the accords reached in February 2007 in the context of the six-party talks, which have the potential to lead to the actual implementation of a Northeast Asia "regional security community." The chapter further argues that U.S. failure to continue to engage with North Korea will strengthen China's influence not only over the North but also over South Korea, assuming North Korea does not opt for war, or more likely, collapse as a "failed state" and thus generate new regional tensions. Moreover, the United States and China need to not only finally settle the North Korean crisis, but also work toward a resolution of Taiwan question. This is because geostrategic and political economic tensions over both Taiwan and North Korea have been exacerbated by the fact that both China and Japan are major energy importers and historical rivals in Asia, coupled with the "insecurity-security dialectic" fostered by U.S. and Japanese decision to deploy BMD systems in the region to counter weapons systems of North Korea, China, and Russia.

Chapter 8, China and Blue-water Dreams: Toward a Sino-Russian Alliance?, critically examines China's post–Tiananmen Square global political-economic influence and burgeoning energy demands and discusses the significance of the March 2006 Sino-Russian cooperation accords and military maneuvers. The latter are in part a response to closer U.S.-Japanese defense cooperation and the potential development of BMD in Asia (as well as eastern Europe). Heading off a potential Sino-Russian alliance that would tacitly, if not overtly, back China's irredentist claims to Taiwan would require closer U.S.-Japanese and Russian cooperation in an effort to *channel* the rise of a highly unstable China as a military and political-economic power—but without provoking major-power war.

Chapter 9, Three Dimensions of "Montezuma's Revenge": Hugo Chávez's Bolivarian Vision, "War on Drugs," and "Illegal" Immigration, discusses the "Bolivarian" goals of the increasingly authoritarian and populist Chávez regime, the war on drugs, and the international threats that Washington faces in its own backyard that could lead Washington to focus more closely on hemispheric affairs and turn toward "isolationism." It then tackles the question of Mexican and Central American migration in the United States, the proposal for temporary work permits, and the question of immigrant remittances and contributions to U.S. social security. It also deals with issues related to the consumption of drugs, drug trafficking, criminality, and "terrorism." It is argued that if there is no effective and sustained development program for Mexico and Central American countries, coupled with effective temporary work programs, there is a real risk that efforts to reduce migration in the United States could significantly cut back remittances that many of these migrants send back to their home countries. This would ironically cause greater political-economic instability, criminality, if not acts of terrorism (and not necessarily by Islamist movements alone) in America's own backyard and within the United States itself.

Chapter 10, American Hypertrophy and Strategic Options: Toward a Geostrategy for Global Peace, first outlines a number of possible scenarios that could lead to wider regional conflicts or even major-power war and then discusses U.S. foreign policy options intended to both avoid the pitfalls of U.S. hypertrophy and to prevent a widening and deepening of contemporary disputes and wars, with a focus on diplomacy to end the war in Iraq and U.S. military face-off with Iran. On the international level, Washington needs to avoid a return to its more traditional pre-World War II position of "isolation" and reach out toward a full-fledged entente with Moscow through a "diplomatic revolution" (bringing Russian and Ukraine into a more cooperative relationship). It also needs to seek out new ways to work with Beijing and to resolve issues involving North Korea and Taiwan. Washington likewise needs to work toward the establishment of new forms of confederations or interacting and interlocking "regional security communities" in the wider Black Sea region, the Mediterranean and the Levant, northeast Asia, and between China and Taiwan, as well as in Central and South America—backed by major-power security and multilateral economic supports—as a means to transform and ameliorate, if not resolve, conflicts throughout key areas of the world, thus indirectly strengthening global governance.

The Postscript: The Obama Administration: Surmounting Nightmarish Scenarios? discusses president Obama's first year in office (2009) as he has attempted to tackle the disastrous foreign policy legacy of the George W. Bush administration.

CHAPTER 1

Triptych of Terrorism

The Three Temptations

Images of terror, mass murder, torture, cities burning, even satellite surveillance, the world inverted—a perverse world of double standards, without ethics or morality. I am transfixed before Hieronymous Bosch's triptych, The Temptation of St. Anthony. Suddenly a revelation: The relevance of Saint Anthony's "temptation."

The first temptation in the "global war on terror" is to assume that the primary threat to the United States and Europe (plus Russia) will come from "radical Islam" and to ignore other threats. This temptation is linked to the corresponding tendency to lump differing Islamist groups and certain Islamic states together—as if they all possess the same short- and long-term local, regional, and international interests and goals.

The second temptation is to *overreact* and to assume a priori that "terrorism" can be fought only by military means—and in effect expanding what should have been a struggle against a specific group into a global crusade against both antistate partisan movements "with global reach" and "rogue" states. Related to this is the temptation to pursue specific national interests that are not at all concerned with the problem of terrorism, which are nevertheless taken in the pretense of fighting terrorism.

The third temptation is to fight the "global war on terror" with "immoral" or "unethical" methods and not in accord with the standards set by international law; that is, to use state-supported acts of "terrorism" and controversial, if not illegal, military technology against "antistate terror."[1] Here, ethical considerations are not always the same as legal ones; yet the *irregular* nature of contemporary "terrorist" warfare provides a pretext for state leaderships not to combat illegal partisan groups in accord with international standards of warfare.

The vital concern raised in this chapter is that the international community must become more creative, more innovative, than the "terrorists" themselves— if the scourge of all forms of indiscriminant violence is ever to be eliminated.

The First Temptation: Differing Species of "Terrorists"

What President George W. Bush called "radical Islamic" groups in his January 2006 State of the Union Address certainly represent a significant threat. The horrific attacks on civilian targets on September 11, and the lesser strikes in Madrid, London, Moscow, Casablanca, Beslan, Bali, and Amman as well as in Riyadh, Mumbai, Bangkok, and Baghdad and elsewhere, have all revealed the reality of that threat.

In August 2006, British authorities foiled another major al-Qaida associated plot to explode ten passenger airliners; British intelligence (MI5) had been monitoring about two hundred networks of disaffected Muslims, generally of South Asian background, some with links to al-Qaida. In June 2007, four men were charged with plotting to blow up fuel tanks, terminal buildings, and the web of fuel lines running beneath Kennedy International Airport, at the same time that they were purportedly seeking finance from the Islamist group Jamaat al-Muslimeen that had attempted a coup in July 1990 against the government of Trinidad and Tobago. There will undoubtedly be more major terrorist attempts that might not be stopped, because these groups are more like multiheaded hydras that germinate spontaneously even after having been beheaded. Yet there will also be those arrested or killed unjustly for crimes they did not commit, or were not planning to commit, thereby setting the stage for acts of revenge.

Here, the worldwide diasporas of people of Islamic background and faith, combined with the evident misery of many Muslims throughout the world despite the incredible wealth and potential of a select number of Islamic countries, makes for an explosive combination that could result in a potentially long-term struggle. Given these general realities, militant Islamist ideology will only begin to subside through (1) efforts to boost general knowledge of the positive contributions of the Islamic world to the international community (against "clash of civilizations" theosophy), combined with secular education projects, to indirectly de-legitimize violent versions of pan-Islamist ideology; (2) more intensive efforts to foster sociopolitical and regional development; (3) efforts to permit greater degrees of good governance and power sharing within Muslim societies themselves; and (4) more engaged diplomatic efforts involving *multilateral dissuasion* and *persuasion* (the concerted use of both positive rewards and negative sanctions and pressures by both major and regional powers) to achieve geopolitical compromise (where possible) in disputes that affect Islamic interests and concerns. And finally, caution must be taken in any effort to prevent and to counteract terrorism of all forms by the use of force—which includes the necessity to self-limit the exercise of state power through effective legal and ethical oversight.(See Chapters 3, 4, 5, and 6.)

Other Extremists

Despite solid evidence that groups with Islamist ideologies are, in fact, increasingly engaged in major acts of "terrorism," there is a perilous temptation for Washington and the Europeans to concentrate attention primarily on only "radical Islamist" groups, however defined. The point raised here is that too great a focus on what the Bush administration has called "radical Islam" (or later

"Islamo-fascism") could permit other potentially dangerous groups and states (without Islamist ideologies) to avoid close scrutiny. In effect, antistate terrorism can take differing anarchist, anti-globalization, communist, socialist or "leftist," nationalist, separatist, racist, fascist, irredentist, anti-immigrant, and religious forms (even including animal rights activists). Some of these groups, which increasingly exhibit nationalist or religious ideologies, could find common cause with groups with Islamist ideologies, but the majority have their own ax to grind.[2] Concurrently, efforts to eradicate such groups through state-supported counterterrorism have historically caused far greater "crimes against humanity" than antistate actions and can take numerous ideological forms as well.

Here, a number of white supremacist groups in the United States still require close scrutiny. There are dozens of such movements in the United States, with an estimated twenty-five thousand members who are often linked to the Christian identity movement. The Federal Office Building in Oklahoma City was bombed in April 1995 by individuals who might have been associated with these so-called Christian groups. In December 2006, for example, there was a conspiracy by an extreme right-wing group to attack the Los Angeles federal building, an Internal Revenue Service office in Utah, and a synagogue in Phoenix, Arizona.

Some extreme right-wing groups see themselves as aligning with pan-Islamist movements against the alleged "world Jewish conspiracy." (In 1999, an FBI report revealed that 239 of the 327 terrorist attacks in the United States between 1980 and 1999 were perpetrated by domestic groups, usually a small number of individuals; most of these groups were aligned ideologically with the extreme right.)[3] In opposition, Jewish extremist groups include Gush Emunim (The Bloc of the Faithful) and the Jewish Defense League, founded by Rabbi Meir Kahane. In addition, non-Islamist immigrant groups within the United States itself cannot be overlooked. These include the Mara Salvatrucha (MS-13), which the FBI considers the most dangerous street gang in the United States, and which has had purported contacts with al-Qaida members. At the same time, immigration in general represents a rallying cry for violent xenophobes. (See Chapter 9.)

While tensions in Northern Ireland finally appear to be winding down (a result of the decision of the Provisional IRA and Protestant Loyalists to accept the decommissioning of their arms), die-hard groups such as the "Real IRA," the Loyalist Ulster Volunteer Force (UVF) and the Ulster Defense Association (UDA) have been more reluctant to turn in their weaponry. Other violent groups include differing Kurdish factions and the Sri Lanka Tamil Tigers, who, in turn, accuse the Turkish and Sri Lanka governments respectively of state-sponsored terrorism. Militants of the Basque *Euskadi Ta Askatasuna* (ETA) opted for violence in December 2006 with attacks on civilian targets—despite the ongoing negotiations between the more moderate political representation, *Batasuna*, and the Spanish government that were then immediately cut off.

Since German reunification more than one hundred people have been murdered in Germany in xenophobic attacks. There are about 150 neo-Nazi groups (plus a thriving skinhead subculture that numbers approximately nine thousand members). These groups are often involved in street terrorism and have been particularly visible (and violent) at soccer games and sports events. There are essentially three far-right political parties—*Die Deutsche Volksunion* (German People's Party), *Die Republikaner* (Republicans) and *Die Nationaldemokratische Partie Deutschlands* (National Democratic Party of Germany).[4] Some of these latter parties have links with extreme nationalists in Russia or in other countries, including Austria, whose Freedom Party led by Jürgen Haider was banned by the EU when it became part of a coalition government. Vladimir Zhirinovsky's Russian Liberal Democratic Party (named, in effect, as a parody of U.S. liberal democracy) has had close links with the *Deutsche Volksunion* (German People's Party). The Russian National Unity Party, *Pamyat* (National Patriotic Front Remembrance) and the National Salvation Front likewise represent extreme nationalist movements. Some of the latter have had links with Serbian extreme nationalists, such as Radovan Karadzic, who has been indicted for war crimes.[5]

Far-right, anti-immigrant movements have been gaining strength in Europe as well. In the EU, the new populist far-right bloc comprises 20 of Parliament's 785 members—and argues that it has deeper support in Europe than its numbers suggest.[6] The leader of the anti-immigrant National Front, Jean Marie Le Pen, barely defeated Socialist candidate Lionel Jospin unexpectedly in the first round of the French presidential elections in 2002; the country then unified behind Republican Jacques Chirac on the second round: 82.2 percent to 17.8 percent. The question of "immigration" in France—which sparked rioting and acts of urban violence in November–December 2006—was a major issue in the French 2007 presidential election campaign as well.

"Radical Islam" and the "Global War on Terror"

Washington's faltering efforts (in 2006) to focus policy on "radical Islam" (shifting from a more general focus on the "global war on terror") were, in part, intended to counter the general decline of domestic support for the Bush administration's foreign policy ventures and to ward off apparently increasing isolationist tendencies among the American public.

For domestic U.S. political purposes, raising the threat of "radical Islam" or "Islamo-fascism" (as opposed to extremism in general) in response to a foiled threat to explode passenger airlines in London in August 2006 makes for strong propaganda to counter public tendencies toward isolationism, but it is not an appropriate means to do so, because it tends to implicate much of the Muslim world. The key problem is that overt linkage of Islam and Fascism might tend to alienate moderate Muslims who resent the association of the religion, Islam, with "fascism"[7] but who still oppose extreme violence, even if they might not support U.S. (or European) beliefs, values, and politics. Adding to the practical difficulties, the focus on "radical Islam" tends to push a number of these divergent groups closer together in the name of the *jihadi* cause. U.S. obsession with "radical Islam" also makes it more difficult to play significant differences between divergent groups and states against each other or to distinguish between those groups that advocate violence and those that do not. Some Islamist groups could become allies, while others could shift sides, depending on the conflicting nature of their interests as they interact with U.S. diplomacy.

Focusing on "radical Islam" alone additionally tends to result in the loss of executive flexibility to deal effectively with various groups with Islamist ideologies and other actual and potential extremist threats, whether by means of bilateral or international diplomacy, international sanctions, police action, special forces, or direct military action, where deemed necessary. The issue raised here is that credible force may be needed to deal with a number of differing threats, but if that force is too spread out or if there is the perception that the United States or the international community is unwilling to use force, the other side could take significant risks. At the same time, however, using force or increasing troops alone could actually exacerbate tensions if not deployed properly and if not accompanied by negotiations with the opposing sides.

The focus on "radical Islam" (coupled with demands for "regime change") also thwarts the very possibility of negotiations, if not the eventual recognition, of militant Islamist regimes (if deemed necessary), while currently weakening the efforts of more moderate Islamist groups to reform those more hard-line regimes. The Bush administration's denunciation of the Iranian regime as a member of the "axis of evil" and threats to preempt Iran's nuclear enrichment program have been countered by Iranian president Mahmoud Ahmadinejad's threats to make Israel "vanish from the page of time" (in literal translation). These taunts—which only appear to justify Iran's membership in the "axis of evil" from the Bush demands administration perspective have been used by the Ahmadinejad regime to counter the demands of domestic Iranian opposition groups for reform and for negotiations with the United States. In effect, hard-liners on both sides refuse to take the first steps toward negotiating their differences. (See Chapters 3 and 4.)

Dialectics of "Insecurity-Security"
Numerous threats of very different magnitudes (particularly given destructive capabilities of both conventional and nonconventional weaponry) appear to be on the rise, but each kind of threat has differing levels and dimensions of effect on differing states and societies. This is ironically true even though the absolute number of conflicts appears to be waning, at least before the war in Iraq.[8] The key point is that the *significance* of acts of terrorism and various conflicts and disputes around the world (which might involve serious arms rivalries, power-based bargaining, and outwardly spiraling *insecurity-security dialectics*) cannot be judged in merely quantitative terms, but must be primarily studied in more *qualitative* terms and in terms of their geostrategic, military, technological, political economic, socioideological, and psychological significance. Some threats are specific to regions; others could be more encompassing.

Here, it is important to emphasize that simple action-reaction models do not totally explain either acts of terrorism and counterterrorism or differing forms of arms rivalries (threats of state terror using weapons of mass destruction [WMD]). If not actions of a madman, acts of antistate terrorism, however violent and indiscriminate, are generally associated with some form of political demand, but might result in retaliation by states or other antistate actors. Partisan groups that use "terror" as a tactic are generally concerned with creating a major psychological impact on those they hope to influence. Such groups often hope to create an inflated perception of power, even if they are relatively weak. Acts of terror can force people to choose sides and thus help gain converts or else strengthen the convictions of the members of those organizations by obtaining greater and greater degrees of external recognition for their actions. Hence groups that engage in acts of terrorism seek to exacerbate perceptions of insecurity (through the dialectics of "insecurity-security"), while concurrently seeking recognition and support for their particular values and goals.

Not too differently, an arms race is not merely intended as deterrence; it is also a tool of *power-based bargaining* or *strategic leveraging* intended to gain some form of political demand or economic concession. (These demands or concessions can include financial aid or assistance or overt diplomatic recognition and respect for a particular state's values, vital interests, and objectives.) Once one state engages in *power-based* bargaining to impel the other side into making concessions manipulating advanced weaponry or WMD as strategic leverage, it might inevitably draw other powers into the fray, directly or indirectly, thus resulting in outwardly "spiraling" buildups of armaments in potential retaliation.[9] In this respect, perceived situations of "insecurity" lead to compensating efforts to obtain "security," thus resulting in a *dialectical* interaction of perceived "*insecurity-security*"—in which the net result could be less security for all.[10]

On the one hand, those efforts to obtain "security" by building up defense capabilities can, in return, result in conditions of domestic *insecurity* in terms of the classic opportunity cost of "guns versus butter," for example, which can then be afflicted by downswings in domestic and international political economic cycles. On the other hand, arms rivalries can also result in counterresponses: The actor (or actors) that initially caused that fear of insecurity could respond once again with a larger buildup of forces, or else other actors might likewise build up their defense capabilities in response to those perceived threats, thus widening the dispute and the potential conflict.

From this perspective, one must also factor in the *dialectical* nature of domestic perceptions and reactions (internal domestic support for, or opposition to, the burdens of a continuing "arms race")—not to overlook questions with respect to the intrinsic financial and technological capacities to engage in such an arms rivalry. Apparent lulls in arms rivalries might result from the lack of finance or technology rather than a lack of political will. Most important, one must consider whether arms limitations and reductions can or should be achieved through diplomatic engagement and whether it is possible to both "trust and verify" through international inspections, for example. Arms rivalries themselves do not necessarily lead to wars, but they can indirectly destabilize financially strapped societies, possibly leading to civil conflict.

Given acts of antistate terrorism, as well as the outwardly spiraling nature of the *insecurity-security dialectic*, what does it actually take to provoke states into conflict? Why do states respond violently to one attack by a state or antistate actor but ignore others or else engage in diplomacy in response to another attack? When do states opt to preempt the other sides' threats to develop WMD or else engage in other forms of retaliation, through acts of sabotage and counterterrorism? When do they let the "spiraling" arms rivalries continue? When do they seek to negotiate and "manage" the tensions through arms limitations or reductions?

Why are some disputes peacefully addressed or ignored, while others widen to involve more than two states or antistate actors in the general region? Which kinds of conflicts could draw in the major powers? Which kind of conflicts could possibly draw in the major powers *against* each other? And which kind impels states to realize that major and regional power cooperation is generally the optimum policy?

Given the post-September 11, 2001, reaction to major acts of antistate terrorism, coupled with the post-Iraq intervention in 2003, justified in the effort to preempt (or really preclude) the development of WMD, the point is to caution vigilance and prudence in the nature of state response to these grave concerns and to underscore the necessity to weigh the magnitude and *relative* danger of differing forms of threats and seek out the most appropriate response. Such responses can range from the use of force to containment, to sanctions, to diplomacy, to intentional appeasement, and to ignoring the threat altogether.

The problem is that more thinking must look at the long term and at what kinds of policies and actions might ultimately undermine the *raison d'être* of at least some antistate partisan groups, and that might change the nature of the *insecurity-security dialectic* in such a way as to manage or reduce tensions in the proper security environment. Efforts to downplay media hype by an effective government media strategy are important but not sufficient to thoroughly resolve deep rooted conflicts by themselves. Most acts of state-supported or antistate "terrorism" and arms rivalries do not exist in a vacuum but in response to specific actions, policies, or general sociopolitical-economic conditions and thus exist in specific geohistorical conditions. How could the present geohistorical and political-economic conditions as well as correlated social, religious, and ideological factors—that ostensibly justify the violent acts of partisan groups and arms buildups among rival states—possibly be changed, altered, or communicated in such a way so as to reduce the chances for wider regional conflicts—if not major power war?

Widening Conflicts

Numerous states and groups have been responsible for assassinations that tend to spark wider or more intense conflicts involving cycles of revenge and counterrevenge. The assassination of General Ahmad Shah Massoud just two days before the September 11, 2001 attacks represented a kind of preemptive strike to weaken efforts by the Northern Alliance to build forces in the fight against the Taliban and al-Qaida. The August 2003 assassination (by an al-Qaida affiliate) of UN envoy to Iraq Sergio Vieira de Mello and other UN representatives was intended to weaken U.S. and UN efforts to establish an ex post facto international legitimacy for the U.S. intervention in Iraq.

The assassination in May 1991 of Indian prime minister Rajiv Gandhi by a female Tamil Tiger suicide bomber played a role in intensifying the Tamil struggle, following Gandhi's decision to deploy Indian peacekeepers in Sri Lanka, which were accused by the Tamil Tiger leadership of committing atrocities. The Tamil Tigers are reputed to have engaged in more suicide bombings in Sri Lanka than Islamist groups or Palestinians had engaged in, at least before the Iraq War; they have likewise manipulated women and child soldiers. Moreover, the fact that the Tamils (with a Tamil diaspora in the United States, EU, and Canada) have attempted to buy sophisticated weaponry from the United States and other sources, has raised fears that they might expand their violent activities overseas. In their struggle for a homeland ("Eelam") so as to safeguard the Tamil race, language, culture, and nation against the Sinhalese majority, the Tamil Tigers could also seek out additional international support to counter Sri Lanka's use of air power against them. Sri Lanka has additionally sought advisers and assistance from Pakistan, indirectly raising Indian suspicions.

The March 2004 assassination of Sheikh Ahmed Ismail Yassin, leader of *Hamas*, by Israel (seen by Palestinians as state-supported "terrorism" in response to legitimate "resistance") augmented Palestinian support for the *Hamas*, which subsequently achieved victory in democratically held elections against their more secular opponents, *Fatah*, also accused by Israel of condoning terrorism. The assassination of former Lebanese prime minister Rafik Hariri (plus other ostensibly "anti-Syrian" Lebanese politicians) sparked tensions between Lebanon and Syria and could result in civil war if a national unity government cannot be established. The pro-Syrian pro-Iranian presence of *Hizb'allah* (which has, in effect, become a state within a state like the PLO before it) along the Israeli border resulted in a renewed, but unsuccessful, Israeli intervention in the Summer 2006, following the *Hizb'allah's* kidnapping of two Israeli soldiers. (See Chapter 5.)

Acts of terrorism in Iraq have deepened the ongoing civil war. Among many horrific actions, the "symbolic" bombing of the Golden Mosque in August 2006 (which represents one of Shi'ite Islam's holiest sites after the shrines of Najaf and Karbala) was most likely executed by pan-Sunni groups, linked to *al-Qaida*. Here, Abu Musab al-Zarqawi had openly stated one of his goals was to incite a sectarian civil war between Iraq's Shi'ites and Sunni Muslims.[11] The attack also fueled tensions elsewhere in the world. President Bush thus stated that bombing was an "al-Qaida plot." Conversely, Iranian president Mahmoud Ahmadinezhad blamed the United States and Israel, as did *Hizb'allah* leader, Sayyed Hassan Nasrallah. The issue raised here is that one attack serves the political purposes of another, thus perpetuating accusations and counter-accusations.

An "eye for an eye," in both the Hebrew and Muslim traditions, appears to make the whole world blind from the perspective of Mahatma Gandhi—thus aggravating the *dialectics* of *"insecurity-security."*

"Radical Islam" in Europe

"Radical Islam" cannot be blamed for all crises ranging from the causes of the Iraq War (by attempting to link Saddam Hussein to Osama bin Laden and al-Qaida, for example) to riots and car burning in the French banlieue (suburbs) in October and November 2005. In regard to the latter crisis, the misleading focus on "radical Islam" will not reach the deeper roots of a much more complex socioeconomic (and geopolitical) problem that has largely resulted from patterns of immigration (which is not entirely Muslim) from countries in North Africa, sub-Saharan Africa, and Turkey, as well as from Asia and to many countries in Europe—and which also includes poor white Europeans as well.

The roots of what is essentially a structural problem lie primarily in the failure to "integrate" a large majority of second- and third-generation immigrants into European societies (in terms of meaningful participation in the social and political affairs of the host country and in terms of mutual respect and recognition of the differing cultures, traditions, and religions). While some "radical Islamist" groups might have taken advantage of the violence (despite efforts of Islamic religious leaders, such as the Union des Organisations Islamiques de France, affiliated with the Muslim Brotherhood, to calm passions in France and elsewhere), the problem of integration cannot really be handled by individual countries alone but now requires assistance from the European Union. From this standpoint, it is necessary to not only create jobs but also help integrate citizens of North African descent (among other minorities) into positions of power and authority as well. Here, a distinction must be made between *jihadists of European nationalities*, who support the struggles (and who might have actually fought) in Afghanistan, Bosnia, or now in Iraq, and who remain militant, and those individuals who want to integrate and be accepted by European society, but who feel rejected or unable to fully participate, largely as a result of degrees of discrimination based on language ability, skills, or cultural background.

Rioting and protests that took place throughout many European and Middle Eastern cities (plus Islamic state boycotts of Danish products and threats to Danish citizens and troops stationed in Iraq) in January and February 2006 in response to the cartoon caricatures of the Prophet Mohammed (published in September 2005 initially in the Danish press) can, in part, be traced to issues involving strict Danish immigration practices, strict laws relating to marriage and citizenship, obligatory Danish lessons, restrictions placed on Imams, and the refusal or opposition of local Danish authorities to permit the building of mosques and cemeteries for Muslims living in Denmark.[12] (In response, Danish authorities argue that some of the problems related to the building of mosques have to do with disputes within the Islamic community itself, as well as with the desire to prevent radical elements from trying to control the mosques.)

The fact, however, that Danish prime minister Anders Fogh Rasmussen (against the counsel of his own advisers) refused to meet eleven ambassadors from Muslim states who had hoped to discuss the cartoon scandal, as well as other problems facing Muslims in Denmark, in October 2005 had helped to exacerbate political-religious tensions. Certainly, Iran and Syria might have manipulated the crisis (as accused by U.S. secretary of state Condoleezza Rice). But "radical Islamist" groups could not have been able to cause considerable damage, if there were not already underlying problems with regard to Danish relations with its two hundred thousand-member Muslim community.

The general crisis affecting Muslims in Europe has involved boycotts of Danish products (Danish pastries are popular in the Middle East), as well as acts of violence, sabotage, riots, death threats, and assassinations—such as the murder of Dutch film director Theo van Gogh. The repercussions of these actions have been exacerbated by militant partisans that claim to speak in the name of "Islam" and who risk provoking a potentially dangerous backlash from extreme nationalist movements throughout much of Europe.

Divide and Rule

It is additionally crucial to avoid the temptation to presume that all Islamist groups necessarily possess the same primary goals and that there is necessarily "solidarity" or "brotherhood" between differing factions. It is furthermore crucial to find ways to separate the "more militant" jihadists from the "less militant" groups and to encourage alternative and "more moderate" voices of the Islamic faith so as to minimize its manipulation for political purposes, through training of the Imam, for example.[13] Here a distinction needs to be made between those more "moderate" Islamic voices that accept the present nature of the state system and its historically imposed territorial divisions (despite the fact that these are generally based on European imperialism or colonialism) and those "radical" jihadist groups that call for pan-Islamist goals and that do not accept often-artificial territorial divisions, which did not exist in the Ottoman empire or among nomadic peoples. In general, "Islamist" groups are divided between differing sociopolitical movements.

Pan-Islamist internationalists at least claim to seek unity among all Islamist groups across the religious spectrum. By contrast, pan-Sunni and pan-Shi'a Islamist groups seek unity across borders for Sunnis and Shi'as respectively. *Islamist patriots* represent those who oppose the interference of third states (even Islamic states) within their particular country's affairs. *Islamist ethnonationalists* seek independence or secession for specific groups from non-Muslim states. And finally, *Islamist "clans"* are primarily tribal in outlook, yet they adopt Islamic religious ideology, even though their specific customs often predate the rise of Islam.[14]

Within the various Islamist groups that accept the present territorial division of states, distinctions can be made between those groups that accept parliamentary systems of governance (and that will accept rival political parties), whether within the "Westminster parliamentary system" or else within ethnic and religious-oriented confessional systems, such as that in Lebanon; those groups and countries that believe in the custom of *shura* (consultation), such as the Persian Gulf monarchies; and those groups and political movements that demand the full imposition of *Shari'a* law (however defined).[15] At the same time, Islamist partisan movements may be divided between extremists such as the Taliban (which, to a large extent, is a creation of the Pakistani secret service, the ISI) and more moderate factions. The Taliban engaged in extreme measures, such as executions, to enforce *Shari'a* law. With a macho Kalishnikov culture (generated by years of armed resistance against the Soviet Union and now the United States and NATO), the Taliban prohibited women and girls from employment, barred women from access to education and health care, and required women to wear the full *burqa* (a custom that predates the rise of Islam) in public. As opposed to *al-Qaida*, which was influenced by its own interpretations of Salafism and Sayyid Qutb,[16] the Taliban, which is primarily Pashtun in ethnic background, have primarily been concerned with independence from the Soviet (and now the NATO and U.S.) occupation, coupled with demands for decentralized tribal or clan rule in the name of a radical Deobandi interpretation of Islam.

There likewise are differences in goals among those Islamist groups that do not accept the present territorial state system. The Taliban issue is complicated by Pashtun efforts to link the regions of northwest Pakistan with those of southern and eastern Afghanistan in the creation of an independent Pashtunistan. In effect, Pakistani support for pan-Islamist internationalists, such as Gulbudden Hekmetyar's Hizb-i Islami, against the Soviet Union partly represented an effort to defuse Pushtun irredentism and provide "strategic depth" for Pakistan's war with India over Kashmir. The American-led intervention against the Taliban in 2001, however, coupled with Pakistani complicity in that intervention, has ironically raised the threat of Pushtun irredentism, potentially breaking up Pakistan.

Differing substantially from the Taliban, some groups, like *al-Qaida*, hope to link as many Islamic states together as possible to form an Islamic *Ummah*, similar to that once ruled by the Ottoman Empire. *Al-Qaida* strategy appears to be that of destabilizing as many vulnerable (deemed "corrupt") Islamic states as possible to gain a foothold wherever possible. Here pan-Islamist movements have sought bases in Sudan, in Kashmir, in Indonesia and the Philippines, in Afghanistan and along the Afghan-Pakistani border, on the Saudi-Yemeni border, and in Somalia (despite Ethiopian intervention backed by the United States in 2007). The predominantly Sunni province of al-Anbar in Iraq (bordering Syria and Jordan) has become a hotbed of pan-Islamists by 2006 despite the April and November 2004 battles for Fallujah against the Iraqi insurgency and subsequent clashes between pan-Islamists and local tribes.[17]

The Islam of Chechen leader Shamil Basayev has been called "inherently communitarian."[18] But it is better described as "inherently sectarian" in that sectarianism seeks divisions among differing groups in striving for total independence (as if such a thing as total independence really existed in a highly interdependent world) while communitarian approaches seek to link differing social and ethnic groups together in closer cooperation where possible (at least in the neocommunitarian definition). Thai Islamist groups that extended their attacks to Baghdad in 2006 appear to be separatists; in January 1990 Islamist groups in the four southern provinces of Thailand had declared a separate state called Langkasuka. By contrast, Jemaah Islamiyah, linked to the 2002 Bali bombing, seeks to establish an Islamic state linking Indonesia, Malaysia, and the Muslim regions of the Philippines as well as Thailand. Consequently, not all groups seek to obtain pan-Islamist goals. Some want "independence" or secession; some seek regional federations (as opposed to pan-Islamist movements that struggle against democratic federations!)

At the same time, however, political and military pressures may press differing groups together. U.S. backing for a Filipino crackdown on Abu Sayyaf, seen as linked to al-Qaida and Jemaah Islamiyah, appears to risk widening the conflict to other actors, the Moro National Liberation Front and militant Moro Islamic Liberation Front. The crackdown on Islamic movements has additionally upset off and on Filipino peace negotiations with the latter, while potentially angering Indonesia and Malaysia. This could provoke yet another coup attempt in Manila for the government's ostensible failure to get tough.[19]

Further distinctions can be made between the specific political circumstances in which the groups are formed and the primary goals of those groups. The Sh'ite Hizb'allah (Party of God) was founded in 1982 after the invasion of Lebanon by Israel. The Sunni Hamas (Zeal) and Islamic Jihad organizations were founded in 1987 with the outbreak of the first Palestinian Intifada; both represent the more militant offshoots of the Muslim Brotherhood, which was founded in 1924 following the break-up of the Ottoman Empire. Moreover, the Brotherhood itself has sought to channel its followers into politics and charity and has attempted to distance itself from the violence associated with one of its foremost thinkers, Sayyub Qutb. Despite its history of resistance to Egyptian leaders Nasser and Sadat (see Chapter 6), the Muslim Brotherhood is generally seen as too moderate and reformist by more radical elites, such the Egyptian al Qaida leader, Ayman al-Zawahiri.[20]

Here, the differing national organizations of the Muslim Brotherhood possess divergent views despite the group's international following and its relatively peaceful quest to achieve a pan-Islamic caliphate. Nevertheless, the Brotherhood is strongly antiliberal and argues that a number of essentially secular governments and Islamic regimes (including Egypt, Algeria, Morocco, Turkey, Malaysia, Indonesia, Pakistan, and Saudi Arabia) dwell in a corrupted psychological condition of greed (in that their elite leaderships have not engaged in personal *jihad* against materialism). This corruption appears manifest in that these governments generally do not appear capable of providing public services such as basic education, health care, environmental protection, and transportation.

Ironically, Bush administration efforts to "democratize" a number of Arab and Islamic regimes since the 2003 intervention in Iraq, coupled with steps to "demonize" a wide range of Islamic movements without drawing distinctions, have had the effect of politically strengthening a number of hard-line Islamist movements and compelling many of these same regimes to take steps to repress *both* moderate *and* hard-line movements to retain power.[21]

Iraq and Splintering Factions

In Iraq, following the U.S. decision to dissolve the Ba'ath Socialist party, Sunni Muslims have splintered into numerous parties, such as the Iraqi Islamic Party, Muslim Clerics Association, Iraqi Council of National Dialogue, and the Conference of the People of Iraq, among others. Numerous Sunni factions have resisted the U.S. "occupation" in Iraq, including those Islamic "patriots" who support the former Ba'ath Socialist regime, or those groups that are aligned with al-Qaida, such as the Jama'at al-Tawhid wa'al-Jihad, of the Jordanian-Palestinian Abu Mus'ab al-Zarqawi (killed by an U.S. air raid in June 2006), who sought to link the pan-Arab pan-Sunni struggle in Iraq to a greater Syria (Syria, Lebanon, Israel, and Jordan.)[22] At the same time, however, Syria, which is 75 percent Sunni, is presently run by Bashar Assad, who is Alawite, which is a minority sect that the Sunni world generally opposes as "heretical." (Al-Zarqawi's Islam has been called "radically cosmopolitan," but it is better described as "pan-Sunni."[23]

At the same time, Al-Zarqawi's group does not appeal to patriotic or nationalist-oriented Iraqi insurgents or tribal groups.)

Despite efforts to sustain unity, Shi'ite Muslims in Iraq have likewise splintered into factions. The main Iraqi Shi'ite party, the United Iraqi Alliance (UIA), led by Abdul Aziz al-Hakim, has three primary components: *Hizb al-Dawah* (HD), the Supreme Council for Islamic Revolution in Iraq (SCIRI), and the party of Moqtada al-Sadr. SCIRI was founded in Tehran in 1982 by Shi'ite exiles from Iraq. SICRI's pro-Iranian Badr militia has, however, clashed with the more "nationalist" Moqtada al-Sadr and his Jayish al-Mahdi militia, particularly between April 2003 and late 2005.

In addition, the more "quietist" Shi'ite traditions of Najaf (as supported by the Grand Ayatollah Ali al-Sistani) compete with the more politically engaged and pro-Iranian traditions of Qom. In January 2007 a new Shi'a group called the *Jund al-Sama*, or Army of Heaven, plotted to kill the Ayatollah al-Sistani, along with other senior ayatollahs in Najaf, before about two hundred of its fighters were killed by U.S. forces. (Much as Christian millennialists support Israel against the Islamic "threat" in the belief that it will help hasten the return of Christ, the Army of Heaven hoped to prepare the way for their messiah, the Mahdi, who had ascended to heaven in the ninth century and is to return to earth to usher in a final confrontation between good and evil.)

Despite conflict between differing sects, practical politics can make strange bedfellows, or can result in opposition among individuals within the same political-religious grouping. Iraqi Muslims (both Sunni and Shi'a) generally seek a strong centralized state, as opposed to Kurdish demands for greater decentralization, if not outright independence. Here, the interim prime minister, Ibrahim Jaafari, a member of the UIA, has opposed a *decentralized* Iraq, along the lines of the Kurdish regions of Iraq, to take place throughout the country. By contrast, the leader of the UIA, Abdul Aziz al-Hakim, proposed the establishment of two new regional confederacies in the Shi'ite south in March 2006. While Sunni Muslim groups have violently opposed a more decentralized Iraq carved out of its eighteen provinces, they also opposed the appointment of Ibrahim Jaafari as a Shi'a prime minister—despite his position in favor of a centralized Iraq. (Kurdish, Sunni, and secular leaders had all accused Jaafari of failing to stop acts of revenge by Shi'a paramilitaries. The fact that the Iraqi parliament was divided into four major factions consequently stalled the appointment of a new Shi'a prime minister until the designation of Nuri Kamal al-Maliki, in late April 2006.) Shi'a groups also split with respect to the political effect of proposed direct U.S.-Iran talks over Iraqi security.[24] Prime Minister al-Maliki has been accused of permitting Shi'a militias and death squads to run amok (knowingly or unknowingly) against Sunni enemies.

Kurds and Ethnic "Gerrymandering"

The rush to execute Saddam Hussein appeared to be symbolic of Shi'a efforts to obtain revenge against his Sunni-dominated rule and previous execution of Shi'a leaders, while at the same time the Kurds, who were likewise oppressed by

Saddam Hussein, were not able to put him to trial as well, so as to achieve a modicum of catharsis. The sudden execution of Saddam Hussein blocked public and legal examination of the brutal campaigns against the Kurds (seen as backed by Iran) during the Iran-Iraq War in the 1980s in which as many as 180,000 Kurds were killed. The use of chemical weaponry during the 1988 Anfal campaign was, however, later examined in the trial of Ali Hassan al-Majid, known as "Chemical Ali," who was convicted on charges of genocide and crimes against humanity in June 2007. The execution of Saddam Hussein also meant a lack of closure for the Americans—so as to obtain a full disclosure of U.S., European, and Russian support for Iraq during the 1980–88 Iran-Iraq War.

Kurdish groups (which can be called "pan- or ethnonationalist" despite their ideological divisions) have been in favor of greater decentralization (having initially obtained greater autonomy after the 1990–91 Persian Gulf War), while seeking irredentist ties with Kurds in Turkey, Iran, and Syria. At the same time, they are divided into generally secular political factions, between the Marxist-oriented Kurdistan Workers' Party (PKK), the ostensibly democratic Kurdistan Democratic Party (KDP), and the nationalist leaning Patriotic Union of Turkey (PUK). These groups have fought among themselves—as well as with both Turkey and Iraq. Most Kurds in Iraq are Sunni Muslims (over five hundred thousand Shi'a Faili Kurds were expelled from Iraq in 1980).

The main Kurdish parties, KDP and the PUK, for example, which appear to be moving toward reconciliation, want the oil-rich trade center of Kirkuk to be incorporated into an "enlarged autonomous" Kurdish region of Iraq, but have not yet publicly demanded outright independence. Kurdish militias have purportedly victimized Arabs and Turkomen in a form of ethnic "gerrymandering"—so that Kurds can better determine the future of the oil-rich city of Kirkuk. Previous elections had blocked minority groups from voting. (Actions of the PKK in Turkey, plus concern for the fate of Turkomen and oil interests, have led Turkey to threaten intervention in northern Iraq. Concurrently, the U.S. troop surge in Baghdad might have helped to push Sunni-backed terrorist actions into Iraqi Kurdistan by July 2007.

Only the Kurdish Sunni Islamist group Ansar *al-Islam*, which opposes the PUK, appears to have some links with *al-Qaida* and might possibly serve Iranian interests in Iraq. (In 2006 this group was, however, rumored to have turned against Iran—supported by Israel and the United States.) The presence of *Ansar al-Islam* in Iraq was used by the Bush administration to "prove" a link between Saddam Hussein and *al-Qaida* before the U.S.-led intervention, yet *Ansar al-Islam* thrived in the mountainous regions of Kurdish Iraq, largely beyond the reach of Saddam Hussein's forces. It is possible that Saddam Hussein had limited contact with this group, but no formal control. By contrast, in addition to harboring the Palestinian terrorist Abu Nidal, Saddam Hussein did directly support the Mujahedin-e Khalq (MEK), an exiled "Islamic socialist" group that opposed Iran's theocracy and that exposed Iran's secret nuclear enrichment program in 2002—ironically, an example in which a "terrorist" organization served U.S. interests. What to do with the MEK represented one of the contentious issues between the United States and the Iranian government after the U.S. intervention in Iraq (see Chapters 2, 3 and 4).[25]

Limited Policy Options

As the primary goal of each partisan group is very different, such groups cannot easily be labeled as generically "radical Islamist"; each group can and should be treated very differently. In implementing a concerted strategy of multilateral dissuasion and persuasion, Washington, the Europeans, and Moscow need to ascertain with which groups it is possible to negotiate (if given the appropriate and mutually agreeable incentives); which groups need to be "contained" making it more difficult for them to engage in "terrorist" activities; and which groups need to be "drawn and quartered," if not eradicated (if possible). Despite apparently common ideologies among some "radical" groups, there is no reason to assume that an absolute "solidarity" exists among various Islamist groups and states.

A policy of "containment" seeks to prevent opposing states from further expanding their power and influence; such a containment policy also seeks to prevent militant groups that have already gained public support from gaining even greater popularity and strength. In the post-cold war era, a number of militant groups have made significant gains (if not victories) in the electoral process. These groups include the African National Congress, with its military wing, *Umkhonto we Sizwe* (based on the Israeli *Irgun*); the Kosovo Liberation Army, with its political directorate, *Drejtoria Politike*; the Irish Republican Army (IRA), with its more moderate political representation, *Sinn Fein*, in Ireland; the *Euskadi Ta Askatasuna* (ETA) "Basque Fatherland and Liberty" in Spain, with its ostensibly more moderate political representation, *Batasuna*; the Islamic Brotherhood in Egypt[26]; *Hizb'allah*, which holds twenty-three seats in the Lebanese parliament but has thus far refused to give up its arms, with its military wing, the Islamic Resistance (*Al-Mowqawama al-Islamiyya*); the coalition of Islamist parties, the *Muttahida Majlis-e-Amal* (MMA) in Pakistan, which supports the Taliban, seeks Kashmiri independence, and opposes the U.S.-Pakistan alliance; *Hizb-i-Islami* in Afghanistan, which has both a military and political wing, with its leader Gulbuddin Hekmatyar who has opposed both the Soviet and NATO and U.S. presence in Afghanistan, after previously being supported by the United States and Pakistan against the Soviet intervention; *Hamas*, with its armed wing *Izz Al-Din Al Qassam* and *al-Fatah*, with its military wing, the Al Aqsa Martyrs Brigades in Palestine.

The rise of political parties often linked to overt or secret "terrorist" organizations or paramilitaries has raised the question as to whether or not the participation of these groups in the government will necessarily moderate their previously militant behavior and thus "contain" their potential militancy. Here, for example, the United States has considered the entire Hizb'allah organization as "terrorist" while the United Kingdom has listed its "external security organization" as "terrorist" but not its Lebanese faction. Or, in some cases, could certain groups usurp power and establish essentially one party or dictatorial regimes, as did Hamas in

Gaza in 2007? Or can military, political, and economic pressures impel these groups to alter their political stance once they enter political office?

A strategy of "drawing and quartering" seeks to split relatively less militant factions from intransigent militants who oppose all forms of compromise. The former Turkish Welfare Party, for example, had been opposed by the Turkish military for undermining the secular nature of the Turkish state; under military pressure, the Welfare Party then split into at least two factions, the reformist Justice and Development Party, which abides by parliamentary systems of governance, and the more traditionalist, Islamic Felicity Party. Secular opponents to the moderate Islamic Justice and Development Party, which now rules Turkey, however, continue to fear steps toward Shari'a law, particularly since Foreign Minister Abdullah Gul did win the presidency in August 2007.[27]

The Irish Republican Army split between the IRA and the more intransigent "Real IRA." The Moro Islamic Liberation Front (MILF) in the Philippines, which seeks independence, split in 1977 from the Moro National Liberation Front, after the latter (under military pressure) advocated a more conciliatory approach toward the government and accepted greater autonomy in 1987.[28] The less extremist members of the Islamic Salvation Front (ISF) ultimately split from the Armed Islamic Group in Algeria, in the long process of ending a tragic civil war, costing between 150,000 and 200,000 lives. Involving both state-supported and antistate "terrorism," the civil war had begun in 1991–92 when it was feared that the Islamic Salvation Front would win a majority in the second round of parliamentary elections and impose Shari'a law, among other actions.

A policy of negotiation seeks to find areas of common accord with militant groups that will accept some form of dialogue. Discussions might, at first, take place in secret or indirectly through third parties. Such a dialogue had taken place between African National Congress, the United States, and the South African government; between the Kosovo Liberation Army and the United States and NATO (despite the fact that the KLA was considered to be a terrorist group by the United States in 1998); the Irish Republican Army and the UK government; and secretly through the Oslo Accords between Israel and the PLO. Negotiations have taken place between the Spanish government and the Basque *Batasuna*. In June 2006 both U.S. ambassador Zalmay Khalilzad and Iraqi president Jalal Talabani claimed the United States and Iraq had arranged secret meetings with some of the insurgent groups in the effort to prevent them from siding with "religious zealots," such as al-Zarqawi and *al-Qaida*. These claims had, however, been denied by Iraqi insurgents, who stated that they would not have met with Iraqi government officials (whom they denounce as "puppets"), but with U.S. officials.[29] (See Chapter 3).

For the most part, the United States has been more reluctant to engage with various terrorist groups or "rogue" states than the Europeans have been. (France, for example, has been accused of dealing secretly with *Hamas*.) Although Moscow opposed dealing with Chechen partisan movements (which it has generally considered "Wahabist" or "Salafist" backed by Saudi Arabia despite the fact that only a minority have been influenced by Salafism since the 1950s and more are influenced by the Hanafi school, if not Sufi islam), Russia was among the first non-Islamic states to engage Hamas following its "surprise" election victory in January 2006—to the dismay of Washington.[30]

Virtual Negotiations

Public officials often claim that they will never enter into dialogue with "terrorists," but governments nevertheless do engage in some form of negotiation, or dialogue, through intermediaries, albeit generally in secret, assuming they can open channels for communication at some point. Some negotiations with "terrorist" factions also take place in "virtual reality"—that is, in the media and in the shadows. This is particularly true if the groups or cells involved are highly decentralized and linked only by a common ideology. The problem is that there may be no one central group or person with whom to communicate.

In this respect, the decision to pull the majority of U.S. troops out of the holy lands of Saudi Arabia and move them to Qatar (and to Iraq) represented a tacit concession—and highly symbolic gesture—to one of bin Laden's key demands. One of the major demands of the kidnappers and assassins of reporter Daniel Pearl in Pakistan in February 2002 was that the United States resume the sales of F-16 fighter jets, or else return the payment that had not been received by Islamabad after Pakistan had purchased the fighter jets.[31] The Bush administration ultimately reversed U.S. policy and pressed Congress to sell F-16s in 2005–2006—ostensibly as a reward for Pakistan's efforts (albeit limited) against *al-Qaida* and Taliban operatives in the "global war on terror" and despite Pakistan's purported role in the spread of nuclear expertise to North Korea, Iraq, Libya, and Iran through the A. Q. Khan nuclear network.

The Second Temptation: Overreaction

If political groups cannot foment a revolution, one immediate goal of antistate partisan organizations that use "terrorism" as a tool is to destabilize governments, to impel a coup d'état, or else to force foreign forces out of a country that are regarded as protecting an "illegitimate" regime. Another possible goal is to provoke military intervention and police reprisals so as to augment domestic repression. Here antistate partisan groups seek to provoke the state or foreign forces to overreact and commit atrocities—and thus impel the state itself to engage in repression and acts of terrorism. This is done in the effort to gain popular support for their side, or else to polarize the society against the government so that the latter loses its effectiveness, support, and perceived legitimacy.

As a means to obtain wider Muslim support for his cause, bin Laden initially realized that he could manipulate Washington—in the foreseen expectation of an U.S. *overreaction* to provocation. Claiming that the "destroyed towers in Lebanon" after the 1982 Israeli invasion had inspired him to "destroy towers in America so that it tastes what we taste and would be deterred from killing our children and women," bin Laden planned his attacks on the World Trade Center and Pentagon in the clichéd expectations of a U.S. "cowboy" style *overreaction*.

These expectations of overreaction were based on President Bill Clinton's actions in striking targets with multimillion-dollar cruise missiles (which would most likely to be scrapped after a certain period of time) in both the Sudan and in Afghanistan in response to the bloody, yet largely "symbolic," bombings of the U.S. embassies in Kenya and Tanzania. While *al-Qaida* operatives expected U.S. counterattacks on Afghanistan (and even predicted the use of nuclear weapons), they did not expect the essentially unilateral U.S. intervention against Iraq; the latter attack was considered a godsend, a "gift from the heavens for *Al-Qaida*."[32] Overreaction to the September 11 attacks combined with apocalyptic fears of WMD in the hands of a "rogue state" permitted Washington to obtain strong domestic and Congressional support in the effort to "preempt" (or really preclude) a formerly "unthinkable" catastrophe of nuclear terrorism without thinking through the immediate and long-term ramifications of such action.

U.S. intervention in Iraq consequently served *al-Qaida*'s ultimate purposes by providing "proof that America is not merely interested in revenge for 9/11—it shows that America wants to besiege Muslims. Second, it has highlighted the quisling status of Arab regimes. Thirdly, Iraq is an ideal place to pin down and attack the Americans."[33] Washington consequently fell into the snare, yet largely going way beyond *al-Qaida*'s wildest dreams.[34]

Political-economic Impact

More indirect, consequences of terrorist actions (and much hoped for overreactions) include the decision of states to adopt protectionist measures and for private firms to augment security measures, hence exacerbating political-social-economic tensions. In business terms, fears of terrorism tend to reduce confidence and increase risk perceptions and risk premiums, thus increasing insurance costs for cargoes and passengers, also leading to lower rates of investment and reduced economic growth and trade flows. Acts of terrorism also create the need to carry higher levels of inventory (because of the potential for terrorism to cause bottlenecks in delivery systems), thus reducing the benefits of "just-in-time" manufacturing processes and undermining supply chain management.[35]

In addition to assassinations, car bombings, suicide missions, air hijacking, other targets of terrorist groups often include oil pipelines or other energy facilities, as in Colombia, Iraq, Afghanistan, Somalia, and Saudi Arabia or along shipping routes, such as the coast of Somalia and the Straits of Malacca—to force up the price of energy and destabilize societies dependent on oil. In February 2007, al-Qaida called for attacks against oil producers that supply the United States, including Canada, Venezuela, and Mexico. This call to arms could possibly attract groups other than those with pan-Islamist ideologies.

Acts of terrorism given high media attention are consequently intended to disrupt the economies of countries that are highly dependent on tourism, such as Sharm El Sheik, Egypt, and Bali, Indonesia. Tourist arrivals in Bali in 2003, for example, declined by 23 percent following the October 2002 attack.[36] Acts of terrorism consequently seek the maximum political, economic and psychological impact with the minimal expenditure, in the hope to impel an overreaction that will destabilize or polarize societies and gain more converts. In this latter respect, al-Qaida's spending for the September 11 attacks has been crudely estimated between $250,000 and $500,000 (for flight training, reconnaissance, transportation, and box cutters).[37] The September 11, 2001, attacks (which resulted in roughly three thousand deaths and $32.5 billion in *insured* damages) not only caused more destruction than any previous act of antistate terrorism in U.S. history but also provided Washington a rationale (if not a pretext) to significantly boost both defense and counterterrorism spending. (In historical terms, acts of antistate terrorism or really sabotage, such as the burning of the *Reichstag* in Nazi Germany and the Manchurian incident that justified the Japanese intervention in China, have generally paled in comparison to acts of state-supported terrorism of Nazi Germany, the Soviet Union, Imperial Japan, the Khmer Rouge, or the more recent one hundred days of Rwandan genocide, etc.)

Moreover, while the United States has frozen more than $140 million in "terrorist" assets in 1,400 bank accounts worldwide, this does not prevent relatively inexpensive and decentralized actions: The March 11, 2004 Madrid bombings cost around $10,000 to $15,000; the estimated cost of the bombings in Bali was between $15,000 to $50,000; the London subway attacks in July 2005 cost less than $2,000.[38] As early as October 16, 2003, just after the U.S. intervention in Iraq, former secretary of defense Donald Rumsfeld raised the question as to whether or not the United States was "winning" the war on terrorism: "Does the U.S. need to fashion a broad, integrated plan to stop the next generation of terrorists? The U.S. is putting relatively little effort into a long-range plan, but we are putting a great deal of effort into trying to stop terrorists. The cost-benefit ratio is against us! Our cost is billions against the terrorists' costs of millions."[39] Despite the fact that "the terrorists" are not at all unified in terms of organizational structure, their seemingly spontaneous acts are often able to provoke excessive counterresponses.

In effect, the Bush administration's decision to expand the "global war on terror" from Afghanistan to the "rogue state" of Iraq has represented a godsend for pan-Islamist forces seeking to undermine U.S. legitimacy throughout the Arab and Islamic worlds and to build a popular following among *jihadi* elements so as to impel the United States out of both Afghanistan and Iraq. In effect, U.S. *overreaction* has played into the hands of *al-Qaida* and other groups and states in political and economic terms, as these groups attempt to use minimum resources for maximum political, economic, and media effect throughout the world, and to *impel* the United States into acts of "collateral damage" and into overextension through a war of attrition—in the ultimate hope to force the United States (and other states) into "isolationist" retrenchment and withdrawal. Another possible ramification of terrorist actions—whether intentional or unintentional—would be to draw major and regional powers into violent collision.

The Third Temptation: Torture and Illicit Means

The United States should resist, as much as possible, the temptation to fight the "global war on terror" by using means that overtly violate international law and that raise accusations of "double standards." The Bush administration has been accused of forming its own minigulag of "Islamic militants" (with detention camps and torture facilities in Bagram Air Base in Kabul, Afghanistan; at Abu Ghraib prison in Iraq; at Camp Delta in Guantánamo Bay, Cuba; and purportedly in eastern Europe along with a global network of secret CIA prisons in other countries.) The latter threaten to become a maxigulag should the United States intervene militarily against Iran's nuclear facilities or should Washington declare a "formal war" against all kinds of radical Islamist groups, as has been suggested by superhawkish "neoneoconservatives."[40] It has been estimated that, as of May 2007, roughly forty thousand individuals could be in U.S. and Iraqi managed prisons with no sign of death squad activity and violence ceasing.[41]

In addition to the prison camps for *al-Qaida*, the "rank and file" of the Iraqi Interior Ministry had set up a concealed network of torture facilities that "are doing the same as [in] Saddam's time and worse," according to Ayad Allawi, the former interim prime minister of Iraq and head of the secular Iraqi National Reconciliation Party. These torture facilities have been designed as an aspect of Shi'a revenge against Sunni atrocities that were committed both before and after Saddam Hussein's reign of terror. In this respect, it is clear that the "double standards" engaged in by both the U.S. and the Iraqi government have only served to inflame sectarian strife between Sunni and Shi'a, ironically turning differing "terrorist" factions of "radical Islamists" against each other, making it even more difficult to reach a stable settlement, and to establish an Iraqi government with perceived legitimacy. (See Chapter 3.)

Washington has thus far refused to abide by the Geneva Convention. In effect, picking and choosing between international laws it will abide by, the United States has argued that the presumed al-Qaida "terrorists" themselves do not abide by Geneva rules (and did not actually sign the convention), so why should the United States? Washington has additionally argued that the provisions of the Geneva Convention do apply to the conflict with the Taliban, but that Taliban detainees, as unlawful combatants, do not fall under article 4 of the Third Geneva Convention.[42] In this respect, the Bush administration has appeared to ignore the fact that it is now engaged in a "new," highly media-covered form of struggle that is quite different from more traditional wars with states and conventional militaries. The actual form of warfare has been *asymmetrical* in that various partisan forces cannot hope to match overall U.S. force capabilities, but force capabilities are often *relative*: Conventional or suicidal attacks against key strategic targets (pipelines, electrical plants, military and police recruitment centers, UN headquarters, centers of communication and population centers)—plus effective use of media—helps to "equalize" the conflict—in the *specific situation*—which is then "blown up" and internationalized by propaganda.

Photos and testimony against any illicit act of U.S. counterterrorism can furthermore be sent around the world by Internet, CD ROM, video, TV broadcasts (with *Al-Jazeera* competing with CNN)—as were the pictures of Saddam Hussein's hanging filmed by portable phone. According to leaked tapes, President Bush discussed the option of bombing *Al Jazeera* itself with Tony Blair.[43] More so than previous forms of communication, the Internet has permitted antistate partisan groups to bypass the requirements of traditional media (television, radio, or print media) and directly communicate with diverse global audiences of members, sympathizers, media, and potentially millions of people, thus internationalizing issues and transcending local communities. In addition to disseminating propaganda by displaying speeches, training manuals, and multimedia resources, the Internet permits groups to raise funds and recruit.[44] The global reach of the Internet additionally makes it more difficult for governments to control "spin."

Every "illegal" act that the United States commits—whether by accidental "collateral damage" or questionable and illicit military technologies, such as use of cluster bombs, depleted uranium penetrators, fuel air explosives—can thus be manipulated by pan-Islamist propagandists (or other groups) to convert more followers, more individuals willing to engage in acts of "terror." For every scrap of information that torture might obtain (along with much more mis- and disinformation), it can also provoke the birth of hundreds of potential "terrorists." The torture of pan-Islamist activists, such as Sayyub Qutb and later Ayman al-Zawahiri, might have caused both (as well as their associates) to seek revenge not only against the Egyptian government for torturing them but also against the United States (and the Western world in general) for supporting repressive regimes and for ostensibly helping to corrupt Islam.[45]

Although all previous wars have involved propaganda in one form or another—in the effort to win "the hearts and minds" of the population and delegitimize the rival's leadership—today's "postmodern" antistate warfare is perhaps even more concerned with psychological and symbolic aspects of a target than with its military value. One of the basic goals of antistate asymmetrical warfare is to underscore double standards and pretensions. When the United States resorts to torture, it undermines the American creed. Yet, what is even more disturbing about the revelations of U.S. torture facilities is the fact that Washington has used methods of torture that seek to denigrate Islamic beliefs and values. How can Washington win the "hearts and minds" (as the Pentagon puts it) of the more "moderate" Islamic populations, if the United States is known to use torture techniques that denigrate Islamic culture in general?

Bush administration neoconservatives—who previously propagandized in support of the war—initially claimed that the United States was taking the "high moral ground" in fighting terrorism in Afghanistan and in eliminating the regime of Saddam Hussein. Although they do not want to claim credit for the way the Iraq War has been fought, neoconservatives are ideologically responsible for the superhawk, or really vulture-like, strategy of "preemption," which was, in reality, a policy of preclusion, if not predation. They are also responsible for the belief that essentially unilateral military intervention in Iraq was to be a "cakewalk" and for the policy of *de-Ba'athification*, as well as for the radical privatization of the "socialist" political economy to include oil industry and for many policies that have generally boosted the Iraqi resistance.[46] But once the Bush administration fully engaged in the "global war on terror" in Afghanistan and Iraq, the United States has increasingly been seen as perpetrating "state-supported terror" and thus acting as a "rogue state" itself. The problem is not so much that the United States has been in danger of losing its presumed "high moral ground" but that it may have lost its ability to play "honest broker" between con-flicting parties.

U.S. Sen. John McCain (R-AZ) put it this way in his effort to change Bush administration policy toward torture:

> To prevail in this war we need more than victories on the battlefield. This is a war of ideas, a struggle to advance freedom in the face of terror in places where oppressive rule has bred the malevolence that creates terrorists. Prisoner abuses exact a terrible toll on us in this war of ideas. They inevitably become public, and when they do they threaten our moral standing, and expose us to false but widely disseminated charges that democracies are no more inherently idealistic and moral than other regimes. This is an existential fight, to be sure. If they could, Islamist extremists who resort to terror would destroy us utterly. But to defeat them we must prevail in our defense of American political values as well. The mistreatment of prisoners greatly injures that effort.[47]

Yet, in his political struggle to ban torture, as he himself was tortured by the North Vietnamese and forced to sign a meaningless confession, Senator McCain was not able to prevail in his defense of U.S. political values. In this case he was forced to backtrack under pressure from both the White House and the Pentagon into accepting a "torture compromise" for the 2006 Military Commissions Act.[48] The senatorial compromise (signed into law October 17, 2006) permits the president to "interpret the meaning and application" of Geneva Convention standards, while the White House additionally sought other ways to circumvent the compromise.[49]

The Bush administration has consequently refused to stop splitting legal hairs and to take steps that conform closer to international law and to UN recommendations.[50] Replacing Donald Rumsfeld after the November 2006 midterm elections, the new secretary of defense, Robert M. Gates, purportedly argued for closing down Guantánamo Bay and bringing trials of suspected terrorist suspects to the United States—for the sake of credibility and because Guantánamo's continued existence harmed the broader goals of the "global war on terror." His efforts were said to be supported by Secretary of State Condoleezza Rice but have been successfully opposed—thus far—by Attorney General Alberto R. Gonzales and Vice President Dick Cheney.[51]

In effect, the use of torture (dubbed "enhanced interrogation techniques" by the Bush administration) has represented an additional form of *overreaction* that is backfiring against U.S. interests by making its allies less willing to cooperate with the United States and by undermining actual and potential multilateral support from the European Union as well as from Arab and Islamic states. Here, many European Union countries (e.g., Germany, Netherlands, the United Kingdom, Spain, and Belgium) have given support to the legal concept of "universal jurisdiction" that forms the conceptual basis for the International Criminal Court (ICC); the United States, however, has opposed the ICC (along with China, Iran, Israel, Libya, and Qatar.) U.S. support for torture also puts U.S. troops in even greater danger than troops of other states should they be captured, since they are more exposed than troops of other states.[52] As it is the leading powers that set global normative standards, the use of torture or other illegal acts gives the green light for other states to engage in similar actions—which then weakens the otherwise strong U.S. human rights case against regimes that even more routinely use torture against their own citizens.

And finally, instead of trying to moralize against states that use torture, the United States, as still the world's leading power, needs to support stronger international and regional institutions as well as nongovernmental organizations that would attempt to persuade all states (including the United States) not to violate human rights. Here, the new UN Human Rights Council appears to be a net improvement over the old UN Human Rights Commission in that it will meet at least three times a year, and because emergency sessions can be called on the request of "only" one-third of the membership (of forty-seven members). At the same time, however, to press states into action on civil emergencies and in the effort to prevent genocide and ethnic cleansing, the Human Rights Council should select internationally prominent human rights activists as members of a human rights advisory body—who would represent a fairer judge of human rights violations than either an UN human rights "commission" or "council" that is linked to the membership of governments alone.[53]

In September 2006 the new Human Rights Council identified a number of states accused of gross violations of human rights in the past or that have recently been engaged in severe repression of various antistate movements. The realistic question is whether this new council can bring a number of these states (perhaps with the legal and political assistance of various civil society organizations) into a dialogue so that they begin to ameliorate prison conditions and violent actions against domestic political opponents. Washington could also attempt to work more closely with the Organization of the Islamic Conference, for example, to create a dialogue between American, European, and Islamic conceptions of human rights. The latter possibility is, of course, made more difficult when the United States—as the world's leading power—stands accused of legalizing "torture," however defined.

Unlike Saint Anthony, the United States cannot withdraw into isolation, adopting the life of a hermit in the desert (although there are increasing domestic demands for it to do so). Washington needs to adopt both short- and long-term diplomatic strategies to deal with the crises posed by both antistate and state-supported "terrorist" actions, including the "blowback" resulting from its own overreaction and blunders. In the interest of ending the "global war on terror" and in sustaining global peace, and in the interest of sustaining a positive U.S. image and credibility, the United States should absolutely resist the temptation to stoop as low as some of its opponents have in the ultimately futile attempt to fight "terror" with "terror," thereby sinking even more deeply into that utterly immoral and grotesque world—as depicted in Hieronymous Bosch's painting, *The Temptation of St. Anthony.*

Postscript: Donald Rumsfeld's Reflections

In a moment of critical reflection, Donald Rumsfeld, after stepping down as secretary of defense, after the November 2006 Democratic victory in the House and Senate midterm elections, caustically stated his regret for having used the term, "war on terror." He explained that the term "'war' conjures up World War II more than it does the Cold War" and that it "creates a level of expectation of victory and an ending within 30 or 60 minutes of a soap opera. It isn't going to happen that way." Here, however, neither World War II nor the cold war represent appropriate historical analogies; in many ways the predilection to look at the "global war on terrorism" through a cold war mind-set is at the roots of the crisis.

Rumsfeld continued to argue that "I've worked to reduce the extent to which that [label] is used and increased the extent to which we understand it more as a long war, or a struggle, or a conflict, not against terrorism, but against a relatively small number of terribly dangerous and violent extremists."[54] Yet, it was not until May 2005 that the Bush administration did attempt to change the term "Global War on Terror" (GWOT) to "Global Struggle against Violent Extremism (G-SAVE)"—but the latter acronym did not stick.[55] Moreover, this belated reasoning is precisely why the Europeans preferred *at the outset* to call this conflict a "fight against terrorism" as opposed to a "war against terrorism"[56]—yet no one in the Bush administration would listen to the EU at that time!

In avoiding the term "Islam," Rumsfeld did recognize that "Terror is a weapon of choice for extremists who are trying to destabilize regimes and (through) a small group of clerics, impose their dark vision on all the people they can control."[57] But Rumsfeld's statement does not appear to recognize the fact that "terror" can be an instrument used by states as well or that a major aspect of the problem of "antistate terrorism" is that of retaliation for "state-sponsored terrorism." At the same time, however, while ignoring his failure to deploy sufficient forces to protect weapons depots, government buildings, and national treasures at the outset of the Iraq intervention, he did recognize that the deployment of more troops "can have exactly the opposite effect. It can increase recruiting for extremists. It can increase financing for extremists." By declaring a "global war on terror," the Bush administration regrettably did conjure up images of World War II. Having turned a battle against a few extremists into a titanic Manichean struggle in the global media, the problem now is how to wind down that war so as to prevent it from becoming a truly global conflict—involving both antistate actors and major powers, possibly with weapons of mass destruction.

CHAPTER 2

The Uncoordinated NATO-EU "Double Enlargement": Toward the Isolation of Russia?

The founders of the post–World War II U.S. "containment" strategy, George Kennan and Paul Nitze, had both opposed NATO enlargement into central and eastern Europe following the Soviet collapse. In February 1997, Kennan asserted that NATO enlargement "would be the most fatal error of U.S. policy in the entire post-Cold War era."[1] On the surface, this statement appears to have been overtaken by the colossal strategic blunder of U.S. intervention in Iraq. (See Chapter 3.) Yet, the global ramifications of U.S. military expansion and NATO enlargement have begun to reveal themselves: Russian leaders have begun to more forthrightly denounce U.S. National Missile Defense (NMD) policy, NATO enlargement, and the 1990 Conventional Force in Europe (CFE) treaty (adapted in 1999).[2] On July 14, 2007, Russia stated that it would suspend its participation in the CFE until NATO ratified the treaty.

In May 1995, the late ambassador Paul Nitze wrote an unpublished draft editorial, in which he stated:

> With the vulnerability of Russia's new democracy, pushing for NATO enlargement will likely exacerbate the existing destructive, internal pressures. A wrong move on our part could easily backfire, triggering a rise to power by Russia's nationalists, sidetracking START II and possibly unraveling other arms agreements—without which NATO will find itself back in a cold war environment. It is far better to act on the belief that Russian nationalists are growing in political power and be wrong by curtailing NATO expansion, than it is to risk European instability in the face of a new confrontation with Moscow. . . . *Our long term objective should be to promote the engagement not the exclusion of Russia in Europe.* (emphasis author's)[3]

Paul Nitze's argument against NATO enlargement was not limited to fears that NATO might provoke a Russian backlash; Nitze's position was also based on the argument that "less is more"—that an enlarged NATO risked its potential overextension in confrontation with new threats should it bring in new members that were essentially "consumers" but not "producers" of security. Furthermore, the more NATO became involved in peacekeeping and in regional "out of area" conflicts (such as the question of Bosnia at the time Nitze was writing), the less attention NATO would pay to strategic nuclear defense, and the less it would be prepared to deter possible conventional and nuclear conflict among the major powers. Strategic military decision making would furthermore be hampered by too many members. The problem raised here is that an increasingly "global" NATO that seeks to defend the expanded borders of a new Europe—at the same time that it both provokes Russia and engages in peacekeeping in the Balkans and in the global war on terror in Afghanistan—risks hypertrophy.

The NATO debate had traumatized the Clinton administration, but it appeared to lay dormant following NATO enlargement to central Europe in 1999 (bringing in Poland, the Czech Republic, Hungary, and former East Germany). This first wave of enlargement was followed by a second wave of NATO enlargement to eastern Europe (and to the Russian borders) during President George W. Bush's first term in 2004 (bringing in Latvia, Lithuania, Estonia, Slovakia, Bulgaria, Romania, and Slovenia). The arguments against NATO enlargement during the Clinton administration debates were countered by then Secretary of State Madeline Albright, who was Zbigniew Brzezinski's protégée. Albright argued that such criticism represented an example of "old thinking" in that it presumed that NATO was still carrying out its cold war mission but that NATO was now in the process of far-reaching reform. The question, however, was really to what extent the increasingly authoritarian Russian leadership (and Russia's allies) regard NATO as thoroughly transforming its cold war orientation as a vehicle to contain or preclude Russian ambitions and to what extent Russia is really being brought "on board." Moscow had requested a "NATO plus 1" relationship as early as 1992; in 1997 Russia was brought indirectly into the decision-making process by membership in the Permanent Joint Council; by May 2002, Russia was brought into the NATO-Russia Council (NRC), meeting all NATO members face to face, yet still without the right to a vote or a veto. As Russia cannot block a NATO decision once it has been made and as the NRC has limited funding and joint tasks, Russia's relationship with the United States and NATO thus remains uncertain and ambiguous.

Proponents of NATO enlargement furthermore argued that its goal was preclusive: Its purpose was to check a feared return of Russian imperialism to the region. From an economic standpoint, enlargement appeared to provide a secure umbrella for regional development and for U.S. and multinational corporate investment. Citibank, General Motors, Pepsi, and Philip Morris were among the major investors in Poland, for example. Although the issue of arms sales was initially played down by NATO spokespersons, the United States nevertheless engaged in a significant number of arms sales in 2003, coupled with elaborate long-term financing, dubbed "the contract of the century," in which Poland purchased forty-eight Lockheed Martin F-16s (instead of the French Mirage 2000–2005 and the British-Swedish Jas-39 Gripen).[4] This was the biggest defense contract signed by a post-Soviet country since the end of the cold war.

The Return of the "Great" NATO Enlargement Debate?

The "great" NATO enlargement debate has appeared to be resurrecting itself. NATO has begun to contemplate membership for Ukraine and possibly Georgia. In March 2007, the U.S. House and Senate supported resolutions calling for the "timely admission" of Macedonia, Albania, and Croatia into NATO (the "Big MAC" enlargement), plus Ukraine and Georgia. The latter two states are more controversial than the Big MAC states from the Russian perspective, as Moscow has largely given up hope of trying to influence the politics of the Balkan states, although it does hope to sustain influence in Serbia. Here, it is not certain that Russia will once again "swallow its pride" (as it did during the previous enlargements, despite declaring the Baltic states a "red line"). While Soviet collapse had significantly weakened Russian defense and economic capabilities, the rise in world oil prices following U.S. intervention in Iraq has ironically helped Russia rebound, so that world oil prices tripled from 2002 to 2006 and Russia's economy grew at a roughly 7 percent rate.

In his February 11, 2007, Munich address, Russian president Vladimir Putin vehemently denounced perceived anti-Russian elements of U.S. foreign policy and appeared to threaten a new cold war, although ostensibly keeping the door open to compromise. The speech decried that "unilateral, illegitimate actions have not solved a single problem, they have become a hotbed of further conflicts" and that "one state, the United States, has overstepped its national borders in every way." In a play for Arab support, Putin then visited Qatar, Jordan, and Saudi Arabia (in part to discuss potential sales of nuclear technology for ostensibly "peaceful" purposes), where he reiterated, "We are seeing a greater and greater disdain for the basic principles of international law. . . . Today we are witnessing an almost uncontained hyper use of force—military force—in international relations, force that is plunging the world into an abyss of permanent conflicts. . . . NATO expansion does not have any relation with the modernization of the alliance. . . . It represents a serious provocation that reduces the level of mutual trust."[5] Putin likewise criticized the U.S. and European positions on Kosovo independence as well as the proposed deployments of missile defense systems in Poland and the Czech Republic.

Putin's Munich address, plus those in the Middle East, referred not only to unilateral U.S. intervention in Iraq, but also to U.S. policies in Bosnia and, in particular, to the war "over" Kosovo in which he claimed Russian interests were bypassed.[6] The statements also referred to the unilateral U.S. decision to withdraw from the Anti-Ballistic Missile (ABM) treaty, coupled with the possible deployment of National Missile Defense (NMD) system components in Poland (the deployment of ten interceptors) and the Czech Republic (a radar system). And last, the statement resulted from the whole process of NATO enlargement in which Soviet leader Mikhail Gorbachev had been promised (by verbal commitments by top U.S. and European leaders, German foreign minister Hans Dietrich Genscher, U.S. secretary of state James Baker, UK prime minister John Major, and German chancellor Helmut Kohl) that NATO would not expand into eastern Europe following Moscow's decision to dismantle the Warsaw Pact.[7] Russia argues that the U.S. and NATO expansion process has represented a direct violation of international law as embodied in the 1997 NATO-Russia Treaty that Russia claims stipulated that the United States would not build any major bases in the territories of the new NATO members at that time. The Russian military has furthermore regarded the expansion of a U.S. network of bases alongside the expansion of NATO "as representing twin or linked processes to encircle and threaten Russia directly if necessary."[8]

Here, the United States (not NATO) has made plans to set up at least ten ballistic missile interceptors in Poland and a radar control center in the Czech Republic (requiring communications satellites) as part of its NMD program by 2011.[9] The United States has justified its proposed NMD plan to counter potential missile threats from Iran and other "rogue" states; senior members of the Russian military believe that ten interceptor missiles in Poland could easily be augmented to one hundred in the future. This could give the United States a potential first strike capability.

In a somewhat humorous response to President Putin's speech, U.S. secretary of defense Robert Gates quipped, "One Cold War was quite enough" and called for a U.S. partnership with many countries, including Russia. By contrast, Polish and Czech leaders viewed Russian statements with alarm, arguing that it was "clearly an attempt to intimidate" and to reestablish Russian "spheres of influence" by "blackmail."[10] More critical analysis argued that the Polish and Czech decision to accept NMD had more to do with placating the Americans (and keeping the United States involved in European security and defense) and that such a missile defense would do more to anger the Russians than to assist east European defense. The Polish and Czech turn toward the United States has been complicated by the weakness of European Union in forging a common foreign and security policy; the lack of an adequate European nuclear deterrent to counter perceived threats; coupled with the French and Dutch failure to ratify the proposed European constitution; and divisions within NATO itself.[11]

Conversely, other critics argued against the excessive costs and underscored the fact that the new NMD systems would *not* be under the control of the NATO alliance, of which the Czech and Poles were members, but solely under U.S. control.[12] In addition to questioning its cost effectiveness, Europeans have questioned what the precise link is between NMD, which is designed to detect and shoot down longer-range ballistic missiles at higher altitudes, and NATO's effort to develop its own deployable medium-range or theater missile defense system (TMD). The following questions have consequently been raised as to U.S. intentions: "To what degree would BMD bring protection to Europe's territory? What is the link to NATO? Would there be information sharing about early warning data? Who would make the decision to launch missile defenses. Will control lie with Washington or Supreme Allied Command Europe (SACEUR) or with a national command post?"[13]

Moreover, if Europe finds itself under a U.S. missile defense shield instead of a NATO one, it would then raise questions as to U.S. efforts to sustain an imperial supremacy in "double restraining" European efforts to achieve relative defense autonomy and make it appear to be dividing Europe between "old" and "new" Europe, in former secretary of defense Donald Rumsfeld's terms—without engaging in "power" and "responsibility" sharing. As the United States had rejected European and NATO offers to assist U.S. forces in Afghanistan, in part due to the nature of the Pentagon's integrated command and communications systems, and as the United States essentially intervened in Iraq unilaterally, this position likewise raises questions as to the willingness of the United States to back its NATO (and EU) allies.

The German response was divided along political lines. The German Christian Democratic Union (CDU) emphasized the question of NATO's role. Defense Minister Franz Josef Jung, of Chancellor Angela Merkel's CDU, stated that he believed the strategic questions should be for NATO to decide (and not the United States alone). By contrast, Kurt Beck, leader of Germany's Social Democratic Party, stated that his party would oppose setting up a proposed U.S. missile defense project in Poland and the Czech Republic "unless a common position is worked out in a dialogue with Russia in advance."[14] The key issue here is to somehow develop a joint framework for U.S., EU, and Russian decision making for both NMD and TMD.

In March 2007, it appeared that the United States would respond to Russian criticism of its defense buildup and NMD by promising to engage in a more diplomatic outreach to Russia and by admitting that Russia deserves "a more thorough dialogue on American foreign policy and national security plans." At the same time, the United States would "stand [its] ground" in talks with Moscow and not be deterred by "Russian threats" regarding the proposed missile defense project. U.S. secretary of state Condoleezza Rice observed that Washington had held ten rounds of talks with Russia on NMD since the spring of 2006.[15] Rice (along with Polish and Czech officials) stressed that NMD talks are a matter between sovereign, independent states. The NATO-Russian Council was thus informed of the plan—that such a system cannot counter Russian strategic-nuclear capabilities. But the diplomatic timing came just at the moment that the United States was seeking Russian diplomatic supports—and support for sanctions against Iran's nuclear enrichment program.[16]

Interestingly, Russia and NATO have explored the possibility of TMD technological cooperation since at least June 2000 and engaged in joint planning and operations exercises in 2004, 2005, and 2006. While Russia hopes that NATO will purchase its S-300 and advanced S-400 Triumph TMD systems (which it claims are among the best in the world[17]), Russia and the United States (without NATO) have also explored cooperation in NMD systems. At the June 2007 G-8 summit, President Putin then proposed that Washington use the Gabala radar station that Russia leases to Azerbaijan. Putin also suggested that missile interceptors could be placed in Turkey or Iraq or sea platforms. Secretary of State Condoleeza Rice stated that it was not yet clear "whether Azerbaijan makes any sense in the context of missile defense."[18] Germany and Canada have thus far rejected hosting the project, although the United Kingdom might reconsider. Iranian missiles could be better countered from Turkey, which has stated that it will not be involved with the program. Other options could include Israel (or possibly the Golan Heights in Syria in the future). In the Caucasus, Georgia could be interested (opposed by Moscow) but so could Azerbaijan (supported by Moscow).

At the July 2007 "lobster summit" in Maine, Putin proposed permitting the United States to use a radar system in southern Russia and to bring more

European nations into the decision-making process on BMD under the umbrella of the Russia-NATO Council. A few days later, Moscow threatened the deployment of short-range missiles in Kaliningrad if the United States did opt to place BMD systems in eastern Europe (and did not share facilities with Russia), ironically the same time that Sochi in the southern Russian Caucasus mountains was selected as the site for the 2014 Olympics Games. By mid-July, Moscow announced that it was suspending its participation in the CFE treaty—in an effort to pressure the United States to negotiate.

As of mid-July 2007, Washington appeared to be considering the placement of BMD systems in the Caucasus region and in eastern Europe but still stalling on the question of BMD cooperation with Russia. The recurrent problem is whether the Pentagon would agree to share technical facilities that appear crucial to U.S. national security, given the Pentagon's emphasis on network centric warfare and complications involved in coalition operations.[19] The Pentagon would need to find a way to enhance interoperability and forge some form of NATO-Russian "dual key" controls, possibly by placing U.S.-controlled NMD or NATO-controlled TMD systems on Russian territory itself.[20] If one could argue that NMD/TMD is not a panacea, that it is excessively expensive, and that cooperation with Russia is in the greater national interest, then compromise could be found.

Geostrategic Aspects of U.S. and NATO Expansion

The Russian military has been concerned with what it considers an "encirclement" by U.S. and NATO military bases and believes that the United States appears to be looking for means to secure pipelines that bring oil and gas to Europe, but that efforts to secure or protect these pipelines could result in U.S. or NATO military intervention in Russian "spheres of influence and security."

On February 19, 2007, the commander of Russia's Strategic Missile Forces, Nikolai Solovtsov, threatened that Russia might withdraw from the 1987 Intermediate-Range Nuclear Force (INF) treaty that had limited medium-range missiles in Europe (a threat previously made in March 2005)—if the U.S. NMD plan goes ahead. Solovtsov also warned that the Czech Republic and Poland could become targets of a Russian missile strike. NATO dismissed Solovtsov's remarks as "extreme language."[21] On February 20, Foreign Minister Sergei Lavrov then reiterated that "we are seriously concerned about plans to deploy elements of a U.S. missile-defense system in Europe and the critical situation that threatens the Conventional Armed Forces in Europe Treaty." He added that "NATO's enlargement, which was undertaken despite the assurances we were given previously, does not help strengthen trust either. We are also concerned about the advance of the alliance's infrastructure toward the Russian border" in the form of new bases in eastern Europe, plus NMD systems.[22]

The U.S. State Department insisted that "the [proposed] system . . . is designed to counter threats from the Middle East or from other potential rogue states. . . . This system is not physically capable of threatening Russia, or threatening any other country for that matter. It's for defensive purposes."[23] Here, however, it is not clear how BMD systems in eastern Europe would protect

Israel and the Gulf monarchies, which would be Iran's primary targets. More importantly, the United States did not address real Russian concerns that correctly or incorrectly appear to see a "conspiracy" between NATO enlargement, the *future* potential of NMD (without Russian participation in such a system), and the CFE treaty.

From the Russian perspective, the real intent of the NMD might be to counter Russian missiles in the not-so-distant future. Here, while NMD can be used for defensive purposes, such systems could also assist a preemptive strike by providing a shield, helping to destroy second-strike retaliatory systems. Russian president Vladimir Putin consequently warned that a U.S.-backed ballistic missile shield in central Europe would foster a new arms rivalry and that the Russian response would be "asymmetric, but effective to the highest degree." The option of bringing back intermediate-range ballistic missiles, coupled with antisatellite systems to destroy U.S. communications systems, would represent an *asymmetrical* approach to counter U.S. military *superiority*.

Moscow has already developed the SS-27 Topol-M (or RT-2UTTH) intercontinental ballistic missile, which it claims could penetrate missile defenses. (Moscow is expected to deploy fifty-two of these missiles by 2007). Moscow also claims to be developing more effective weapons systems although its *Bulava* nuclear submarine and SLBM systems have suffered from technical problems. In May 2007 Russia successfully tested its new mobile ICBM, the RS-24, which Putin stated was "aimed at maintaining the balance of forces in the world" as it was capable of either a first or second strike and of penetrating BMD systems with purportedly up to ten multiple warheads (MIRVs). It then tested the R-500, a short-range cruise missile, said to be capable of evading air and missile defenses. As its aging ICBMs are in need of replacement, Moscow hopes to press Washington into renewing START I, which expires in 2009 and limits the numbers of warheads and restricts the location of deployments. Moscow's demands for a debate in a multilateral format on the BMD issue have been opposed by Poland that sees the issue in terms of "vital" national security interests and transformed international security threats. Warsaw believes Moscow is attempting to undermine U.S./ NATO defense ties that protect it against both Russian and German pressures and influence.

Putin also argued that the United States had planned to deploy NMD long before growing oil revenues gave Russia a chance to increase its defense spending—which was still twenty-five times less than Washington's defense spending, according to Russian calculations. This is because the system was planned in response to "rogue" states, but not excluding Russia.

NATO Enlargement to Ukraine?

From a domestic political-economic perspective, NATO enlargement, particularly to include Ukraine, also represents a threat to the Russian military industrial complex. The breakup of the Soviet empire has undermined Moscow's formerly integrated military-industrial complex (which was on the verge of bankruptcy), but it also makes it more difficult for Russia to produce nuclear-powered submarines and submarine-launched ballistic missiles, because contractors are now spread out across the Commonwealth of Independent States (CIS).[24] Furthermore, if Ukraine should join NATO, Kiev would most likely have to end defense industrial collaboration with Moscow—that is, unless Russia joined NATO as well, in a new form of "membership."

Moreover, there is a real danger that local and regional disputes (over irredentist claims, securing oil production and distribution, as well as fishing rights) could eventually "internationalize" as a result of the membership of eastern European states in NATO (and the EU). Here, there are evident tensions between eastern (and western) Europe and Russia over Russia's ability and willingness to supply oil and natural gas at reasonable prices. There is a real risk of conflict widening because of Russian perceptions that NATO now possesses strategic capabilities to attack deep into the Russian heartland.

Moscow's concerns were clearly expressed by Konstantin Sivkov of the Russian General Staff's Center of Military Strategic Studies in July 2005 after Russia refused to ratify a border treaty with Estonia:

> The Alliance has achieved strategic depth of operations in Russia. U.S. tactical aircraft operating from NATO airfields may now reach Moscow, Tula, Kursk, and other cities of central European Russia. This is an important factor from a geostrategic point of view. . . . It means that there are no more strategic barriers between Russia and NATO. What [might] it lead to? It may lead to escalation of border disputes with NATO countries [say because of certain territorial claims, or problems with oil production at sea, and fishing matters] into armed conflicts. Dangers of this sort exist in the Baltic region [Estonia claims the Pyatlov District of the Pskov Region] and in North Europe. . . . The situation is such that a local conflict may promptly become international. When it happens, it will be the alliance as such or the United States that will be putting forth demands, not the initiator of the conflict. Weapons may be used if Russia refuses to make concessions—space weapons first and foremost.[25]

Tensions with Estonia further flared from April to May in 2007 when the Russian government was accused of engaging in cyber sabotage against banks and Estonian institutions (costing one bank at least $1 million) after the Estonian government relocated a Soviet-era war memorial. This resulted in protests by the vocal ethnic Russian minority, who believe themselves to be discriminated against in the post-Soviet era. While the source of the attacks was more likely pro-Russian hackers than the Russian government itself, pro-Estonian hackers also struck Russian Web sites; the Estonian leadership then sought NATO and EU support against "cyber-terrorism," even pressing for article 5 security guarantees.[26] Planting computer viruses and overloading systems with excessive information, causing computer and Internet shut down and blockage might herald a new form of "cyberwarfare" that can be directed by states or individual partisan groups.

Another issue is that of tactical nuclear weaponry. The Russians argue that the United States is in a quest for nuclear and BMD superiority. Yet, while the United States has clear superiority in strategic warheads (4,183), it also possesses several hundred tactical warheads deployed in Europe (out of roughly 500 altogether). By contrast, Russia appears to be in a position of inferiority in terms of intercontinental ballistic missiles (ICBMs) in that it possesses 3,340 strategic warheads (many systems have been placed on launch on warning), but it possesses clear superiority in tactical warheads (2,330), which it claims are largely for "defensive" purposes in Europe, but which theoretically have wider use than that.[27] (Calculations of "superiority" and "inferiority" are, however, really impossible to determine in that one can only tell which side has a true advantage by testing weaponry in actual warfare. In this sense, "balance of power" calculations of relative superiority and inferiority have always possessed an element of imagination, if not myth.)

Toward the Collapse of Arms Control Treaties?

Much as Paul Nitze had forewarned, NATO enlargement, now coupled with expansion of U.S.-controlled NMD systems in Europe, could lead Russia to withdraw from a number of arms control pacts, including the crucial 1987 INF pact that Paul Nitze himself had helped to negotiate that was intended to limit the spread of intermediate ballistic missile systems throughout the world. Although Moscow has urged the United States to negotiate a replacement for the 1991 Strategic Arms Reduction Treaty (START I) that is to expire in 2009, the Bush administration has thus far refused to discuss this issue. Having withdrawn from the ABM treaty in mid-2002, after having announced its withdrawal in December 2001, the Bush administration has, in effect, left the fate of the United States (and the world) in the hands of an unproved technology in which there are numerous potential countermeasures and asymmetrical responses. By not formally renegotiating a new treaty, the Bush administration left Russia in the lurch without written mutual guarantees and guidelines as confidence-building measures.

There is the additional question of the uncoordinated NATO-EU strategic relationship. What happens if major disputes occur between Russia (or other non-NATO, non-EU states) and EU members such as Sweden, Finland, and Austria, which are not also members of NATO or U.S. security systems? Would the EU be capable of backing up the security concerns of these states? Would the EU need U.S. and NATO backing? Would the United States (and not NATO) defend these states? Here, U.S. policies appear to be dividing EU members who are not also members of NATO (possibly opening the door for Russia to play on the political differences).[28] From this perspective, what appears to be developing is a dangerous dialectic of "insecurity-security"—ostensibly stemming from the Iranian missile threat that could result in an outwardly "spiraling" arms race extending to more and more countries.

It consequently appears certain that the next U.S. presidency will need to address these issues to make up for the Bush administration's legacy of opposing international treaties. On the one hand, the option to engage Russia is opposed for fear that agreements reached with one government might be changed by the next one, particularly in the case of unstable political-economic conditions. On the other hand, holding out for a "better" deal with a "more democratic" government in Russia could aggravate the dispute, particularly when differing factions consider certain points legitimate, resulting in the rise to power of even harder line factions. Here, it appears that Russian perceptions of "encirclement" by U.S. alliances and superior military capabilities coupled with fears of eventual political-economic "isolation" can only be counteracted by stronger Russian participation in the NATO-Russia Council. The latter needs greater political support on the U.S. side and more funding to engage in joint projects so as to reduce mutual suspicions and enhance cooperation.

With regard to START I, Russia prefers a new treaty to reduce strategic nuclear warheads to less than 1,500 each, with additional limits on delivery systems, plus more intrusive measures, such as on-site inspections, while the Bush administration rejected further weapons limits and preferred new, more informal confidence-building measures that would allow for "visits" to each other's weapons storage sites.[29] The next U.S. administration will thus need to reconsider its approach to the ABM treaty, TMD, NMD, START, the INF treaty, and the CFE treaty (including the issue of eliminating tactical nuclear weapons in Europe) in addition to dealing more realistically with the Russian troop presence in the "frozen conflicts" and give more attention to banning or controlling weapons in outer space.

A Baltic-Black Sea Alliance?

Immediately following Soviet collapse, Moscow attempted to build the Commonwealth of Independent States, which would include Kazakhstan and other central Asian states. The CIS largely failed, however, to a large extent as a result of Ukraine's desire for a "civilized way of divorce." Moreover, in the 1991 to 1994 period, Ukraine threatened to retain its nuclear weaponry left over from the Soviet era, until it was dissuaded to give it up by Moscow (which threatened military strikes) and persuaded by the United States (which promised aid and assistance.)[30] Once it had agreed to give up its nuclear weaponry, Ukraine received security assurances from all five nuclear-weapon states parties to the Treaty on the Non-Proliferation of Nuclear Weapons (NPT) as a non-nuclear weapon state party. The United States and the United Kingdom, together with Russia (and by France unilaterally) took the decision in Budapest to provide Ukraine with security assurances as a non-nuclear weapon state party to the NPT. Ukraine then renounced nuclear weapons and acceded to the NPT. This represented the formation of a "regional security community" backed by the UN Security Council. The fact that Ukraine gave up its nuclear weapons capabilities did not, however, prevent peaceful and democratic "regime change" to take place a decade later in the 2004 "orange" revolution. U.S. and European support for the ostensibly pro-Western candidate in Ukraine in the December 2004 elections, plus Ukrainian interest in joining NATO, once again raised suspicions of U.S. backing for a Georgia-Ukraine-Uzbekistan-Azerbaijan-Moldova (GUUAM) alliance, and of a NATO-GUUAM-Japanese "encirclement." (GUUAM was then changed back to GUAM once Uzbekistan dropped out in May 2005, after having joined in 1999.[31]) Warsaw, Brussels, and Washington had all supported the pro-Western "reformist" Viktor A. Yushchenko of the Our Ukraine Party, while Moscow and Minsk strongly supported the candidate Viktor F. Yanukovich of the Party of Regions.

Russia been accused of using oil pressures and finances to pressure Ukraine into a more neutral stance. Moscow has subsequently been blamed for a series of pipeline incidents in which oil or gas supplies were temporarily cut off (in Ukraine, Moldova, Georgia, and Armenia) and thus seen as intentionally pressuring these states. On the one hand, Russia has cut oil and gas subsidies and moved prices closer to world market levels in accord with "capitalist" principles; on the other, it has been accused of "energy imperialism" and undermining fledgling "democracies"—at least until it also cut energy subsidies for its own ally, Belarus.[32]

Ukrainians generally oppose the basing of the Russian Black Sea Fleet (as well as its air, intelligence, and naval infantry components until at least 2017) in Crimea, which is controlled by Kiev but still claimed by Russian nationalists. The Crimean base raises fears that Kiev could be drawn by Moscow into conflict with third parties. In addition, in October 2003, despite the fact that the two sides had finally agreed in January 2003 on the delimitation of their 1,300-mile border, Moscow opted to "resolve" a territorial dispute in the Sea of Azov unilaterally—by constructing a causeway under the protection of Ministry of Emergency Situation troops in the Kerch Strait. Here, the control of the Tuzla Island leads to control of the Kerch Strait, which is the only shipping route between the Azov Sea (with untapped oil and natural gas reserves) and the Black Sea. If Ukraine controls the Kerch Strait, then the warships of NATO would be able to move freely into the Azov Sea deep inside Russian territory. While leading Ukrainian nationalists to seek NATO membership, Russian actions did not obtain a public rebuke from NATO.[33]

The presidents of Ukraine, Georgia, Poland, and Lithuania launched the "Community of Democratic Choice" in August–December 2005 (an organization formed in accordance with the principles of the Community of Democracies—an informal U.S.-backed forum launched in 1999 to promote liberal goals such as support for civil society, free and fair elections, independent judiciary, transparency, and accountability of governance.) Georgian president Mikhail Saakashvili and Ukrainian president Viktor Yushchenko sought to create "an alternative Commonwealth of Independent States (CIS) without Russia." The "orange revolution" then led Ukraine to look more closely to joining NATO as opposed to accepting the more general security assurances of the UN Security Council, of which Russia was a member. Kiev, at least initially, had hoped to enter NATO (before Viktor F. Yanukovich became prime minister in 2006), having entered into an intensified dialogue in 2005 similar to that Poland, the Czech Republic, and Hungary engaged in before joining NATO.

Here, however, Russia began to augment support for its "pro-Russian" candidate in Ukraine. In August 2006, President Yushchenko ironically brought in his political adversary, Yanukovych (who had strong support in the pro-Russian regions of Donetsk, Kharkiv, Lugansk, and Crimea), to form a government as an increasingly powerful prime minister. The tilt back to Russia has been expressed by Yanukovych, as the new prime minister of Ukraine, after the meeting of the NATO-Ukraine Commission on September 14, 2006:

> We have to convince the society and when I say convince the society that means we
> should not really juxtapose two different ways like the part . . . the membership in
> NATO and our policy of good relations with Russia. And if we manage to find a
> way of bringing these two positions together, then this will be a policy that will be
> comforting, not only for a party, but for the country in general. We should not
> develop a policy that would create a blind alley in the relations between Russia and
> the European Union or in the relations between Ukraine and European Union ver-
> sus Russia. We should build a reliable bridge between Russia and the European
> Union and I have stated that often and often again.[34]

Tensions, however, flared again in 2007 between President Yushchenko and
Prime Minister Yanukovych when the former ordered the dissolution of the
Ukrainian parliament, an action resisted by Yanukovych's supporters—with the
threat of violence in the background when it appeared that Interior Ministry
troops began to take sides in May.

From Moscow's perspective, placing the NATO summit in Riga, coupled with
public U.S. support for NATO membership action plans for both Ukraine and
Georgia, following the placement of U.S. bases in Poland, Romania, and Bulgaria
symbolizes the potential formation of a Baltic Black sea alliance backed by
NATO and the EU.[35] Moreover, neo-Wilsonian pressure for national independence and for "democratization" has tended to mask irredentist claims: civil society and ethnonationalist pressure groups in Finland, Estonia, and Latvia have all
claimed Russian territories, and there also are Polish-Belarusian claims and counterclaims left over from Stalin's reannexation of western Belarus.

By seeking to influence Ukrainian politics, Russia appears to be doing everything possible to check potential NATO membership for Georgia and Ukraine.[36]
The question is thus how to develop a shared regional space with Russia, not
against it—in letting Russia join NATO in a "new" form of membership as well.

The Question of Irredentist Claims

As the United States and NATO began to debate the issue of NATO enlargement, the 1995 Study on NATO Enlargement emphasized that new NATO
members would have to give up irredentist claims. But here NATO provided no
mechanism for states to resolve these claims with their non-NATO neighbors.
Furthermore, NATO does not really provide a means to resolve such disputes
among its own membership, as indicated by Greek-Turkish disputes over Cyprus
that have flared periodically since the 1958, 1963, and 1974 crises and that have
threatened to flare up again in the past few years. Even if states do not publicly
raise territorial claims, civil society movements might continue to lobby for
changes in boundaries or support for fellow ethnic groups and cousins on the
other side of the border. This is particularly true in central and eastern Europe,
where state boundaries have changed frequently in the twentieth century alone.[37]

As the United States, NATO, and the EU (separately) continue their venture
into former Soviet (and tsarist Russian) space, they need to take into account: (1)
the unintended consequences of actual and potential U.S., NATO, or EU power

projections that might result in political schisms between pro- and anti-United States, NATO, and EU factions within NATO and EU members as well as among nonmembers; (2) the future power and threat differential between those states that join NATO and the EU as "full" members (or who link to U.S. defense systems) and those that do not; (3) the ability of states to use aspects of strategic leveraging to manipulate the United States, NATO, and the EU into backing their specific interests; and (4) the geostrategic implications of different forms of irredentist claims or territorial disputes among central and eastern European states, including those affecting Russia or its allies, as well as disputes among NATO and EU members themselves and with third parties.

The latter can be divided into roughly five interrelated categories of territorial disputes and irredentist claims: (1) disputes directly affecting Russia; (2) disputes among central and eastern European countries against potential or actual Russian allies (or claimed spheres of influence and security), thus more *indirectly* affecting Russia; (3) claims or tensions among the eastern European members of NATO and the EU themselves; (4) potential conflicts of interest *between* NATO members and non-NATO EU members; and (5) potential disputes and tensions between NATO members, prospective NATO members, and third parties.[38]

Here, a number of territorial disputes continue to raise Russian concerns. Russia has opposed perceived Nordic state support for autonomy or independence for Karelia, Komi, Murmansk, and St Petersburg itself. Estonia, for example, has claimed the Pyatlov District of the Pskov region; at the same time the Russians in Estonia represent 30 percent of the entire population, mostly concentrated in Narda. On June 27, 2005, six weeks after signing a border treaty with Estonia, Russia announced that it was revoking its signature, withdrawing from any obligations stipulated in that treaty, and demanding renegotiation from scratch. Moscow had criticized the Estonian ratification law's preamble, which made references to Estonia's uninterrupted legal continuity during the Soviet occupation. Moscow then refused to submit the treaty to the Duma to prevent the European Union from interceding with Russia to ratify the treaty.[39] Latvia publicly claimed the Abrene territory until ostensibly renouncing it in 1996. A new Latvian-Russian treaty was signed in March 2007, but agreement was still problematic from the Russian perspective. Germany, Poland, and even Lithuania all have historic claims to Kaliningrad, which no longer shares a border with Russia. This has raised Russian fears of loss of sovereignty and a possible secessionist movement, while the EU fears illegal migration, cross-border crime, drug smuggling, pollution, the spread of AIDS and other diseases, and human trafficking.[40]

Russia's loss of military outposts and harbors on the Baltic Sea (and on the Black Sea adjoining Ukraine) have increased the relative strategic nuclear and military importance of the Kola Peninsula, thus tending to pressure Nordic states more directly. Russia furthermore possesses energy interests to protect in the Barents Sea and in the German-Russian "Nord Stream" Baltic Sea gas pipeline, which represents a potential cause for concern in Sweden in that it crosses the Swedish economic zone. Speculation that Russia could possibly use the pipeline to gather intelligence on Swedish military capabilities has raised a debate as to whether Sweden should spend more on homeland security or should look closer to NATO. Moreover, as the search for oil and gas continues in the "High North," NATO-member Norway and Russia have not yet resolved an undersea border dispute in the Barents Sea.[41] The perception that Russia and Germany have signed a deal over the heads of those states lying between them has raised historic eastern European fears of a Russian-German condominium. Sweden, Poland, Estonia, Latvia, and Lithuania have additionally raised concern about the environmental risks of the undersea project (as a result of submerged nuclear submarines and atomic waste, for example).

From the Russian perspective, Finland and Sweden have shifted away from their formerly neutral status during the cold war by joining the EU but also by supporting the three Baltic states for NATO membership—a fact that indirectly draws NATO to support Swedish and Finnish interests as well. In February 2007, President Putin once again warned that Finnish membership in NATO would be bad for Russian-Finnish relations but that the decision was up to the Finnish people. NATO had offered nonmember Partnership for Peace states, such as Sweden and Finland, the option to take part in operations of the nineteen thousand-man NATO Reaction Force (NRF)—an option that could open the door to NATO membership, but an option generally opposed by both Finns and Swedes, in part because of perceptions of "bellicose" U.S. leadership. At the same time, Sweden hopes to expand defense cooperation with its neighbor, NATO member Norway, just as it presently shares radar surveillance data with EU member Finland and seeks to expand Swedish-Finnish military monitoring projects.

Poland and Belarus

Of concern are disputes between Russian allies and NATO and EU members. Most significant of these are the burgeoning tensions between Poland and Belarus, due, to a certain extent, to claims and counterclaims left over from Stalin's reannexation of western Belarus. At first, Polish-Belarusian relations appeared to ameliorate following the initial waves of NATO enlargement. Yet, over time, tensions began to rise, particularly once NATO began to integrate Poland more closely into its defense structures. The new U.S.-Polish defense relationship has been symbolized by the arms "contract of the century" (in which Poland chose F-16s over French Mirage and Anglo-Swedish JAS-39 Gripen). Moreover, from Warsaw's perspective, its membership in NATO helps to check a Russian-Belarusian-Ukrainian alliance along its borders. To counter such a phenomena, the United States and Poland have actively assisted "pro-Western" and pro-Polish social movements in both Belarus and Ukraine.

Belarusian autocrat Alexander Lukashenko began a crackdown on pro-Polish and other democratic groups in Belarus in fear that U.S. and European efforts to stage a Ukrainian "orange-style" revolution that could overthrow his regime by democratic means. In December 2006, the U.S. Congress passed H.R. 5948, the Belarus Democracy Reauthorization Act of 2006, which is intended to provide sustained support for the promotion of democracy, human rights, and the rule of law in the Republic of Belarus, as well as to encourage the consolidation and strengthening of Belarus' sovereignty and independence. The bill authorizes assistance for fiscal years 2007 and 2008 for democracy-building activities, including support for nongovernmental organizations, youth groups, independent trade unions and entrepreneurs, human rights defenders, independent media, democratic political parties, and international exchanges.[42] (Open U.S. assistance can be risky in that these groups can be considered subversive by Belarus authorities.)

Concurrently, despite the 2002 Belarusian-Russian "New Union Treaty," Russia did not want to subsidize the Belarusian dictatorship forever and thus doubled energy prices to reach market levels in 2007 as it did for Ukraine, Moldova, Georgia, and Armenia, consequently risking a deteriorating relationship with the autocrat, Lukashenko. The Russian action likewise harmed relations with Poland, Germany, and the EU following the temporary cutoff of gas and oil to Belarus, making Europeans look to alternative energy sources, including nuclear power.[43]

There appear to be three options for Belarus: (1) let Russia "Russify" the country and integrate it more closely into Russian defense and economic structures; (2) begin a U.S.-EU dialogue with the dictatorship once dubbed as the "last dictatorship in Europe" and member of the "outpost of tyranny"; and (3) begin U.S.-EU-Russian discussions as to how to jointly develop and reform the country, perhaps by establishing a Belarusian-Ukrainian economic space that would be open to U.S., EU, and Russian investment. As the first two options are "zero sum" and could provoke conflict, the third option needs to be attempted.

European vs. U.S. Approaches

While Washington tends to see Moscow as a rival in the Black Sea region, the "core" states of the EU, France, and Germany have sought to counterbalance Russian fears of isolation and exclusion through Franco-German-Russian summitry—in the understanding of Russia's legitimate right to keep its own sphere of influence around its borders and to balance the extension of the Atlantic Alliance to the east. Franco-German-Russian talks have, however, not been entirely successful and have been regarded as going over the heads of eastern Europeans in that these states are not included in discussions.[44]

In this regard, the German-Russian pipeline (to connect with the United Kingdom) that is to be built by Gazprom and Germany's Wintershall and E.ON Ruhrgas under the Baltic Sea (a project the Reagan administration purportedly attempted to sabotage during the Soviet era)[45] would exclude Poland, the Baltic states, and Ukraine; eliminate the transit fees for these states; and forge a kind of energy condominium over Poland, which depends on Russia for roughly 70 percent of its gas needs. As an alternative, Warsaw, along with Baltic states, has suggested an "Amber pipeline" that would pass through the territories of Latvia, Lithuania, and Poland. Polish experts say that such a pipeline would be much cheaper than the Baltic one. But prospects for such a pipeline, and hence prospects from reducing oil and gas dependence on Moscow, appear dubious, at least in the midterm. The only clear alternative to an excessive dependence on Russian oil and gas is the development of alternative fuels and energy-related technologies, coupled with measures to use energy more efficiently.

Following the 2006 energy crisis with Ukraine (which is highly energy inefficient), Poland proposed a European energy treaty for both EU and NATO members (thus excluding Russia) that would contain (among other provisions) a mutual energy security clause that would resemble NATO's article 5. In this case, signatories would support each other "in the event of a threat to their energy security from natural or political causes."[46] While it is necessary to cooperate more closely on energy questions, it seems unclear as to how a potential military intervention would necessarily resolve a Russian, Belarusian, or Ukrainian failure to supply oil or natural gas, whether the cutoff is accidental, by terrorist action, or on purpose. Here, the best option would be first to diversify energy sources and develop alternative technologies; the second best option would be to strengthen cooperation with Moscow, Ukraine, and Belarus, where possible.

The latter approach has been backed by German chancellor Angela Merkel in opposing the more confrontation approach of the Polish government under prime minister Jaroslaw Kaczynski. In addition to expanding Russo-German fields of research, education, and culture, the German Foreign Ministry has been in favor of concluding a new treaty with Russia establishing a free-trade zone that would seek out an energy partnership that would not only secure energy supplies for Germany but that would also assist Russian investment in energy. Germany has thus hoped to integrate Russia into an "international regulative framework that defines energy security as the outcome of a cooperative partnership between producers, transit states, and customer states."[47]

Germany would additionally seek to establish confidence-building measures (initially as part of civilian assistance measures and disaster relief), so as to develop closer cooperation within the framework of European Security and Defense Policy (ESDP). As Russian and German trust grows, this could eventually include joint peacekeeping or even peace-enforcement missions. A Russian-German cooperation package would likewise be accompanied by a "Modernization Partnership" aimed at developing rule of law and democracy in Belarus, Moldova, and Ukraine, and the Southern Caucasus. The key (and difficult to overcome) dilemma will be to get Poland and the EU (as well as the United States) to work together in engaging Russia for this policy to be successful.[48]

Here, however, EU-Russian relations have not been moving forward. The May 17–18, 2007 EU-Russia Summit at Volzhsky Utyos, in the Samara region of Russia, hoped to achieve new EU-Russia agreement to replace the current Partnership and Cooperation Agreement. It sought to deal with issues (Russian import tariffs, domestic energy pricing, and bank regulations) concerning Russia's WTO accession; the Kyoto Protocol; cooperation in the field of freedom, security, and justice; visa dialogue; traffic congestion at EU-Russia borders; space and regional development; and international issues, such as Kosovo, the Iranian nuclear program and the Middle East. The Summit, however, failed to produce any tangible results largely because of continued political-economic tensions between Poland and the Baltic states with Russia.

Sociopolitical Disputes among NATO-EU Members

There are also a number of problematic tensions between NATO and non-NATO members, as well as among NATO and EU members themselves that could weaken alliance cohesion. In addition to those briefly outlined in relation to north and central Europe, southeastern Europe possesses a number of unresolved disputes that could spark tensions and possible conflict.

As new NATO and EU members, both Romania and Bulgaria hope to anchor themselves in NATO and the EU in order to deal with their domestic problems. Both need to improve rule of law and attempt to control drug smuggling and corruption. Bulgaria appears particularly concerned with Turkish ethnonational influence in its southern regions.[49] Both states oppose a Russian-Turkish condominium over the Black Sea and see the need to link themselves with NATO and the EU, along with Ukraine, where possible. On the one hand, both states play a role as connecting points to trade and energy between Europe and the wider Black Sea region; on the other hand, both must also work to block the "new threats" stemming from that same region (drug smuggling, organized crime, human trafficking, as well as potential "terrorist" activities)—in effect placing them on the front line between the Black Sea and Europe.

Romania has a number of disputes with its neighbor, Ukraine. Disputes between the two over Serpent Island have been discussed by the International Court of Justice.[50] NATO and EU member Romania seeks support from the EU to help find a formula to assist the ethnic Romanian presence in Moldova and in Ukraine, particularly in the province of Northern Bukovina in Ukraine that was part of Romania before World War II. Romanians are also present in Serbia, in the Timok River region, and in the province of Serbian Banat. While its relations with Russia have been cool (in part because of Romanian support for Moldova, which is roughly 40 percent ethnic Romanian), Romania does seek a positive partnership with Russia, but it also wants to develop alternatives to the current Gazprom monopoly (as do most states!). Romania also hopes to engage directly in the Transnister negotiations and needs NATO-EU backing in order to do so.[51]

To the west of the Black Sea region, the issue of Hungarian irredentism is not yet resolved, and this affects Romania and east European stability in general. The riots in Budapest in 2006 not only represented a protest against political economic mismanagement, the "lies" of the government, and the financial problems associated with entering the Euro Zone, but were targeted also, in part, against the 1920 Treaty of Trianon and the perceived failure of the present government under Prime Minister Ferenc Gyurcsány of the Hungarian Socialist Party to address the issue of ethnic Hungarian minorities in southern Slovakia, Transylvania, Romania, and Vojvodina, Serbia. Hungarian ethnonationalists (backed by Americans of Hungarian background) have supported for independence of Slovenians, Croatians, Macedonians and Albanians, and Montenegrins as well as the Albanian community in Kosovo.[52]

Both the Romanian and Hungarian ethnic questions are difficult enough for the EU to handle (as they do not appear to be a NATO concern), but these problems are heightened by the general economic malaise confronting eastern Europe.[53] In addition to Hungary, there have been antiliberal backlashes in

Poland (a government with a number of extreme nationalist and religious representatives) and in Slovakia (the building of a coalition with social democrats, nationalists, and right-wing populists).

A New NATO Strategy: Geostrategic Importance of the Black Sea Region

After NATO expanded to fill the "strategic void" in central and eastern Europe, the attention of the United States, NATO, and European Union (as well as Russia) has increasingly been drawn to the Black Sea—what has been called the "Bermuda triangle" of Western security studies. Then, following its March 2003 intervention in Iraq, the United States began to downsize its forces in the "old" Europe (except Ramstein Airforce base in Germany, site of nuclear weapons storage). The Pentagon has thus begun to shift bases from the United Kingdom and Germany (downsizing seventy thousand troops) to Italy; it has begun to implement more cost-effective bases in the "new" Europe: Poland, Hungary, Romania, and Bulgaria. The United States has also begun to deploy troops throughout central Asia and the Caucasus and has considered drawing Ukraine, if not Georgia, into NATO.[54]

The Black Sea region has an area of nearly twenty million square kilometers, with roughly 350 million people, and it straddles two continents. Its foreign trade runs about US$300 billion annually. The region is also the second-largest source of oil and natural gas after the Persian Gulf region and thus offers an alternative source to Persian Gulf energy resources.[55] The region possesses the key commercial rivers that flow into the Black Sea (the Danube, Dniester, and Dnieper)[56] and largely controls the trans-Ukrainian oil and gas pipelines running to the energy markets in the north of Europe. Russian energy export facilities lie at Novorossiysk (which is hemmed between the Ukrainian Crimea and Georgia). The Blue Stream natural gas pipeline links Russia and Turkey under the Black Sea. The projection that Europe could be importing some 90 percent of its oil, 60 percent of its gas, and 66 percent of its coal from sources beyond Europe itself by 2030 (assuming that Europe cannot soon develop viable alternatives to oil and natural gas) indicates the importance of the region.[57] Moreover, EU countries import 25 percent of their energy needs from Russia, which might rise to 40 percent in 2030 (another 45 percent comes from the Middle East).[58] Only the Baku-Tbilisi-Ceyhan (BTC) pipeline from Azerbaijan thus far links to the Mediterranean and provides an alternative to Russian-backed routes.

U.S. concern with the Black Sea region represents at least part of the reason for the U.S. redeployment of military forces from Germany and western Europe (as discussed previously) to lesser bases (with less-developed infrastructure but longer term ten-year leases) in Eastern Europe following the 2004 "minibang" that brought Black Sea states Romania and Bulgaria into NATO. Apart from bases in Poland, bases in Romania and Bulgaria in particular are more cost effective and closer to "hot spots" in southeastern Europe (the Balkans), central Asia (the Caspian Sea)—as well as to what neoconservatives have dubbed the "greater Middle East." At the same time, NATO appears to be overstretching its political-military effectiveness as it moves closer to the Russian and Belarusian borders and the Black Sea region.[59]

Soviet disaggregation has meant that Moscow no longer dominates the Black Sea region in face-to-face confrontation with NATO member Turkey. Instead, Russia is almost entirely landlocked and shares the Black Sea littoral with five other independent states: Turkey, Bulgaria, Romania, Georgia, and Ukraine. In a larger geostrategic and geoeconomic perspective, the actual and potential wealth of the region, plus the fact that it is rapidly becoming Europe's major transport and energy transfer corridor from the Caspian Sea, central Asia, and the "greater Middle East," consequently makes the Black Sea region the focal point of major power and regional rivalries. It is likewise the region of the so-called frozen conflicts (the Transnistria, Abkhazia, South Ossetia, and Nagorno-Karabakh), plus those conflicts in Chechnya and Dagestan. It is additionally the region through which pass illegal immigrants, human traffickers, narcotics and weapons, as well as various "terrorist" groups.

Continuing Crisis: The "Frozen Conflicts"

The frozen conflicts (plus Chechnya and Dagestan) of the Black Sea region all involve Russia to a certain extent. The reality is that the majority of these crises cannot be resolved without some form of Russian participation, input, or agreement and thus provide Russia with varying degrees of strategic leverage to assert its interests elsewhere.

The Russian troop presence in Abkhazia and South Ossetia in Georgia and in Transnister in Moldova, as well in Nagorno-Karabakh between Armenia and Azerbaijan, combined with Russian demands for a *droit de regard* over much of ex-Soviet eastern Europe (the Baltic states, Belarus, Moldova, and Ukraine) have thus far represented the major rationale for NATO members to refuse to sign the adapted Conventional Force in Europe (CFE) treaty. Here, Russia has demanded that all eastern European states sign the adapted CFE pact before entering NATO. New NATO members refused, however, arguing they would have greater bargaining leverage with Russia once they joined NATO. (Russia had previously promised to withdraw forces from these regions in Istanbul in 1999 after revising the CFE treaty.) Russia argues that issues regarding Moldova and Georgia have no relation with the CFE treaty since the latter countries are not members of NATO, and that NATO itself is in violation of the 1990 treaty since its expansion into eastern Europe and the movement of NATO troops to bases in Romania and Bulgaria from Germany.[60]

Russia has backed independence for the Transnistria against Moldova and for the independence of Abkhazia and South Ossetia against Georgian interests (accusations denied by Moscow, which claims it is protecting Abkhazians against Georgian revenge).[61] Moscow is also seen as backing Orthodox Armenia (Russia's primary strategic partner) in the dispute over Nagorno-Karabakh versus Muslim Azerbaijan. Here, ironically, in a cross-civilizational alliance, Iran and Russia have tended to join forces against Azerbaijan, as well as against the Chechen independence movement in support of landlocked Christian Armenia. And although brutal Russian military operations in Chechnya have largely subsided with a pro-Russian government in power, Chechen "terrorist" activities have not entirely ceased. While Moscow's policy has flip-flopped for and against Kosovar secession, possible Russian support for Kosovar independence could possibly be contingent upon demands for the independence of other regions.[62] The issue of Macedonian, and now Kosovar, independence may influence the question of Russian support for South Ossetia and Abkhazia against Georgia, as well as Transnistria against Moldova as a means to control the Nistru River trade routes to the Black Sea.[63]

From the U.S. perspective, Georgian membership in NATO would strengthen NATO's dangerous (and potentially overextended) new flank, permitting NATO to reach toward the Caspian Sea and toward central Asia beyond in the "global war on terror" and in countering drug and arms trafficking. Following the coup attempt in 1998 against former Georgian president Eduard Shevardnaze, the Georgian leadership called for NATO or the United States to station peacekeepers in Georgia to protect Caspian oil transport. In December 1998, representatives from the GUUAM Group held talks about setting up a special peacekeeping force to protect the oil export pipelines. Proposals were made to work with NATO to set up this force within the framework of the Partnership for Peace program. At least since 2004, Georgia has been accused of increasing rather than decreasing its military spending. Tbilisi has likewise been accused of seeking a military rather than a political solution to Abkhazia and South Ossetia. Unnamed Western officials have questioned Georgia's commitment to human rights and "whether Georgia is really a democracy."[64]

After the January 22, 2006 attacks on a Georgian pipeline, President Mikhail Saakashvili immediately implicated Russia. Russia, which has periodically accused Georgia of harboring Chechen "terrorists" in the Pankisi valley, in turn, put the blame on pro-Chechen insurgents in North Ossetia. Then in late September 2006, four Russian military officials were accused by Georgia of spying; Russia declared a blockade. Flights between the two countries were halted at midnight Moscow time on October 3; Russia has also severed maritime, road, and railway links as well as postal communications with Georgia. The Russian blockade on Georgia additionally hurt landlocked Armenia, because Georgia is Armenia's main land route to Russia.

On the positive side, after releasing the four Russians, President Saakashvili said, "There are no threats that can intimidate Georgia." But he also pointed out that he wanted a good relationship with Russia. "We do not need Russian military officers but we need Russian tourists . . . (and) Russian business. Russia and Georgia are historic partners." In a conciliatory gesture, Georgia also agreed to allow Russian peacekeepers in Abkhazia to monitor the strategically key Kodori Gorge region of Abkhazia (which had been taken by Georgia in July 2006) alongside UN peacekeepers, something it had previously opposed. Organization for Security and Cooperation in Europe chairman in office and Belgian foreign minister Karel De Gucht urged Moscow to cancel its blockade and "defuse the situation."[65]

Mr. Saakashvili appeared to be engaging in a form of brinkmanship intended to strengthen his popular base, draw stronger U.S. support (by insisting on the Russian "threat" to obtain membership in NATO as soon as possible) while not confronting Russia directly, at least in military terms. However, Georgia also appeared to playing a dangerous game given the larger geostrategic and political economic complexities and interests throughout the region. Rather than working to bring the region into closer cooperation, his approach risks polarization of the region into pro-Russian and pro-U.S. and European camps, further fueling secessionist movements. (By mid-2007, tensions increased as Georgia accused Russia of firing several missiles into its territory.)

This rivalry in the Caucasus is further illustrated by purported offers by Georgian Foreign Minister Gela Bezhuashvili in May 2007 to base U.S. BMD systems on Georgian territory, most likely as a backdoor step into NATO.[66] Moscow then countered by proposing Azerbaijan instead as a potential base for BMD systems, thus further exacerbating the regional and global "insecurity-security dialectic." The dilemma is that these "frozen conflicts" will continue to be manipulated by Russia, but these disputes really cannot be resolved until the United States, Europe, and Russia finally sit down to the negotiating table and begin to forge a more concerted policy toward the Black Sea region.

NATO and the "Wider Black Sea"

U.S.-Turkish relations have deteriorated significantly since the first Persian Gulf War in 1990 (following the cutoff of Turkish trade with Iraq, the failure of the United States to provide promised compensation, and ostensible U.S. support for an autonomous Iraqi Kurdistan not to overlook the war's effect on the Kurdish independence movements inside Turkey). These issues have raised a real question mark as to the future of NATO-Turkish relations and of the security of the Black Sea region in general. By contrast, Russian-Turkish relations and trade have been improving considerably since the end of the cold war when Moscow feared that Ankara would assert its pan-Turanian claims to central Asia. Yet Russia now ranks as Turkey's third largest source of imports, ahead of the United States. Russian-Turkish trade is worth billions of dollars and includes construction, tourism, and natural gas. Turkish imports from Russia account for close to 70 percent of Turkish gas consumption (in part through the underwater Blue Stream gas pipeline).[67]

The burgeoning Turkish-Russian relationship includes defense cooperation. On February 27, Russia and Turkey held naval exercises in the Black Sea; by March 2006, NATO member Turkey, along with Russia, openly opposed the extension of NATO's naval Operation Active Endeavor (OAE) from the Mediterranean into the Black Sea.[68] Here, the OAE had been supported by both Bulgaria and Romania, as well as by Ukraine and Georgia. The latter two Black Sea littoral states tend to regard Russian and Turkish efforts to check NATO as a means to establish a Russo-Turkish condominium over the Black Sea Economic Cooperation Pact. This fact has raised the question, which has priority: the Atlantic alliance or Russian-Turkish naval hegemony in the Black Sea.[69]

Ankara has argued that OAE is unnecessary as it duplicates the already-existing Black Sea Naval Force of all six Black Sea riparian states and through Black Sea Border Coordination and Information Center (BBCIC) that already possess NATO connections. Moreover, Ankara argues that the OEA violates the 1936

Montreux convention that permits Turkey to control the straits. This raised the question as to whether the United States and EU need to demand a review of the Montreux Convention (at the risk of alienating both Turkey and Russia). Or, by contrast, whether the United States should encourage Turkey and Russia to take the maritime lead rather than expanding OEA into the Black Sea. Rather than seek to *fully integrate* the region into NATO and EU security structures through a *top down* approach,[70] this latter approach would represent a *bottom up* approach that seeks to build interlocking systems of security from the perspectives of the regional actors themselves.[71]

Because of the region's strategic importance, the United States and NATO have tended to focus on Ukraine and Georgia as potential new members to the exclusion of other states in the Black Sea region, risking further NATO overextension and Russian (if not Turkish) backlash. In the background of the dispute over hegemony in the Black Sea region remains the crucial intra-Slavic dispute between Ukraine and Russia over the Crimea. Moscow now controls only a small part of the northeastern shores of the Black Sea—plus naval facilities that have been leased from Ukraine in the Crimea, after Khrushchev handed the Crimea over to the Ukraine to the dismay of Russian nationalists. At the same time, Russia's oil export facilities in Novorossiysk have been crucial for its burgeoning economic recovery.[72]

The strategic-economic concern related to potential membership of Ukraine and Georgia in NATO is that the Novorossiysk port is hemmed between the Ukrainian Crimea and Georgia. The United States and NATO would then be in a position to interdict Russian exports from Novorossiysk (cutting off one of the major lifelines of the Russian economy)—should Ukraine or Georgia join NATO. This fact (among others discussed previously) helps explain extremely strong Russian opposition to NATO membership for these states, as well as its support for Abkhazian secession as a buffer with Georgia. It is consequently not surprising that Russia has expressed opposition to a "Ukraine-Georgia alliance" in the fear that Kiev will demand a review of the treaty on Russia's lease of Crimean naval infrastructure, which was signed on May 28, 1997, for a period of twenty years and that Tbilisi would rely on the support of Ukraine to demand that Russia vacate the military "facilities" in Georgia.[73]

Despite the favorable support of the United States and partly because of the situation in Afghanistan, which is draining NATO resources and attention, Georgia or Ukraine did not get the go ahead to join NATO at the November 2006 NATO summit in Riga. Neither did the "Big MAC" countries of Macedonia, Albania, and Croatia—which appeared to be next on the list, having more or less completed their Membership Action Plans (MAPs).

Not overlooked by NATO enlargement advocates is the fact that the BTC pipeline, one of the few non-Russian controlled pipelines, goes through Georgia from Azerbaijan and the Caspian Sea. According to Western and Russian sources, an agreement had purportedly been reached that arranged for the United States and NATO to secure the BTC pipeline. In the future, the United States and NATO would also safeguard the Baku-Tbilisi-Erzurum gas pipeline (Georgia, Azerbaijan, Turkey and Kazakhstan). The key dilemma is that these routes pass near the site of secessionist movements in Abkhazia (which fought a civil war with Georgia from 1992 to 1993) and in Ossetia. The port of Supsa is just twelve miles from a buffer zone between Abkhazia and Georgia. Abkhazia, which claims to be a "democracy," has demanded to be a sovereign republic with minimal ties to Georgia. For its part, Georgia has expressed a willingness to grant Abkhazia some autonomy. Moreover, the United States is allegedly going to provide Azerbaijan with small submarines intended to guard its oil fields. As both Russia and Iran (which has completed an oil pipeline to Orthodox Armenia) regard the regional equilibrium shifting toward U.S. interests in the Caspian sea and the Caucasus, a local cross-civilizational arms race between regional allies—with Iran and Armenia on the Russian side versus Azerbaijan and Georgia on the U.S./NATO side—should not be ruled out. This could potentially pit the United States and NATO versus Russia and the Collective Security Treaty Organization (CSTO), which includes Armenia, Belarus, Kazakhstan, Kyrgyzstan, Tajikistan, and Russia.[74] Much could depend on whether the United States will cooperate with Russia on BMD and other issues.

In another scenario, Turkey could enter the fray of Balkan and Caucasus strife and has threatened military intervention in Northern Iraq against the Kurdish Workers Party. With Armenian genocide resolutions passing the National Assembly in France in October 2006 (but stalled by the French Senate) and pending in the U.S. Congress, Turkey claims that Armenia has territorial ambitions toward eastern Turkey. With its EU membership application on hold, Turkey increasingly finds itself "encircled" with conflict: Ankara fears that an increasingly independent Iraqi Kurdishstan will give greater support to Kurds fighting for secession in eastern Anatolia; Ankara likewise opposes Armenian irredentist claims. It also opposes a French-Greek Cypriot defense and military cooperation pact, which Ankara sees as a threat to regional security.[75] Moreover, the secular Turkish "deep government" of military officials fears the rise of Islamist and Kurdish movements inside Turkey itself. (See Chapter 1.)

The fact that the Black Sea region is rapidly becoming Europe's major transport and energy transfer corridor (as well as for the transport of drugs and black market activities) from the Caspian Sea, central Asia, and the "greater Middle East" to the Mediterranean consequently makes the entire area the focal point of major-power and regional rivalries. The peace and stability of the region will largely depend on whether or not NATO, the EU, Turkey, and Russia can ultimately find ways to jointly cooperate against burgeoning threats of region instability, secessionism, criminal activities, and terrorism and work together in areas of mutual interest, particularly in regard to energy transport.

The Balkans

In 1995 President Clinton had promised the U.S. Congress that U.S. forces would remain in Bosnia for only one year. U.S. forces did not withdraw until 2004, largely to focus on Afghanistan and Iraq, to be replaced by EU forces. In February 2007, in yet another sign of military overstretch, the EU announced plans to cut by almost two-thirds the number of peacekeeping troops in Bosnia and Herzegovina—in part to increase the number of forces deployed in Afghanistan. This was to be done despite signs that intersectarian tensions between Bosnian Croats, Muslims, and Serbs increased, particularly at the beginning of the campaign period for parliamentary elections to be held on October 1, 2007. These tensions, coupled with the failure of Bosnian political parties to agree on major changes to the constitution, and to form a unified national police force, led the fifty-five-nation Peace Implementation Council to extend the powers of its Office of the High Representative—who has the right to make laws and dismiss local politicians—for another year—although the council had previously planned to phase out its powers in 2007.[76]

Furthermore, in another sign of military overstretch, if not renewed violence, the issue of "meaningful autonomy" for Kosovo has continued to plague UN efforts under special envoy and former Finnish president Martti Ahtisaari to reach a compromise between Serbs and Albanian Kosovars. The UN plan had envisioned the establishment of a European Security and Defense Policy Mission that would monitor all areas related to the rule of law and that would have the authority to assume responsibilities to ensure the maintenance and promotion of the rule of law, public order, and security. NATO would provide a secure environment in support of Kosovo's institutions—until those institutions were capable of assuming the full range of security responsibilities.[77] In February 2007, however, the Serbian parliament rejected the UN plan by a vote of 255 to 15. Both the Kosovar Serbs and Albanians protested against the UN plan.

Likewise, in February 2007, the International Court of Justice demanded that Serbia comply with its obligations under the Genocide Convention by turning over General Ratko Mladic and other individuals accused of war crimes—or face the possibility of UN sanctions. In March 2007, NATO discussed the issues of Kosovo and Serbian military cooperation with NATO (Serbia had joined NATO's Partnership for Peace Program in 2006), but NATO also focused on the continued Serbian failure to capture Mladic. At the same time, however, the EU hinted that Serbia could become a candidate for EU membership in 2008, raising the possibility of the resumption of renewed trade talks, depending on cooperation with the United Nations, and raising questions whether the capture of Mladic remains a precondition for EU talks and closer ties with NATO.[78]

To Russian regret, contact group mediators failed to forge a loose confederal arrangement, which would permit Serbian minorities in Kosovo some relative "autonomy within the autonomy," in regard to Serbia and Kosovar Albanians. While its policy has flip-flopped, by threatening opposition to Albanian Kosovar independence in the UN Security Council, Russia could be trying to build arguments to support secession for Abkhazia and Southern Ossetia against Georgia and for Transnistria against Moldova, in exchange for Kosovar independence. A Pandora's box of additional secessionist movements might well be opening throughout the entire region, which will be exacerbated by Serbian (and Russian) opposition to UN peace plans. Here, for example, should Kosovar Albanians opt for independence, then the Kosovar Serbian minority would also seek to secede or else join Serbia. The other "frozen conflicts" could suddenly thaw.

Russia and NATO Enlargement

Following Vladimir Putin's Munich speech in February 2007, editorialist Thomas Friedman brought the "great" NATO enlargement debate back to the public arena in the United States. Friedman pointed out that by pressuring Russian president Boris Yeltsin to accept NATO expansion, the Clinton administration had helped to undermine Russian liberals and democrats, thus opening the door to former KGB agent Vladimir Putin: "We told Russia: Swallow your pride, it's a new world. We get to have spheres of influence and you don't—and ours will go right up to your front door."

Here, NATO enlargement, in particular, has been used to inflame Russian patriotic and nationalist convictions. Thomas Friedman thus depicted the sense of humiliation caused by NATO enlargement from the Russian perspective, and Russian resentment of "double standards." Friedman then stated his rationale for having opposed NATO enlargement in the 1990s: "There is no major geopolitical issue, especially one like Iran, that America can resolve without Russia's help. So why not behave in a way that maximizes Russia's willingness to work with us and strengthens democrats, rather than expanding NATO to countries that can't help us and are not threatened anymore by Russia, and whose democracies are better secured by joining the European Union."[79]

Here, opponents of NATO enlargement had essentially argued in the 1990s for an alternative, yet more realistic, approach to security for all of Europe. The expansion of the EU, plus the strengthening of NATO's Partnership for Peace initiative, in cooperation with both the Europeans and the Russians, would have represented a much less provocative approach to central and eastern European security than the expansion of NATO's integrated military command to these states. The real question was not "to expand" or "not to expand" NATO. The real question was whether to draw these states into "full" NATO membership and ultimately into an integrated command structure *or* to expand U.S. and NATO security guarantees, in coordination with the Europeans and Russia to central and eastern Europe, in the formation of separate regional command structure and extension of security guarantees backed by NATO, the EU, and Russia, in a form of "associated membership" with NATO.[80]

Much as Nitze, Kennan, and others predicted, since the rise of Russian president Vladimir Putin, Russian liberals and democrats have largely been sidelined. Putin's approval ratings have hovered around 75 percent. No elites have thus far been able to challenge him. NATO enlargement, fears of the further disaggregation of the Russian empire—as symbolized by Russia's brutal efforts to repress Chechen secessionist movements—as well as the ostensible failures of economic liberalization in the 1990s—as symbolized by the collapse of the ruble in 1998—have all represented factors leading to a new authoritarianism, which should cause real concern but not exaggeration.[81] Putin's crackdown on some of the "oligarchs" who enriched themselves during the Yeltsin years, plus efforts to reassert national controls over oil resources, has additionally frightened both Russian and foreign investors, all the more so as other *nomenklatura* appear to be taking their place but without reforming the whole system.[82]

At present, Putin appears to be challenged by a number of former Russian oligarchs, including exiled Russian billionaires Leonid Nevzlin (formerly of Yukos) and Boris Berezovsky. The latter publicly stated in April 2007 that he was plotting Putin's ouster by force from London.[83] These two have supported the "liberal" Mikhail Kasyanov, who was Putin's prime minister from 2000 to 2004, for president in 2008. Kasyanov has also been supported by the leader of Russia's United Civil Front, Garry Kasparov (former world chess champion). In a movement that gained more strength with the Dissenter's March in December 2006, both Kasparov and Kasyanov of the "liberal" People's Democratic Union have joined "Other Russia"—an opposition coalition group that includes the far-left Vanguard of Red Youth, the far-left Workers' Party, and the National Bolshevik party. On the economic side, Putin's market-oriented reforms have alienated a wide range of groups: pensioners, students, teachers, trade unions, and private residents, as well as Yeltsin-era oligarchs. On the political side, the Russian government has been accused of corruption and of murdering journalists critical of Russian actions in Chechnya. These groups see the Putin administration as supporting state megacorporations and not small businesses, stifling freedom of speech, and as undermining democratic institutions by abolishing direct elections of provincial governors, among other issues.[84]

The question now is whether it is possible for the United States and European nations to work with a more authoritarian regime that will be changing leadership in 2008.[85] Will Vladimir Putin be able to keep his foot in power in the forthcoming government? Or will an even more overtly anti-United States, anti-European, pro-Eurasian leadership come to power? Or will Russia take a more "liberal" outlook and look closer to the United States and EU? While domestic Russian politics will predominate, much will still depend on how future Russian policy makers interpret U.S. global strategy, particularly with regard to the deployment of BMD systems, and the potential formation of a "Baltic-Black Sea alliance" as well as in regard to Russian fears that the United States might once again try to play the "China Card" against Moscow. Here, however, U.S. efforts to deploy BMD systems in both eastern Europe and in Japan and Australia appear to be pressing Russia and China into even closer defense cooperation.[86] (See Chapter 8 and *postscript*.)

Toward a NATO-Russian Entente

The question remains whether Russia can be brought into the NATO command structure, or whether it will remain a suspicious outsider, only partially informed by the NATO-Russia Council—which permits Russia "a voice, but not a veto." The fact, however, that Moscow has insisted that it wants to engage in more proactive NRC-led operations—in which it can co-decide on every stage and participation in operational planning from BMD to issues affecting eastern Europe and the Black Sea—indicates room for potential compromise.[87]

If Russia is to move closer to the United States and NATO, the NRC would need to engage with Turkey, as well as Romania and Bulgaria, in airspace reconnaissance, border controls, and coastal security in the effort to check drug smuggling, organized crime, trafficking in women, and "terrorist" activities. In this regard, the United States should work through the NRC to support Turkish initiatives, such as the Black Sea Naval Task Force (BlackSeaFor), and *Black Sea Harmony* as a regional grouping involving the Black Sea littoral states.[88] Such an approach would seek to accommodate U.S., European, and Russian geostrategic and political-economic interests through use of relevant EU programs, coupled with EU cooperation with Turkey, while assisting Black Sea political cooperation and socioeconomic development.[89] As full Turkish membership in the EU has been put on hold, one option would be to bring Turkey into an associate EU membership with limited voting rights on issues that directly affect the country and the "wider" Black Sea region while still limiting Turkish migration to Europe. Here, Turkey could take the political economic lead in forging a new Mediterranean union that would seek to forge regional cooperation agreements between North African and Levant states (see Chapters 5 and 10). The NRC, the EU, and Russia can thus begin to engage the Euro-Atlantic Partnership Council and Partnership for Peace Working Group composed of littoral states and others in the greater Black Sea region in the effort to implement a full-fledged "regional security community" for the entire BSEC *under a separate command structure* backed by NATO, Russia, and the EU security guarantees. Here, the European Commission is currently developing measures to strengthen the European neighborhood policy toward countries pinched between the EU and Russia.

The German Foreign Ministry has additionally announced that the German EU presidency will propose a strategy for central Asia that will specify the EU's interests in its relations with Kazakhstan, Turkmenistan, Kyrgyzstan, and Tajikistan.[90] NATO, Russia, and the EU will thus need to work with Kazakhstan and regional groupings such as the Shanghai Cooperation Organization, where possible. To finally bring peace to the region, the NRC should consider the option of deploying Partnership for Peace peacekeeping forces under UN or OSCE mandates—alongside Russian forces—in the "frozen conflicts." Following the 1990s, Russia has asserted "sovereign democracy" by limiting the control of multinational corporations over its energy resources and industry and has likewise restricted the presence of nongovernmental organizations, in addition to pressuring states, such as Kazakhstan, to keep them from making energy deals with U.S. and European firms. In addition to pressuring British Petroleum, Russia used the threat of environmental litigation to permit Gazprom to buy a majority share of Shell's investment in Sakhalin Island.[91]

Working with Russia does not, however, necessarily exclude the quest to build alternative pipeline routes and, even more important, diversifying energy resources and technologies. Yet, such a quest is difficult to achieve because of the conflictual nature of the states in the Caspian and Black Sea regions. Diversifying energy resources and technologies needs to be taken with regard to oil and gas in general, no matter who is the supplier. The development of alternative energy resource supplies and energy-saving technologies can, in turn, help moderate the Russian strategic-energy stranglehold on a number of states, in addition to limiting U.S. and European dependence on the Persian Gulf. Moreover, if the United States and EU want to secure access to Russian energy supplies, then the United States and EU will also need to open their economies to Russian investment, while Russia, in turn, opens up to investment to help diversify its economy once

Moscow enters the World Trade Organization. This means the difficult process of building trust on both sides.

Such a bold approach would consequently help reinvigorate the largely moribund NATO-Russian relationship, strengthen the Euro-Atlantic Partnership Council and Partnership for Peace, and move toward boosting deteriorating U.S. and NATO-Turkish relations. Yet, with the United States concentrating its attention and resources on the "global war on terror" and with its focus primarily on Afghanistan, Pakistan, Iran, and Iraq, however, and with the EU suffering from "enlargement fatigue," there is a real danger that not enough diplomatic attention and resources will be invested in the "wider" Black Sea area that links the Caspian Sea, the "greater" Middle East and eastern Europe—and in overall U.S.-EU-Russian relations.

CHAPTER 3

Iraq: Sinking Deeper into Mesopotamian Quicksand

Losing Domestic Support for the Intervention

More than three years after the U.S. intervention in Iraq in March 2003, with more than 3,700 U.S. troops killed, more than 27,000 wounded (many severely), and between 150,000 to 655,000 Iraqis directly or indirectly killed by the conflict—and at a long-term cost of between $700 billion to $2 trillion—the majority of Americans now believe that U.S. intervention in Iraq was a major strategic error.[1]

While the war had initially been justified to eliminate weapons of mass destruction (WMD), no WMD of any military significance were uncovered. U.S. intervention in Iraq has been shown to be *preclusive*, if not *predatory*, rather than *preemptive*, as initially claimed by the administration of George W. Bush.[2] The U.S. leadership likewise claimed that it was engaging in "regime change" in the effort to establish "democratic federalism" and market "liberalization," but these idealistic goals have appeared nearly impossible to achieve.

The Bush administration additionally hoped to boost Iraqi oil production, in part to pay the costs of the war effort, but oil production has thus far failed to rise to the previous level of 3.7 million barrels per day as produced by the regime of Saddam Hussein prior to U.S. intervention, largely due to political-economic instability, corruption, smuggling, poor management, and sabotage.[3] In addition to increasing Indian and Chinese demand, plus a lack of refining capacity in the United States and political-economic instability in Nigeria and Saudi Arabia, oil prices have probably averaged about $10–15 higher per barrel[4] than they would have if Iraqi oil had come pouring onto the world market, as expected by pro-Iraq War neoconservatives. Although not part of the official rationale, U.S. intervention in Iraq was additionally intended to ultimately break OPEC, by exploiting cheap, low-sulfur, high-quality Iraqi crude, as well as limiting as much as possible Chinese, Russian, and European political-economic influence and control over Iraq's high-quality, low-cost crude.

The intervention in Iraq essentially sidetracked the United States away from the war against *al-Qaida* and has aggravated the global threat of terrorist activities, in that Iraq has now become a training ground for future *mujahideen*. And finally, as the intervention in Iraq possessed no clear achievable goal and exit strategy (as the Powell Doctrine demanded for the first Persian Gulf War in 1990–1991) and as its reconstruction "plan" was largely ad hoc and ill-conceived (particularly its de-Baathification policy), the mission has wasted extraordinary financial resources and military capabilities that are much needed elsewhere—thus risking *hypertrophy*.

The essentially unilateral U.S. intervention in Iraq has furthermore split NATO and has drawn the United States and its dissipating number of coalition partners into Mesopotamian quicksand with no clear end in sight. Not only that, because of the extent to which the crisis is absorbing attention and finance, there is a risk that U.S. foreign policy will tend to view nearly all foreign policy questions (and not just those dealing with the Middle East) through an Iraqi prism, thus raising very uncertain prospects for a coherent U.S. foreign policy elsewhere. The funding necessary for both domestic U.S. concerns and international development programs, for example, might end up going to serve U.S. purposes in Iraq.

Before his January 23, 2007, State of the Union speech, President George W. Bush's popular approval ratings were among the lowest of any contemporary president before his annual address.[5] Exit polls following the November 6, 2006, elections (in which the Democrats won in both houses of Congress)[6] had indicated that the Iraq War (which was important to two-thirds of voters) did hurt Republican candidates, but that corruption and scandal involving Republicans represented even bigger issues. A combination of these latter issues might have cost President Bush much of his electoral base: Almost one-third of all white evangelical Christians voted for Democrats.[7] This appeared to prove warnings by Republican leaders that the president's policies both at home and abroad were alienating significant parts of the Christian conservative Republican base.

Corruption scandals cost the Republicans and President Bush one of his strongest supporters, Congressman Tom DeLay (R-TX), a Christian conservative, who was the former Republican majority leader in the House. DeLay had to step down from office after a Texas grand jury indicted him in late 2005 on charges that he had violated campaign finance laws. Moreover, the whole nature of special interest lobbying has come under questioning, which could likewise weaken the power base of a number of politicians. In its first major action, on January 18, 2007, the new Senate overwhelmingly passed sweeping changes to ethics and lobbying rules and was thus able to ban many of the favors that lobbyists do for lawmakers and to question the practice of earmarking money for special projects. While DeLay's fall from power represented a major blow to the Christian coalition (which was also known for unquestioning support for Israeli policies), it remains to be seen whether the new legislation could weaken Christian conservatives as well as the effectiveness of important lobby groups, such as the American Israel Public Affairs Committee, among others, which have been highly influential in developing Israeli and U.S. policy toward the Middle East in general.[8] (See Chapter 4.)

That Republican senator Sam Brownback (KS) also stated opposition to President Bush's policy is symbolically important as well. It was Brownback who took Republican Bob Dole's seat in the Senate in 1996 and who first supported the Iraq Liberation Act and helped to raise $100 million for the Iraqi National Congress. Brownback endorsed the Iraq Study Group's demand, in his words, for a "very aggressive, regional diplomatic effort." Brownback's opposition to President Bush's Iraq policy (as he is one of the 2008 presidential candidates that is preferred by Christian conservatives) thus began to draw these voters away from supporting George W. Bush.

President Bush also lost general support from another important group: some 55 percent of families who possess military veterans or active service soldiers disapprove of Bush's handling of Iraq, and 54 percent say the war hasn't been worth the cost.[9] The fact that a number of retired military officers and other former government officials spoke out against Bush administration foreign policy, urging direct talks with Iran "without preconditions," was likewise indicative of the erosion in the president's support.[10] Moreover, the Joint Chiefs of Staff had reportedly been at odds with the White House over the concept of a "surge" of more than 21,500 troops (plus support staff) for Iraq.[11]

That a freshman senator, and a very early critic of unilateral intervention in Iraq, Jim Webb (D-VA) was chosen to deliver the Democrats' response to President Bush's 2007 State of the Union Speech was likewise illustrative of the growing domestic opposition to the Iraq War.[12] Webb's speech also revealed a deeper opposition to other Bush administration policies, including the growing gap in salaries between CEO's and labor,[13] inadequate health care and corruption and lobbying (issues that generally hurt Republicans more than Democrats).

Related to the political economy of the Middle East were Webb's demands that more significant steps be taken (than President Bush has taken) to reduce dependence on oil imported from the Middle East and to develop alternative energy resources.[14] The latter represent policies that Al Gore would have most likely taken had he not "lost" the 2000 presidential bid in Florida. Such policy disputes could signify a turn toward concentrating more on domestic than on international affairs. These contentious issues could forewarn of domestic paralysis and vicious infighting in the final years of the Bush administration mandate in which both the president and vice-president (in a form of *imperial diarchy*, as opposed to a "unitary" presidency[15]) attempt to dig in their heels in support of a bellicose Manichean "faith-based" foreign policy intended to counter the Democratic challenge to Republicans in the 2008 presidential elections.

State of the Union

In the immediate aftermath of President Bush's January 2007 State of the Union address, however, there appeared to be a slight improvement in the president's standing. President Bush's address spoke of the necessity to engage more U.S. troops as a means to stabilize the situation. The president took personal responsibility for the present crisis (ostensibly relieving subordinates), but did not articulate a long-term strategy or really explain how the "troop surge" was to play a role in the longer-term goals of stabilizing Iraq and the region as a whole.[16]

The president stated bluntly (without providing substantial evidence) that "Iran is providing material support for attacks on U.S. troops. We will disrupt the attacks on our forces. We'll interrupt the flow of support from Iran and Syria. And we will seek out and destroy the networks providing advanced weaponry and training to our enemies in Iraq." The speech itself made no mention of negotiations with Iran or Syria, nor did it consider larger issues, such as how to achieve peace between the Israelis and Palestinians. The president consequently sought to manipulate public opinion to gain some leverage versus a Democratic majority in Congress and to threaten a veto over congressional legislation that might appear to undermine his foreign policy in Iraq, Iran, and elsewhere. Although divided, the U.S. public appeared to give the president the benefit of the doubt, but only if he could show some form of "success" in the very near future.

Despite Democratic opposition, and rebellion within the ranks of the Republican Party, the president, as commander in chief, still possesses considerable room to maneuver. There are many political games the president could play regardless of the positions that Congress takes. President Bush still has the support of Vice President Dick Cheney, plus key Republican senators, plus that of "Independent Democrat" Senator Joe Lieberman. Conversely, if Congress does ultimately mount an effective opposition to the president's foreign policy (in seeking withdrawal of U.S. forces by 2008), it will ultimately be rebellion among Republicans ("Republicans against the war")—even more so than the opposition of Democrats—that can put real pressure on the White House.

Can Congress Alter U.S. Policy toward Iraq?

Will the new Congress with its democratic majority succeed in changing the Bush administration foreign (and domestic) policy? The task of critiquing the Bush administration policy has been greatly assisted by the bipartisan *Iraq Study Group Report*, which was cochaired by James Baker (R) and Lee Hamilton (D).[17] By presenting alternatives to the Bush administration policies, the *Iraq Study Group Report* has helped to open a crack in the predominant neoconservative and Christian conservative discourse that has thus far characterized the Bush administration policy. The *report* has permitted Democrats and a small number of Republicans to seek out a more flexible and realistic approach to policy toward the so-called greater Middle East—even if not all congressmen necessarily agree with all of its recommendations. Former Indiana congressman Hamilton has additionally challenged Congress to more strongly exercise its constitutional responsibilities in the effort to check the excess of presidential power.[18]

At a January 11, 2007, hearing of the Foreign Relations Committee, for example, Senator Webb openly challenged Secretary of State Condoleezza Rice to "more actively engage" in diplomatic efforts in the Middle East. Although Senator Webb did not agree with all the points raised by the *Iraq Study Group Report*, he believed that failing to engage in dialogue has worsened the situation in the region by driving Syria toward Iran. Webb consequently argued for negotiations with both Syria and Iran that would seek to split the "unnatural alliance" between them, while concurrently providing strong support for Israel. But with respect to the latter, Webb also supported renewed diplomatic efforts to bring a peaceful solution to the Arab-Israeli conflict.[19] Other senators, such as Sen. Bill Nelson (D-FL) and Republican senator Arlen Specter (PA) believed that negotiations with both Iran, and particularly with Syria, were possible.[20]

Troop Surge Debate

The problem, however, is that both Democrats and Republicans who oppose the president's foreign policy toward Iraq and toward the "greater Middle East," in general, have been divided as to what tactical approach to take to better influence and pressure White House policies. As the Senate is divided between Democrats and Republicans fifty-one to forty-nine (but some of these politicians might shift sides on foreign policy issues), most senators initially sought a "bipartisan"—rather than a confrontational—approach. Moreover, pro-Bush Republicans threatened to block or "filibuster"[21] any resolution that opposes President Bush's "troop surge" or other issues.[22] An additional concern is that many Republicans and moderate Democrats oppose measures that might cut funding for U.S. forces abroad, thus harming the troops.

In terms of Iraq, the primary focus of Congress has been the surge of 21,500 troops as requested by the president. Estimated costs could range from $9 billion to $13 billion for a four-month deployment and from $20 billion to $27 billion for a twelve-month deployment, depending on the total number of troops deployed and including additional costs that would be incurred during the buildup and drawdown phases. In addition, the surge might require as many as 15,000 to 28,000 additional support personnel. As of May 2007, the troop "surge" was set to last for up to a year with combat-troop numbers rising to 98,000 by the end of 2007. Adding in support troops, the overall total of troops was expected to rise from 162,000 now in Iraq to over 200,000. The Pentagon might furthermore be planning to maintain up to 40,000 troops in Iraq (plus private security contractors) for many years—possibly several decades.[23]

As Democratic, and former National Security, adviser Zbigniew Brzezinski has pointed out the deployment of 21,500 more troops is of "limited tactical significance and of no strategic benefit. It is insufficient to win the war militarily." On the Republican side, Senator Specter, the ranking Republican on the Senate Judiciary Committee, stated that the White House needed to accept Congress' role in shaping war policy and share decisions: "We're all looking for a plan that will work. . . . The current plan is not working, and 21,500 additional troops—it's a snowball in July. It's not going to work."

The first round of the battle between pro- and anti-troop surges took place on Monday, February 5, 2007. Yet, the Republican and Democratic opposition to Bush administration policy failed to obtain enough votes to bring even a bipartisan nonbinding compromise resolution.[24] On February 1, 2007, Republican senator John W. Warner of Virginia initiated a nonbinding bipartisan resolution (backed by Senator Carl Levin [D-MI], member of the Senate Armed Services Committee). Both Warner and Levin said they believed that a majority of Democrats and Republicans could possibly support a resolution that would clearly state Senate opposition to the "troop surge" and press for alternative policies. Although the Warner-Levin resolution did not please more militant

Democrats, Democratic supporters of the Warner-Levin resolution argued that it was important to demonstrate a broad, bipartisan majority against the troop increase. The bipartisan resolution was regarded as necessary to get the discussion on the floor of the Senate and check attempts by the White House and pro-Bush Republicans to block or "filibuster" any congressional resolution that opposes Bush's troop surge. The procedural vote on the Warner-Levin resolution subsequently divided along party lines. The Democratic leadership found themselves eleven votes short of the sixty (out of one hundred) needed to begin a debate on the bipartisan resolution. Forty-seven Democrats and two Republicans voted to open debate on the resolution; forty-five Republicans and one independent (Senator Lieberman) were opposed. (Senators Susan Collins [R-ME] and Norm Coleman [R-MN] were the only two Republicans to support the Democrats, despite promises from other Republicans.)

Republican strategy was largely designed to fracture the Democratic opposition by drawing Democrats in different directions. Sen. Mitch McConnell (R-KY), the Republican leader, urged the Senate to consider two competing Republican alternatives that were regarded by Republicans to be more supportive of the president. One of those alternatives, by Sen. Judd Gregg (R-NH), declared that Congress should not cut off any funds for forces in the field. By contrast, the resolution of Sen. John McCain (R-AZ), set eleven conditions for the Iraqi government to meet if it wanted to retain U.S. support.[25]

Yet, Republican supporters of the "troop surge" worried that such a vote could undermine presidential authority; it would, in effect, "declare Gen. David Petraeus's new strategy a failure before it has a chance to be implemented," as U.S. Senator Lindsey Graham (R-SC) put it.[26] Sen. Jon Kyl (R-AZ) added that "[T]he worst thing would be for the Senate by 60 votes to express disapproval of a mission we are sending people to lay down their lives for."[27] Senator Lieberman likewise supported the president's policies as advocated in the 2007 State of the Union address. Lieberman emphasized values of democracy versus Islamist extremism in arguing that "it would be disastrous to our national security if we fail in Iraq."[28] Here, Lieberman put his finger on the nature of the problem: the Bush administration cannot admit failure in Iraq—even if it did not possess a guaranteed plan for success.

The main dilemma is that many senators and congressmen (whether Republican or Democrat) have been reluctant to press too hard to impel a change in Bush administration policy for fear of harming the troops already deployed or else of damaging morale. Defense secretary Robert M. Gates, who replaced Donald Rumsfeld, warned that even nonbinding action by the Senate would "embolden the enemy." Supporters of the president argued that critics seek to "micromanage" foreign policy, thus undermining presidential flexibility and legitimacy. The Republican Party consequently put intense pressure on recalcitrant Republicans to impel them to support the president's surge. Even those Republicans who want to pull troops out of Iraq but engage them in the war against *al-Qaida*, have been accused of being "weak" on defense issues.[29] As ex-White House adviser David Gergen put it, "A vote that attracted up to 10 or 12 Republican senators would be a major political blow, damaging to the president, would hurt him in Iraq, would send a clear signal to [Iraqi prime minister] Maliki and others in Iraq that this president is hanging on at home. And that weakens his negotiating—it weakens his leverage position."[30] Here, domestic aspects of strategic leverage appears to be a crucial factor in international bargaining.

The fact that partisan politics once again played a key role in preventing the formation of a viable alternative strategy forewarns of ineffective and indecisive foreign policy in the years to come.

Congressional Threats

Despite the pressure from the president, a number of Republicans have, however, begun to switch away from "neoconservative" discourse to what can be called more "flexible" realism as advocated by the bipartisan *Iraq Study Group Report*. The main reason that a number of Republicans are beginning to break with the president is the fear that the Democrats will defeat them in the 2008 elections if they are seen as too closely supporting Bush administration policies, particularly in regard to Iraq. (Twenty Republican Senators will face new elections in 2008.) As opinion polls have indicated, there is a burgeoning opposition to the U.S. intervention in Iraq, to the troop surge (particularly as its costs become known), and to the real possibility that the Bush administration policies might either inadvertently (or "accidentally on purpose") result in war with Iran.

Despite the initial setback for opponents of Bush administration policy with regard to the bipartisan Warner-Levin resolution, the House and Senate both approved nonbinding resolutions in February and March 2007 to protest the troop surge and to impel the administration to withdraw from Iraq.

In mid-February, after intensive debate, the House, which has a solid Democratic majority, resolved in a nonbinding resolution: "Congress and the U.S. people will continue to support and protect the members of the United States Armed Forces who are serving or who have served bravely and honorably in Iraq; and (2) Congress disapproves of the decision of President George W. Bush announced on Jan. 10, 2007, to deploy more than 20,000 additional United States combat troops to Iraq." Then, in late March 2007, with a veto threat from President Bush, the House of Representatives barely passed (218 to 212) a $124 billion emergency spending bill that sets strict binding benchmarks for progress in Iraq, establishes readiness standards for deploying U.S. troops abroad, provides better health care for returning troops, and requires the withdrawal of U.S. combat forces from Iraq by the end of August 2008.

Once again, on March 27, the Senate, by a close vote of fifty to forty-eight, unexpectedly rejected a Republican effort to block any mention of a possible date to withdraw from Iraq from the military spending bill. The Senate thus called for a gradual withdrawal of U.S. troops from Iraq within 120 days of the measure's enactment, with a nonbinding goal of pulling out by March 31, 2008.

The divisions among Republicans appeared bitter. Senator Chuck Hagel (R-NE) had been the first Republican to publicly break with President Bush, over the surge. But he still surprised Republicans by voting for a specific date to pull U.S. forces out of Iraq, joining with the majority of Democrats. The Independent Democrat, Senator Lieberman, voted against the measure, while Republican Sen. John McCain called it the "Date Certain for Surrender Act." On the one hand, the date is nonbinding and serves to pressure the president to seek a diplomatic solution for a "no-win" situation—in which the majority of Iraqis appear to want the United States out as well. On the other hand, it forewarns of a deeper clash with the president and of domestic political paralysis—in which the fault is the president's for not being able to get diplomacy on track.

After the passage of the congressional measures, Defense Secretary Robert M. Gates warned both the Senate and the House that if they did not approve the 2007 Supplemental Appropriations bill by April 15, service members would "face significant disruptions, and so will their families."[31] Congressional victories, however, fall significantly short of the two-thirds majority that would be required to overturn a highly likely presidential veto once the Senate reconciles its bill with that of the House and submits the modified version for executive approval. At the same time, however, Congress might have forced President Bush into a closer dialogue with the Congressional opposition. Congress will likewise need to put pressure on the Fiscal Year 2008 Defense Authorization bill and the Fiscal Year 2008 Defense Appropriations bill.

More Militant Opposition

A number of the more militant opponents of the Iraq War seek to cut off funding altogether, which Congress could do through its "power of the purse." A number of resolutions seek to push for binding legislation to cap troop levels or else require President Bush to return to Congress for approval before committing troops; other resolutions want to force a new vote to authorize the war or begin bringing troops home. If funds cannot be cut, then a number of members of Congress want to engage in hearings, investigations, and resolutions that condemn an escalation of the war much as Congress did during the Vietnam War. At least one congressman, Dennis J. Kucinich (D-OH), has threatened impeachment proceedings (with regard to U.S. threats toward Iran).[32] Critics of the president argue that the president himself has already undermined his own authority through his incompetent policies. The question remains: If the strategy is not guaranteed to be successful, then it is time to consider other options.

Concurrently, there have also been calls to revive the draft, which could include women as well as immigrants hoping to obtain expedited citizenship (see Chapter 9), coming from "democratic patriots." Representative Charles Rangel (D-NY), the incoming chair of the House Ways and Means Committee, opposed the Iraq War but also argued for bringing back the draft because of claimed unequal sacrifice of poor blacks and Hispanics who are joining the professional army.[33] A draft, which would take time to implement, might be useful for peacekeeping forces only (under a UN flag), but it would not meet the skilled requirements of the new professional army. Yet, if things go for the worse in Iraq, Iran, or elsewhere in the "global war on terror," a potential patriotic nationalist alliance between Congressman Rangel and Senator Lieberman, plus other Republican neoconservatives and eagle-like Democrats could be foreseen.

Success or Failure of the Troop Surge?

The surge concept failed in 2006; Operation Together Forward II resulted in a 43 percent increase in violence in June through October 2006. The present surge was met with considerable violence in January through August 2007. In April, in addition to numerous attacks outside the Green Zone, a suicide bomber was able to penetrate the parliament cafeteria, indicating a major breech in security.

The report of the independent special inspector general for Iraq reconstruction, Stuart Bowen, had stated that even though more Iraqi troops and police could be trained, equipped, and fielded, it was unclear whether these forces and troops could sustain a secure environment independent of coalition forces. The report, furthermore, stated that demands to go on leave and "immature personnel management policies" accounted for up to 40 percent of police not being present for duty. The report cited estimates up to 20–25 percent of the national police "needed to be weeded out," because the national and local police apparently are infiltrated by, and possibly coordinated with, sectarian militias. The report likewise observed that public confidence in the ability of the Iraqi government to provide for public safety and the rule of law was below 40 percent nationwide, and that, in Sunni and mixed Shi'a-Sunni areas of the country, confidence remained even lower.[34] The point raised here is that police (and army) training is key to true Iraqi independence and an end to the bloodshed. The president's position is that U.S. forces cannot withdraw until benchmarks for the Iraqi police can be met; but it appears they might not be met.[35]

The problem is that any claim to success would be uncertain. By focusing on securing Baghdad, it was argued that the troop surge plan could push insurgents out of the city and into the surrounding provinces of Al-Anbar, Diyala, and Salah ad-Din. Insurgents would thus be suppressed in one area only to reemerge somewhere else (such as Iraqi Kurdistan) or try to wait it out until the Americans leave. U.S. forces furthermore do not possess the language, cultural skills, or the sociopolitical legitimacy to deal with the population. Another issue is that U.S. junior officers have been convinced that the Bush military escalation in Iraq would actually hand over portions of Baghdad to Iraqi security forces infiltrated by the Jayish al-Mahdi army.[36]

Moreover, the surge has resulted in considerable population displacement: "Almost 18,000 individuals have been displaced in January-mid February since the beginning of the US surge in the fifteen central and southern governorates. . . . An estimated 290,000 people have been displaced in these governorates since February 2006 with a further 84,000 having been forced to leave their homes in Iraq's three northern governorates . . . an additional one million people could be displaced this year in a country where pre-2006 displacement figures had reached about 1.4 million."[37] Such pessimistic estimates had been predicted by Bush administration critics before the war but were dismissed as exaggerated immediately after the initial phase of the intervention. Here, to close off the Iraqi border from a potential wave of immigrants and to counter infiltration of al-Qaida or other insurgents into its eastern oil-rich Shi'a region, Saudi Arabia has planned to build a high-tech $700 million 900-kilometer fence.

There is a real danger that Iraq could implode, involving both civil war and outside intervention: "Iran has set up an extensive network of safe houses, arms caches, communications channels, agents of influence, and proxy fighters. . . . The Sunni powers of Saudi Arabia, Jordan, Kuwait, and Turkey are all frightened by Iran's growing influence and presence inside Iraq . . . [and] have begun to create a similar network, largely among Iraq's Sunni population. Turkey may be the most likely country to intervene overtly. Turkish leaders fear both the spill-over of Kurdish secessionism and the possibility that Iraq is becoming a haven for the PKK."[38] In April the deputy chief of the Turkish General Staff, Gen. Ergin Saygun, called for military intervention in northern Iraq to squelch 4,500 Kurdish Workers Party (PKK) "terrorists," raising outrage in Iraq.[39]

But would Turkey be content with such an intervention, or would it want more? And what would be Iran's response? (Here, the distribution of oil in the region further exacerbates potential regional conflict. Iraqi oil is largely concentrated in Shi'a and Kurdish regions of Iraq [attracting Iran and Turkey]; Saudi oil tends to be concentrated in predominantly Shi'a eastern province of Saudi Arabia, susceptible to Iranian influence, while Iranian oil tends to be concentrated in predominantly ethnic Arab [not Persian] Khuzestan, which had attracted Saddam Hussein.) From this perspective, the U.S. military presence is not preventing covert Turkish and Iranian penetration. Moreover, while the American troop presence might be stopping more overt intervention by Turkey so far, it will not necessary stop direct intervention by Iran, particularly if the United States crosses the border to hunt down terrorist havens in Iran. Here, strong Bush administration rhetoric against Tehran appears to cover the less than "successful" troop surge.

In short, it is dubious the troop surge will enhance the chances for "success" in Iraq, particularly if not accompanied by fully engaged regional diplomacy, and it weakens U.S. force readiness for other potentially more dangerous situations around the world. In their testimony before the U.S. Senate Foreign Affairs Committee, James Baker and Lee Hamilton argued that, "The Study Group, the President, and Prime Minister Maliki agree on key measures the Iraqis need to take. Those measures include: legislation to share oil revenues among all Iraqis; provincial elections later this year; reform of the de-*Ba'athification* laws; and a fair process for considering amendments to Iraq's Constitution. The Study Group calls on the United States to consult closely with the Iraqi government to develop additional milestones tied to calendar dates."

The question remains: What if the Iraqi government does not meet the benchmarks as demanded by President Bush and Congress? In the past, as pointed out by Senator Carl Levin, Iraq previously failed to meet the following benchmarks[40]:

- Iraqi president Jalal Talibani said in August 2006 that Iraqi forces would "take over security in all Iraqi provinces by the end of 2006." That pledge has not been kept.
- Prime Minister Maliki said last June that he would disband the militias and illegal armed groups as part of his national reconciliation plan, and in

October he set the timetable for disbanding the militias at the end of 2006. That commitment has not been kept.

- The Iraqi Constitutional Review Commission was to present its recommendations for changes in the Constitution to the Council of Representatives within four months of the formation of the Government last May. The Commission has yet to formulate any recommendations.
- Prime Minister Maliki put forward a series of reconciliation milestones to be completed by the end of 2006 or early 2007, including approval of the Provincial Election Law, the Petroleum Law, a new *de-Baathification* Law, and the Militia Law. Not one of these laws had been enacted by the deadline.
- The Iraqi army pledged six battalions in support of U.S. and Coalition efforts during Operation Forward Together last summer. In fact, Iraqis provided only two battalions.

By July 20, Pentagon commanders testified before Congress stating that they needed until at least until September to determine if there was any really progress in the troop surge. In addition, U.S. ambassador to Baghdad Ryan Crocker argued that Congressional benchmarks were largely artificial constructs that "precisely defined benchmarks . . . do not serve as reliable measures of everything that is important—Iraqi attitudes toward each other and their willingness to work toward political reconciliation." In opposition, Senator Biden (Dem.) asserted, "We're not staying . . . you [Ambassador Crocker] don't have much time." Senator John Warner (Rep.) stated, "Our concerns are about their inability to come together and resolve things." The fact that six cabinet members backed by Moqtada al-Sadr left the government of prime minister al-Maliki in April 2007 (demanding that the United States withdraw) has made it more difficult for the United States and the Iraqi government to control the actions of the Jayish al-Mahdi Army. By August, Sunni members of the Accordance Front also pulled out of the al-Malaki cabinet due to the government's failure to meet twelve key Sunni demands; members of the secular Iraqiya bloc led by Ayad Allawi also withdrew. In all, nearly half the cabinet lost confidence in the government.[41] On the one hand, the al-Maliki government has appeared incapable of reconciling the differing Sunni and Shi'a factions (despite a statement of broad poliitcal unity by the remaining Kurdish, Shi'a, and Sunni factions in the cabinet). On the other hand, the more senators threatened that government, the more it tacitly threatened to turn toward Iran for support. The issue is how long can Washington sustain a government without perceived legitimacy?

Another major concern is military overstretch and how concentration of forces on Iraq will affect U.S. global strategy: In his testimony before the Senate Foreign Affairs Committee, Congressman John Murtha (D-PA), whose decision in late 2005 to turn against the war and call for U.S. forces to be withdrawn from Iraq is seen as a major turning point for congressional attitudes toward the war, warned: "While we are fighting an asymmetric threat in the short term, we have weakened our ability to respond to what I believe is a grave long term conventional and nuclear threat. At the beginning of the Iraq War, 80 percent of *ALL* Army units and almost 100 percent of active combat units were rated at the highest state of readiness. Today, virtually all of our active-duty combat units at home and *ALL* of our guard units are at the lowest state of readiness, primarily due to equipment shortages resulting from repeated and extended deployments to Iraq."[42]

On the one hand, Iraq War spending has weakened force readiness; on the other hand, the Pentagon's February 6, 2006, Quadrennial Defense Review (QDR) appears provocative, with its emphasis on nuclear weapons and cold war-style armaments, coupled with the deployment of the U.S. national missile defense system—without having proven its effectiveness against cruise missiles and stealth systems. Despite efforts to transform the U.S. military in twenty-first-century circumstances in order to deal more effectively with "asymmetrical warfare," the Pentagon appears caught between near- and long-term requirements.[43]

In mid-February 2007, Congressman Murtha planned legislation that would force the president to seek the authorization of Congress before widening the war to Iran. Murtha also planned to put conditions on the president's request for $100 billion more to pay for the Iraq War in 2007 and that would require more time between deployments for military units, more equipment, and better training. This would help lead to a cut in the number of U.S. military units in Iraq. The intent of such legislation "would force the administration to consider alternatives" for its current policies in Iraq.

Biting the Bullet: Toward Negotiations with Iran and Syria over Iraq?

In part pressed by the political effect of the Baker-Hamilton report, as well as by domestic opinion, U.S. secretary of state Condoleezza Rice's trip to the Middle East in January 2007 represented a *belated* reconnaissance mission for future discussions. The Iraqi and Iranian governments began talks. New regional negotiations with Saudi Arabia and other governments took place (possibly including Israel), coupled with revival of the Quartet group. Saudi Arabia has begun to more openly engage in regional peace talks in part in the fear that the United States will withdraw its forces from Iraq, thereby strengthening Iran's hand. Riyadh has talked to *Hizb'allah* and Syria and has been hosting talks between the two Palestinian factions in Mecca. In March 2007, Saudi leader King Faisal met with Iranian president Mahmoud Ahmadinejad.

The initial March 10 conference on Iraq was ostensibly set up by the Iraqi government itself (to help the United States save face) and included representatives of Iraq's neighbors, Iran and Syria, as well as other regional states, plus representatives of the Islamic Conference and the Arab League, as well as the five permanent members (P-5) of the UN Security Council. The United States and Iran, at least publicly, did not meet bilaterally to discuss Iran's alleged involvement in supporting Iraqi militias, nor did the conference discuss largely regional issues outside the Iraqi context. The conference issued a general statement promising regional cooperation. Prime Minister al-Maliki issued the following statement: "Iraq is now on the frontline of the battle against terrorism. That's why Iraq needs support from the international community, neighboring countries, brotherly countries to stand by Iraq to face terrorism, because if terrorism spreads, it will spread in the whole region."[44] Following the meeting in March, Iraq (urged by the United States) also announced its intention to invite the Group of Eight (Canada, France, Germany, Italy, Japan, the United Kingdom, the United States and Russia) to a conference of foreign ministers in April.

The question is, of course, how effective U.S. diplomacy will prove, given opposition abroad and at home. What the United States must do most urgently is to engage in talks among all Iraqi leaders (including those rebel or "terrorist" groups *outside* the Green Zone) in order to *jointly* set a date for U.S. military disengagement (and that would result in a removal of U.S. bases from Iraqi territory, but not from the entire region). The United Nations can assist the U.S. force withdrawal, but only if the United States can obtain UN Security Council support. U.S. congressional pressure on President Bush can help achieve this goal, but only if the president acts.

The Next Two Years

In the mind of the American public and the U.S. Congress, much will depend on whether the Bush administration's military buildup in the Persian Gulf, coupled with a troop "surge" is ultimately branded "successful." Although it initially spoke of a "moonwalk" strategy, which consisted of building up first before phasing out,[45] by May 2007, the Pentagon foresaw a long-term Korea-like commitment (but without clear dividing lines)—claiming that some 80 percent of Iraqi groups (including a number of Sunni militias and the Jaysh al-Mahdi army) were ready for reconciliation while groups such as al-Qaida in Iraq were not.[46] While the latter assessment appeared much too optimistic, the United States also began to arm those tribal or "nationalist" Iraqi Sunni groups who would oppose al-Qaida fighters, at the risk of fostering civil war between Sunni and Shi'a forces or permitting those Sunni groups to eventually turn against U.S. interests once (and if) U.S. forces begin to downsize. The al-Maliki government, Kurds and Shi'a have all complained that the United States is arming former Ba'athists. The results have been dubiously effective and possibly counter-productive.[47]

The Bush administration has been engaged in a dangerous two-forked game of post-cold war brinkmanship ostensibly intended, on the one hand, to stabilize Baghdad and other turbulent regions of Iraq in part by setting possibly artificial benchmarks for the Iraqi government to follow in order to end sectarian warfare and, on the other hand, to pressure Iran into negotiations over its nuclear enrichment program, as well as to press Iran to withdraw its support for *Hizb'allah* in Lebanon and for Shi'ite militias in Iraq. (See Chapter 4.)

Ironically, U.S. pressures on the Iraqi government to meet U.S. defined benchmarks have led the al-Maliki government to threaten to turn to Iran for support. This has left the United States in a dangerous dilemma: either back a weak and ineffective government in Baghad or else start truly engaged discussions with Tehran. In effect, the Bush administration has opted to challenge Iran from a "position of strength," using military pressures, UN sanctions, major arms sales to Saudi Arabia and other Gulf states and Israel, plus thus far unsuccessful efforts to press Saudi Arabia to reduce the price of oil to destabilize the Iranian economy. Yet as Zbigniew Brzezinski warned the U.S. Senate Foreign Relations

Committee: "If the United States continues to be bogged down in a protracted bloody involvement in Iraq, the final destination on this downhill track is likely to be a head-on conflict with Iran and with much of the world of Islam at large." (See Chapter 4.)

The Bush administration has denied what it calls the "urban legend" that it is preparing for war with Iran. But will its policies of a general military buildup and brinkmanship and opposition to diplomacy inadvertently lead to an escalation of sectarian conflict within Iraq? Or will the failure of the Iraqi government to meet benchmarks or milestones as requested by the United States be blamed on Iranian-backed militias? Will the Bush administration be able to recognize the right moment to engage in full-fledged negotiations with Damascus and Tehran—if it really intends to negotiate at all? And will the Iraqis be able to settle their scores peacefully? Or will sectarian warfare continue until the strongest party wins, possibly resulting in the breakup of the country and regional intervention by Iran or Turkey? Or, more positively, can the central government be effective enough to forge confederal accords and help foster major compromises between essentially Shi'a, Sunni, and Kurdish communities, as well as other groups and factions with a modicum of protection for those minorities caught in the crossfire? (See Chapter 10.)

The danger is that Republicans and Democrats will focus on the next presidential and congressional campaigns and largely forget about Iraq and the rest of the world. U.S. diplomacy could stall miserably in waiting for a new U.S. leadership to take the helm in January 2009. Without sufficient preliminary steps toward a more concerted and multilateral "owlish" approach to the burgeoning crisis in the Persian Gulf and Middle East, and throughout much of the world, new risks associated with indecision, if not ostrich-like isolationism, and extreme policy flip-flops, could then come to the forefront. (See *postscript* for President Obama's steps to withdraw American forces from Iraq.)

CHAPTER 4

Iran: Nuclear High Tension
and Holocaust Polemics

Cruise Missile Diplomacy or a New Diplomatic Offensive?

The United States and Iran appear to be engaged in a high stakes and dangerous game of post–cold war "brinkmanship" that could either result in some form of compromise or else continue to degenerate into a further escalation of tensions, if not direct conflict. In accord with traditional hawkish strategy, the Pentagon has attempted to make the *threat* of war as *credible* as possible in order to press Tehran to make concessions.

At the same time, however, secretary of defense, Robert Gates, has reiterated his statement that recourse to war would be a "last resort." A White House spokesperson likewise decried the "urban legend" that President George W. Bush had already signed the papers to go to war with Iran in June 2005. Secretary of Defense Robert Gates stated in Baghdad in December 2006 that the naval presence in the Persian Gulf was not to be interpreted as a response to actions by Iran but represented a message to all countries in the region that the United States will sustain its military presence in the long term while it concurrently is engaged in a "surge" in ground forces in Iraq. (See Chapter 3.)

By March 2007 a second U.S. carrier strike force accompanying the USS *John C Stennis* arrived in the Gulf to join the carrier USS *Eisenhower* and its group (with possibly a third or fourth carrier group to be added). Extra U.S. F-16 fighter planes have also reportedly flown into Turkey, ostensibly for joint exercises. Patriot antimissile systems are purportedly being deployed in the region. The more than 21,500-soldier troop "surge" (plus support personnel) was partly to be directed against Shi'a militias operating in Iraq with perceived Iranian assistance. (See Chapter 3.) The Bush administration has accused Iranian Revolutionary Guards and Iran's Ministry of Intelligence and Security of supporting attacks by the Mahdi army and the Badr brigades against U.S. forces in Iraq (and of supporting *Hizb'allah* against the Israeli occupation of Lebanese territory). The United States has consequently engaged in raids on offices of Iranian diplomats in Iraq (an apparent tit for tat for Iranians taking U.S. diplomats hostage in 1979). These actions have been coupled with rumors of U.S. forces crossing into Iranian territory and of the United States giving support to anti-Iranian dissident groups. All these factors indicate a tougher posture toward Iran intended to "bargain" from a hawkish position of "strength."

In response, in January 2007 Iran's elite Revolutionary Guards began three days of military exercises southeast of Tehran to test the operational capabilities of Zelzal and Fajr-5 missiles.[1] Its navy is reportedly engaging in "swarming" techniques using rapid boats designed to attack large, slow-moving naval vessels. The regime has apparently accelerated its centrifuge program to enrich uranium. Here, the international community is concerned with the fact that Iran might have produced as much as two hundred tons of uranium ready for enrichment at its Natanz reprocessing facility. If turned into weapons-grade uranium (using roughly one thousand centrifuges), the amount could eventually produce more than a dozen nuclear weapons.

In January 2007, UN sanctions measures were placed to restrict Iran's ability to trade in sensitive nuclear materials and to freeze the assets of Iranian officials and institutions linked to its nuclear and missile programs, but not to curtail investments and financial support. These sanctions were symbolically important in that Russia—and even more significantly, China—voted (for the first time) for sanctions.[2] By March 2007 all fifteen members of the UN Security Council voted for sanctions (under UN Resolution 1747), including South Africa (leader of the nonaligned movement), Indonesia (world's most populous Muslim nation), and Qatar (wealthy Sunni Islamic neighbor between Iran and Saudi Arabia).[3] This signaled to Tehran that its primary backers in the international community, China and Russia, as well as other regional powers, are wary of its threats to develop nuclear weapons and ballistic missile capabilities, particularly as Iran's missile programs are providing part of the rationale for U.S. BMD systems.

The key issues are formidable and difficult to negotiate. The United States demands that Iran curtail its nuclear enrichment program, that it cease its support for Shi'a militias in Iraq and for *Hizb'allah* in Lebanon, and that it recognize the State of Israel (in exchange for a "two state solution"). Yet, the bipartisan *Iraq Study Group Report*, has advocated diplomatic engagement with both Syria and Iran and has at least pointed the way toward an alternative strategy of engaging with the "enemy." Contrary to Bush administration strategy, James Baker has warned *against* trying to negotiate with Iran from a "position of strength."

In part because of congressional pressures, it appears that the Bush administration has started the diplomatic process. Following rumors that Iranian nuclear negotiator and national security member Ali Larijani might have met secretly with Condoleezza Rice in Riyadh in January (or that Saudi Arabia was mediating between the two), the United States announced in February 2007 that it would meet with both Iran and Syria on the Iraq question only—on the invitation of the Iraqi government as part of a larger conference that would include other regional states, plus representatives of the Islamic Conference and the Arab

League, as well the five permanent members of the UN Security Council. Following the initial meeting in March, Iraq said it might also invite foreign ambassadors plus the Group of Eight (Canada, France, Germany, Italy, Japan, the United Kingdom, the United States, and Russia).

Secretary of State Condoleezza Rice emphasized that the March 2007 Iraq conference would only discuss the situation in Iraq, and thus the conference did not represent a step toward the U.S. diplomatic recognition of Iran. At the same time, however, the Iraq conference still appeared to represent a face-saving measure that prevented the Bush administration from having to take the first steps toward talks leading to possible negotiations with the very states (Syria and Iran) that have been so vehemently denounced by bellicose Bush administration rhetoric. It is still hoped that a first step toward a U.S.-Iranian compromise over Iraq—to prevent a larger bloodbath and refugee crisis—could lead to compromises on other issues, including the nuclear question.

The March 2007 Iraq conference thus raised the prospects for further "talks" but not necessarily "negotiations" on issues beyond Iraq. Yet, it is dubious that mere talks over Iraq will be able to resolve the complex web of disputes and issues confronting both sides. The deeper problem is how to move from mere discussions to negotiations dealing with specific issues and then on to *diplomatic recognition* and *mutual respect*—in terms of the long-run goal of trying to build a more peaceful and cooperative relationship with Iran in the effort to forge a "regional security community" in cooperation with the Gulf Cooperation Council (GCC). There is a real danger of a "dialogue of the deaf"—that talks will lead nowhere but to further preparations for war. On May 28, 2007 the Bush administration began the first U.S. talks with Iran in twenty-seven years and announced another meeting in mid-July, ostensibly over the Iraq question alone.

From a domestic U.S. perspective, in addition to debating the reality of the Holocaust (not to overlook inviting the leader of the Ku Klux Klan to speak!), Iranian threats to make "the regime occupying Jerusalem vanish from the page of time" (in literal translation citing Ayatollah Khomeini) have worked to provoke a broader anti-Iran backlash in the United States and elsewhere. Such a backlash can potentially bring Democrats and Republicans closer together in supporting President Bush—if he does opt for military force or, more likely, if he is drawn into war "accidentally on purpose." The bellicose nature of the rhetoric on both sides thus makes it more difficult for peaceful diplomacy to succeed—despite the fact that opinion polls indicate that the U.S. public generally opposes war with Iran.

The Bush administration claims that it still has the legal authority to attack Iran, given the executive power granted by Congress in the "war on terrorism." This position, however, was challenged on January 11, 2007, when Sen. Joseph Biden (D-DE) urged President Bush to answer whether he possessed the authority to send troops into Iran or Syria without congressional approval. Sen. Barack Obama (D-IL) likewise warned President Bush not to "stumble into active hostilities with Iran without having aggressively pursued diplomatic approaches, without the American people understanding exactly what's taking place. . . . We do not want to see precipitous actions that have not been thought through, have not been discussed, have not been authorized."[4] In early March 2007, Sen. Jim

Webb (D-VA) introduced a bill prohibiting the use of funds for military operations in Iran without congressional approval.[5]

The danger now is that of a face-off. Although neither side really appears to want war, any spark could set it off, and there are many groups in the region (and in Iran itself) that believe they might benefit from a U.S.-Iranian conflict.

Nuclear Power Is Not the Wave of the Future!

Despite both Iranian (and Bush administration) claims, nuclear power is not the wave of the future. Most nuclear plants will be mausoleums in twenty-five years, in that the pace of decommissioning will exceed updated replacements! As the nuclear question ostensibly lies at the heart of the present tensions between Iran and the United States, it appears worth questioning whether nuclear energy is, in fact, in the interest of Iran, regardless of the issue as to whether Iran's nuclear enrichment program is really intended to serve a nuclear weapons program.

Iran (and other oil-producing states) do need to diversify energy production in addition to diversifying their economy into other domains; yet, it does not seem to be a wise investment to put too much money into nuclear technology. This is primarily because the latter is destined to become more and more expensive because of the costs of construction, problems concerning nuclear waste disposal, and the costs of reparation and renovation, if not decommissioning, of aging power plants. The U.S. and European effort to reduce the use of fossil fuel consumption, at first glance, has appeared to strengthen the argument for nuclear development. However, the new Generation IV plants, which are claimed to be safer, more economical, less wasteful, and proliferation resistant are not expected to be in service until 2030.

In addition to German and European reconsideration of nuclear power after energy was cut off from Russian sources in 2006–2007 (see Chapter 2), Bahrain, Egypt, Jordan, Kuwait, Oman, Qatar, Saudi Arabia, Syria, Turkey, Yemen, and the seven sheikdoms of the United Arab Emirates have all begun to express an interest in acquiring nuclear technology. In February 2007, Russian president Vladimir Putin visited Saudi Arabia to discuss nuclear technology sales.[6] Yet, a number of factors indicate that, with a truly concerted effort on the leading technological states, the world's energy infrastructure could be weaned away from dependence on fossil fuels—without an excessive dependence on the global spread of the "peaceful" atom.

The future is really in the hands of a number of different forms of alternative energy resources. In January 2003, President Bush announced his $1.2 billion four-phase "Hydrogen Posture Plan." The latter, combined with the microchip revolution and other alternative technologies and methods to save fuel consumption, coupled with producer and consumer tax incentives, is intended to create a whole new hydrogen-based energy infrastructure between 2030 and 2040.[7] This, of course, assumes that the Hydrogen Posture Plan obtains significant and sustained financing (that is not reduced by the costs of the Iraq occupation and other defense-related and social burdens). It also depends on the relative availability and costs of other technical options, such as increasingly competitive biofuel, geothermal, and solar technology.

While the price of oil and natural gas probably will remain high for the foreseeable future (unless Saudi-Iranian rivalry leads Saudi Arabia to increase production to cut into Iranian revenues), it is also probable that the worldwide supply of uranium might only last about fifty years at present rates of consumption; this likewise makes too much investment in nuclear power shortsighted. With increasing demand, and general instability in energy markets, the price of processed uranium rose from $10 a pound in 2003 to $40 in 2006 to $120 in May 2007.[8] Chinese projections for massive investment in nuclear power could likewise drive prices up. (See Chapter 8.)

Moreover, as indicated by the cases of Iran and North Korea, but also Israel, India, Pakistan, and Saudi Arabia, among other countries, the fact that the "war" and "peaceful" atoms are closely interrelated provides additional incentives to move away from the worldwide nuclear and plutonium infrastructure. In addition, centralized nuclear plants make perfect targets for terrorist activities, if not "preemptive" strikes. In this respect, in the new age of terrorism and "preemption," it will soon be time for nuclear energy to wither away.

From this perspective, the future of energy production lies in a combination of wind, geothermal and solar energy, and biofuels in combination with the development of advanced fuel-efficient technologies, such as hybrid gas-electric and fuel cells, as well as the microchip revolution designed to save energy as well. The problem is not to think in terms of one option, but to use many technologies in combination—as each energy resource has its strengths and weaknesses. Here it is better to have wind generators or solar absorbers in one's backyard than oil facilities or nuclear power plants!

Once these alternative energy sources are more fully developed, oil and gas prices will begin to tumble. Iran, in addition to other states that are largely dependent on the export of oil and natural gas, may not be prepared to diversify in time: "There will be an irreversible trend of lowering oil and gas prices and revenues. Major Gulf exporters such as Saudi Arabia are not prepared for the impending collapse in energy prices, and neither is Iran, Nigeria, Venezuela, or Russia."[9] These points raise questions about the political stability of these oil-producing countries and likewise raise the prospects of future energy-related conflict in the transition phase away from the petroleum based economy.

The fact that Iran (as well as Venezuela and Russia) engages in heavy domestic subsidies can also represent a curse if sanctions are placed on investments of Iran's energy sector, as threatened by the U.S. Congress. Cheap energy means that there are no incentives to make efficient engines, while a cut in energy subsidies can cause significant social protest. Iran uses almost as much energy as China does per day, although China's population is eighteen times larger![10] Once again, a drop in oil prices depends on the need to invest heavily in energy alternatives—a prospect that appears more likely given the likely scenario that the costs of oil will remain high because of the increasing difficulties and expenses involved in extraction of petroleum, increasing worldwide demand and, to a large extent, because of continued political-economic instability in many major oil-producing states, not to overlook financial speculation. Iran itself has shown some interest in solar and geothermal energy,[11] yet, under its present leadership, it appears to be concentrating its attention upon dual-use nuclear power, for both energy—and potential military—purposes, stimulating other states in the region to do the same.

Iran's Nuclear Program

The Islamic Republic of Iran had initially opposed the shah's nuclear program and refused to honor Westinghouse contracts, upsetting Washington, which had broken off diplomatic relations after the seizure of U.S. embassy personnel in Tehran. At that time, there had been a tacit alliance between U.S. ecologists, the antinuclear movement, and anti-imperialists with the anti-shah movement.

Tehran then began to reconsider the nuclear option at the start of the 1980–1988 Iran-Iraq War. Israel's so-called preemptive strike (which was really preclusive) on the Iraqi Osirak nuclear site in 1981 effectively led both Baghdad and Tehran to accelerate the nuclear option (contrary to the general view).[12] By 1982, two years into its bloody conflict with Iraq, Iran turned to India, China, and Pakistan for technological support. About fifteen thousand to seventeen thousand Iranian students were sent abroad for training in nuclear physics.[13]

As Iran sought to develop a nuclear capability, the Bushehr nuclear site was "mysteriously" bombed, in former National Security adviser Richard Perle's words, six times from March 1984 to November 1987 during the missile strikes of the Iran-Iraq "war of cities."[14] In September 1985, Iran, Syria, and Libya stated they would obtain nuclear weapons to counter Israel's "nuclear threat," while Iraq (and Pakistan) purportedly obtained financing from Saudi Arabia for their nuclear programs.

Since the Iran-Iraq War, however, while Iraq largely abandoned its program in the 1990s, the Iranians contracted with Russia to construct a reactor at Bushehr and then promised to buy an additional five Russian-made reactors in the 1990s once the Bushehr reactor was completed. The offer was made to hook the Russians into backing the Iranian nuclear program, much as the shah had promised to order U.S. and German reactors in the 1970s. Much like the shah's program, Iran's nuclear energy program has aimed to produce seven thousand megawatts at twenty nuclear power plants by 2025, according to a decision taken by the Iranian Atomic Energy Council in August 2004.

While Russian nuclear technology might have improved somewhat since Chernobyl, it is also not clear that Iran would want to become dependent on Russian nuclear expertise.[15] Here, Iran purportedly entered into a dispute in 2007 with Russia (denied by Tehran) over the payments for the Bushehr project (worth $1 billion), in part caused by Iran's decision to pay transactions in more expensive euros, not dollars. Moreover, by late March 2007, Russia warned Iran that it would not deliver nuclear fuel for the Bushehr power plant unless Iran stopped enriching uranium. There were also reports that Moscow was pulling its experts from the nearly finished reactor site. In addition to proliferation concerns (if not fears of an U.S. or Israeli attack), the reason may be that Russia hopes to become a leader in the business of nuclear fuel production and spent fuel storage and thus does not want Tehran to emerge as a competitor.[16]

"Genetic Genocide"

If spread into the natural environment, nuclear radiation (whether in the form of the "peace" or "war" atom) represents a form of genetic genocide. The radioactive Chernobyl clouds still hang over much of Europe—even if the radioactive particles cannot be seen.

As is the case with many nuclear plants still in service, there are legitimate concerns about the safety of the Bushehr plant, which was "bombed mysteriously" during the Iran-Iraq War and is potentially subject to "terrorist" strikes or earthquakes, assuming that it does not leak as a result of technical failure. The safety of the plant is not guaranteed: The Bushehr plant (a Russian-built 1,000-megawatt plant constructed in place of German architectural designs) is certainly causing anxiety in neighboring Kuwait and the United Arab Emirates, as well as within Iran itself.[17] (At least two earthquakes were reported in 2004 in the Bushehr region.) Spokespersons for the United Arab Emirates have proposed establishment of an early warning system with Iran in case of radioactive leakage.

From this perspective, it seems that it is in Iran's interest to accept European or international technological assistance for its nuclear program (to find the best quality technology)—without demanding national control over the enrichment process. Enrichment and waste reprocessing can then be carried out by multinational firms overseen by the International Atomic Energy Agency.[18] A second option would be to have Russia or another state oversee the enrichment process, a proposal that has not been accepted by Tehran as of this writing.

Iran has thus far argued that it could enrich uranium and sell it at a price that is 30 percent less than multinational companies. If this amount is not subsidized as is Iran's oil industry, then this factor would need to be considered in the diplomatic negotiations.[19] By mid-April 2006, Iran claimed that it had enriched uranium to 3.5 percent, using a bank of 180 centrifuges hooked up so that they "cascade."[20] By May 2007 the total number of operating centrifuges could come to three thousand, which, if operating continuously for a year, could produce about one bomb's worth of highly enriched uranium.[21]

Nuclear "High Tension"

Iran has initiated a strategy of nuclear "high tension" in its rivalry with the United States and in its quest for regional predominance. The strategic purpose appears to be that of raising political-economic tensions to keep oil prices as high as possible and to concurrently assert Iranian influence throughout the Middle East and Persian Gulf. Here, high oil prices tend to assist inefficient producers as opposed to more efficient multinational energy conglomerates. As a form of post–cold war "brinkmanship," this is to be done without resorting to conflict, while keeping the option to develop nuclear weapons open.

The Iranian leadership of President Mahmood Ahmadinejad thus appears to be purposely provoking "high tension" in its public pronouncements. Since at least August 2005, Tehran has flip-flopped, playing nuclear enrichment as a card of strategic leverage against the United States, but then, after making provocative statements, the leadership has generally pulled back away from direct confrontation. Such a strategy may well be the inadvertent product of policy disputes among rival and competing domestic political factions within Iran, but it helps to explain frequent flip-flops in Iranian policy and media pronouncements.

In 2006, UN Security Council (plus German) proposals to provide financial and trade incentives for Iran in return for Iran's suspension of its uranium enrichment, for example, split Iranian factions. Extreme right-wingers, who are led by President Mahmood Ahmadinejad and backed by the Revolutionary Guards (the Pasdaran), opposed compromise of any form. Pragmatists (led by former president Akbar Hashemi Rafsanjani) argued Iran should accept the compromise and seek changes. An anti-Ahmadinejad coalition that represents pro-secular intellectuals (generally close to former president Mohammad Khatami, who supported a "dialogue of civilizations") argued that Tehran should offer a counterproposal. In the meantime, the supreme leader, Ayatollah Ali Khamenei (backed by provincial clerics), has appeared to be playing each of the factions against each other. The latter is supposed to be the ultimate judge along with the Guardian Council of religious leaders, which selects those individuals who can run for public office.

Whether this flip-flop strategy is purposeful or inadvertent, it is highly risky. The game of nuclear "high tension" appears to be harming Iran's image in much of the international community. It likewise appears to be resulting in significant capital flight from the country. In November 2005, President Ahmadinejad introduced a scheme to provide shares in the national industries to Iran's poor, allowing them twenty years to repay the cost of the equities. In itself, this appears to be a positive initiative (even if it is one that would strengthen his power base), but then rumors spread that he would do the same thing in Iran's private industrial holdings. The latter rumor led to capital flight from Iran to Dubai, estimated to be from $200 billion to $700 billion. Capital flight was further accelerated by President Ahmadinejad's remarks about making "the regime occupying Jerusalem vanish from the page of time."[22]

The December elections 2006 showed a decline in Ahmadinejad's support among the middle class, but some of his core supporters in the lower-middle class and the working class are not that dissatisfied with him. It is "not his conservatism per se, but his radicalism is beginning to rub people the wrong way. The confrontational rhetoric, the anti-Semitism and the opprobrium that he brings internationally to Iran is not something that's appreciated by the public."[23]

Hostage Trauma

It is not clear that the Iranian leadership comprehends the extent to which the U.S. government and general population were traumatized when Iranian militants took U.S. embassy personnel hostage. At the time, it was regarded as if America itself was being held hostage, (*Nightline*, hosted by Ted Koppel became a news media sensation for discussing the hostage crisis nightly.) Considerable hostility built up over the fact that no one expected the embassy personnel to be held for as much as 444 days. In many ways, Ronald Reagan's neoconservative (and Christian conservative) movement took advantage of the hostage crisis to build up its strength by denouncing President Jimmy Carter's perceived weakness and inability to deal effectively with the Islamic Revolution. In this way, the crisis pitted Shi'a fundamentalism against Protestant evangelical fundamentalism, at least on the ideological level. (As many of these same groups had supported George Bush Jr. at least before the Iraq intervention, confrontation with Iran might help him to rebuild some of his domestic support.)

Once Ronald Reagan built up his electoral support in the south and west of the United States, President Carter lost the election, but then he negotiated the Algiers Accord of January 19, 1981, promising U.S. nonintervention in Iranian affairs and the immediate release of the U.S. hostages. Under *Point I: Non-Intervention in Iranian Affairs*, "The United States pledges that it is and from now on will be the policy of the United States not to intervene, directly or indirectly, politically or militarily, in Iran's internal affairs."[24] As Carter looked totally weak and impotent, Reagan basked in glory, particularly as the U.S. embassy personnel were returned safely to Algeria, to be greeted by Jimmy Carter. But this took place on the day of Reagan's inauguration so that President Carter would not get any credit, thus humiliating the Democrats.

On the one hand, there is the allegation of former Iranian president Bani Sadr that former Carter administration National Security adviser Zbigniew Brzezinski gave Saddam Hussein the green light for the Iraqi invasion of Iran. (Unfortunately, it is too late to ask Saddam Hussein after his bungled execution whether the allegation is correct—assuming he would have told the truth.) On the other hand, it was the Reagan administration that opened the door for Israel to sell weapons to Iran, which then set the stage for the later Iran-Contra affair. (This latter fact indicates that some neoconservatives who served in both the Reagan and Bush Jr. administrations might possess back channel links with Tehran.)

Whatever the case, whether or not the United States initially gave the green light for Iraq to attack, it is clear that Washington engaged in a balance of power strategy that was largely designed to weaken both Iraq and Iran and prevent either side from becoming the clear winner. Iraq's actions were ostensibly intended to counter Iranian support for Kurdish groups and Shi'ites within Iran, while Hussein himself coveted Iranian Khuzistan. In 1982 and 1983, once Iran began to make advances, with some offensives spearheaded by Iraqi Kurds, the United States tilted primarily toward Iraq (with special envoy Donald Rumsfeld visiting Iraq in 1983 to promise arms shipments). The United States not only ignored Iraqi atrocities and war crimes, but it also took Iraq off the list of states supporting terrorism. Washington accordingly regarded Saddam Hussein as the "lesser evil" in comparison with the Ayatollah Khomeini—so as to prevent an Iranian victory.

Ironically, the Iran-Contra affair (exposed in 1986), in which arms sales to Iran helped to raise secret funds to the Nicaraguan Contras, engaged in fighting the Sandinista government, almost led to the downfall of Ronald Reagan—as Congress demanded an investigation by calling for grand juries in 1986 and 1987. Following the August 1990 Iraqi invasion of Kuwait, President George H. W. Bush Sr. opted to intervene in 1991 under a UN mandate to force Saddam

Hussein out of Kuwait. Yet, President Bush Sr. then refused to go to Baghdad (a position backed by then secretary of defense Richard Cheney at that time) to eliminate Saddam Hussein altogether. But it was this refusal to go to Baghdad that helped provoke the neoconservative backlash that would press for the overthrow of the Iraqi regime—ironically in interests of Iran (and al-Qaida) but possibly opposed by Israel.

After attempting to sponsor two (failed) coups in Iraq, the Clinton administration attempted to engage in a dialogue with the Islamic Republic following the election of President Khatami in 1997. U.S. secretary of state Madeleine Albright apologized for the 1953 U.S. intervention that installed the shah in power after overthrowing Prime Minister Mohammed Mossadeq.[25] But these apologies were not considered sufficient by Iranian authorities (who had also opposed Mossadeq) as a step toward an opening of diplomatic relations.

Iraq: Regime Change

President Bill Clinton had tried but failed to eliminate Saddam Hussein by a *coup d'etat* and began a systematic bombardment of Iraq in November 1998 once Congress passed the October 1998 Iraqi Liberation Act. Even though some of the same neoconservatives in the Bush administration had strongly supported Saddam Hussein in the 1980s, including Donald Rumsfeld and Dick Cheney, by the 2001–2003 period, the administration of George Bush Jr. opted to overthrow the Iraqi regime—linked with efforts to restructure the "greater Middle East" through regime change. The quest to hunt down Osama bin Laden then took second place to the quest to overthrow Saddam Hussein.

Ironically, unlike the Iran-Iraq War, these events generally played in Iran's favor. The elimination of both Saddam Hussein and the Taliban could have opened the door to compromise with Tehran—if the views of recalcitrant hardliners *on both sides* had been neutralized. In the spring of 2003, Washington openly received (through their Swiss representation in Iran) a one-page document from Tehran

that laid out an agenda for a diplomatic process intended to resolve all of the bilateral differences between the United States and Iran on a comprehensive basis. The Ayatollah Ali Khamenei offered to open up Iran's nuclear plants for inspection, control *Hizb'allah*, accept a two-state solution to the Israeli-Palestinian conflict, and cooperate against *al-Qaida*. The ayatollah Khamenei also issued a *fatwa* against nuclear weapons.[26]

Yet, rather than testing the offer and seeing exactly what could be bargained, and what could not, both vice president Dick Cheney and Defense secretary Donald Rumsfeld opposed engaging in direct talks at a high level.[27] Although Tehran was willing to help the United States defeat the Taliban in Afghanistan and support the interim Afghan government, the Bush administration still labeled Iran as a member of the "axis of evil" on February 1, 2002, because of its support for Hizb'allah, its purported arms sales to Palestinians in Gaza, and its nuclear and ballistic missile programs. In essence, U.S. plans for a "democratic" greater Middle East clashed with Iranian calls for hegemony over Shi'a in Lebanon, Iraq, Bahrain, and the oil rich eastern province of Saudi Arabia.

Dilemmas of "Backdoor" Multilateralism

The second-term Bush administration engaged in a new multilaterally oriented strategy, in part, because it has found itself bogged down in "peacekeeping" in Iraq and that it needs international supporters almost wherever it can find them. Consequently, the United States began to follow the European lead with respect to negotiations with Iran, at least initially, before deciding to engage in negotiations in the UN framework (along with Germany).

In February 2005 French defense minister Michele Alliot-Marie stated that negotiations were hampered by lack of trust on both sides: "The Europeans don't want to concede anything in negotiations or give up something so long as the Iranians don't accept the controls that are being demanded. . . . And the Iranians don't want to give up a nuclear enrichment program because they are unsure that they will get anything tangible in return."[28]

On the one side, Iran has been confronted with the risk of UN sanctions; on the other, the United States and Europe are likewise confronted with the threat of higher oil prices, a pressure point that Tehran had hoped to use to divide the UN Security Council[29] (which failed in 2006–2007). Yet, rather than attempting to engage in unilateral actions, the United States belatedly agreed in 2006 to work in a "backdoor" multilateral framework with its European allies (the EU-3 of France, Germany, and the United Kingdom), and then the UN Security Council plus Germany.

Here, the Europeans have been more willing to negotiate directly with the Islamic Republic than has the United States. Unlike the United States, Europeans in general have not thought that sanctions will be very effective. Moreover, should Iran obtain nuclear weapons, the United States is still more willing to pre-empt an Iranian nuclear capability than Europeans are, even at the risk of greater political-economic instability and conflict. At the same time, Europeans generally do not think they can reach a deal with Iran unless the United States firmly backs it, and unless the United States ultimately engages directly with Tehran as well—taking steps toward diplomatic recognition. The Russians have also been opposed to Iran's possession of a nuclear capability, as have the Chinese. But in general, both Moscow and Beijing have been more opposed to international sanctions than have been the Europeans.

The Americans, British, French, and Germans have also been divided as to how to work with Russia and China on the Iranian question, in that the United States has criticized Russian and Chinese weapons sales to Iran. In addition to helping to build "peaceful" Iranian nuclear plants, Moscow is a major trading partner of Iran. Russia and Iran also possess common interests in regard to the Caspian Sea and, somewhat ironically, in regard to Azeri oil interests, as well as Chechen secessionist movements, for example, which they both hope to "double restrain." Both Russia and Iran oppose Sunni-backed pan-Islamic movements.

Iranian officials had therefore hoped that the October 2004 major China-Iran natural gas and oil deal (worth $100 billion) would lead the European countries, India, Japan, and even Russia to reconsider their relations with Iran and not support sanctions. Iran additionally has sought to join the thus far weak Shanghai Cooperation Organization (SCO) of China, Russia, Tajikistan, Kazakhstan,

Kyrgyzstan, and Uzbekistan. The latter appears designed to forge a counterweight to the U.S. and NATO presence in central Asia.[30] Russian diplomatic influence with Tehran has, at least until mid-2007, been really one of the major keys in helping to find a compromise on the nuclear question. This has been true despite a major "cooling" of relations with Moscow over BMD and other issues. (See Chapter 2.)

In January 2006, the UN Security Council voted to apply limited sanctions against the Islamic Republic. Concurrently, the United States stated that limited UN sanctions would be just the beginning of more severe pressures: the Bush administration then tried to persuade major banks around the world to cut off more lending and export credits to Iran in the hopes of further damaging its oil infrastructure and thus isolating the country even more. Here, the United States and Europeans have still been divided as to the nature and extent of UN sanctions, because the United States has pressured the EU to augment financial sanctions and to curb billions of euros of export credits for Iran; they have also been divided as to whether to threaten, if not use, military force.

UN sanctions would have to be targeted at specific industries (such as the highly subsidized oil industry or companies owned by the Revolutionary Guards), but it would be difficult to enforce a general sanctions regime on Iran as this would upset states that seek to trade with Iran (with Dubai as an intermediary). Given the considerable underground black market economy in nuclear power technology, plus Iranian scientific expertise, it may be difficult to block nuclear development. A general sanctions regime could anger the general population that seeks access to U.S.-European-style consumer goods, and which is already confronted with high degrees of unemployment. The Iranian government would seek to exploit this dissatisfaction by blaming the United States and Europeans for Iran's economic crisis. (See *postscript*.)

Bush Administration Threats

In addition to U.S. forces in Iraq and Azerbaijan, the United States has based its Fifth Fleet in Bahrain; the U.S. Central Command is based in Qatar; and the U.S. Navy is based in the United Arab Emirates, at the deep-water port at Jebel Ali. Patriot antimissile systems have purportedly been based in Kuwait, Saudi Arabia, and Qatar.[31] In effect, while building up aircraft carrier battle groups in the Persian Gulf, the United States is encircling Iran with multiple forces.

The United States has additionally threatened to openly support "civil society" movements inside Iran, as a means to destabilize the regime and impel regime change. After European-Iranian nuclear talks failed in January 2006, Secretary of State Rice urged the Senate Foreign Relations Committee to secure $75 million in aid for Iranian pro-democracy activities and movements. This committee had previously stalled the bill for a year owing to opposition from the State Department, which did not want negotiations with president Ahmadinejad to be jeopardized by congressional action that would potentially make it America's official Iran policy "to support efforts by the people of Iran to exercise self-determination over the form of government in their country" as demanded by Iran Freedom and Support Act, a bill that would toughen sanctions against the Iranian regime, provide "financial and political" assistance to civil society organizations, and help fund the broadcast of free television and radio into Iran.[32] (It is interesting to note that Washington did support civil society movements during the cold war, but secretly, not openly, as was the case for the Solidarity movement in Poland. Concurrently, to counter U.S. efforts to support antiregime civil society movements in Iran, Tehran has opted for a crackdown of dissident groups, including student movements and Sufi Muslims, for example. Open U.S. support for the Iranian opposition could thus prove counterproductive, thereby delegitimizing reformers who oppose the government.[33])

The Pentagon appears to be developing options for conventional, and possibly nuclear, strikes against Iranian nuclear infrastructure and other targets.[34] U.S. military options range from covert actions, to preemption and surgical strikes, to direct military intervention. As the United States remains bogged down in Iraq (with NATO in Afghanistan), however, direct intervention with overstretched ground forces appears highly dubious. Surgical strikes likewise appear dubious, given the fact that such actions could further destabilize Iran and the region and force the price of oil to skyrocket even further. Less overt military actions, including covert actions and sabotage, support for minority opposition movements inside Iran, however, cannot be entirely ruled out.

Iranian Countermeasures

U.S. intelligence agencies believe that the Iranian Revolutionary Guard Corps (the Quds Force) has been supplying Shi'ite groups with Iranian-designed weapons, called improvised explosive devices or what U.S. soldiers themselves call EFPs, or Explosively Formed Penetrators. It is believed that the Iranian authorities have been aware of the Quds Force operations, but it is not clear at what level of the Iranian government this activity is being conducted. (While the Bush administration has accused Tehran of fueling sectarian violence in Iraq, the National Intelligence Estimate [NIE] has played down the significance of Iran's role,[35] thus giving the *Iraq Study Group Report* greater credence.)

What does appear to be certain is that, during 2006, Tehran adopted a more assertive policy of directly confronting the United States inside Iraq, which is aimed (1) at raising the cost of U.S. involvement in the Middle East; (2) teaching the Bush administration a lesson about the cost of regime change; (3) putting pressure on U.S. forces to leave; and (4) dissuading the Bush administration from taking a more confrontational policy toward Tehran by revealing that Iran can upgrade attacks on U.S. forces in Iraq.[36] Iran's elite Revolutionary Guards have engaged in military exercises southeast of Tehran to test the operational capabilities of Zelzal and Fajr-5 missiles.[37] The Iranian navy is reportedly engaging in "swarming" techniques using rapid boats designed to attack large, essentially immobile, naval vessels.

Here, in case of sanctions, or tougher pressures, including the use of military force, Iran has several powerful cards to play (as the world's fourth largest oil supplier) if it opts to curtail oil production in an effort to augment prices further. If provoked, Iran has threatened to cut production by 2.6 million barrels a day to force prices upward; but here Saudi Arabia appears more willing to raise production levels to meet world demand in Iran's place if necessary.[38] (Ultimately Iraq could raise oil production but not until its warring factions can reach a political settlement.) If the United States eventually goes to war with Iran, the price of oil could reach $90 to $120 per barrel (or higher), further destabilizing the world economy.

Tehran could also strengthen its support for Hizb'allah, the Islamic Jihad, and possibly Hamas; it could likewise further destabilize Iraq, if not intervene directly. The fact that Israel, India, and Pakistan have acquired an nuclear weapons capability all militate in favor of Iran's acquisition of weapons of mass destruction (WMD) from Tehran's perspective, despite the potentially destabilizing consequences for the region—which could result in a general race to obtain arms or WMD by a number of key states in the region.

Should Iran obtain nuclear weaponry, it has been purported that the Israelis purchased Dolphin submarines from Germany in 1999 and 2004 that are reportedly capable of carrying nuclear-armed cruise missiles as a second-strike capability.[39] Israel, however, does not have the air-fueling capability to strike all Iranian nuclear facilities. In addition to Israel and the United States, French president Jacques Chirac likewise warned Iran at least obliquely, "The leaders of states who would use terrorist means against us, as well as those who would envisage using . . . weapons of mass destruction, must understand that they would lay themselves open to a firm and fitting response on our part. . . . This response could be a conventional one. It could also be of a different kind."[40]

In effect, the United States, Israel, and France all threatened Iran in some way or another. In the case of Israel, the Iranian threat has opened the issues as to whether Israel should put an end to what is called its policy of "nuclear ambiguity" or "opacity" and thus publicly announce its nuclear arsenal of over one hundred nuclear weapons as a deterrent. Moreover, Iran would have to assume that any nuclear attack on Israel would result in U.S. retaliation.[41]

It should furthermore be underscored that if Iran really had the nuclear and ballistic missile capability to strike Israel (it might need at least three to ten more years, if not more, according to some estimates, to make weapons-grade uranium), a nuclear attack would also wipe out the one million Palestinians who live inside Israel and those on its borders as well, if not Hizb'allah at the same time, thus annihilating those whom Iran is supporting, while Iran itself would be annihilated in a devastating counterstrike. To paraphrase a saying that came out of the Vietnam War, the use of nuclear weapons would, in effect, destroy the Palestinians in order to save them.

Holocaust Polemics

James Baker's argument "that it is not appeasement to talk to one's enemies" does not seem to have been heeded by the Bush administration. The latter has generally followed the advice of the lobby group, the American Israeli Public Affairs Committee (AIPAC), among other neoconservative and Christian conservative lobby and pressure groups. AIPAC directly opposed key recommendations of the *Iraq Study Group Report*, particularly in reference to possibility of negotiations with Iran and Syria; it only reluctantly supported the "two state solution" to the Middle East conflict as backed by the president himself in 2002, but with significant qualifications that place obstacles in the path of Israeli-Palestinian dialogue and reconciliation.[42] Following the advice of AIPAC, the Bush administration has thus far opposed engaging Syria in diplomacy, in part because of Syrian support for partisan groups in Iraq and supplies to Hizb'allah, plus thus far unproven accusations of the Syrian leadership's involvement in the assassination of former Lebanese prime minister Rafik Hariri (despite Israel's own secret talks with Syria). (See Chapter 5.)

The influence of AIPAC (among other pressure groups) on U.S. politicians, both Republicans and Democrats, is considerable. In discussing Iran at a dinner sponsored by the AIPAC, U.S. senator and presidential candidate Hillary Rodham Clinton declared, "U.S. policy must be clear and unequivocal: We cannot, we should not, we must not permit Iran to build or acquire nuclear weapons. . . . In dealing with this threat . . . no option can be taken off the table."[43] Former U.S. senator and Democratic presidential candidate John Edwards has been quoted as saying to a conference on the "Balance of Israel's National Security" that the "rise of Islamic radicalism, use of terrorism, and the spread of nuclear technology and weapons of mass destruction represent an unprecedented threat to the world and Israel. At the top of these threats is Iran. Iran threatens the security of Israel and the entire world. Let me be clear: Under no circumstances can Iran be allowed to have nuclear weapons."[44] Sen. Evan Bayh (D-IN) described Iran as "everything we thought Iraq was but wasn't. They are seeking nuclear weapons, they do support terrorists; they have threatened to destroy Israel, and they've threatened us, too."[45]

Here, however, lobby groups cannot be blamed *alone* for lack of progress on U.S.-Iranian diplomacy. The question is how radically U.S. policy would change without them. The comments and actions of the present Iranian regime itself make for easy counterpropaganda. Contrary to the stated intent of Iranian president Mahmoud Ahmadinejad, who claimed that his remarks are neither anti-Semitic nor anti-American,[46] his officially sponsored "Review of the Holocaust: Global Vision" effectively undermined any potential support Iran might obtain from the U.S. public. Not only did the Holocaust conference deeply offend the Jewish community throughout the world (including the Iranian-Jewish community, which numbers about twenty-five thousand), but it also offended Black Americans (a large percentage who are Muslim) through the official invitation of David Duke, the Imperial Wizard of the Ku Klux Klan. Ahmadinejad also claimed that his intent was to show the extent to which non-Jewish groups suffered. But in so doing, the conference offended those very non-Jewish groups that identify with the millions also persecuted by the Nazis (the mentally handicapped, gypsies, gays, Jehovah's witnesses Slavs, Communists, Socialists)—in addition to enraging German authorities (possibly toughening the German stance on sanctions).[47]

Former Iranian president Mohammad Khatami, among other Iranian authorities, directly or indirectly, denounced the conference.

"Insecurity-Security Dialectic"

The so-called Greater Middle East does not need a renewed spiraling arms race and a renewed dialectics of "insecurity-security." Should Iran be considering "peaceful" nuclear power development as a means to help amortize a nuclear weapons program (to lower the costs of weapons-grade enrichment), questions as to what nuclear weapons will mean for its own security, as well as that of the region, should be raised, regardless of the U.S. and Israeli standpoints.

The point raised here is that possession of a nuclear weapons capacity has not prevented either wars of mutual subversion or regime change caused by internal dissent and resistance. Moscow's massive nuclear arsenal designed for overkill did not prevent the Soviet Union from imploding. Pretoria's nuclear program did not prevent Apartheid in South Africa (which possessed eight nuclear bombs) from collapsing following President Frederik Willem de Klerk's decision to abandon the nuclear program in 1993 before the victory of Nelson Mandella.[48]

The shah's efforts to develop a nuclear infrastructure (buying Westinghouse and Siemens reactors), combined with his own threat to acquire nuclear weaponry in the mid-1970s, did not prevent the Islamic Revolution. Initially, the Ayatollah Khomeini had opposed the shah's nuclear power program, although this position changed after the outbreak of the Iran-Iraq War. In this regard, Iran's nuclear program was intended to counter Iraq's nuclear program and not that of Israel; only following the 2003 Iraq War has Iran tried to justify its ballistic missile and nuclear enrichment program as a means to deter both the United States and Israel, but it might well end up provoking both these countries rather than deterring them.

From this perspective, it is dubious that the possession of nuclear weapons by Iran will help to stabilize its domestic sociopolitical situation through populist appeals to Iranian nationalism and by rallying the domestic population in favor of nuclear energy as a sign of prestige and "modernity." If the Iranian government believes it can stave off popular dissent through nuclear reactor development, it appears dubious that it will succeed. Investment in nuclear power is more likely to aggravate, rather than ameliorate, socioeconomic tensions. There are other ways to build national pride and to secure respect and a positive place in the international community.

It is even more dubious that nuclear weapons will help to stabilize the "greater Middle East" or make Iran more secure. The fear that Iran is secretly enriching uranium to obtain weapons-grade material has also upset France, Germany, and the United Kingdom and increasingly Russia and China as well. A nuclear Pakistan could also reconsider its relations with Iran as well, should Tehran finally opt for nuclear weapons and delivery capabilities, leading to an even more tense relationship with Pakistan, rather than the contrary. Iran's alleged quest for a nuclear weapons status might ultimately raise a military counterreaction in Turkey and Saudi Arabia—if not in Iraq itself.[49] Saudi Arabia, in particular, has been taking a more vocal stance against Iranian efforts to achieve predominance in Iraq and throughout the region.

The United Arab Emirates, Kuwait, Oman, and Saudi Arabia might spend up to $60 billion for defense purposes in 2007.[50] These states seek their own deterrent in case the United States cannot protect them against Iranian attack, which has engaged in naval maneuvers, possibly designed to block the Strait of Hormuz through which 40 percent of the world's oil passes. The Gulf states (which are tightening their federation through monetary union) fear that a nuclear armed

Iran would attempt to assert its hegemony over the region and engage in efforts to support pan-Shi'a secessionist movements in the oil-rich eastern regions of Saudi Arabia and in Bahrain in addition to supporting Shi'a groups in Iraq. Here, the United Arab Emirates and Iran are in a very dangerous dispute over the control of three Persian Gulf islands, Greater Tunb, Lesser Tunb, and Abu Musa. Tehran has argued that the three islands dominate the entrance to the Persian Gulf and the lanes through which the bulk of Iran's oil exports and its vital imports pass, and thus are vital to Iranian security. Abu Dhabi, however, argues that three islands are not directly at the entrance to the Strait of Hormuz, where the Iranian port of Bander Abbas and the island of Qishm lie (which is a free trade zone and site of ecological tourism)—and thus are not strategically positioned. It has been argued that the island of Sirri, for example, could provide the same strategic protection as the three islands.[51] From the UAE perspective, the islands give Iran a base for projecting power to the south. The Iranians counter that the three islands could provide a second line of defense for Bander Abbas.

It is thus not accidental that Qatar, Kuwait, Bahrain, and the United Arab Emirates have also opted to forge common political economic policies and that all joined NATO's June 2004 Istanbul Cooperation Initiative (ICI) designed to promote security and regional stability through bilateral cooperation with NATO in areas where the alliance has particular skills and expertise. Saudi Arabia and Oman have also expressed interest in working with NATO as well.[52]

Breaking the Logjam

With the deployment of a second battle carrier group in the Persian Gulf, plus Patriot antimissile systems, plus efforts to press for stronger UN sanctions, combined with the arrest of Iranian diplomats in Baghdad, the Bush administration appears to engaging in a dangerous game of *coercive diplomacy*—or what can be called a new form of *brinkmanship* in post–cold war circumstances—aimed at impelling Iran to give up its nuclear enrichment program before Tehran develops a nuclear weapons capability, thus impelling the regime to compromise, from a hawkish "position of strength." Taking the owlish stance of a flexible realism, James Baker and Lee Hamilton, however, have argued against negotiating with Iran from a position of strength: "Sometimes the argument is made that Iran has momentum in the region, and the United States should not negotiate until it has more leverage over Iran. We disagree."[53]

The problem remains: Is the Bush administration playing post–cold war brinkmanship, seeking to pressure a deal without actually going to war? Or is it intended to physically wipe out Iranian nuclear facilities through the use of cruise missiles? Would the targets be comprehensive or selective? (It appears very dubious that the United States could even attempt to occupy Iran—as it has Iraq.) If the United States does opt for cruise missile diplomacy (with or without UN Security Council support), is the United States willing to risk the Iranian counterterretaliation in the form of regional and global acts of terrorism—or possibly the targeting of U.S. allies in the region? Would U.S. strikes mobilize the Iranian population against the United States, creating permanent hated and animosity? Would the Bush administration take the risk that war could block Persian Gulf shipping lanes, with consequent energy shortages and price hikes, estimated to rise as high as $90 to $120 per barrel? Or even higher if Saudi petroleum facilities are attacked?

On the other side, despite President Mahmoud Ahmadinejad's own form of belligerent propaganda, there have been reports that he is being pressured by the Guardian Council, as well as by the student opposition, among other factions, to modify his rhetoric and policy. (Ahmadinejad was said to have won the 2005 presidential elections by surprise—perhaps even a surprise for the ruling Guardian Council.)[54] These factions may be seeking a face-saving compromise (such as suspending all major enrichment activities but keeping a handful of centrifuges in operation, or else suspending enrichment long enough to get UN talks going). It is not clear, however, whether the United States and the UN Security Council appear willing to accept a compromise position. Despite splits within the Iranian leadership, the latter has continued to reject President Bush's preconditions for negotiations that demand an immediate suspension of its nuclear enrichment program. Furthermore, the Bush administration seeks to negotiate from a position of strength, but with oil at $60–$70 a barrel (or higher), Washington is concerned that no sanctions can truly harm Iran. If negotiations (or the "dialogue of the deaf") drags on, then, over time, Iran would move closer to producing a nuclear weapons capacity.

To break the logjam, the United States will ultimately need to engage in direct negotiations with the regime, as proposed by the Iraq Study Group, and thus begin to break the latter's isolation—assuming, of course, that Tehran accepts. The United States' elimination of both the Taliban and the Iraqi regime of Saddam Hussein, the two principal enemies of Iran, should have opened the doors to a U.S.-Iranian rapprochement in the aftermath of the U.S. military intervention Iraq in 2003, as previously argued.[55] Tehran has subsequently been looking for a face-saving way to open relations with the United States since 2003, but this has thus far been denied.

In the very near future, the United States and the European troika cannot rely on "backdoor" multilateralism or even Saudi-Iranian discussions. Much as it did with North Korea (see Chapter 7), Washington, in particular, will need to engage in a more "front-door" multilateralism that will involve direct U.S. diplomatic engagement (probably in secret at first). Iran's former chief nuclear negotiator, Hassan Rowhani, had proposed solutions in an effort to defuse the current standoff with respect to Iran's peaceful nuclear activities (in his personal capacity). In April 2007 Rowhani called for a ten-point plan for the creation of "Persian Gulf Security and Cooperation Organization," comprising the six Gulf Cooperation Council (GCC) States, Iran, and Iraq in line with the UN Security Council Resolution 598 (paragraph 8) of July 1987 and that would permit IAEA inspections and supervise production of nuclear fuel.[56] But such a proposal has thus far been regarded as a means for Iran to assert its regional interests and to offset U.S. influence among the Gulf states. For such a community to become feasible, Iran would need to retract its pursuit of regional predominance or hegemony.

The dilemma is that the United States needs Iranian assistance to help stabilize the region, particularly in Iraq, but also in Afghanistan and the Persian Gulf in general. Iran likewise needs a peaceful regional environment without actual or potential threats that jeopardize its need for political economic reforms and the diversification of its economy. U.S.-Iranian rapprochement would additionally look toward concerted ways to help end the continuing Israeli-Palestinian conflict, among other regional disputes. In the past, countries have renounced their nuclear programs only after having experienced a substantial lessening of external threats.[57]

To obtain Iranian consent for European or international controls to be placed over the Iranian nuclear fuel cycle, the United States might ultimately need to engage in direct negotiations with the regime and thus begin to break the latter's isolation, as has been urged by IAEA chief negotiator Dr. Mohamed El-Baradei. In the latter's view, the United States needs to engage in more direct diplomacy and thus offer more, along with the Europeans, to obtain greater trust and confidence. In June 2007, El-Baradei stated that Iran, the IAEA, and the UNSC are at a "stalemate." Tehran could be running close to three thousand uranium-enriching centrifuges by the end of July: "The next few months will be crucial . . . Iran is building a capacity, a knowledge" of enrichment that is irreversible, and they are not providing the IAEA "an assurance that this is a peaceful program." He forewarned, "The longer we delay, the less option we have to reach a peaceful solution." El-Baradei stated that Iran is three to eight years from achieving a nuclear weapons capability, thus there is still time for negotiation: "Even the idea of people talking about using force . . . it would be catastrophic, it would be an act of madness, and it would not solve the issue." While Iran has continued to insist on its legal right to engage in the enrichment process, El-Baradei argued that the Iranian nuclear program must be made more transparent and that Iran should engage in a "time out" on enrichment as there is no urgency to build capacity and "self-imposed moratorium" on the number of centrifuges built while the UNSC takes a time-out on the imposition of sanctions.[58]

Efforts to dissuade Iran from controlling its own nuclear fuel cycle might ultimately mean *regime recognition* as opposed to *regime change* (but without necessarily ruling out far-reaching *regime reform*)—given the appropriate negotiated conditions and conditional security *assurances* leading to *security guarantees*. The option of granting UN security guarantees for Iran, combined with U.S. diplomatic recognition, may be a possibility—but only if the right conditions can be formulated. Such conditions, among others, include giving up Iranian national controls of the enrichment process (or permit enrichment under strict IAEA supervision), plus all pretensions to develop nuclear weapons. Among geopolitical concerns, this might mean curtailing Iranian support for *Hizb'allah* in the assumption that a settlement can take place on the continuing Israeli presence in Lebanon. Other conditions might include recognition of the State of Israel, coupled with clear steps toward an Israeli-Palestinian peace settlement. Iran has previously stated that it will support whatever peace accords with Israel the Palestinians agree to (while concurrently arming Hamas). Accordingly, while U.S. *regime recognition* of the Islamic Republic of Iran involving *conditional security guarantees* would rule out *regime change* by force, no potential U.S.-Iranian "deal" could rule out the continuing possibility of *regime reform* led by Iran's own highly active civil society.[59] The United States really has no control or permanent influence over domestic Iranian social and political movements. Here it would also be up to Tehran itself to negotiate with Iran's distinguished overseas émigrés, who, for the most part, have been urging the Iranian leadership to make significant political and economic changes from differing perspectives.

The Bush administration belatedly began its first formal negotiations with Iran over the Iraq crisis in late May 2007, while continuing to denounce Iranian military supports for Iraqi Shi'a militias, Hamas, Hizb'allah and the Taliban, leading commentators to believe that it was setting the ground for war. While secretary of state Condolezza Rice and under secretary of state Nicolas Burns are said to support continued diplomatic efforts, superhawks and vultures in vice president Dick Cheney's office were said to be still pressing for preemptive strikes.[60]

By July 2007, however, Iran stated that it would accept IAEA inspections; the next step is to find ways to cooperate in Iraq and elsewhere.

Toward a Regional Peace?

While the establishment of a "nuclear free weapons zone" remains a dubious possibility in that Israel will continue to sustain an undeclared nuclear deterrent, it is possible that states of the Middle East, including both Israel and Iran, could accept a "no first use" pledge of WMD. One future possibility to explore would thus be a "no-first use" pledge against the use of all forms of WMD (nuclear, chemical, or biological) that would be signed by all states in the region of the "Greater Middle East." In this context, Israel could sign such an agreement—but without admitting that it possessed nuclear weaponry. A nuclear Pakistan could also sign. Moreover, if it did ultimately open up all of its nuclear facilities to IAEA inspectors, Tehran could obtain the international security guarantees of the United States, United Kingdom, France, Russia, and China. Such security guarantees would be similar to those obtained by Ukraine once the latter gave up its nuclear weaponry in 1994.

It is also possible, but highly unlikely, that Israel could agree to put its facilities under IAEA nuclear safeguards—if it signed a revised nonproliferation treaty and if given adequate U.S. security guarantees. Nevertheless, security guarantees for both Israel and a new Palestine could be granted through the NATO-EU-Russian deployment of multinational peacekeepers, which could include Turkish troops, for example, under a general UN mandate, in a newly independent Palestine, and the formation of multilateral regional "security communities." Such a multinational force would act to prevent continuing acts of terrorism and counterterrorism that have taken place since Israel withdrew from Gaza. (See Chapter 5.)

Yet, such a scenario evidently appears a bit too optimistic at present. If there should be solid evidence of Iranian deceit, then the United States and the European *troika* of Germany, France, and the United Kingdom will need press Iran harder. Yet to ultimately obtain Russian support for putting even greater diplomatic and economic pressure on Iran might mean that the United States might have to find a *quid pro quo* with Russia. Yet, what kind of *quid pro quo*, and how much the United States might concede, if anything, to Moscow, remains to be seen. Would it include, for example, the promise not to expand

NATO to the Ukraine? Or a new form of Russian membership in NATO? Or a decision not to deploy BMD in eastern Europe? If given the right incentives, Russia could move closer toward the United States and EU on Iran and other issues, particularly given the fact that Russia does not want Iran to become a competitor in nuclear fuels. (See Chapter 2.)

It will take some time for the United States and Iran to resolve their differences; it is certain that hard-liners on both sides oppose all reconciliation for the immediate future. If the Bush administration is unable or reluctant to engage in negotiations, it is possible that President Bush might seek to destroy Iran's nuclear facilities as his last parting shot as a lame duck president aimed at restructuring the "greater Middle East" with the argument that no other president will be in a better position to stop Iran's efforts to achieve regional hegemony.[61] Even if President Bush, or the next president, does not intend to intervene militarily, the problem is that once U.S. forces are deployed, it is difficult to pull back after already committing regional allies in the defense buildup (much as Henry Kissinger argued as a last-minute rationale for U.S. intervention in Iraq). But more likely, there is a real danger that either U.S. or Iranian forces could be drawn into action by "terrorist" groups such as *al-Qaida* (or other third parties) who thrive on confrontation—even though neither Iran nor the United States really desire war.[62]

CHAPTER 5

Israel and Palestinian Fratricide: Beyond the "Two State Solution"?

Something There Is That Does Not Love a Wall

Outside the window of a Bethlehem hotel, which once possessed a panoramic view of Rachel's tomb, graffiti is scribbled across the massive rampart near the watchtower. In the center is one citation: "Mr. President: Tear Down this Wall!" The historical irony is apparent: The reference is to Ronald Reagan's demands that Soviet president Mikhail Gorbachev tear down the Berlin Wall. The difference, however, was that the Berlin Wall was essentially built by East German authorities to keep their population *in*, while the Israeli government has built its wall to keep Palestinians *out*. But the wall has been built on portions of territory still claimed by Palestinians. (See Chapter 10.)

In the Israeli-Palestinian context, the wall appears symbolic of deeper tensions and disputes that appear intractable, but require patience, determination, and real leadership to address. Here, the major obstacle to peace in the region (and the world) lies symbolically in Jerusalem, much as Riah Abu el-Assal, bishop of the Episcopal Church of Jerusalem and the Middle East, put it to UK prime minister Tony Blair in February 2003 just before the U.S.-UK intervention in Iraq. At that time, Bishop El-Assal asserted that "the shortest way to Baghdad goes through Jerusalem" and that "[o]nce peace comes to Jerusalem, peace will come to the whole world."[1] The bishop's comments were intended to counter Blair's assertion that peace in the Middle East would come only *after* intervention in Iraq and the removal of Saddam Hussein from power in Baghdad. The point here is not based on mysticism. As the differing religions and sects of Christianity (Orthodox, Catholic, Protestant), Islam (Sunni and Shi'a), and of a likewise varied Judaism (among other religious groups) all possess interests in Jerusalem, a peaceful settlement would help to bring together much of the world.

Resolving the Israeli-Palestinian conflict, as well as intra-Palestinian strife, would help draw "moderate" (even if illiberal) Arab and Islamic opinion away from violent pan-Islamic factions and would represent a major step toward winding down the "global war on terror." In terms of the Arab-Israeli conflict more specifically, the United States and Israel tend to point to intra-Arab and intra-Islamic conflicts and tensions and lack of "democracy" as the root cause of the Middle East crisis and of "terrorism"; yet, by contrast, the Arab world tends to point to the injustice caused by the democratic state of Israel and the Israeli-Palestinian conflict as the root source of the Middle East conflict. The reality is, as usual, somewhere in between. At the same time, however, while both sides continue to point the finger at the other, it has become increasingly evident that the "global war on terror" is irrevocably interwoven with the Israeli-Palestinian conflict. Working to resolve that conflict could possibly be achieved by means of a loose West Bank Palestinian–Jordanian confederation linked to a U.S.-EU-Turkish backed Mediterranean initiative. Now that the "two state solution" appears infeasible following the seizure of Gaza by Hamas in June 2007, such an alternative approach might help bring Fatah and Hamas closer together in a situation in which Fatah and Hamas appear to be digging their own trenches in the West Bank and Gaza.

From this perspective, the United States, along with Russia, the United Nations, and the European Union, and with the assistance of other regional actors such as Saudi Arabia and Turkey, will need to take more decisive political-economic steps to bring a peaceful resolution to the Israeli-Palestinian conflict, as well as to intra-Palestinian strife, while not losing sight of the need to address other key disputes and apparently burgeoning conflicts in the Arab-Islamic worlds through the establishment of wider regional security communities in the Euro-Mediterranean and the Persian Gulf.

Road Map for Peace: Not Past Phase I

As a follow-up to the failed Camp David summit in July 2000, the Road Map for Peace had set out a three-stage process to resolve the Israel-Palestinian conflict and to end the occupation of the Palestinian territories that began in 1967.[2] The principles of the Road Map for Peace—which called for an independent Palestinian state living side by side Israel—were thus first outlined by U.S. president George W. Bush on June 24, 2002, in the midst of the violent *Intifada*. (At his own Camp David summit, President Bill Clinton had attempted, but failed, to surpass President Jimmy Carter's successful 1978 Camp David summit that brokered a peace accord between Egypt and Israel).

Here, Yasser Arafat's refusal (despite his promises to Clinton to do so) to sign onto the July 2000 Camp David summit, combined with Ariel Sharon's politically and religiously provocative September 28, 2000, visit to the Temple Mount and Al-Aqsa Mosque in the Old City of Jerusalem, had helped to spark the Al-Aqsa *Intifada*. The often-overlooked Taba summit in January 2001, in which Israeli-Palestinian compromise might have proved feasible, was largely doomed to failure, given the outbreak of that violent uprising (which lasted from September 2000 until 2005).[3] Events in February 2007 surrounding the Al-Aqsa Mosque once again threatened a third Intifada—or more likely provide a rallying point for pan-Islamist militants around the world.

As the United States and Israel insisted that the Palestinian Authority (PA) begin a process of "democratization" as part of Phase I, the plan began to be implemented in the March through April 2003 time period, with the appointment of Palestinian prime minister Mahmoud Abbas (Abu Mazen) by Palestinian leader Yasser Arafat in the formation of a new PA. Abbas was then elected president of the Palestinian National Authority in January 2005, but the fact that Israel did not change its position in terms of supporting a land for peace resolution worked to weaken his authority. Moreover, the concept of "democratization," however, was largely conceived as a form of "pacification" in that Israel and the United States had assigned Mahmoud Abbas the task of attempting to rein in various Palestinian factions that Israel had accused of acts of terrorism. This led Hamas to accuse Fatah and its Preventive Security forces of repressing Hamas militants in collaboration with Israel and the United States. Not only was Abbas unable to prevent violence, but Hamas, in particular, grew stronger and won the January 2006 Palestinian elections by peaceful democratic means. In mid-June 2007, Hamas then staged a coup against Fatah for control over Gaza, leading Islamic militants to proclaim a "second liberation" following Israeli withdrawal.

The Road Map process was originally based on the foundations of the Madrid Conference; the principle of "land for peace;" UN Security Council Resolutions 242, 338, and 1397; and other agreements previously reached by the parties. The latter included the March 2002 peace initiative of Saudi Arabia's Crown Prince Abdullah that had been endorsed by the Beirut Arab League summit (although not signed by Iraq or Iran). This initiative had also called for the acceptance of Israel as a neighbor living in peace and security, in the context of a comprehensive settlement. Also included was a call to forge closer military and security ties among Arab states, including nuclear cooperation.[4] The 2002 initiative represented a vital element of international efforts to promote a comprehensive peace on all tracks, including the Syrian-Israeli and Lebanese-Israeli tracks. The subsequent unofficial 2003 Geneva Accords sought to press the two parties further along the Road Map.[5] The March 2002 accords were then reconfirmed in the March 2007 Arab summit.

Phase I of the Road Map demanded that the Palestinian leadership issue an unequivocal statement reiterating Israel's right to exist and to cease violence. It also called on the Israeli leadership to issue an unequivocal statement affirming its commitment to the two-state vision of an independent, viable, sovereign Palestinian state living in peace and security alongside Israel and calling for an immediate end to violence against Palestinians everywhere. Phase II sought the "option of creating an independent Palestinian state with provisional borders and attributes of sovereignty, based on the new constitution, as a way station to a permanent status settlement," while Phase III called for permanent status resolution (in 2005!), including an agreement on borders, Jerusalem, refugees, and settlements and to support progress toward a comprehensive Middle East settlement between Israel and Lebanon and Israel and Syria, to be achieved as soon as possible.

The Road Map, however, has evidently not yet pointed the way to peace, and the Quartet (the United States, Russia, the United Nations, and the European Union) appear to have lost their direction. Weak Israeli leadership, plus ever-widening fissures on the key issues (Jerusalem, borders, and return of refugees) have only accentuated the factional disputes both between and among the Israelis and Palestinians since the Camp David summit in 2000. Moreover, the splintering of the PA permitted Hamas and the Islamic Jihad to strengthen their position in Gaza. To make matters worse, Iranian political-economic influence has thus far tended to usurp that of Saudi Arabia, even with the signing of the Mecca Accords in 2007.

From this perspective, the Road Map has not even gotten past Phase I. Moreover, given fratricidal conflict between Fatah and Hamas, the "two state solution" (as if national "independence" is really possible in a globalized world) appears dead in its tracks. Some form of confederal resolution as a transitional agreement appears more feasible.

Withdrawal from Gaza

The death of Yasser Arafat in November 2004, coupled with Ariel Sharon's unilateral withdrawal from Gaza in the summer of 2005, had initially appeared to raise hopes for a peaceful settlement to the ongoing crisis. Yet that withdrawal effectively divided Israeli political opinion and almost cost Sharon his leadership of the Likud Party to his challenger Benjamin Netanyahu by a close vote of 51.3 percent to 47.6 percent. Sharon's subsequent coma further undermined the Israeli leadership whose cohesion and effectiveness has appeared to have declined since the assassination of Yitzak Rabin in November 1995 by an Israeli "terrorist" opposed to the 1993 Oslo Accords.

In splitting Israeli opinion, the unilateral Israeli withdrawal from Gaza has consequently raised questions as to the effectiveness of the Israeli leadership to put an end to the conflict without the more-engaged and direct diplomatic engagement of the Quartet group. The fact that the withdrawal had not been well coordinated with the Palestinians, or with the Quartet powers as part of a larger diplomatic settlement, did not augur well for the future. The PA did not have the police capability to control potential acts of terrorism once it took control in Gaza. Here, it appears that a more-controlled Israeli withdrawal from Gaza, with a peaceful transfer of assets that had been coordinated with the PA and the UN, would have been in Israeli and international interests.[6] The withdrawal, had it been accompanied by a similar withdrawal in the West Bank, could have taken place with the backing of international peacekeepers under a joint NATO-EU command as well as under a general UN mandate.

Once Israeli forces withdrew unilaterally, however, the PA had consequently not been able to prevent Hamas, and other factions, from shooting rockets into Israel from Gaza, resulting in a swift Israeli reprisal. Moreover, exacerbating tensions between rival Palestinian factions, the PA refused to pass control over decision making regarding the distribution of land in the Gaza strip to a committee made up of all the Palestinian factions, as proposed by Hamas, the Islamic Jihad, and other groups. This has led the latter groups to accuse the PA of corruption in attempting control valuable real estate.

Israeli attacks on the PLO's secular leadership before (and after) Arafat's death considerably weakened the secular PA, while Israeli strikes against Hamas' leadership (such as the Israeli assassination of Sheikh Ahmed Yassin in March 2004) made Hamas even more popular among Palestinians. The Quartet group failed to help reform Fatah and build Fatah's capabilities to provide social and welfare services (through NGO assistance, for example) so as to better compete with those of Hamas. These factors all helped to strengthen support for Hamas relative to the secular leadership of the Fatah Party led by Mahmoud Abbas after Arafat's death. Hamas, by contrast, was able to obtain popular support precisely because roughly 90 percent of its work is in social, welfare, cultural, and educational activities.[7] These factors, in addition to the complex electoral system, helped Hamas win the January 2006 elections.

Israeli's unilateral and uncoordinated withdrawal has subsequently permitted Gaza to become a hot bed of pan-Islamic radicalism in which the major militias of Fatah, Hamas, Islamic Jihad, as well as the Popular Front for the Liberation of Palestine, began to expand a network of bases (which provide launch pads for rocket attacks) in some of the territory of former settlements. *Al-Qaida* and other groups purportedly have been able to infiltrate the region, with both Ayman al-Zawahiri and Osama bin Laden denouncing sanctions on Hamas and urging Hamas not to accept agreements between the PA and Israel—and not to provide the secular Fatah any legitimacy for having sold out the Palestinian cause. Fratricidal Palestinian strife in Gaza could additionally afflict Palestinian relations with Egypt, a factor leading Cairo to attempt to mediate between Israel, Hamas, and the PA, as it did in the effort to achieve a truce in 2005. Here, while Hamas claims no links to al-Qaida, Egypt fears that Hamas (with the help of the Egyptian Muslim Brotherhood) could help further radicalize its own population.[8] As reconciliation efforts failed in late 2006 until June 2007, the UN and Israel proposed the deployment of an international peacekeeping force along the Egyptian-Gaza border—a proposal opposed by Hamas who considered it to represent a potential "occupation."

The Wall

Initially, the PA did appear to win out over Hamas in municipal elections held in the West Bank in late September 2005 despite (or because of) Israeli raids, which had detained roughly 441 suspected members of Hamas or the Islamic Jihad. (Fatah obtained 54 percent of the vote compared to Hamas' 26 percent). Following Israel's withdrawal from Gaza, the PA appeared to obtain greater credence for its objectives of achieving peace through diplomacy.

Yet, a major factor helping Hamas to win the January 2006 elections was the expansion of Israeli settlements, which the peace accords signed by Fatah did not stop. While Israel had begun to withdraw from some of the lesser settlements in the northern West Bank (Samaria), the establishment of new Jewish settlements appeared to indicate that Israel had no intention of totally withdrawing. Since 1995, some twenty-seven settlements had encroached on territory confiscated from Bethlehem, a major factor in dooming the Oslo Accords, and assisting the hard-line stance of Hamas. In the first three months of 2005, construction in the West Bank settlements increased by 83 percent, when in Israel proper, housing construction was said to have decreased by a quarter. (Palestinians claim that over thirty thousand new housing units were planned for the West Bank.)[9]

The expansion of settlements cuts back agricultural and industrial development and, combined with the wall, discourages tourism in the Palestinian sections. Moreover, Israeli's violent actions against Hamas ironically tended to build the latter's credibility at the same time that relations between Hamas and Fatah became increasingly fractious. At the same time, in areas such as Bethlehem, the Muslim population now outnumbers the Christian population (roughly 70 percent to 30 percent), which finds itself caught between Israeli expansionism, on the one hand, and Muslim revivalism on the other. With a deteriorating economy, many Christian Palestinians have chosen emigration.

Israel has thus sought to strengthen some of the major West Bank settlements, while concurrently building a massive wall. The infamous separation barrier (known by several names depending on one's perspective: On the Israeli side, The "Security Fence," "Separation Wall"; on the Palestinian side: "Annexation Wall," "Apartheid Wall") is to take in some 7 to 8 percent of the West Bank, plus fifteen thousand Palestinians (according to Israeli sources). This raised the question as whether these lands would ever be returned to Palestinians, or whether there will be a trade-off for other Israeli lands (and of what quality), in accord with the principle of "land for peace."

Opponents of the wall, which zigzags through areas not even close to the 1967 borders, argue that Israel intends to use it to expropriate up to 47 percent of the West Bank, while simultaneously setting up new systems of permits and restrictions on the movement of Palestinian civilians. Because the "separation wall" is roughly 70 percent complete in Jerusalem, the wall additionally raises the specter of a new, and perhaps more insidious, complex of American Indian-type reservations in which Palestinians would be separated from both Israel and their own lands by divided cantons.[10] Israel likewise retains intrusive control over any decisions to operate any future port or airport. The PA attempted to address the question of Israeli control over Gaza's ports and crossings if a Palestinian state is to become viable, plus control its own system of taxation.

January 2006 Elections

Almost immediately following the electoral victory of Hamas in January 2006, U.S. secretary of state Condoleezza Rice went to the Middle East in mid-February hoping to obtain Arab state support for cutting back on funding to Hamas. Here, the United States is prevented by statute from assisting "terrorist" organizations. While the United States and Israel had hoped to pressure Hamas to recognize accords signed by Fatah, Hamas refused to do so. On the one hand, Hamas argued that Israel itself has not completely abided by its agreements with the previous Palestinian leadership.[11] On the other hand, Hamas also refused to change its charter that asserts that the land of Palestine represents an Islamic *waqf* that cannot be renounced or abandoned.[12]

Here, Arab countries, including Egypt, argued for giving Hamas at least one hundred days to see how it would run the government and were generally reluctant to place sanctions on the Hamas-led PA largely in fear that isolating the new Palestinian government would benefit militant opposition groups as well as Iran. Tehran had promised to fill the void of any loss of international aid and called for all Islamic states to accord yearly financial assistance to the Hamas-dominated government.[13] Yet, in mid-April 2006, Hamas had difficulty paying its 165,000 public workers, including about 80,000 in the security forces, many loyal to Fatah. (Since 2000, overall costs of the conflict for both Israel and the Palestinians have been quite high.[14])

Israel immediately sought to pressure Hamas economically once the latter was elected. Tel Aviv opted to cut about $55 million a month in tax revenues funds that are crucial to the Palestinian budget. In April 10, 2006, Israel broke off contacts with the PA altogether, although it stated it would sustain "personal" ties with Mahmoud Abbas.[15] The problem, however, with this latter measure, as former president Jimmy Carter pointed out, is that it sends the wrong signal to the average Palestinian. These tax revenues are generated by the Palestinian economy and do not represent funds received from international donors. (Incidentally, former president Jimmy Carter had attempted, but failed, to bridge a similar gap between Hamas and PLO chief Yasser Arafat at the time of the Oslo Accords.[16])

Russia (backed by France), Turkey, Egypt, and Qatar had opted to meet with Hamas, despite U.S. and Israeli efforts to isolate the government.[17] China invited Hamas' foreign minister, Mahmoud Zahar, to visit China in May 2006. The French, who backed the Russian initiative, were accused of secretly meeting with Hamas. The United States and EU have consequently been looking for ways to assist the Palestinian population, most likely through the UN and nongovernmental organizations, but in such a way as not simultaneously to assist Hamas. Yet, as most forms of external support still require interaction with the Palestinian administration, it seems impossible to isolate Hamas altogether.

The fact that Russia took the initiative to meet with Hamas appeared to represent a double-edged sword. On the one hand, it was argued that Russian influence could help nudge Hamas and the Palestinians toward compromise with Israel, assuming Moscow could eventually obtain the strong backing of the Quartet as a whole, ostensibly as an "honest broker." Or Russia could also be seeking to change its image in the Arab world and thus seeking to divert pan-Islamic attention toward the United States and Europe. The Russian connection with *Hamas* could also be, in part, a result of increasing ties between Moscow and Tehran, which has been seen as increasingly backing *Hamas*, in addition to *Hizb'allah*. Following the formation of the "unity" government, Russia continued to support meeting with Hamas despite U.S. reticence.

The most difficult process has been that of diplomatic engagement. The dilemma is that it was largely Washington that initially pressed the secular Fatah leadership to engage in democratic elections, despite the lack of a formation of an effective state infrastructure and despite the strong reluctance on the part of Fatah itself to accept elections. Thus, after more than forty years, Fatah lost its position of predominance over other Palestinian factions following the January 2006 Palestinian legislative elections, despite the fact that roughly 57 percent of the Palestinians voted for differing "secular" parties, as opposed to only 43 percent for Hamas.[18]

The World Bank has predicted that growth in Palestinian GDP per capita would fall from 6.3 percent in 2005 to 4.9 percent in 2006, and then would turn negative in subsequent years, with the possibility of 40 percent unemployment in the worst-case scenario. The World Bank itself has had legal difficulties in sustaining its aid and assistance programs to Palestinians because of U.S. antiterrorist laws, as it appears impossible to avoid dealing with Hamas, which has been listed by Washington as a terrorist organization.[19]

Yet, it appears dubious that Israel would want a totally failed state on its borders—even if walled off.

Mecca Accords

It had been Hamas that had carried out the largest number of suicide bombings over the five years before the declaration of a truce on February 8, 2005. Of the ten suicide attacks in Israel and the West Bank from the February 8, 2005 to April 2006, none had been organized by Hamas. Eight of the attacks were carried out by the radical Islamic Jihad, which has close ties to Iran, and a ninth was claimed by the Al-Aqsa Martyrs Brigade, which is regarded as being aligned with Fatah. The tenth attack of April 17, 2006, was claimed by *both* the Islamic Jihad and the Al-Aqsa Martyrs Brigade in revenge for Israeli actions in Gaza.[20] Much as Fatah could not control Hamas, Hamas can not necessarily control the Al-Aqsa Martyrs Brigade; the latter, in return, could possibly be aligning with the Iranian-backed Islamic Jihad.

Like Israel, the United States refused to enter into direct dialogue with Hamas, but it kept channels open to the PLO through the president of the PA, Mahmoud Abbas. The United States has thus tended to regard the Palestinian leadership much like Siamese twins. The risk was that such a policy might further split the Palestinian leadership, particularly as Hamas at least initially took over the key ministries, largely isolating Fatah. Once Hamas obtained power in the January 2006 parliamentary elections, it overwhelmingly voted in early March to strip Mahmoud Abbas of the expanded powers that he had previously been granted by the legislature. The latter event appeared to represent an opening salvo for Hamas in an intensification of intra-Palestinian fratricide, particularly once Abbas threatened to use his authority to dissolve the Parliament in mid-April 2006.

It was not until February 2007 that the Saudi government was able to bring the differing Palestinian factions to what appeared to be a general settlement. From the Saudi perspective, the problem was how not to fall for the temptation of absolutely isolating Hamas, but to attempt to engage it diplomatically (along with Israel), using a mix of rewards and sanctions (dissuasion and persuasion) in the effort to moderate Hamas' policy. This has led Saudi Arabia and the United States in very different directions.

Although the unity agreement initially appeared to achieve a temporary truce between the two warring Palestinian factions, the Mecca Accords confused both Israel and the United States, which insisted that the unity government accept the conditions laid out by the Quartet that any Palestinian government must recognize Israel, renounce violence, and honor previous Israeli-Palestinian agreements. The key problem was that the platform of a Hamas-Fatah government agreed at Mecca only contained a promise to "respect" (not clearly defined) previous peace deals with Israel, at best implying recognition. In other words, Hamas reluctantly accepted those agreements, but was not fully committed to those accords and asserted the right to resist foreign occupation. The question was raised: Was Hamas getting milder or playing politics in its call for "open dialogue?"[21]

In response, Secretary of State Condoleezza Rice stated that the United States had not yet decided how it would treat a new unity Palestinian government that included Hamas. U.S. uncertainty appeared due to the fact that Fatah and Hamas had not agreed on how to organize Palestinian security forces and because Hamas could hold a number of the key ministries, including the ministry of the interior, if these positions were not made independent.[22] The United States then went so far as to promise arms and training for Fatah against its rival, Hamas—an option that the CIA had warned against.[23]

Failure of the Quartet

The Quartet's three conditions have largely become regarded as a meaningless slogan that does not deal with the realities on the ground and that will not help resolve the dispute between Hamas and Fatah—as these conditions do not address the key and pressing problem of Palestinian borders and *mutual* Israeli-Palestinian recognition. In this regard, what was most needed from Hamas was not so much an agreement to the three conditions of the Road Map to Peace, but the Hamas' acceptance that Mahmoud Abbas could negotiate for all Palestinians and its willingness to abide by any negotiated peace treaty, provided that it is ratified by a referendum of the Palestinian people.

By contrast with the U.S. position, the question that had been raised immediately after the Hamas parliamentary victory in 2006 was "whether it was better to support a Palestinian government that preaches peace but can't deliver it? Or a Palestinian government that stands for the destruction of Israel but just might maintain an indefinite cease-fire?"[24] From this perspective, the problem was to judge Hamas on its actions, not on its words. If Hamas kept to a cease-fire, then, it was argued, the existing official aid program should remain intact, but no *new* aid or assistance should be granted. Hamas would also need to limit its contacts with Iran.[25] Yet, given sanctions, it may be even more difficult for Hamas to control various terrorist factions without the deployment of international peace-keepers, assuming it wanted to. At the same time, the question remained whether Hamas could accept something approximating Israel's 1967 borders—assuming Israel will ultimately unilaterally withdraw its own claims to most of the West Bank and Jerusalem and in exchange for other territories as the new Kadima Party, led by Ehud Olmert after Ariel Sharon's coma and incapacitation, has promised. In April 2007 Prime Minister Ehud Olmert, while engaging in the first round of planned regular meetings with Palestinian president Mahmoud Abbas, stated that Israel was ready to discuss the March 2007 Saudi-Arab peace plan but offered nothing concrete. Without concerted Quartet group pressures, however, it is dubious that the Israeli leadership will follow through on its promises despite the real possibility that, like Arafat before him, Abbas could eventually lose his credibility and authority, leading to "failed states" in both Gaza and the West Bank.

For its part, the Bush administration appeared to be encouraging an "Arab peace" track by trying to get Saudi Arabia involved in the negotiations, although the Saudis and the United States did not see eye to eye. Saudi Arabia did not set up the Mecca Accords and the unity government to meet U.S. and Quartet demands (that is, to recognize Israel's right to exist, abandon violence, and accept all agreements previously signed by the PA) but to try to prevent intra-Palestinian strife and check Iran's influence. This raised questions as to whether the United States and Israel would deal with the new government in which the Hamas appeared to hedge on recognizing the State of Israel.

Riyadh was, at least initially, able to bring together Fatah and Hamas in the Mecca accords, but it also opened discussions between Hizb'allah, Syria, and Iran. In March 2007, at the Arab summit, Riyadh also opposed the "illegitimate foreign occupation" of Iraq (angering U.S. officials), and warned against nuclear proliferation in the region and against war with Iran, likewise urging Israel to accept a "land for peace" settlement to the Palestinian crisis.

The fact that Washington and Riyadh still appear far apart does not augur well for a peace settlement.

Hamas and Gaza

While Israel, ignoring international pressures, dealt with its own internal divisions following its poorly conceived and poorly executed intervention in Lebanon in the summer of 2006 against Hizb'allah, Fatah and Hamas continued a violent face off that divided the PA. This permitted Hamas to seize Gaza from the control of the PA in mid-June 2007, leaving Fatah in control of the West Bank.

Here, it appears increasingly likely that Fatah will continue to rule the West Bank (with possible resistance in Nablus and other areas) while Hamas rules Gaza. Israel appears willing to engage in compromise accords with Fatah, while still pressuring Hamas, yet risking sociopolitical and economic chaos and the further militarization of pan-Islamist movements, and division among Palestinians.

Given the fact that Hamas is in control in Gaza, it appears that the "two state solution" needs a significant revision. Another option might be considered: a loose Palestinian confederation with Jordan as a transition to help build and develop the West Bank. This possibility appears viable as Jordan once controlled the West Bank and east Jerusalem before the Six-Day War. The idea had been proposed by King Hussein to Secretary of State James Baker in 1992, and had been supported by Simon Perez (now Israeli president). It was brought up again in 1999 by Yasser Arafat in accord with an old Palestinian National Council resolution, possibly to test the reaction of the new Jordanian leader, King Abdullah, immediately after King Hussein's death. (Arafat's initiative had been opposed by the Muslim Brotherhood.)

While initially supporting the option, King Hussein might have turned against it in reaction to the secret Oslo accords between Israel and the PLO and for fear of excessive PLO influence among Palestinians living in Jordan[26] (and in remembering events that led to the Jordanian Black September in 1970–71). Now, however, with the more "moderate" Fatah and more "extreme" Hamas divided, Jordan might find a confederal arrangement in its interests, assuming Jordan will obtain significant political, financial and security support from the Quartet group and other donors to help it ward off serious threats of terrorism, if not the possibility of Palestinian irredentist claims to link with Palestinians in Jordan that might stem from a fully independent Palestinian state. Hamas, now in control over Gaza, will most likely remain dangerously isolated for a period of time, albeit supported by Iran, but it could ultimately join such a confederation. Much will depend on whether Egypt, Syria, Qatar, and Saudi Arabia can work to moderate Hamas—or whether Hamas might eventually help to radicalize Egypt, if not more indirectly, Saudi Arabia. If possible, rather than seeking to strengthen the divisions, it is still crucial to bring Hamas and Fatah closer together, and thus try to moderate Hamas, so that Palestinians can speak with one voice—otherwise the conflict will continue to degenerate. This could occur only if Israel does make significant concessions to Fatah as promised.

The Question of Syria and the Golan Heights

In the summer of 2006, I had just opened an anthology of Arabic poetry that included the powerful poem "The Desert" by the Syrian poet Adonis, on the 1982 Israeli siege of Beirut. It was on that day that Israel, largely unexpectedly, launched attacks against Lebanon, striking Beirut in addition to *Hizb'allah* positions in southern Lebanon, following the capture of two Israeli soldiers.

These largely disportionate actions, with the overt support of Washington (as well as with the tacit support of the Arab states opposed to the Iranian-backed *Hizb'allah* movement), had been preceded by Israeli attacks in 1968, 1973, 1978, and 1982.[27] The key difference is that this time the Israeli operation could hardly be called even a "limited success." In many ways, Israel's failure to destroy *Hizb'allah* positions helped to undermine the previously undefeatable image of the Israeli Defense Forces (the *Tzahal*).

Most interestingly, the attack came during a period of intensive Israeli-Syrian negotiations, which then were called off (purportedly by the United States). Indicating a willingness of Israel to reach peace with its neighbor (much as it was able to reach peace agreements with Jordan, Egypt, and Turkey), the draft Israeli-Syrian deal was said to propose an Israeli withdrawal from the Golan Heights (occupied since the Six-Day War in 1967). The area would then be turned into a demilitarized, Syrian-administered park that Israelis could visit without a visa. In return, Syria would cut off its support to anti-Israeli groups such as Hamas and Hizb'allah and would take steps to distance itself from Iran. A formal peace treaty would also be signed. The deal would have also permitted Israel to retain control over use of the waters of the Jordan River and the Sea of Galilee and an early-warning station (against missile attack) would be built in the area and operated by the United States.

The major disagreement was said to be over Syrian demands that Israeli forces leave within five years, while Israel hoped to stay fifteen more, because of the area's important strategic location, plus the fertility of its soil (producing Golan Heights wines, for example), in addition to possessing a ski resort, which is rare in the region. The peace talks had allegedly been initiated in January 2004 and began in earnest in September 2004; they came to a halt in the midst of the thirty-four-day Israeli intervention against *Hizb'allah* and when Israel argued that the talks could no longer proceed covertly in 2006. It was then suggested that senior officials from both the Syrian and Israeli side meet with U.S. officials. Discussions were then said to have come to an abrupt end, but only after the Americans were brought in. Needless to say, both the Israeli and Syrian governments initially denied having accepted such a "nonpaper."[28]

Had this Israeli-Syrian peace accord succeeded, it would perhaps have been similar to that advocated by the later *Iraq Study Group Report* in December 2006. At that time, James Baker argued that diplomacy could draw Damascus away from its strategic alliance with Iran and help resolve the conflict with *Hizb'allah*: "If you can flip the Syrians, you will cure Israel's *Hizb'allah* problem." James Baker also argued that Syrian officials believed they could persuade Hamas' militant external wing to accept Olmert's conditions for direct engagement with the Palestinians, an effort then taken up by Saudi Arabia in Mecca in mid-February 2007. (In addition to James Baker, Senators Arlen Specter (R-PA) and Jim Webb (D-VA) called for breaking the "unnatural alliance" between Syria and Iran, contrary to the AIPAC position.)

By contrast, anti-Syrian neoconservative hard-liners have opposed diplomacy with Syria and have argued that the latter represents its real enemy in that it directly backs *Hizb'allah*. These individuals generally argue that Syria is behind all efforts to destabilize Lebanon. Hard-liners also argue that it was the Syrian leadership that assassinated former Lebanese prime minister Rafik Hariri (who had close contacts to Saudi Arabia), and thus cannot be trusted to quit Lebanon altogether, which they had "seized" during the first Persian Gulf war in 1991 when then secretary of state James Baker sought to bring the Syrians into the coalition against Saddam Hussein. Here, one position contends that Syria moved into Lebanon with a wink of the eye—"appeasement" from Washington (James Baker). The other position argues that Syria betrayed the United States (and James Baker). Some Lebanese contend that Syrian repression in Lebanon was worse than that of Saddam Hussein in Kuwait.

Thus, hard-line neoconservatives argue that the summer 2006 Israeli war with *Hizb'allah* should have been widened to strike Syria, thus indirectly weakening Iran as well and effectively checking Iranian influence in the Middle East. It was thus purported that neoconservatives remaining in the second-term Bush administration following Rumsfeld's dismissal did encourage the government of Israeli prime minister Ehud Olmert to extend its war beyond Lebanon's borders in the first days of the Israel-*Hizb'allah* conflict. In such a way, Israel would have served both Israeli and U.S. interests in the region, but failed to do so.[29] From the hard-line neo-conservative perspective, Israeli actions thus were not sufficient—and backfired completely.

It is, however, unclear how such a war on Syria (even if Israel could rapidly defeat Syria without the latter being able to retaliate) would have succeeded in checking *Hizb'allah*. On the contrary, Syrian defeat would create a totally "failed state" (as opposed to a partially "failed state"). Damascus would be unable to control its borders even if its government wanted to—thus exacerbating instability and not at all enhancing Israel's security. It is also not absolutely certain exactly who had al-Hariri assassinated. Certainly other groups (possibly allied with military officials in the Syrian government) thought they would profit more from his death than the Syrian leadership of President Bashar Assad would.[30]

In addition, the Israeli attack indirectly worked to strengthen Hamas and other Islamic factions within the Palestinian camps, so that the Lebanese government engaged in significant clashes with the Palestinian group Fatah al-Islam in 2007. Fatah al-Islam has purportedly been supported by Syria, which disclaims those accusations, to regain hegemony over Lebanon. The group itself claims no affiliation with Syria or al-Qaida but has been publicly supported by the latter.[31] The situation has raised fears of a renewed Lebanese civil war.

In September 2006, Syrian president Bashar al-Assad stated that peace talks with Israel could conclude within six months—if they were ultimately to resume from where they left off in July 2006. Al-Assad furthermore stated that Syria would attempt to guard its border with Lebanon but that he could not make an oath to halt all arms smuggling from Syria into Lebanon: "If there is a real desire to smuggle [weapons], neither Security Council resolutions nor surveillance nor the whole armies of the world can prevent this."[32] Here, once again, is the problem of a partially failed state in that it is also difficult for al-Assad to stop arms smuggling into Iraq, even if he had the will to do so. One option may be to bring Syria closer to NATO's Mediterranean Initiative and the Partnership for Peace for better training in managing borders. At the same time, however, the threat of a Lebanese civil war and of an Israeli-Syrian conflict has not entirely dissipated as Hizballah has begun to rebuild its military capability.

Third Intifada over Al-Aqsa Mosque?

The tires were still smoldering from the afternoon's protest. In mid-February 2007, in the East Jerusalem neighborhood of Wadi Joz, the head of the northern branch of Israel's Islamic Movement, Sheikh Raed Salah, accused Israel of attempting to build the temple on the Temple Mount "while drenched in Arab blood" and purportedly called for an intifada to save the Al-Aqsa Mosque. Public Security Minister Avi Dichter then asked Attorney General Menachem Mazuz to investigate whether Salah's comments constituted incitement and sedition. The problem arose as Israelis began working to repair the Mugrabi ascent, a ramp next to the Al-Aqsa Mosque, the third holiest site in Islam, while concurrently excavating the area in an archaeological search (work that began in 1967), ostensibly for historical artifacts. The event immediately set off demonstrations and threats of a third *intifada*—perhaps not so accidentally timed in an effort by pro-Iranian factions (or al-Qaida) to break up the Mecca Accords that were backed by Saudi Arabia.

Following the outbreak of violence, in mid-February, Turkey's ambassador to Israel stated that he had visited the site of the Mugrabi ascent to investigate whether the ramp caused any damage to the foundations of the Al-Aqsa Mosque. Israel stated that it would put the work area under open video camera surveillance. At the same time, Muslim groups throughout the world have opposed any changes, such as a building of a synagogue, in the vicinity of Al-Aqsa Mosque because the site is considered part of an Islamic *Waqf* and accepted as such by Israel.

Certainly, the Temple Mount under the Al-Aqsa Mosque is also one of Israel's most holy sites, while the whole area is considered holy by Christians, Jews, and Muslims. Hence, the dilemma is to find a way to implement final status provisions for Jerusalem. In affirming that "sovereignty" over the site belongs to "god" (or the world's religions), it might be possible to permit Palestinians operational control but to establish an international religious mechanism that would seek to adjudicate disputes.[33] Or, as the late Yasser Arafat had argued, Jerusalem could be the capital of two states, with a status like Rome—which also hosts the Vatican. If feasible, this could help tremendously to improve U.S., European, and Russian relations with the Islamic world.

Toward a Middle Eastern "Security Community"

While Israel engaged in Lebanon, and was then caught up in domestic political scandals and critique of its new leadership, the two major Palestinian factions engaged in a quasi-civil warfare (with the United States arming Fatah and Iran and other states arming Hamas). In June 2007 Hamas gained control of Gaza, while Fatah retained control of the West Bank. This, ironically, makes Hamas directly responsible for Gaza residents. On the one hand, external pressures could lead Hamas to ultimately look to the United States and EU for funding and support. On the other, Hamas could continue to seek out Iranian assistance and engage in domestic repression despite its leadership claims that it does not seek to establish an "Islamic emirate" in Gaza.

One option is to forge a loose Palestinian-Jordanian confederal arrangement. Here, the Palestinians on the West Bank could initially link with Jordan to form a confederal state with close political, economic, and security ties and perhaps interlinked parliamentary assemblies. With Jordanian political leverage, West Bank Palestinians could negotiate their borders and then declare "independence" from Israel while forming their own national assembly that was, at least initially, linked with that of Jordan. This confederation, in turn, could look toward a larger union with a U.S.-EU-Turkish backed Mediterranean initiative. This new confederation would then reach out to both Israel (to cooperate on outstanding issues) and to Egypt and Gaza (to ameliorate living conditions and gradually demilitarize Hamas). As there is really no such thing as "national independence" in the age of "interdependence," many states are looking to regional economic agreements and security communities. Why not the Palestinians as well?

International Peacekeeping

One way to resolve the continuing crisis is thus for the United States, EU, Russia, and UN to engage international peacekeeping forces under a general UN mandate. This would assume that Israel would already have completed its unilateral withdrawals in the West Bank, as the new Kadima Party has promised, and as the Quartet attempts to mediate between Israel and the Palestinians with respect to a broad range of questions involving compromise over Jerusalem, Palestinian refugees and the right to return, work permits in Israel, trade, electricity, water rights, prisoner exchange, and so forth. This, in effect, would forge a "loose confederation" resulting from the continued need to cooperate.

If accepted by all parties, the dismantling of the "terrorist" infrastructure of various partisan Palestinian groups can be assisted by multinational peacekeeping forces, as urged by the unpublished Annex X of the unofficial 2003 Geneva accords. Partnership for Peace troops could be placed under a joint NATO-EU-Russian command under a general UN mandate; they could incorporate troops from a number of Arab and Islamic countries, and link both Israeli and Palestinian security forces. Such forces could be placed along the newly delineated borders of the West Bank and ultimately Gaza as well as potential borders in Jerusalem. Troops from neutral countries such as Sweden and Finland might be suitable, as might Turkish and Egyptian troops, as they are both Muslim but not opposed to Israel. (German peacekeepers would not want to be placed in a position where they might harm Israelis.) Such a peace-enabling force (with the number of troops raging from 2,500 to 7,000) would seek to protect both Israelis and Palestinians from acts of "terror" and "counterterror" through clear rules of engagement. Such a peace-enabling force would likewise seek to prevent the infiltration of al-Qaida and other militant groups into the region. Such forces would have an open-ended UN mandate and would not leave unless *both* states requested their withdrawal.[34] Moreover, working with Russia in the Israeli-Palestinian crisis where Russian Orthodox have significant interests (and where the Israeli population of Russian background is quite significant) can additionally help draw Russia into cooperation in other areas as well.

The key international political problem, however, is that the United States and NATO need to overcome its image as a "dishonest broker."[35] In March 2006, for example, Palestinians had accused the British and U.S. governments of colluding with Israel in the Israeli seizure of Ahmed Saadat, the leader of the Popular Front for the Liberation of Palestine and four others, from detention. The British government had removed their supervisors from a prison in Jericho, citing security reasons. In return, armed Palestinians kidnapped at least eleven foreigners in the West Bank and Gaza. The Israeli government stated it raided the prison to prevent Hamas from releasing prisoners accused of assassinating an Israeli minister of tourism. The British denied complicity. The problem is that the incident raised questions as to willingness of international forces to protect Palestinians and accept Palestinian political decisions, thus weakening trust. As the situation stands now, Israel can intervene militarily throughout Palestinian territories at will, maintaining a permanent state of siege—complicated by intra-Palestinian strife. While permitting such a fratricidal conflict to take place without mediation could cynically be regarded as "divide and rule" from some perspectives, the third parties to win from intra-Palestinian fratricide have been Hamas, *al-Qaida* and other militant movements, as well as Iran.

Security for the Region

Peacekeeping alone in Palestine will not resolve the regional crisis. It might additionally be necessary for NATO, the EU, and Russia to protect the entire region, and all parties involved, from ballistic missile threats, should the Islamic Republic of Iran ultimately opt to make the dangerously destabilizing decision to develop nuclear warheads and other weapons of mass destruction (WMD) that potentially threaten not just Israel, but the Palestinians and Arab states as well as the Europeans.

Although there is still some hope for a diplomatic settlement, it is quite possible for Iran to obtain nuclear weapons in the next three to ten years. While Israel could join NATO in response to rise of ballistic missile threats throughout the region, this option would tend to polarize relations between the U.S. and European versus the Arab and Islamic worlds. By contrast, a less provocative option would result in the formation of a "regional security community" that would seek to defend those states willing to join (Israel, Palestine, Jordan, Egypt, and perhaps Saudi Arabia, the GCC countries, Syria, and Jordan) from both external as well as domestic threats of terrorism. Such a regional security regime would press all states in the region (including Israel, Syria, Saudi Arabia, and Iran) to declare the "no first use" of WMD. In order for Iran to join as well, it would need to be accompanied by some form of U.S.-Iranian security guarantees or "nonaggression pact"—as well as UN-backed multilateral security guarantees for the Islamic Republic. (See Chapter 4.)

Sincere efforts to resolve the Israeli-Palestinian-Syrian confrontation and intra-Palestinian strife would show the Arab world that the United States, EU, Russia, and the UN are willing to engage in *real diplomacy*, involving multinational peacekeeping and *multilateral dissuasion and persuasion*. A diplomatic resolution to the conflict would symbolically show the way to an end to the "global war on terror," pointing the way to the potential resolution of other major conflicts involving Arab and Islamic interests. An Israeli-Palestinian peace settlement, perhaps based on a loose confederation with Jordan with indirect ties to Israel and Egypt, and linked to the proposed Mediterranean union, with strong Turkish backing, would show the Arab and Islamic worlds that the United States, Europe, Russia, and the UN are really serious about engaging in peace and thus help to split the less radical, Islamic factions from the more extremist groups, which appear to be gaining influence in Afghanistan, Iraq, as well as in Palestine, if not Pakistan and elsewhere. It will take real leadership in Washington to begin to engage in a truly *conciliatory* strategy worthy of the name.

CHAPTER 6

An Ever-widening Zone of Conflict, Terrorism, and Black Market Activities: From Central Asia to Sub-Saharan Africa

Extension of the Zone of Conflict

The manipulation of religious beliefs (and civilizational movements) represents a form of strategic leverage used by elites throughout history. Yet, the manipulation of religious belief represents an aspect of strategic leveraging that generally went unrecognized during the cold war but that has come to haunt the world in the post–cold war era. In particular, U.S., Saudi, and Pakistani support for militant Sunni pan-Islamist forces in Afghanistan against the brutal Soviet intervention (provoked in part by the United States) has set forth a chain reaction among a number of political and social movements and countermovements that now appears nearly impossible to control.

The consequences of the unleashing of pan-Islamist forces in Afghanistan, and indirectly throughout much of the world, can be seen following the September 11, 2001, attacks on the World Trade Center and the Pentagon as well as in the "terrorist" attacks on civilian targets in Madrid, Bali, Casablanca, Moscow, Beslan, London, Riyadh, Baghdad, and other cities. Not only did pan-Islamist groups turn against their former supporters, the United States and Saudi Arabia (and continued their struggle against Russia after Soviet collapse), but tensions between Sunni-led states and Shi'a Iran have also been reignited since the U.S.-led overthrow of the secular (yet Sunni) leader, Saddam Hussein, who once was Iran's most immediate enemy.

Not only have the conflicts in what neoconservatives in the administration of George W. Bush have called the "greater Middle East" begun to interlink with conflicts in central Asia, the Balkans, and the Caucasus, consequently drawing the United States and NATO into these regions, but these conflicts have also begun to interlink with conflicts as far away as sub-Saharan Africa (as well as those in Thailand, the Philippines, and Indonesia, plus Xinjiang province in China). In February 2003, for example, Osama bin Laden was purported to have decreed that oil-rich Nigeria (with a Muslim population of roughly 50 percent) represented one of six countries that needed to be "liberated" from America's "enslavement."[1]

With regard to Africa, the geostrategic aspects of "global war on terror," combined with the political-economic search for guaranteed access to petroleum resources, have begun to interlink. While the collapse of the Ottoman empire and subsequent imperial rivalries after World War I helped set off ongoing conflicts in the Middle East and Persian Gulf regions, the Soviet collapse helped set off conflicts in central Asia, the Balkans and the Caucasus, and more indirectly in Africa. Here, collapse of the Warsaw Pact, and subsequent reduction of NATO and Warsaw Pact arsenals, led to a flood of small arms to Africa and the south, while the number of small arms manufacturers increased significantly in the latter regions. In addition to the rise of interstate and societal conflicts in Africa that have followed the collapse of cold war regimes (for example, Mobuto Sese Seko's Zaire), the illicit nature of "black" and "gray" market activities have helped to augment the demand for light weaponry—in part to protect the ivory trade from the Lake Chad region and Central African Republic, the diamond trade from Angola, and the transshipment of narcotics from Afghanistan and Nigeria (and increasingly Latin America) to Europe.[2]

Growing Global Demand for Energy

The United States, with only 3 to 4 percent of the world's population, consumes roughly a quarter of the world's oil, but it possesses only 3 percent of the global oil reserves. To satisfy its growing energy needs, the United States imports 58 percent of its oil (ten million barrels per day). U.S. natural gas imports come from Canada, yet its oil comes from four key countries: Canada, Mexico, Venezuela, and Saudi Arabia. (Gulf of Mexico reserves add 50 percent to U.S. reserves, but they can only be developed at considerable cost). Gas also represents some 96 percent of U.S. transportation energy (a source that needs to be drastically reduced through use of biofuels, flex fuels, fuel cells and other alternative technologies.) European Union countries, as a whole, currently import 50 percent of their energy needs and could import 70 percent by 2030. Furthermore, 45 percent of what EU countries import comes from the Middle East (25 percent of their energy needs come from Russia, which might rise to 40 percent in 2030).

The dilemma is that the Middle East still holds some 67 percent of the world's proven oil reserves, while the Persian Gulf holds 90 percent of the spare oil production capacity. This is true despite worldwide efforts to diversify to the Caspian Sea, to Russia (the second largest oil producer after Saudi Arabia), as well as to Iraq, Libya, Nigeria, Angola, and other African countries. Despite possible overestimation of reserves, the rich Caspian Sea region (the South Caucasus and central Asia) contains about 3–4 percent of the world's oil reserves and 4–6 percent of the world's gas reserves. The search for alternatives to Middle Eastern and Russian oil and gas on land (and under the sea) has led to the development of the Atasu-Alashankou oil pipeline (China and Kazakhstan), the Baku-Tbilisi-Ceyhan (BTC) pipeline, the Baku-Tbilisi-Erzurum (BTE) pipeline (Georgia, Azerbaijan, Turkey, and Kazakhstan), and the Nabucco gas pipeline (European

Union, Turkey, Bulgaria, Romania, Hungary, and Austria), among others.[3] In effect, many energy-dependent countries are caught between Charbydis and Scylla—Russia and the Middle East (Iran or Saudi Arabia)—unless they can begin to further diversify their energy infrastructure.

Although the countries involved deny the allegations, Russia may also be attempting to create a "gas OPEC" by attempting to coordinate gas production with states such as Kazakhstan, Turkmenistan, Uzbekistan, Iran (and possibly Algeria and Qatar), because it is estimated that natural gas will meet 70 percent of the growth in energy consumption in the coming decade.

In an effort to monopolize energy production, Russia has increasingly put pressure on Kazakhstan and Turkmenistan to make sure that all pipelines travel through Russia, reducing European chances to lessen its dependency upon Russian gas and oil (through the Nabucco pipeline, for example).[4] Moreover, as Moscow has sought to consolidate major energy resources under state controls, pressure on Shell's Sakhalin-2 project in 2006, for example, has made multinational energy firms such as British Petroleum very hesitant to increase their investments. (See Chapter 2.) While the United States and the EU seek an "open door" policy to energy resources, Russia, China, and Iran hope to sustain a "closed door" so as to monopolize Central Asian and Caspian Sea resources, making possible cooperation between the United States, NATO, the EU, and the Shanghai Cooperation Organization more difficult.

Ironically, the more the EU seeks independence from Russian energy sources, coupled with both political and technical difficulties in terms of transport costs and logistics, in supplying the U.S. market, the more Russia is pressed (or presses itself) into a closer energy symbiosis (with China in particular), at the same time that a Sino-Russian energy symbiosis serves to boost the development prospects of the Russian Far East and East Siberia. As these latter regions face depopulation, de-industrialization and infrastructure degradation, Moscow hopes to consolidate its controls so as to preserve the unity of the country.[5] Along with the proposed deployment of U.S. BMD systems in both Europe and Asia, these factors increase the likelihood of a stronger Sino-Russian alliance unless Washington and the European Union can find incentives to draw Moscow away from its embrace with Beijing.

Worldwide Military Bases

Rising energy demand has consequently led to the worldwide proliferation of military bases that appear to be designed as much to protect oil supplies and Sea Lines of Communication (SLOC) as to guard against acts of terrorism. In addition to expanding bases into eastern Europe (see Chapter 3), Washington is building military bases in the Balkans, Caucasus, and central Asia, including Azerbaijan (some fifteen thousand troops), Georgia, Uzbekistan, Kyrgyzstan, Tajikistan, and Kazakhstan. By January 2008, as many as 200,000 troops (plus private contractors) could be deployed in Iraq; by mid-2007, U.S. forces in Afghanistan could exceed 25,500—so that total foreign forces exceed 40,000 (including the 34,000-strong International Security Assistance Force (ISAF) force under NATO control).[6] Washington has reportedly built bases in Pakistan as well. The Pentagon also plans to reinforce its bases in Hawaii, Guam, Diego Garcia (in the Indian Ocean), and in French Djibouti at the Horn of Africa (deploying 5,000–6,500 troops). Washington has also hoped to regain basing rights in the Philippines (after being forced out of Subic Bay in 1992). Semipermanent bases are to be maintained in Algeria, Morocco, Tunisia, Senegal, Ghana, Mali, and Kenya. One of the primary goals in Africa is to protect an unstable Nigeria, expected to provide some 25 percent of the United States' oil needs in the future (up from 16 percent). The United States also appears to have plans to build a naval base in the Gulf of Guinea. The strategic goal appears to be to place U.S. and NATO forces in position to guarantee access to oil and supply routes, to counterbalance both Russia and China, and to check pan-Islamic movements.

On sea, the security concerns involving SLOCs, coupled with the transport of energy resources and raw materials and globalization of ocean trade, have made "chokepoints" such as the Strait of Hormuz (between Iran and Oman) and the Strait of Malacca (between Indonesia, Thailand, Malaysia, and Singapore) exceedingly important in geostrategic and political-economic terms—because roughly 40 percent of the world's total trade and half of the world's trade in oil and natural gas transit through the Malacca Strait, while 40 percent of the world's oil trade transits the Strait of Hormuz. This is not to overlook the renewed importance of the Panama and Suez Canals, which have recently begun to upgrade their capacity to take on increased maritime traffic.

Not generally noted is that the world's "black" and "gray" market economy that has begun to develop in conflict areas of central Asia, the Caspian and Black Seas, East Asia, Africa, and Latin America has become increasingly interlinked to maritime insecurity and the threat to shipping caused by piracy. Piracy has resurrected itself on the high seas along the coasts of Indonesia, the Philippines, Bangladesh, the Malacca Strait, the South China Sea, India, Ecuador, Nigeria, Somalia, and the Red Sea. Piracy often involves organized mafias, including experienced sailors and partisan groups willing to engage in acts of "terror." (In addition, numerous interstate and civil wars involving conflicting partisan groups are taking place alongside a number of important sea lanes and threaten shipping. The waters off Somalia, where a number of Islamist groups thrive, have been considered among the most dangerous in the world.)

In effect, naval strategy requires the right to affirm or deny access to SLOCs, if necessary. It might also require a forward naval presence to secure burgeoning global demand for resources and oil, in particular. Short of an alternative energy revolution, natural gas and oil must travel by generally more expensive overland pipelines or else by undersea pipelines and much cheaper ocean-going tankers—as must most other heavy products and produce. Both land and sea routes thus need to be secured against the potential for sabotage by states or antistate partisans. But sea routes are generally less expensive and easier to protect off shore.

Potential tensions arise as regionally challenging states, such as China, Japan, and India seek to secure the ocean resources or islands adjacent to their territory by means of developing blue water navies to guarantee the profitability and long-term access to those resources, as well as to guarantee their general security from overseas attack. The issue is that these efforts often take place in rivalry with U.S.

efforts to sustain its naval hegemony and its ability to secure vital resources and sea lines of communication through forward naval deployments. In this regard U.S. naval efforts to take on a revitalized role in securing maritime traffic and in guarding against expanding maritime and "terrorist" threats in the post–cold war era could play a role in either enhancing political and economic stability—or else exacerbating instability.[7]

Roots of the Crisis in Soviet Collapse

The cold war has generally been stereotyped as an ideological conflict between capitalism and democracy versus communism and totalitarianism. Yet, during that period, the United States and its allies were able to play Protestant, Catholic, and differing Islamic beliefs against "atheistic communism" in an effort to implode the multiethnic, multireligious Soviet empire. Soviet Communism's attempt to repress or control almost all forms of religious practices and beliefs made for easy propaganda that permitted the United States and its allies to better counter communist influence within their own countries. Soviet repression of religious beliefs likewise opened the door for the United States to provide covert support for various ethnic and religious groups and civil societies within the Soviet empire, in addition to those groups that were resisting its expansion.

Changes in Soviet policy under President Mikhail Gorbachev, followed by Soviet collapse, at least initially appeared to bring peace to a number of conflicts dating from the cold war. Most notably, international sanctions led by the United States and the multilateral Western Contact Group, negotiations to put an end to South African conflict with Namibia and Mozambique, plus "managed revolution" in South Africa in which the United States engaged in initially secret diplomacy with the African National Congress, all helped to abolish the system of apartheid and prevented a feared blood bath, while seeking to stabilize the southern cone of Africa.[8]

At the same time, however, despite the retraction of Soviet support for revolutionary movements in Africa after the cold war, the collapse of anti-Soviet U.S.-backed bastions of power (for example, Mobuto Sese Seko's regime in Zaire) have helped set off renewed conflicts. Centered primarily in eastern Congo (formerly Zaire), what was once called "World War III in Africa" (1996–2004), directly or indirectly involved at least nine African nations (Rwanda, Democratic Republic of Congo, Angola, Burundi, Namibia, Sudan, Uganda, and Zimbabwe, with peace talks held in South Africa). In addition, it took another decade for Angola—whose bloody civil war had been fueled by the U.S., Soviet Union, and "blood diamonds"—to finally put an end to the conflict in 2002.

Toward the end of the cold war, after defeat in Vietnam and perceived Soviet gains throughout much of the developing world, the administration of Ronald Reagan (picking up from the efforts of Jimmy Carter's administration to forge an alliance with the People's Republic of China) sought to "revitalize containment." The United States thus intensified its multipronged containment strategy and began to manipulate religious ideology as a tool to "roll back" and undermine Soviet power and influence.

One prong of the new "rollback" strategy was to support predominantly Catholic populations and civil society movements, such as Solidarity in Poland to undermine Soviet control over Eastern Europe. The new-found U.S.-Catholic alliance—relations with the Vatican were established in 1984—likewise sought to roll back perceived pro-Soviet gains in other predominantly Catholic countries in areas such as Central America. Another prong was to tacitly back NATO-member Turkey's "pan-Turanian" civilizational claims into deep central Asia, which dated from years of Ottoman influence and before. An additional prong was to use Sunni Islam to undermine Soviet controls over central Asia by supporting the mujahedin "freedom fighters"—in a tacit Christian-Sunni Muslim alliance against the "evil empire."

The latter strategy involved a forked attack: Not only was U.S. support for Saudi Arabia and Pakistan intended to undermine Soviet controls over central Asia, but it was also intended to contain and encircle predominantly Shi'a Iran. By backing Saudi Arabia and by aligning with Pakistan—in addition to backing the secular regime of Saddam Hussein (whose elites were, for the most part, Sunni Muslim, but aligned with Iraqi Christians)—the Christian-Sunni Muslim alliance sought to contain the Islamic Republic of Iran and its support for pan-Shi'a movements throughout the region.

In essence, the United States coaxed Moscow into intervention in Afghanistan, then built up a worldwide alliance against it.[9] This alliance included Saudi Arabia, Pakistan, Turkey, and China (at least in the early 1980s), thus exacerbating Soviet fears of "encirclement." The strategy ultimately "succeeded" in collapsing the Soviet Union into fifteen separate republics; at the same time, however, Soviet disaggregation opened a *zone of conflict* deep within central Asia that has increasingly interlinked with pan-Islamic movements in the Middle East, the Balkans, the Persian Gulf, and Africa. Ironically, by supporting essentially secular political parties and nationalist movements, Moscow had played a role in containing many of these pan-Islamic political forces during the cold war. Soviet collapse and the loss of its political support for secular pan-Arab parties, combined with U.S. or Saudi support for many pan-Islamic movements, however, has permitted many of those same pan-Islamic movements to begin to flourish more independently following the Soviet collapse.

The Soviet intervention in Afghanistan in 1978–1979 thus coincided with increasing tensions between Iran, Saudi Arabia, and Iraq. This is particularly true after the Iranian Islamic Revolution in 1979 that raised religious tensions in the region. Then during the 1980–1988 Iran-Iraq War, Iran supported the Kurdish and Shi'ite political movements in Iraq while Iraq invaded Iran to seize oil-rich Iranian Khuzestan, with its largely ethnic Arab population. The Iran-Iraq War consequently exacerbated Sunni-Shi'ite rivalries throughout the Islamic world, with Saudi Arabia seeking to encircle Iran through the support of both (secular) Iraq and an increasingly fundamentalist Pakistan. While Washington also looked the other way, Saddam Hussein (then regarded as the "lesser evil" with respect to the Ayatollah Khoemeni) engaged in horrid war crimes against Kurdish and Shi'a factions that were regarded as being aligned with Iran in the devastating missile attacks of the Baghdad-Tehran "war of cities."

Both Iran and the Saudi Arabia likewise assisted the anti-Soviet mujahedin "freedom fighters"—but more in rivalry than in mutual collaboration. In effect, the Iranian Islamic revolution led both Saudi Arabia and Pakistan to further "Islamicize" their respective regimes to contain the ideological threat posed by Iranian Shi'ite Islamic militancy, initially led by the Ayatollah Khoemeni. The fact that Iran took U.S. diplomats hostage additionally helped to provoke a Protestant fundamentalist and "neoconservative" backlash in the United States, bringing to power Ronald Reagan (despite the fact that President Jimmy Carter also called himself "born again.")

The United States itself was willing to back "radical" Sunni Muslim groups as well as the Saudi-backed "Wahhabist" movements against pan-Shi'ite Iran. The United States looked the other way as Saudi Arabia, one of its major arms clients, engaged in significant violations of human rights, refused to engage in democratic reforms, and backed Hamas (because Hamas did not support Saddam Hussein's invasion of Kuwait), as well as other radical Islamist groups—in Chechnya, for example. (Ironically, Hamas itself was initially backed by Israel as a means to check the secular Fatah, led by Yasser Arafat. Moreover, the Muslim Brotherhood, which likewise backed Hamas, was initially aligned with the Free Officers Movement of Gamal Abdel Nasser until the latter failed to Islamicize the Egyptian Constitution as promised; the Brotherhood was then backed by Egyptian president Anwar al-Sadat to counter the influence of Nasserites and Communists in Egypt, that is, until Sadat opted to turn against it—resulting in his assassination.)

Both the United States and Saudi Arabia financed the Pakistani Inter-Services Intelligence (ISI), which supported some of the most extreme Islamic factions. U.S. and Saudi assistance for Gulbuddin Hekmatyar, for example, whose Hezbi Islami was the largest recipient of U.S. military assistance and one of the most militant groups, was channeled through Pakistan during the war on Afghanistan. During the Afghan war, the CIA became concerned that General Muhammed Zia ul-Haq had been diverting a large share of the weapons to Hekmatyar, whose organization's strategy appeared to be aimed at dividing the rest of the Afghan resistance so that it could take over in Kabul—with General Zia's support. The Pakistanis, by contrast, argue that this was the CIA choice.[10]

The United States and Pakistan had likewise worked alongside Osama bin Laden in the 1980s, who was primarily a financier of the "Arab-Afghan" resistance, Mekhtab al Khidemat (MAT) at that time—before he founded al-Qaida (The Base) in 1988–89 as a kind of veteran's organization for Afghan mujaheddin, moving his operations to Afghanistan in 1996 after being expelled from the Sudan. This action helped forge secret ties between Islamic Sudan and the United States. Initially, despite the xenophobic nature and ideological character of the Taliban, the United States had hoped that a "stable" government would serve U.S. oil interests in the region; yet before September 11, Afghanistan became a center for a number of differing terrorist organizations, and not only al-Qaida.

The United States and NATO in Afghanistan (Post-September 11)

Following U.S. intervention in Afghanistan in 2001, the U.S. and NATO forces have supplied both peacekeeping and "peacemaking" forces for the Afghan government of President Hamid Karzai, which is still unable to control many Afghan provinces. Although it did not participate in the early stages of the intervention except for use of some German and French special force operations, NATO's mission expanded to the southern provinces and then, to much of the country, as the United States began to focus more on Iraq. (NATO's decision-making process was considered a liability by the United States, which also had concerns over interoperability because of the revolution in military affairs and U.S. concepts of network centric warfare.)

While Operation Enduring Freedom had targeted Taliban forces from the air with heavy bombing, the Pentagon kept the use of U.S. special forces limited. Two months after Enduring Freedom began, the United States installed a new Afghan coalition government in power in Kabul, yet rejected the use of U.S. ground forces to eliminate al-Qaida and remaining Taliban that had not dispersed. Instead, the Pentagon relied upon anti-Taliban Afghan fighters who worked to disperse al-Qaida fighters, but who also might possibly have assisted their escape. In any case, by not deploying its own forces, the United States lost control of the ground; both Mullah Mohammed Omar (leader of the Taliban) and Osama bin Laden (leader of al-Qaida) escaped.[11]

Gulbuddin Hekmatyar's Hezb-i Islami, which has purportedly claimed to have helped bin Laden and Mullah Omar escape, has remained one the major factions resisting the U.S. and NATO peacekeepers in Afghanistan and along the Afghan-Pakistan border following the initial defeat of the Taliban. These groups, along with the former Taliban, continue to receive protection from the Pashtun tribes in Pakistan's lawless Northwest Frontier Province. Taliban and al-Qaida headquarters appear to be located in Quetta, Pakistan, at the Bolan Pass near the border of Iran and Afghanistan. Furthermore the Taliban—which appears to be resurgent following the increase in the production of opium—openly controlled at least fifteen districts in southern Kandahar.

The dilemma is that the decision of the administration of George W. Bush to opt for intervention in Iraq prevented the United States and NATO from fully concentrating on al-Qaida and the Taliban, permitting the resurgence of the latter. Moreover, the U.S. and international development assistance that does eventually arrive in specific provinces does not necessarily lead to the establishment of security in every community. Lack of development assistance, or at least its lack of adequate distribution, combined with NATO air strikes and significant collateral damage upon civilians and Drug Enforcement Agency (DEA) efforts to destroy lucrative poppy crops, which obtain as much as ten times the profits as cereal crops, has tended to alienate "moderate" leaders and the Afghanistan population—despite the general unpopularity of the Taliban.

U.S. efforts to eradicate poppies have been opposed by the government of Hamid Karzai, in part due to fears that herbicides will poison legitimate crops, cattle, and drinking water. Opposition to drug eradication was also due to the fact that narcotics traffickers and organized crime groups with their own armies or links to the Taliban work secretly with top government officials and can bribe police and other authorities, creating, in effect, a narco-state. Proposals to produce opium-based drugs, such as morphine, for legitimate usage have been opposed with the argument that the world-demand for opium-based medicines is fully met. According to the U.S. embassy in Kabul, the price difference between licit and illicit opium is so substantial that Afghan farmers would not quit the black market and the legalization of opium derivatives would merely expand and entrench the drug trade and undermine ongoing efforts to bring security and sustainable economic development.[12]

The problem, however, is that efforts to bring security and sustainable economic development do not appear to be working in Afghanistan as opium production has increased substantially and as both the Taliban and al-Qaida appear resurgent. The deeper roots of the crisis stem not only from the fact that Afghanistan produces 92 percent of the world's opium (with the two major trade routes through Russia and Turkey to Europe), but from the worldwide black market demand for illegal drugs in general. The growing linkages between the international drug trade, illicit black market activities, mafias, and "terrorist" organizations appear to require a radical reassessment of not only U.S. and NATO strategy, but also domestic U.S. and EU drug policies, with an eye toward the possible legalization of "less dangerous" narcotics as means to limit addiction, combined with education campaigns against all forms of drug use, including cigarettes and alcohol. Such a policy would be intended to sever links between newly legalized business, mafias and partisan "terrorist" groups. (See also Chapter 9.)

In 2006 nearly 140 suicide attacks occurred in Afghanistan, as compared with 27 in 2005. The explosive concoction of warlords, increased opium profits, and weak central government has permitted Taliban and pan-Islamist insurgents to move throughout the country and target policemen, international workers, and U.S., NATO, and Afghan troops. Afghan insurgents have been using suicide attacks and detonating roadside bombs by remote control, similar to insurgents in Iraq. Moreover, in 2005 the United States opposed granting Hamid Karzai and the central Afghan government a "dual key" in determining which homes to search and targets to strike to limit "collateral damage" and popular protest, which could undermine his already-limited political support. The United States argued that Afghan governmental controls would hamper, if not expose, secret operations.[13]

The United States is additionally concerned that Pakistan has not been willing to crack down more firmly on al-Qaida and Taliban movements operating on its own territory as well as in Afghanistan, while Pakistan is concerned over its potential disaggregation because it has no real control over the northwest frontier territories that are close to the Afghan border, based on the historically problematic Durand line that has thus far checked irredentist Pashtun claims to unity. (See Chapter 1.) The failure to use force effectively then led Pakistan to try to find a diplomatic solution in South Waziristan (April 2004) and North Waziristan (September 2006) that seeks to co-opt Taliban supporters (efforts critically received by Washington in that they lacked enforcement measures and provided too many concessions to jihadi militants).[14]

Evidence additionally suggests that Pakistani intelligence agencies—in particular the powerful ISI and Military Intelligence—have been supporting a Taliban restoration. The latter agencies argue that the jihadist movement allows Islamabad to assert greater influence on Pakistan's vulnerable western flank by providing "strategic depth" against India. Here, the 1999 Kargil crisis in Kashmir (fought after both Pakistan and India exploded nuclear weapons in 1998) continues to play in the background of India-Pakistani relations and with Pakistan's relations with militant Islamic groups who are attempting to destabilize the present regime of President and General Pervez Musharraf. The 1999 Kargil crisis almost brought the two nuclear powers into direct conflict; yet was mediated behind the scenes by the United States.[15] In essence, despite the 1999 Lahore Declaration to jointly manage military-strategic relations between India and Pakistan, Islamabad had hoped to use its nuclear weapons as leverage to strengthen its position on Kashmir in the UN through the Kargil crisis and the *threat* of nuclear war, but failed on all counts, further isolating itself. New Delhi saw the crisis as a betrayal of its efforts to extend trust to Islamabad, while pan-Islamist groups (including members of the Pakistan ISI) regarded the crisis as a failure of Pakistani leadership to obtain its rightful claims to Kashmir. Along with the U.S. failure to root out the Taliban and al-Qaida in Afghanistan, the failure to resolve the Kashmir question has strengthened the pan-Islamic cause *within* Pakistan. Moreover, despite efforts to reach a reconciliation of Kashmir and other questions since 2003, Indian-Pakistani nuclear capabilities have not prevented or deterred significant acts of terrorism and counterterrorism on both sides.

In late 2006, literally risking his neck in confrontation with pan-Islamist jihadis, but also refusing to engage in power-sharing with other legitimate political parties, Musharraf declared that Pakistan would give up its claims to Kashmir—if reciprocated by concrete steps by India. The proposal appeared to represent a crucial step in winding down the "global war on terror" in that it would limit Pakistani strategic desires to support jihadi groups in Kashmir (and implicitly in Afghanistan). Second, peace over Kashmir might help draw down the Indian-Pakistani nuclear and conventional weapons rivalry, reducing the real possibility of confrontation. On the Indian side, it appeared that New Delhi might accept some territorial modifications along the Line of Control (LOC), but did not go further to accept possible autonomy for Kashmir as a whole. Here, the two sides would need to agree on the parameters of Kashmiri autonomy, to be overseen by Indian, Pakistani, and Kashmiri (and international?) observers. The United States, EU, Russia, and China should work to press both sides into reconciliation.

The conflict has been accentuated by the fact that, by 2006–7, al-Qaida has been able to regroup its command structure in northwest Pakistan, supporting Taliban, Pushtan irredentist, and pan-Islamist movements in Afghanistan, Kashmir and inside Pakistan. Under increased U.S. pressure to crack down on extremist Islamist movements, Pakistani president Musharraf engaged in a major raid on the Red Mosque in Islamabad in July 2007, thereby risking future confrontations with vengeful pan-Islamists who seek to overthrow his leadership.

Russian Response to the Collapse of the Soviet Empire

With China as the initiator of the project, Beijing and Moscow consequently focused their attention on building the Shanghai Cooperation Organization (SCO), formed in Shanghai in 1996. The SCO seeks to reassert Russian and Chinese control over central Asia. Moscow has also forged a Collective Security Treaty Organization (CSTO) that includes Armenia, Belarus, Kazakhstan, Kyrgyzstan, Tajikistan, and Russia.

By August 1999 the "Shanghai Five" (China, Russia, Kazakhstan, Kyrgystan, and Tajikistan) pledged to cooperate in fighting terrorism, drugs, arms smuggling, illegal migration, national secession, and religious "extremism"—in addition to demarcating borders and regulating trade relations. The Shanghai Five were later joined by Uzbekistan in 2001—and then they combined to call themselves the SCO to represent their organization as a counterpoint to the Organization for Security and Cooperation in Europe (OSCE). The SCO could ultimately parallel NATO if it continues to expand defense coordination over the next decade. Mongolia, Pakistan, and Iran all obtained observer status in 2004–2005; all three seek full membership. India is likewise an observer, while the U.S. application was rejected. The July 2007 SCO summit concentrated on coordinating political, security, and energy policies for its members and observers.

Between June 22 and 24, 2005—following the "Rose" and "Orange" revolutions in Georgia in 2003 and in Ukraine in 2004, respectively—Moscow began to transform the largely defunct CIS forum into the CSTO Collective Security Council. As the CIS began to disintegrate, Georgia and Moldova demanded the removal of Russian bases. (See Chapter 2.) Turkmenistan then sought neutrality. The CSTO Collective Security Council has looked toward stronger military-economic cooperation; it has sought to develop integrated air defense systems, to improve rapid deployment forces, and to engage in peacekeeping missions. Following the September 11 attacks, Russia worked with the United States against al-Qaida and the Taliban in Afghanistan and has provided useful intelligence. In this regard, Moscow generally accepted the expanding U.S. military presence in the Caucasus and central Asia—although not without reservations among its old guard.

Both Russia and China acquiesced to U.S. military bases in central Asia, with China engaging in a rapprochement with NATO in 2003. NATO, China and Russia thus appear to be cooperating against the possible return of the Taliban to power in Afghanistan at the same time both Russia and China appear to be tightening their links to key central Asian states (perhaps as much in rivalry than cooperation). While its leadership appears to be of divided opinion, Moscow has, to a certain extent, shown an interest in CSTO cooperation with the United States and NATO, especially in Afghanistan. Whether the United States and Russia can sustain a modus vivendi remains to be seen. A sustained U.S.-Russian partnership depends to a large extent on their individual approaches to Uzbekistan and Turkmenistan (following the death of President Saparmurat Niyazov), Ukraine, and Georgia.

Russia, China, and India

In the mutual fear of secessionist movements and pan-Islamist "terrorism," Russia has additionally sought to bring China and India together, despite their geohistorical disputes, along with other states in central Asia.

Post-Soviet governments in Uzbekistan, Kazakhstan, Kyrgyzstan, and Tajikistan have thus engaged in crackdowns on both peaceful dissenters and pan-Islamist groups. China has continued its crackdown down in Xinjiang in which the East Turkestan Islamic Movement made up of Uighur Muslims has been depicted as a "terrorist" movement (with purported links to bin Laden) by the both the U.S. State Department and Chinese authorities. In Chechnya, a variety of groups, a few with purported links to al-Qaida, resist Russian intervention and have tried to widen the conflict to involve Dagestan and Georgia. In addition to actions of the Islamic Movement of Uzbekistan (IMU), one of the most dangerous groups is Hizb ut-Tahrir al-Islami—the Islamic Party of Liberation—a five thousand- to ten thousand-member strong group that operates in Uzbekistan, Kyrgyzstan, Tajikistan, and oil-rich Kazakhstan and that seeks to establish a Shar'ia-based caliphate. China is primarily concerned with pan-Islamist and Uighur secessionist movements in Xinjiang, potential "secessionist" movements in Tibet, and Taiwanese "independence." India is primarily concerned with the Kashmir crisis with Pakistan as well as with Sri Lanka, whose militant Tamil secessionist movements have been seeking "self-determination."

Russia's concern has thus been to stem the rise of pan-Islamic and secessionist movements in the Caucasus and throughout central Asia in addition to stabilizing political conditions for the passage of oil pipelines from the natural gas and oil-rich Caspian Sea region. (Here, the United States might have initially overestimated the amount of regional reserves, raising excessive expectations for profit and hence exacerbating the chances for conflict). Moscow has accordingly sought to make deals with Turkey (with its growing economy and energy needs), India, Iran, and Saudi Arabia at the same time that it has attempted to play "divide and rule" in the Caucasus and central Asia.

Ankara's expression of interest in January 2005 to also join the Shanghai Cooperation Organization shows the development of closer Russian-Turkish political-security and economic ties. Russian-Turkish ties have become closer particularly following U.S. military intervention against Iraq in 1991 and support for "democratic federalism" in Iraq—which Turkey fears will result in an independent Kurdish state. Russia and Turkey possess a potentially symbiotic relationship: Turkey needs Russian oil and gas, while Russia seeks Turkish agricultural and consumer products. (See Chapters 2 and 3)

Russia-Iran

The crux of the U.S.-Russian geostrategic dispute lies with Iran, which remains the major Russian ally in the Persian Gulf region, despite Iranian-Russian disputes over ownership of oil reserves and fishing rights (such as caviar) in the Caspian Sea. Russia represents Iran's major arms supplier and has assisted its "peaceful" nuclear energy program (along with China) in addition to assisting

Iran's ballistic missile capabilities. Moscow has regarded support for Tehran as the means to counter Saudi and "Wahhabist" influence in Chechnya and in central Asia. Tehran's tacit support for Russia's intervention in Chechnya represents one reason for the Russian reluctance to reduce its nuclear energy and technical ties with Tehran, including the sale of missile defense systems.[16] (Tehran and Moscow oppose Azerbaijan while both support Armenia.) At the same time, however, Russia has opposed Iran's possession of nuclear weapons, but it only began to vote for UN Security Council sanctions (along with China) in December 2006.

The U.S. presence in central Asia has *thus far* appeared to represent a stabilizing factor in the soft underbelly of the Russian federation—as long as Russia, China, and the United States possess common "threats" in the region. China has signed agreements and territory swaps with Kyrgyzstan, Tajikistan, and Kazakhstan. Russia, in turn, has sought to strengthen ties with Uzbekistan and Kyrgyzstan, which are strong supporters of Russia's views on the war on terrorism. The Kyrgyz leadership has supported the concept of preemptive strikes, and the Uzbek leadership has urged the creation of a common list of terrorist organizations. If so, it would be the Collective Security Treaty Organization (CSTO) of Armenia, Belarus, Kazakhstan, Kyrgyzstan, Tajikistan, and Russia that would engage rapid-reaction forces.[17]

Uzbekistan, in particular, has become a focal point of interest with regard to both regional and global powers because of its geostrategic and political-economic significance. It possesses major energy and mineral resources, and it is the state that is best positioned to predominate over the entire central Asia region in geostrategic terms. The United States, China, Japan, and Russia have thus all been competing for influence there. After the September 11, 2001, attacks on the World Trade Center and Pentagon, Uzbekistan had initially permitted the Pentagon to establish the largest military base in central Asia on its territory, and it cooperated with the NATO stabilization force in Afghanistan. In late July 2005, however, Uzbekistan formally evicted the United States from its K-2 military base that had served U.S. combat and humanitarian missions to Afghanistan (see Chapter 2).

While Russian influence has increased in Uzbekistan, the United States has tended to lose out over time because of its criticism of Uzbek human and political rights, particularly after the bloody protests in the province of Andijan in May 2005, in which as many as five hundred people were reportedly killed. The United States argues that the Karimov regime has tended to use the "war on terrorism" as a cover to repress all Uzbek opposition and that if it does not reform itself, it will face greater resistance. Thus, in 2005 the United States withheld almost $11 million in aid. Uzbekistan then dropped out of GUUAM in May 2005 (see Chapter 2). In 2006 Washington threatened to withhold as much as $22 million in aid if the Karimov regime did not comply with provisions on political and economic reforms that it committed to undertake in its 2002 strategic partnership agreement with Washington.[18]

For its part, Russia seeks to check pan-Islamic infiltration of its soft Islamic underbelly in Chechnya and other Russian republics, where more than 10 percent of global oil reserves are concentrated. Russian hegemony over Uzbekistan permits it to oversee pan-Islamist and anti-Russian movements in Afghanistan,

Pakistan, Iran, and other countries and to help "mediate" regional conflicts. By forging a strong security accord with Uzbekistan (stronger than those with Tajikistan, Kazakhstan, and Kyrgyzstan), Russia could either defend Uzbekistan or possibly intervene in regional affairs. Although it is dubious that Iran and China would intervene in Uzbek affairs, Russia also seeks to check U.S. influence and could play the Uzbek card by supporting the large Uzbek diaspora in neighboring countries in central Asia—if deemed necessary.[19] This possibility could embroil the region in a wider conflict.

Another potential spark of conflict is Turkmenistan.[20] Because China is looking toward central Asia for markets, resources, and security, because the Russians seek to regain former Soviet spheres of influence if possible, and because the United States and EU seek oil and gas from the Caspian Sea region through the wider Black Sea connection (see Chapter 3), U.S., EU, Russian, and Chinese interests could potentially clash. The death of Turkmenistan president Saparmurat Niyazov might have opened the doors to a more intensified interstate rivalry, as each of the states can now vie for influence, potentially squeezing Russia out of the "Great Game of Go" in which the nineteenth-century Anglo-Russian "Great Game" has been superseded by U.S., Russian, EU, Chinese, Japanese, Iranian, Saudi, and Turkish rivalries.

Soviet Collapse and the "Greater Middle East"

The Soviet collapse and breakup into fifteen republics, coupled with a retraction of the Russian role in general Middle Eastern affairs, has opened the door to the emergence of various pan-Islamic movements, among other oppositional forces. A number of militant anti-Russian, anti-Western groups have arisen throughout an enlarged central Asian and "Greater Middle East" and African "zone of conflict." During the cold war, Soviet (and French) backing for Iraq's secular pan-Arab regime had helped to keep pan-Islamic forces at bay, while Saddam Hussein backed militant secular or pan-Arabist factions of the PLO and groups such as Abu Nidal, in addition to the Iranian Mujahedin-e Khalq (MEK), an exiled "Islamic socialist" group that opposed Iran's theocracy. Moscow tended to back Yassir Arafat and the PLO, thus keeping various pan-Islamic groups in check. Saudi Arabia supported both the PLO and Saddam Hussein during the latter's war with Iran. Then, following the Iraqi invasion of Kuwait, Saudi Arabia began to cut assistance to the PLO and support Hamas: Unlike Arafat, Hamas did not support Saddam Hussein.

Furthermore, Soviet collapse meant a cutback in Russian influence in the Middle East and retraction of diplomatic and financial support for the PLO. The loss of Soviet (and Russian) support, as well as that of Iraq, represented one of the background factors that led indirectly to the decline of the PLO relative to Hamas. After more than forty years, Fatah lost its position of predominance over other Palestinian factions following the January 2006 Palestinian legislative elections. Initial Saudi (and Israeli) support for Hamas was, to a certain extent, replaced by Iranian support after Hamas opposed the Oslo peace process by 1993 and since the second Palestinian intifada in 2000. In addition, Israeli attacks on PLO's secular leadership before (and after) Arafat's death considerably weakened the secular Palestinian Authority, while Israeli strikes against Hamas' leadership ironically made Hamas even more popular among Palestinians, as compared with perceived corruption within Fatah. Not only did Hamas win the 2006 parliamentary elections but it also seized control in Gaza in 2007. (See Chapter 5.)

While Soviet withdrawal from Afghanistan in the late 1980s more directly permitted the rise of the Taliban, which has begun to resurge even following U.S. intervention in 2001, the collapse of the Soviet empire more indirectly permitted the rise of the Muslim Brotherhood in Egypt, both Sunni and Shi'a Islamic parties in Iraq, Hizb'allah in Lebanon, the Islamic Muttahida Majlis-e-Amal (MMA) in Pakistan, and Hamas in Palestine. Most significantly, U.S. intervention in Iraq in 2003 has represented a "godsend" for pan-Islamist movements and has opened the door to both militant Sunni and Shi'ite Islamic groups, plus international Islamist groups, among others, such as the Kurdish-based Ansar al Islam and the Al-Zarqawi network. (See Chapter 1.) The failure to find a resolution to the Palestinian, Kashmiri, and Afghan crises could mean war without end—given the fusion of political demands with apparently uncompromising religious belief. Here, Saudi-Iranian rivalry over Iraq appears to be intensifying, with the danger of moving beyond Iraq. While U.S. intervention against both the Taliban and Saddam Hussein eliminated Iran's major enemies and could have theoretically led to a general compromise (as offered by Iran in 2003), U.S. military pressures, combined with an Iranian quest for regional hegemony and support for Shi'a movements in Iraq and potentially in eastern oil rich province of Saudi Arabia, have led to a new regional arms buildup among the Gulf states. (See Chapter 4.)

A political-religious chain reaction has consequently gained momentum since the 1979 Iranian Revolution and the 1979 Soviet intervention in Afghanistan—in which the United States pitted a highly politicized pan-Islamist movement against "atheistic Communism" and Shi'a Iran—and once pan-Islamic movements not so unexpectedly turned against the United States and Europe, as well as Russia.

U.S. Military and Political-economic Involvement in Africa

The fate of the African continent is becoming increasingly significant to U.S. national security. The "global war on terror," the worldwide spread of AIDS and other communicable diseases, and the political economy of oil and other valuable resources have all put Africa on the U.S. map of geostrategic and political-economic priorities.[21] With output of more than four million barrels a day, sub-Saharan Africa already produces as much oil as Iran, Venezuela, and Mexico combined.

In military terms, there were at least twenty U.S. military operations in Africa between 1990 and 2000. Since 2000 there have been ten military operations in Africa. Most of the twenty-four major armed conflicts recorded worldwide in 2001 on the eve of September 11 were on the African continent, with eleven of those conflicts lasting eight years or more, killing more people in Africa than in the rest of the world combined. An estimated 4.7 million people died during the 1990s in the war in the Democratic Republic of the Congo alone.[22] These conflicts have begun to link up with the conflicts taking place in the "greater Middle East," central Asia and increasingly Latin America because of the rise of a massive black and gray market economy (in drugs, small arms, and other illegal goods and services) and the ongoing "global war on terror" (which to a certain extent, ironically permits that black market economy to thrive)—combined with the search to secure alternative sources of petroleum.

Because of Africa's burgeoning geostrategic and political-economic importance, the Pentagon has been considering the creation of a new military command there to "streamline the focus and give appropriate undivided attention to the continent."[23] Condoleezza Rice, who served as assistant secretary of defense for African affairs in the Bill Clinton administration, stated that "the existing system of having Africa divided among three commands is dysfunctional and nonsensical."[24] Up to 2006, the European Command, Central Command, and Pacific Command divide responsibility for Africa, leaving these commands overlapping and overstretched. The new U.S. Africa Command, or AFRICOM, would supervise strategic developments and military operations across the entire continent. At the same time, the issue of secure access to oil appears interlinked with the fear of pan-Islamist movements. The United States has consequently sought to establish a new naval base in the Gulf of Guinea and has engaged in the Africa Crisis Response Initiative (ACRI) as well as African Contingency Operations Training and Assistance.[25]

The Pentagon has been concerned that Africa, with its Muslim population of roughly 250 million, will become the next region for al-Qaida recruitment, particularly after the 1998 attacks on the U.S. embassies in Kenya and Tanzania, coupled with the infiltration of al-Qaida and other groups into the region and the Horn of Africa. The feared al-Qaida and Islamist threat has consequently resulted in the establishment of the Combined Joint Task Force-Horn of Africa (CJTF-HOA) in 2002 and Operation Enduring Freedom-Trans-Sahara (OEF-TS) in 2005. Here, the $500 million Trans-Sahara Counter-Terrorism Initiative is intended to provide military expertise to nine Saharan states, such as Mali, Niger, and Chad, whose desert regions are believed to harbor pan-Islamic groups because of the lack of efficient controls over their territory and borders, coupled with tribal and insurgent solidarity.

Even if they could not cooperate on the question of intervention in Iraq, the United States and France appear to be linking forces in Africa following the collapse of the Mobutu regime, part in rivalry, part in cooperation. While the French have been accused of manipulations leading to genocide in Rwanda and intervening in the civil war in Ivory Coast (once the development model of Africa), the Horn of Africa has also become an area of particular concern to U.S. and EU policymakers, given the battle for state control in Somalia between Islamists—who have suspected links to al-Qaida—and the country's failing transitional government. The United States maintains Camp Lemonnier in Dijbouti (alongside the French) in the effort to guard the Horn of Africa.

In what was once an external war between Ethiopia and Somalia over the Ogaden on the strategically positioned Horn of Africa became an internal war following Eritrean secessionism and the breakdown of the Somalia state, setting off a war among clans within one of the few ethnically homogenous states in the world, but in which the rival clans are backed by neighboring or foreign actors.

Now, following the failure of U.S. operations in Somalia during the Clinton presidency (resulting in the "Somalia syndrome"), followed by the failure of the January 2004 power-sharing agreement among two-dozen warlords that had been reached after talks in Kenya, the Supreme Islamic Courts Union (ICU) seized control of Mogadishu and much of southern Somalia in May through June 2006 and attempted to implement Shari'a law there. As part of a secret directive granted to the Pentagon since 2001, the United States has attempted to root out al-Qaida leaders, while also backing Ethiopian forces in an effort to eradicate the ICU, but this appears to have caused a popular anti-Ethiopian backlash among Somalians.

In former French North Africa, the Salafist Group for Call and Combat (GSPC) has crossed from Algeria into Tunisia. The GSPC was backed by al-Qaida deputy leader Ayman al-Zawahiri's message of September 11, 2006, in which he defined the Algerian group as "a bone in the throat of American and French crusaders." Likewise, in Morocco a network with links to al-Qaida and the GSPC has been uncovered. Pan-Islamist "terrorist" suspects have been caught in the Spanish enclave of Ceuta, north of Morocco, on the path of illegal immigration into Europe. The GSPC might likewise be operating in Mauritania and the Sahel region.[26]

Here the global war on terror and warfare over the Western Sahara in Morocco have been joined by the efforts of African men and women to escape economic depression and lack of development and employment prospects by attempting to sail clandestinely into Europe. How many will become recruits for "terrorist" organizations?

China, the United States, and the Sudan

As more than one third of China's crude oil imports come from Africa, Beijing has entered into the African political-economy in potential rivalry with the United States and EU through support of such countries as Sudan (in which China is the country's largest arms supplier and purchaser of oil), Libya, Algeria, Mauritania, Chad, Ethiopia, Angola, Congo, Nigeria, Gabon, Sao Tome and Principe, and Equatorial Guinea. Because one of the reasons for U.S. intervention in Iraq arguably was to preclude Chinese and Russian control over oil reserves (see Chapter 3), potential problems in Africa can be foreseen, in part because China and the United States have been at odds over China's support for Sudan. Sudan, which started exporting oil in 2003, is expected to more than triple its oil output by 2020. Beijing has invested $3 billion in Sudan's oil industry, which supplies China with 7 percent of its needs.

Believed to be supported by the Sudanese government, the Janjaweed have massacred as many as two hundred thousand fellow Muslims, with hundreds of thousands refugees fleeing to Chad, in the hunt for oil in the Darfur region. Despite international efforts to prevent massacres in Darfur, Sudan, it has been difficult to gain support for peacekeepers from the UN Security Council, particularly because Beijing has threatened to veto UN measures against Sudan since 2003, and Sudan fears that UN peacekeepers (backed by the United States) will become permanent and not "impartial." Beijing has argued that the situation will only get worse if it cuts its supports for the Sudanese government.

While the finger has been pointed at China (which has been accused of arming the Sudanese government's efforts to clear away Nuer and Dinka people along the "serpentine path"[27] of the China National Petrochemical Corporation's [CNPC] oil pipeline), Washington might also be at fault as well. In addition to first-term Bush administration efforts to denigrate UN peacekeeping efforts (which have been for the most part much more effective and less corrupt than the U.S. intervention in Iraq has been!), it has been alleged that U.S. efforts to obtain information on al-Qaida and other Islamist groups from the Sudanese government has led the United States to appease the "regime" with regard to violent "ethnic cleansing" in Darfur, but simultaneously seeking to protect Christian groups in the South.[28]

Here, however, the United States, China, the UN Security Council, and the Sudan began to reconsider their position because of the gravity of the massacres and the risk of the conflict spreading to Chad and beyond—and because the Sudanese government may not be able to protect Saudi, Middle Eastern, and Chinese oil installations and assets alone after Sudanese rebels attacked and briefly held the Abu Jabra oil field in November 2006, for example. The U.S. oil company Chevron had left Sudan in the 1980s as a result of the violent civil war; China's CNPC could be forced to withdraw as well.

In June 2007, the Sudanese government accepted a joint UN-African Union (AU) peacekeeping force of at least twenty thousand troops and police. Here, Sudanese rebel factions hoped that the UN would take a stronger role; the Sudanese government, however, pressed for AU command and control with African troops primarily. As Chinese peacekeepers have been deployed in Haiti, East Timor, Bosnia-Herzegovina, Liberia, Afghanistan, the option of deploying Chinese troops under UN command for Darfur should be considered.

Should permanent members of the UN Security Council block future UN human rights and peacekeeping missions, one option to consider is use of the 1950 "Uniting for Peace Resolution" that permits the General Assembly to overrule UN Security Council members.

Sub-Sahara Africa

While interstate conflict on the southern cape of Africa appears to have stabilized (except for high levels of urban violence in South Africa[29] and repression in Zimbabwe, whose economy has become a basket case), inter- and intrastate violence abounds in central and western African regions. Conflict between Rwanda and Congo dealt primarily with primary raw materials. Conflict in the Sudan, like that between Rwanda and Congo, threatens to widen, involving Chad and other regional states. A number of offshore disputes between São Tomé and Nigeria, Cameroon and Nigeria, and Equatorial Guinea and Gabon over oil reserves could cause significant conflict in the coming years.[30]

Coming out of its violent civil war, in which the United States ironically supported the losing UNITA faction against the ruling MPLA, Angola, as Africa's second-largest oil producer, is expected to double output by 2020 as the center of the oil boom. Equatorial Guinea, Chad (a pipeline with Cameroon is increasing its volume supplied to Atlantic ports), and Sudan, which started exporting oil in 2003, are expected to more than triple their output by 2020.

Nigeria, which is presently Africa's leading exporter of crude oil, is expected to increase its daily output, depending, in part, upon its deep socioeconomic conflicts. Moreover, as Gabon, Equatorial Guinea, Congo-Brazzaville, and Cameroon are not OPEC members, this production could help break OPEC's virtual monopoly over pricing, along with the rise of alternative energy technologies. Of African countries, only Nigeria and Angola (which joined in 1971 and December 2006, respectively) belong to OPEC; the United States has quietly tried to persuade Nigeria to break ranks. Domestic conflict in Nigeria results from interethnic rivalries, oil, and corruption, if not the infiltration of pan-Islamist organizations. The Movement for the Emancipation of the Niger Delta (MEND), for example, has sought to destabilize the country since 2005 by attacking oil facilities, among other actions; it has demanded ownership rights over Niger Delta oil and compensation from Shell Inc. for oil spills. Here, however, Niger delta oil produces 80 percent of Nigeria's Federal Reserves and 95 percent of its exports; yet the regions and communities (such as the Ogoni, and more numerous Ijaw, peoples) that produce this oil are among the most destitute in the entire Nigerian Federation. Three dominant ethnic groups tend to control the riches of the countries, leading to a general militarization of the society and the rise of private militias and gangs.[31] The possibility of a "failed" Nigerian election in April 2007, with its "first civilian-to-civilian" government transition, was regarded as a significant threat to U.S. national security.[32]

Over the next twenty years, Equatorial Guinea could become Africa's third largest producer (ahead of Congo and Gabon), with 740,000 barrels a day.[33] Here, it is important to note that the Gulf of Guinea possesses estimated reserves of twenty-four billion barrels; it is likely to become the world's leading deep-water offshore production center. The sociopolitical issue is that much of this oil is offshore: This means there is much less political pressure against exploiting resources without the repatriation or reinvestment of profits. Already, one of the historical legacies of colonialism and neocolonialism is the lack of reinvestment and repatriation of revenues, and hence lack of development. Here, Africa has lost an estimated $150 billion in capital flight, with around 40 percent of private wealth held outside the continent—a higher percentage than in any other region.[34]

Economic and Development Issues

What might possibly differ between AFRICOM and other U.S. military commands is that it is expected to possess a civilian component that would help coordinate nonmilitary functions such as diplomacy and economic and political aid. But here, it is not clear that U.S. assistance programs are truly effective, and they could be counterproductive in that they might serve short-term U.S. interests and not those of the Africans themselves, except perhaps in immediate crisis situations. Moreover, too great an U.S. military presence without substantial and effective social and economic assistance could prove provocative, attracting sabotage and acts of terrorism.

Here, generally as a result of Africa's history as a victim of imperialism and colonialism (from both the Arab and European worlds), combined with massive postcolonial corruption, much of the great potential of the African continent has been abused. Unlike Asia, no significant entrepreneurial class emerged in the post–World War II period. Between 1960 and 2005, for example, per capita incomes in Africa rose only 25 percent, as compared to East Asia, where they rose 850 percent.[35] It appears that sub-Saharan Africa will not be able to achieve the UN Millennium Development Goals by 2015—let alone even by 2050!

The problem is then how to engage in debt relief and poverty alleviation while at the same time encouraging "good governance." According to the National Intelligence Council 2020 report, "there remains a focus on debt relief in exchange for poverty-alleviation 'good governance' strategies. Africa's external debt stands at US$300 billion. Over 80% of the heavily indebted poor countries (HIPC) are in the region, and the continent's total debt service ratio in 1999 (debt as a percentage of exports of goods and services) was 13.9%, uncomfortably close to the 15–20% mark that is considered unsustainable. Around US$40 billion in debt has already been forgiven under the HIPC initiative."[36]

In general, the focus of development assistance has been on debt relief and technical assistance that goes to U.S. or European agroindustry, corporations or even well-paid nongovernmental organizations (NGOs). The assistance programs rarely go to meet long-term needs in terms of sustainable development but generally represent "stopgap" measures in times of crisis such as emergency food assistance: "Of US $25 billion in aid to Africa only US $6 billion or US $7 billion is 'real money' because US$7 billion goes to technical assistance by advanced countries to their own companies or nationals; US$9 billion is debt relief on debt that is not being repaid; and US$2 billion is emergency food aid and may be smaller or larger depending on the extent of a crisis."[37]

Moreover, it is possible for food aid to generate dependency as opposed to agricultural productivity. African (and Latin American) produce is often in competition with highly subsidized U.S. and Europe agricultural products, or else it cannot be exported because of a number of nontariff barriers to free trade in the United States and Europe. A deeper issue for African development is how to generate fairer trade, plus new productivity, combined with ways to permit temporary work permits to export labor to capital rich, labor poor regions while controlling illegal immigration.

U.S. oil companies—Exxon-Mobil and Chevron-Texaco, and operators such as Amerada Hess, Marathon, and Ocean Energy–are expected to invest more than $10 billion in African oil by 2007. U.S. investments are not new but appear to be growing in magnitude. In political-economic terms, however, U.S. investment has tended to go where it has the most profitable interests, not to the regions that necessarily need it the most. Thus, roughly 80 percent of U.S. Multinational Corporate (MNC) investment goes to Nigeria, Angola, and South Africa. The latter countries are of primary interest to the United States partly because African oil in Nigeria and Angola is closer and more secure than oil from the Middle East.

In addition to oil, sub-Sahara Africa also has potential for biofuel development, particularly Angola, Mozambique, and South Africa. Yet, much as has been the case in China and to a certain extent Brazil (see Chapters 8 and 9), the biofuel and ethanol industry in South Africa has been accused of contributing to the rapidly rising cost of basic necessities for the poor by driving the food prices of staples such as maize and sugar up 28 percent and 12.6 percent in 2006, thus laying the ground for domestic disputes, if not conflict.[38]

Regional Security Communities in a Widening Conflict Zone?

In addition to Sudan, a number of conflicts within Africa have already begun to draw the United States into either direct engagement (because of the significance of geostrategic or political-economic interests involved) or else, more indirectly, in backing UN or regional operations. The UN has increasingly become over-stretched: In October 2006, the UN had 93,000 personnel in the field, 70,000 in the military. It furthermore anticipated being involved in at least eighteen operations, including full deployment in Lebanon and Timor-Leste, plus Darfur, meaning 140,000 military, police, and civilian peacekeepers; a 50 percent increase, at budget over $6 billion.[39]

About 17,000 UN peacekeepers operate in the Congo, overseeing the peace process after the end of a bloody five-year war in 2002. As argued by the Brahimi report, there has been difficulty raising peacekeeping forces because external peacekeeping does little to solve the core developmental problems or even address problems related to the African capacity to manage their own security. Peacekeeping must focus more on "self-help" (especially in Africa) and must be informed more about the challenges of peace-building, particularly after a close examination of the defects of the Somali fiasco and the Nigerian-led Economic Community of West African States (ECOWAS) Monitoring Group (ECO-MOG) operation in Liberia.[40]

Moreover, even where these brutal conflicts, which, in effect, amount to "gang rapes" by state elites, rival ethnic groups, pan-Islamic militants, multinational corporations, and mafias, have ended or wound down in intensity, the problems of hunger, malnutrition (resulting in stunted growth and mental retardation), unsafe drinking water, AIDS, lack of basic medical care that could help cure erad-icable diseases, inadequate clothing and housing, and general political-economic collapse—continue to generate new human and ecological crises.

These crises appear in many ways to be self-generating unless the peace and security can be restored country by country, region by region. Here, the estab-lishment of regional or UN-backed security communities may be the only hope to establish stability for the resource-rich, yet economically ravished, African con-tinent as a whole, in that continual political-economic instability generally does not result in the repatriation of profits and investments for infrastructure devel-opment. One problem, however, is that both U.S. and UN forces are over-stretched. At the same time, there is a real danger that the U.S. military presence might exacerbate conflicts and tensions by appearing to side with "oppressive" and "corrupt" states in the effort to guarantee energy supplies and free trade—instead of playing "honest broker" by bringing disputing factions into compro-mise and instead of seeking effective ways to redistribute offshore oil revenues for purposes of the sustainable development for the entire region.

On a deeper level, many of the factors that cause conflict in Africa (and else-where) are a result of political, economic, and social *exclusion* and lack of effective democracy. Here, the U.S. government's September 2006 "National Strategy for Combating Terrorism" has seen its long-term approach in the global war on terror as advancing effective democracy by overcoming alienation by "empowering individuals" and giving them an "ownership stake in society," establishing rule of law, supporting freedom of independent media, and fostering respect for human beings (against ideologies that justify murder).[41]

Political inclusion and "advancing effective democracy" by overcoming alienation by "empowering individuals" and giving them an "ownership stake in society," however, results from *participation* in the political process and *power-sharing* with differing individuals *and* communities. Here, once again, the concern is that the United States will not necessarily attempt to fully engage disputing factions and alienated groups in real dialogue with those in power through multilateral forums and contact groups, and that the U.S. emphasis will be on providing support for certain powerful individuals and *not* for whole communities. Moreover, mere participation in elections is not always sufficient in that majority votes do not guarantee stability or security, particularly in cases where significant minorities have been oppressed by majorities or vice versa—as in South Africa, Algeria, Burundi, Nigeria, and Rwanda, to mention a few. The problem is that minority communitarian rights might need to be guaranteed by *autonomy* or *confederal* arrangements—and enforced by regional and international police and peacekeepers, if national governments are unwilling to do so. (Here also lies the importance of truth and reconciliation in countries such as South Africa and now Algeria—although the Algerian version hardly lives up to that of South Africa).

Political, economic, and "human" security, involving *power-sharing* and *confederal* arrangements, as well as fair distribution of revenues, can furthermore be enhanced through the implementation of "regional security communities." Africa has a number of nascent regional security communities that need greater international support to become more effective. The history of efforts to achieve regional integration, however, has been a very poor one in Africa—in part because of the history of imposed borders and interstate rivalries. The Economic Community of West African States (ECOWAS), with Nigeria being the central actor; the Southern African Development Community (SADC), with South Africa being the central actor; the Intergovernmental Authority on Development IGAD in the Horn of Africa, with Ethiopia being the central actor; and the East African Cooperation (EAC) represent nascent regional security communities, as does the Economic Community of Central African States (ECCAS). At the continental level, the sole organization is the African Union. In addition there is another grouping of over seventeen states known as the Community of Sahel-Saharan States CENSAD, made up of West, North, Sahelian, and some Horn of Africa states. The important influence of the Arab League and the Islamic Conference Organization in Africa also needs to be taken into consideration. Here, however, problems can arise if interests of national actors are not carefully counterbalanced by those of the larger international community, as well as those of individual states.[42]

Moreover, while the predominance of oil as the primary source of energy and U.S. and European hegemony have been blamed for the lack of regional cooperation in Africa, an enlightened American policy could seek to foster regional integration, "not along the lines of OPEC (but) . . . formulated at the regional level."[43] Based on increased oil revenues and in the effort to attract foreign investment, regional organizations like ECOWAS, ECCAS, and SADC could set up common projects through the creation of special funds, tax packages, trade agreements, privatization legislation, and harmonized oil policies.[44]

Will an increasing U.S. (or NATO) military presence help bring conflicts to an end? Or will it exacerbate those conflicts? Can the United States and NATO cooperate with the Shanghai Cooperation Organization and Collective Security Treaty Organization in Eurasia? Can regional security communities be established in Africa? Will the U.S. presence be perceived in positive terms, as providing the finance and technologies to enhance much-needed development through community-oriented entrepeneurship that repatriates much of its profit and truly advancing effective democracy by "empowering individuals" but that shares power between majority and minority groups and provides all individuals with an "ownership stake in society"? Or will the U.S. presence be perceived in imperialistic terms (in effect, supporting only certain powerful individuals and *not* whole communities) as a means to counter Chinese, European, and Indian political-economic influence, and as a reinforcement of corrupt leaderships in the effort to exploit oil and valuable raw materials—in effect following the footsteps of all previous European empires in Africa? Can regional security communities be established in Africa? Would all states be willing to cooperate in such security communities or will these interstate regional organizations fall apart because of the ambitions of regional hegemons or the failure to obtain significant international backing?

CHAPTER 7

North Korea: Beyond "Backdoor" Multilateralism

In February 2007 U.S.-North Korean relations ostensibly took a sudden turn for the better, ironically despite (or because of) North Korea's nuclear test on October 9, 2006.[1] To a large extent because of Chinese mediation, the six-party talks then began in November 2006; between February 8 and 13, 2007, all parties (China, the United States, Russia, Japan, South Korea, and North Korea) finally agreed to implement the joint statement of September 19, 2005.[2]

As part of the deal, Pyongyang needs to seal its primary nuclear reactor at Yŏngbyŏn-kun, permit international inspections of its nuclear facilities, and provide information on all of its nuclear programs within sixty days. In exchange, North Korea will be provided with fifty thousand metric tons of heavy fuel oil, which would be part of a larger commitment of one million tons of oil only if Pyongyang agrees to disable the Yŏngbyŏn-kun plant. The deal furthermore stipulates the need to establish five working groups to implement the joint statement. These working groups involve some of the major issues confronting the security of Northeast Asia: (1) denuclearization of the Korean Peninsula, (2) normalization of DPRK-U.S. relations, (3) normalization of DPRK-Japan relations, (4) economic and energy cooperation, and (5) implementation of a Northeast Asia peace and security mechanism.

As significant as they are, the accords reached by the six-party talks did not immediate put an end to Pyongyang's insistence that the United States cease "targeted sanctions" placed in September 2005 on its illicit banking and black market activities in order to return to those talks. Moreover, Pyongyang does not need to totally dismantle its nuclear program. It only needs to seal the Yŏngbyŏn-kun reactor. This means North Korea does not need to give up its existing nuclear weapons at this time.[3] By March 23, 2007, the six-nation discussions were stalled once again when North Korea demanded that $25 million (from suspected money laundering and counterfeiting) be transferred to Pyongyang from

Macao.[4] With the estimated costs of the intervention in Iraq estimated at \$1 to 2 trillion, it would be horrifically absurd if a dispute over \$25 million helped set off a nuclear arms race in Asia, even if it is a question of "principle" and illicit and "black" market activities, possibly leading to a secret deal in which the United States would guarantee North Korea access to international financial markets. As the sixty-day deadline approached, it was not clear North Korea would abide by the agreement; China encouraged patience.

Nevertheless, the February 2007 deal revealed that the George W. Bush administration had finally bit the bullet with regard to North Korea and found itself impelled to negotiate with one of the countries that it previously considered as a member of the "axis of evil" and "outpost of tyranny." Having overextended itself in Iraq, and in the process of pressuring Iran into negotiations through a significant military buildup in the Persian Gulf, the Bush administration could not risk confrontation with North Korea at the same time and, in effect, has engaged in a more owlish, if not dovish, strategy of "appeasement" as opposed to pressing for superhawkish "regime change."

The question as to why it took so long to finally reach an agreement appears to have as much, if not more, to do with the Bush administration's internal bureaucratic politics—as well as the inadequacies in intelligence gathering—as it does with North Korean threats and intransigence. This appears true, because the United States might have overestimated North Korean nuclear capacities in the fall of 2002, when it accused North Korea of secretly developing weaponry using enriched uranium, in addition to pursuing a nuclear weapons capability based on plutonium processed by larger, more easily detectable, reactors. At that time, Washington cut off oil supplies, while the North Koreans retaliated by banning IAEA inspections and pressing ahead to build their first plutonium bomb.[5]

These latter sanctions put a temporary end to the essentially multilateral approach as previously pursued by the administration of Bill Clinton (despite Clinton's own threats to engage in preemptive strikes). While President Clinton was primarily engaged in the Middle East talks (but failed to resolve either the Middle East or the North Korea crises in the last year of his mandate), Secretary of State Colin Powell attempted to carry on the progress achieved by Clinton's secretary of state, Madeleine Albright, with regard to North Korea, only to unexpectedly find his multilateralist position overruled by the neoconservative unilateralists of the first-term Bush administration. The Bush administration consequently engaged in a unilateral crusade against rogue states (Iraq, Iran, and North Korea) with presumed potential weapons of mass destruction (WMD) capabilities, but without having clear and certain evidence in each case. It largely ignored the nondeclared nuclear weapons capabilities of Israel, as well as the declared nuclear capabilities of India and Pakistan—and began to accept the latter as *fait accompli.*

Having given up "regime change" by military force (thus pleasing Beijing), Washington, along with its partners, will need to continue to press for North Korean "regime reform." Although there remain suspicions that North Korea might have a double-track system to develop nuclear weaponry, increased confidence between the different parties could result in North Korea abandoning that program as well (if such a program exits), as well as whatever weapons it might still have in its possession. Such confidence could come about through the establishment of a far-reaching "regional security community," or what the State Department calls a "Northeast Asia Peace and Security Mechanism." If North Korea can ultimately obtain security guarantees from the United States and from other major powers, plus significant economic and energy assistance, it could opt to end its nuclear weapons program altogether, resulting in formal U.S. recognition of the North Korean regime and an end to sanctions and isolation.

Furthermore, North Korea's illicit financial and black market activities can be discussed separately from the nuclear question, as the United States did to obtain agreement in February 2007. In June 2007, the United States finally overcame domestic and international obstacles to find a way to return the $25 million to North Korea, while engaging in secret one-on-one talks in Pyongyang in an effort to make certain that the North Koreans will give up their estimated eight nuclear warheads.[6] By June 2007, North Korea offered to open its nuclear facilities to international inspections; yet negotiators had difficulties agreeing to a North Korean nuclear disarmament schedule.

The February 2007 accords appear to have finally pointed the way for "front-door" multilateralism to engage Washington (and not just Beijing and Moscow) in more direct talks with Pyongyang (as opposed to "backdoor" multilateralism in which the United States did not directly deal with North Korea). "Front door" multilateralism thus appears to represent a step in the right direction assuming the process can continue, even if that might eventually mean the normalization and legitimization of Kim Jung-Il's regime in the not so long term.

Unfortunately, however, because of the erratic and recurrent flip-flops in North Korea's bargaining position (in part in response to perceived U.S. threats and in part because of internal Korean power struggles), the North Korean threat to develop nuclear weapons and a ballistic missile capability remains in the background as part of the "insecurity-security dialectic" that involves mutual Japanese, Russian, and Chinese suspicions as well. North Korea's erratic posture, combined with Sino-Japanese tensions over Taiwan (see Chapter 8), could still spark a spiraling arms race—if the six parties do not sustain close attention to events both in and around the Korean Peninsula and move rapidly to the establishment of a Northeast Asia "regional security community." The latter would seek to forge a reassociated and "confederal" Korean state and simultaneously look toward a resolution of the Taiwan question with China so as to minimize the real chances of a North Korean state collapse and major-power conflict in Asia.

End of the Cold War: The Isolation of North Korea

It is important to trace the evolution of U.S. policy prior to the February 2007 accords to show why North Korea accelerated its nuclear weapons program as a result of fears of insecurity caused by the withdrawal of Soviet security guarantees combined with U.S. intervention in Iraq in the 1990–1991 Persian Gulf War, which raised fears of U.S. attacks on North Korea. The normalization of U.S. relations with North Korea would represent one of the major factors that could help persuade North Korea to totally eliminate its nuclear program and help to stabilize the region. The refusal of the United States to normalize relations with

North Korea (even if working through a multilateral six-party context) has thus far not only permitted China to increase its influence over the North, but indirectly over South Korea as well.

As the cold war came to an abrupt and largely unexpected end (at least in Europe), the United States opted not to reciprocate the largely unilateral steps of Soviet secretary general Mikhail Gorbachev to make peace in Asia. In addition to seeking to resolve the "three obstacles" to peace with China (by working to withdraw Soviet forces from Afghanistan, as well as Vietnamese forces from Cambodia, and by taking steps to resolve the Sino-Soviet-Mongolian border disputes), Gorbachev additionally normalized relations with South Korea in September 1990 and significantly downgraded relations with North Korea. With respect to nuclear energy, the Soviet Union persuaded North Korea to sign the Nonproliferation Treaty (NPT) in 1985 in exchange for Soviet assistance in the construction of a light-water reactor; but work stopped abruptly once Pyongyang fell behind on its payments.[7]

With Soviet security ties abandoned, the 1961 Treaty of Friendship, Cooperation and Mutual Assistance between China and North Korea became the latter's only remaining mutual security agreement. Not unexpectedly, Pyongyang regarded Gorbachev's actions as an affront, if not a betrayal, of international Communist "solidarity." North Korea consequently began to shift its defense strategy away from a primary focus on South Korea and toward a focus on the "north" (which could hypothetically include the Soviet Union, Japan, and China).

Concurrently, U.S. intervention in Iraq in the 1990–1991 Persian Gulf War (coupled with Moscow's refusal to back Saddam Hussein) raised fears of a possible U.S. attack against North Korea. A retraction of Soviet security assurances, coupled with a more assertive U.S. global strategy, consequently led North Korea to accelerate its efforts to obtain a nuclear weapons and missile delivery capability. (North Korea's nuclear program was initiated in the 1960s in the aftermath of the Korean War and in reaction to U.S. General Douglas MacArthur's threats to "contain" China with a ring of nuclear explosions across North Korean territory. Moreover, Saddam Hussein's invasion of Kuwait followed by U.S.-led multilateral intervention parallels North Korea's own invasion of South Korea followed by U.S.-led UN engagement.)

Needless to say, Gorbachev's radical change of Soviet foreign policy held no esteem in Pyongyang; yet its positive features were not really appreciated in Washington either. Washington (then secretary of defense Dick Cheney backed by Robert Gates) began to opine that the threat of instability within the USSR had begun to replace the Soviet global "threat." Rather than taking Gorbachev's overtures as an opportunity to forge peace agreements throughout the Asian region through U.S.-Soviet cooperation, as then secretary of state James Baker argued, the United States began to see Moscow's burgeoning links with Beijing (which would strengthen through the administrations of Boris Yeltsin and Vladimir Putin) as a potential new "threat."

Soviet links with China appeared more ominous as the previously close U.S.-Chinese relationship had begun to sour toward the end of cold war. U.S. relations with China had begun to plummet for the worse following China's sale of

Silkworm missile systems to Iran in 1987 and Eastwind intermediate-range ballistic missiles to Saudi Arabia in 1988. U.S.-China relations then grew even sourer following the events of Tiananmen Square in June 1989. Gorbachev's visit to China in May 1989, coupled by an "unofficial" visit of North Korean general secretary Kim Il-Sung to Beijing in November 1989, further raised U.S. suspicions of a new Sino-Soviet and Sino-North Korean relationship in the making. It thus appeared that Moscow was attempting to play the "China card" against Washington.

At the same time, however, as U.S.-Chinese relations soured, Seoul took the opportunity afforded by the end of the cold war to seek out better relations with Pyongyang. In July 1988 South Korean president Roh Tae Woo called for North-South exchanges, family reunification, the development of inter-Korean trade, as well as contact in international forums. President Woo likewise offered to discuss security matters with the North. Begun in September 1990, North-South Korean talks resulted in the 1991 Agreement on Reconciliation, Nonaggression, Exchanges, and Cooperation (the "Basic Agreement") and the 1992 Declaration on the Denuclearization of the Korean Peninsula (the "Joint Declaration").[8] South Korea thus began a process of engagement with the North (what would initially be called the "sunshine policy"). Yet, the United States itself did not respond in kind by *directly* reaching out to North Korea in an effort to bridge the divided Korean Peninsula, in an engagement that could have sought to check China's burgeoning influence on both North and South Korea.

The United States did take some unilateral actions, such as the removal of tactical nuclear weapons from South Korea in 1991, to help provide some confidence-building measures between the North and South, but Washington did not take steps that would in any way formally normalize relations with Pyongyang. By 1993, after U.S. intelligence detected activities in the reprocessing facility in Yŏngbyŏn-kun that indicated North Korea was possibly reprocessing spent fuel rods, the Clinton administration demanded that North Korea open its nuclear reactor facilities to International Atomic Energy Agency (IAEA) inspections. The fact that Yŏngbyŏn-kun nuclear facilities had not been hooked up to the country's electrical grid raised suspicions that their primary purpose was to extract weapons grade plutonium from spent fuel.[9]

It was also at roughly that time that the United States began to suspect a North Korean-Pakistani connection: North Korean missiles in exchange for Pakistani nuclear weapons expertise. Since the late 1980s, North Korea had become one of the leading exporters of missile technology and components (based on Soviet and Chinese designs) to Iraq, Egypt, Iran, Syria, Libya, UAE, Yemen, and Pakistan. For its part, Pakistan purportedly began to amortize its nuclear weapons program by selling nuclear weapons technology abroad. It was then that Pakistan and North Korea purportedly made a deal: A. Q. Khan's blueprints for making nuclear weapons in exchange for ballistic missile technology, based on North Korea's *Nodong* missile.[10]

The Clinton administration at first considered the option of a preemptive strike against the Yŏngbyŏn-kun nuclear facilities but ruled that option out for fear that any fissile material produced by North Korea could be transported elsewhere. North Korea responded to U.S. accusations by threatening to drop out of the NPT treaty. U.S. negotiations with Pyongyang were then assisted by former president Jimmy Carter and consequently led to an ostensible freeze of North Korea's nuclear program in 1994. By 1999 the United States was permitted to inspect a suspected underground nuclear site at Kumchang-ri but found nothing.[11] While he had been able to reach out to normalize relations with Vietnam in 1995, President Clinton was unable to begin the process of normalization of U.S.-North Korean relations, as he had hoped, before the end of his second term in office. During this period, South Korean president Kim Young-sam (1993–1998) feared a U.S.-North Korean arrangement to the exclusion of South Korean interests in reunification.[12]

The Question of China-North Korean Relations

With Washington unable (but not entirely unwilling) to engage with Pyongyang more directly, coupled with a serious decline in U.S.-Chinese relations, as well as the collapse of Russian-North Korean relations, North Korea increasingly became one of the major points of strategic leverage that Beijing could use to pressure U.S. policy in regard to a number of political-economic issues, including the question of China's "reunification" with Taiwan, however defined. For China, the issue of North Korea's political-social-economic stability has been more crucial than Pyongyang's threat to develop nuclear weapons.

Despite their purported close "lips and teeth" relationship during the cold war, post–cold war Sino-North Korean relations have not been entirely good-natured. China itself followed Soviet and Russian footsteps and recognized South Korea in 1992—to take advantage of South Korea's growing market, high technology, and financial investment. China likewise cut its subsidies for the North, but it also placed investment in special economic zones. In such a way, North Korea would remain dependent on China for its energy needs and investment.[13] By 2003 China would ironically displace the United States as South Korea's largest trading partner. This, in effect, made South Korea's export-led economy highly dependent on China's burgeoning consumer market and its quest to achieve a *xiaokang* society in which a majority of the Chinese population becomes "middle class" by Chinese Communist standards.[14] (See Chapter 8.)

Soviet disaggregation in 1991 had further exacerbated North Korean security concerns. In hoping to enhance Russia's economic opportunities, Boris Yeltsin continued steps toward South Korea, as initiated by Gorbachev, and chose Seoul as the first destination for travel abroad in Northeast Asia, as opposed to Tokyo, in part because of the continuing Russo-Japanese dispute over the Kuril Islands and Northern Territories. This change in Russian foreign policy then meant an almost complete collapse of Moscow's strategic leverage over North Korean policies, as indicated by a significant drop in Russian-North Korea trade. Moscow was subsequently left out of important international negotiations on the future of the Korean Peninsula in the 1990s, including the Agreed Framework of 1994 and the four-party talks among North Korea, South Korea, the United States, and China.[15]

By the mid-1990s, Russian foreign minister Yevgeny Primakov attempted to rebuild Russian influence on the Korean Peninsula and throughout Eurasia in general. President Vladimir Putin then sought to restore relations with Pyongyang while simultaneously seeking to maintain cooperative ties with Seoul. Russia has thus looked to sustain a more traditional balanced diplomacy between the two Koreas. By October 2004 Moscow reported a deal to link the Trans-Siberian Railroad with Rajin, a port in northeastern North Korea. In November 2005 Russia proposed a joint Sakhalin oil pipeline project with both North and South Korea. Here, it appears that a tacit Sino-Russian alliance is seeking to obtain hegemony over both Koreas, while simultaneously seeking to reduce Japanese influence, coupled with the strengthening of the Shanghai Cooperation Organization and its expansion to new members (possibly including Pakistan, Mongolia, and Iran). A burgeoning Sino-Russian alliance was made manifest by the March 23, 2006, visit of President Vladimir Putin to Beijing in which Russia and China signed twenty-two cooperation agreements. The latter included significant exchanges in energy cooperation to supply China's burgeoning demand, plus defense technology and military coordination.[16]

On the one hand, the fact that the Soviet Union, Russia, and China opened relations with South Korea helped to exacerbate North Korea's fears of political-military isolation. Pyongyang consequently strove to achieve an autonomous military capability against all potential threats. U.S. estimates of North Korean military expenditure range upward to 25 percent of its GNP. North Korea's quest for both energy and military "independence" has additionally led it to develop both the "peace" and the "war" atom. The "peace" atom is regarded as helping to amortize the costs of a nuclear weapons program (the "war" atom) in addition to helping to provide nuclear technological expertise. Washington has feared that North Korea could eventually export fissionable materials and other nuclear infrastructure despite Pyongyang's claims to the contrary.

Moreover, despite its strong dependence on China, and despite mutual support after the United States (accidentally?) bombed the Chinese embassy in Belgrade in 1999, Pyongyang's relations with Beijing still tended to swing up and down. This fluctuation in Sino-North Korean relations has largely taken place as the North Korean economy itself began to deteriorate. Much as the Soviet Union feared the collapse of East Germany (followed by German reunification and NATO enlargement), China has similarly feared the possibility that North Korea might also collapse. China consequently fears that North Korean collapse will result in a massive refugee crisis, followed by Korean reunification and U.S. military expansion to the north. At present, an estimated 200,000 to 300,000 North Korean refugees reside illegally in northeastern China; North Korea's political economic collapse could send hundreds of thousands more to the borders, which could likewise destabilize the situation in South Korea as well.

Reduced subsidies from the Soviet Union and China (subsidies that had initially permitted North Korea to become highly urbanized, unlike China) additionally woke the North Korean bureaucracy up to the need to seek out greater, trade and international investment, albeit under state controls. North Korea thus joined the UN in 1991, as well as other international organizations and regional forums, and permitted nongovernmental organizations (NGOs) to provide food aid and other forms of assistance. (Joining the UN was a major step forward from the North's perspective, as the Korean War was fought against the North under a

UN flag.) Pyongyang likewise sought out energy assistance from both China and South Korea and set up special economic zones, similar to the Chinese development model.

From this perspective, North Korea has now recognized the need to move away from its concept of "self-reliance" or *juche*, and toward greater "interdependence." While China and South Korea represent the primary rivals in North Korea's opening market, Swiss, Swedish, Irish, and German firms are also beginning to compete. North Korea's agricultural production has made "steady improvement" since 2000, up from three million tons five years ago to 4.4 million tons in 2006, although still falling short of the minimum five million tons needed to feed its people. Despite its repressive nature, the regime has showed some signs of religious liberalization, permitting more churches and temples.[17]

To further reduce its dependence on China in particular, Pyongyang ironically needs to obtain security guarantees and supports from Washington (as well as Russia, Japan, and South Korea). *But to move toward greater interdependence North Korea would require guaranteed economic, agricultural and energy "security"—in addition to multilateral security guarantees that the country would not be attacked or the regime destabilized. The latter could be achieved through the formation of a "regional security community" consisting of a North-South Korean "confederation" backed by the United States, China, Russia, and Japan under a general UN mandate.*

Post-September 11, 2001

In contemporary post-September 11 circumstances, Washington has feared that North Korea, in a desperate financial situation, will sell anything and everything—illicit drugs, ballistic missiles, and nuclear materiel—to any interested buyers, such as *al-Qaida*, despite Pyongyang's disclaimers to the contrary. The Bush administration accordingly demanded that North Korea give up its illegal activities and nuclear program before it will be willing to grant any further aid or concessions. At the same time, the Bush administration's undiplomatic rhetoric and overt actions worked to aggravate the situation. While South Korea feared a U.S.-North Korea rapprochement over its head during the Clinton years, Seoul feared that President Bush's policies would block real chances for North-South cooperation and reconciliation.

In his 2002 State of the Union address, President Bush listed North Korea as a member of the "axis of evil," along with Iran and Iraq. By the summer of 2002, the CIA concluded that North Korea had begun to produce weapons-grade materiel. In November 2002 the United States, Japan, and South Korea then voted to suspend shipments of fuel oil to North Korea. President Bush declared that oil shipments would be cut altogether if the North did not agree to put a halt to its weapons ambitions. At the same time, however, President Bush also issued a statement that the United States had no intention of invading North Korea, so as to indicate that Washington might ultimately provide North Korea with more formal security guarantees.

Such a "promise," however, did not appear very sincere to Pyongyang, which wanted more concrete terms: North Korea demanded the signing of a "nonaggression" pact with the United States and argued that the United States had not kept its side of the 1994 Agreed Framework. The latter agreement had stated that the construction of light-water reactors would be completed in 2003, but the project was years behind schedule. By December 2002 the North threatened to reactivate nuclear facilities at Yŏngbyŏn-kun for energy generation. Pyongyang argued that it had no other option to fulfill its energy needs due to the U.S. decision to halt oil shipments. In January 2003 South Korea asked China if it could use its influence on North Korea. Russia, which had gradually restored its influence, likewise offered to help convince Pyongyang to find a way to put an end to its nuclear program. The IAEA threatened the possibility of sanctions. North Korea then announced it would withdraw from the NPT, but it did not offer explanations as to what extraordinary event justified its withdrawal from the treaty without following the requirements of article 10.1.[18] (This raised the deeper legal question of how the UN and IAEA should respond to a withdrawal from the NPT—without adequate justification.)

South Korean president-elect Roh Moo-hyun proposed a face-to-face meeting with Kim Jong-Il, but this effort failed to break the impasse. In his January 2003 State of the Union address, President Bush declared that "America and the world will not be blackmailed." The IAEA found North Korea in breach of nuclear safeguards and referred the matter to the UN Security Council. At this point, North Korea fired a missile into the sea between South Korea and Japan and then fired a second missile in March. That same month the United States and South Korea engaged in military maneuvers at the same time that the United States intervened militarily in Iraq. The Pentagon placed F-117 Stealth aircraft and B-1 and B-52 heavy bombers in the region on a high state of alert—as an ostensible deterrent against any possible North Korean aggression during the U.S. "preemptive" war against Iraq.

In the immediate aftermath of the U.S. intervention in Iraq in 2003, U.S. neoconservatives continued to press for possible military intervention against North Korea. One option proposed to engage in "regime change" by using extreme military pressures that were designed to confuse the Korean military and then to instigate a *coup d'état* (by means of Operations Plan 5030).[19] Another option foresaw the scenario of engaging in a series of preemptive strikes. Ironically enough, this option would be undertaken should China not be able to use its economic leverage to persuade Kim Jong-Il to give up his nuclear program—or else stage a Chinese-backed "regime change" through a *coup d'état*.[20] The latter scenario of a Chinese-backed *coup d'état* presumed that Beijing truly feared that a nuclear-armed Korea might destabilize regional relations, so that it would be willing to overthrow the "Dear Leader" and the first "Communist dynasty."

China, however, has agreed to pressure North Korea, but only to a point: Beijing has not yet appeared willing to pressure North Korea to the point of rupturing relations or destabilizing the country. In early 2003, largely as a result of the realization that a North Korean nuclear program could provoke both Japan and South Korea into developing a nuclear capability as well, Beijing warned Pyongyang that renewed provocations toward the United States could strain Chinese-North Korean relations. To send a clear message, China then temporarily shut off an oil pipeline from its Daqing oilfields to North Korea for three days in March 2003, officially citing technical problems.[21] (Russia has played similar games using energy as *strategic leverage* versus the Baltic states, Ukraine, Georgia, and Belarus. See Chapter 2.)

For its part, the UN Security Council expressed concern about North Korea's nuclear program, but it did not condemn Pyongyang for pulling out of the NPT. North Korea then signaled that it was ready for direct talks with the United States, which began in Beijing in April 2003. At the time, U.S. officials stated Pyongyang had admitted to possessing nuclear weapons, but that it was ready to destroy its nuclear program in exchange for normalized relations and economic assistance from the United States. Washington, however, refused to engage in direct bilateral talks, arguing that this would encourage "bad behavior." This led China to play the host of a three-party meeting (which excluded Russia and Japan). By May 2003, without any concrete response from Washington as to its demands for diplomatic recognition, Pyongyang threatened to tear up the declaration on the Denuclearization of the Korean Peninsula (the "Joint Declaration") that had established the North-South Joint Nuclear Control Commission (JNCC) and that had been mandated to verify the denuclearization of the peninsula. In July 2003 South Korea claimed that North Korea had started to reprocess a "small number" of the eight thousand spent nuclear fuel rods at its facilities in Yŏngbyŏn-kun.

By August 2003 North Korea then agreed to six-way multilateral talks on its nuclear program; these involved South Korea, the United States, Japan, China, and Russia. At these talks, the United States promised to resume heavy fuel oil and food aid and agreed in principle to a bilateral nonaggression pact. Washington agreed to compensate North Korea for its loss of electric power and both the United States and Japan would normalize relations with Pyongyang. In turn, North Korea would agree in principle to scrap its nuclear program and institute a freeze on its nuclear facilities and materials. Pyongyang would permit inspections and then dismantle its nuclear facilities upon the completion of the light-water reactors promised under the 1994 Agreed Framework. North Korea would also conclude a treaty to halt its missile production and sales. Yet, because the United States then refused to engage in *direct* substantive discussions, North Korea once again threatened to test a nuclear weapon.

By December 2003 North Korea appeared to offer to "freeze" its nuclear program in return for a list of concessions from the United States—in addition to a promised offer of a security guarantee and a nonaggression pact. By the February to June 2004 period, the second and third rounds of multilateral six-party talks took place. Here, the United States made a brand new offer that would permit North Korea to obtain fuel aid—but only if Pyongyang froze, and then dismantled, its nuclear program. In other words, in what seemed to be a new step-by-step approach designed to reduce tensions, the United States was no longer demanding that North Korea completely dismantle its nuclear weapons program before it would address North Korea's security and energy concerns.

The new U.S. offer proposed a two-stage dismantlement and elimination of North Korea's nuclear program in which a general three-month freeze was to be followed by the elimination and removal of all existing weapons as well as the plutonium program, the uranium enrichment program, and all civil nuclear facilities. These programs would be subject to verification by an undefined international body. The United States and other states would promise not to invade or attack; each side would respect the territorial integrity of the other parties. The United States, Japan, and other states would assist North Korea with its energy needs; North Korea could then be shown a route through which it could be removed from the U.S. list of "state sponsors of terrorism." (North Korea had been placed on the list in 1988). Sanctions would be gradually removed.

While leaving open the possibility of further discussion, North Korea rejected the U.S. proposals, arguing that it was being forced to take "unilateral" steps, that U.S. policy in respect to uranium enrichment was "unreasonable," and that the United States had not thoroughly renounced its hostile policy toward North Korea—in deeds as opposed to mere words. North Korea then reiterated its demand for compensation in the form of heavy oil and electricity. At this point, it appeared that North Korea had taken offense to Japanese plans to purchase BMD systems from the United States. North Korea saw the latter systems as a step toward undermining its own missile deterrent: a BMD system could potentially be used in an offensive manner by protecting a preemptive strike.

During these talks, Pyongyang argued that it was "entitled" to possess a powerful nuclear deterrent program to deter a preemptive U.S. attack (as illustrated by the U.S. intervention in Iraq). Pyongyang stated that it was entitled to pursue a "neither confirm nor deny" policy concerning the specifics of its nuclear capabilities (much like the U.S. Navy neither confirms nor denies the presence of nuclear weapons aboard its ships). North Korea likewise raised allegations that South Korea had its own nuclear program—an accusation denied by Seoul (Seoul admitted to having such a program in the 1970s).

In early 2005 the Bush administration dubbed North Korea, along with Belarus, Burma, Myanmar, Zimbabwe, Iran, and Cuba, as "outposts of tyranny," once again offending Pyongyang. By February 10, 2005, North Korea declared itself a nuclear power and pulled out of the six-nation talks, stating that it was "prepared to mobilize all of our military force against any provocative moves by the enemy."[22] Some South Korean analysts stated that North Korea was bluffing: It was too early to consider North Korea as a nuclear power, as it has neither tested the nuclear devices nor provided any solid evidence of their possession.[23] This opened the question as to whether the UN should apply sanctions—or whether the United States would intervene militarily. Later in February 2005, in another of its many flip-flops, Pyongyang indicated that it *might* return to the discussions. The second-term Bush administration then stated that it had new tools to pressure Korea into compliance (targeted financial pressures through the Proliferation Security Initiative), once again raising the threatening rhetoric but backed by actions to go beyond words.

Steps toward Northeast Asia Security Community?

By early 2005 President Bush began to refer to Kim Jong-Il as "Mr. Kim Jong-Il." But this was then interpreted as a joke in response of North Korean demands that their leader be considered with respect, after North Korea was first labeled a member of the "axis of evil" and then as an "outpost of tyranny."[24] In March 2005 U.S. secretary of state Condoleezza Rice proposed the resumption of multilateral talks—but at the same time that the United States and South Korea engaged in annual military maneuvers. As opposed to the assertive unilateral strategies of the first Bush administration, the second-term Bush administration began to somewhat lessen its harsh undiplomatic rhetoric and assert greater diplomatic support for a strategy of multilateralism, largely in the realization that the United States would need as much help as possible from its allies in order to pacify Iraq and deal with other crises.

But here Washington needed to move away from "backdoor" multilateralism (that is largely dependent on China's ability and willingness to pressure North Korea) toward "front-door" multilateralism in which Washington begins to engage North Korea in more-direct talks, while at the same time remaining as much as possible within a multilateral framework. This is the approach Pyongyang itself has demanded since the 1970s, when it sought a formal U.S.-North Korea peace treaty to replace the 1953 armistice that ended the Korean War.[25] (As shall be argued, such an approach should be regarded not only as means to resolve the Korean entanglement, but ultimately that between China and Taiwan.) On September 19, 2005, the fourth round of six-party-talks then agreed to a joint statement aimed at the denuclearization of North Korea and the Korean Peninsula. It was argued that this agreement could set the stage for a "concert of the willing"[26] or what I prefer to call a "regional security community."

At that time, the United States appeared to oppose any "peaceful" nuclear program. Instead, it has offered provisional multilateral security assurances; nonnuclear energy programs; heavy fuel oil; progressive removal of economic sanctions; economic, humanitarian, agricultural, and technical assistance; and, ultimately, normalization of relations in exchange for a clear commitment by North Korea to dismantle its entire nuclear program. Both South Korea and Japan offered significant incentives. Before these talks, Japan and the United States thought the issue should be taken before the UN Security Council; South Korea was opposed.

Here South Korea has begun its own initiative toward the North. The latter started to institute market-economy reforms since 2002, but it will only reform its economy, to the extent that it does not undermine the Kim Jong-Il regime. Wage and price controls have been relaxed in the North, and private markets are being tolerated. South Korean tourists have been flocking across the Demilitarized Zone to Mount Kumgang, which said to be the site of "twelve thousand miracles" and a home of Buddha. Closer North-South relations appear to be very popular among both the population and the corporate South Korean leadership. On March 28, 2006, South and North Korea began building a major $20 million water treatment facility in the North Korean border city of Kaesong.

With North Korean labor costs about half those of China, South Korean firms are increasingly beginning to shift investments from China to North Korea, thus placing investments in special economic zones, such as the Kaesong complex.[27] The North also appeared willing to let South Korean firms explore for minerals and iron ore in exchange for consumer products. These steps represented the best way to forge inter-Korean political-economic ties and to draw North Korea closer to the South and toward the international community. Such steps could also represent the prelude of the formation of a *confederal* Korean state that would link the two Koreas into closer political-economic cooperation, while North Korea continues steps toward reform.

The problem, however, is that either U.S.- or UN-imposed economic sanctions could sever burgeoning inter-Korean trade and cultural ties, in addition to augmenting North Korea's dependence on China. These actions would, more indirectly, increase South Korean export dependence on China's growing domestic market as well.[28] Moreover, it is clear that part of China's strategy of nonideolgical engagement with capitalist South Korea is to take advantage of the desire for better North-South relations in order to better neutralize the South.

Also problematic have been U.S.-South Korean trade relations, which represent two-way trade worth $72 billion and a door for the United States to enter the burgeoning Asian market but which also affect South Korean relations with the North. South Korea has sought increased access for textile producers in the U.S. market, among other trade advantages, while the United States has sought removal of nontariff barriers that have obstructed the access of U.S. automobiles, drugs, and U.S. agricultural products in the Korean market (issues that are being negotiated in the Korea-U.S. Free Trade Agreement, KORUS FTA). Because Korea was once the third largest export market for U.S. beef, the United States also wants to reopen that market, which has become a very sensitive political issue in Korea.[29] In addition, and more directly related to North Korea, the United States does not recognize goods produced in Kaesong as being made in South Korea. Moreover, as it controls the southern half of the Demilitarized Zone (DMZ), the United States could additionally stop traffic from the South to the North. From the U.S. perspective, the potential inclusion of the Kaesong Industrial Complex in the free trade agreement (FTA) negotiations between the United States and South Korea, as requested by Seoul, will raise thorny issues related to the treatment of labor.[30]

In a strongly worded response to U.S. pressures on North Korea, South Korean president Roh warned in January 2006, "The South Korean government does not agree with some in the United States who appear to want to take issue with North Korea's regime, apply pressure, and who occasionally wish for its collapse. . . . If the U.S. government attempts to resolve the problem that way, there will be friction and disagreement between South Korea and the United States."[31]

In this respect, in addition to North Korean intransigence, the U.S. imposition of targeted "sanctions" on North Korea in September 2005 worked to disrupt the six-way talks.[32] From the U.S. perspective, these "sanctions" were intended to target the alleged counterfeiting and distribution of U.S. dollars printed in North Korea by the Banco Delta Asia. Washington consequently ordered all U.S. institutions not to deal with the Banco Delta Asia in Macao, which had also been accused of being a transfer payment center for narcotics and weapons trades. These "sanctions" also led other international banks not to deal with North Korea, so as not to be tainted with an image of corruption. According to David Asher, head of the U.S.-North Korea Working Group, "North Korea is the only government in the world today that can be identified as being actively involved in directing crime as a central part of its national economic strategy and foreign policy. . . . In essence, North Korea has become the Soprano state—a government guided by (Korean) Workers Party leaders, whose actions, attitudes and affiliations increasingly resemble those of an organized-crime family more than a normal nation."[33] Here, U.S. sanctions appeared to be attacking all trade relations of the regime and not just illicit ones. Thus, in North Korea's views, they represented a provocation and a predictable justification for testing its first nuclear weapon. North Korea saw the sanctions as a tool used by neoconservatives within the Bush administration to block regime recognition.[34]

U.S. financial pressures reportedly worked to turn North Korea toward China for billions of dollars in aid and investment; in return, Pyongyang also granted China concessions to North Korean mineral resources. The South Korean Bank of Korea reported that North Korea has become increasingly dependent on China for its economic survival, which could weaken inter-Korean cooperation. Concurrently, North Korean trade with Japan has consistently diminished, thus further deepening Pyongyang's economic dependency on China. Moreover, in October 2005, in its quest to seek out oil concessions throughout the world, China stated that new oil reserves had been uncovered in Bohai Bay, which lies between North Korea and China, and is believed to hold up to 5 billion barrels of oil.[35] At this time, in exchange for its diplomatic and financial support, Beijing reportedly pressured Pyongyang to agree to restart the six-party talks on its nuclear program.[36]

Despite this growing Chinese-North Korean cooperation, which is based on mutual use and not Communist "solidarity," North Korea does not want to become too dependent on China. Thus, on March 9, 2006, in what was dubbed a rare U.S.-North Korean "briefing" (but not a "negotiation") at the U.S. mission to the UN, North Korean spokesmen made four demands that the United States: (1) remove "financial sanctions," (2) institute a joint U.S-North Korean task force to examine counterfeiting, (3) give North Korea access to the U.S. banking system, and (4) provide North Korea with technical assistance to help identify counterfeit bills.

The meeting at the UN took place as North Korea fired surface to air missiles (reportedly "accidentally") toward either China or toward the Sea of Japan. At this time, in a strong criticism of Bush administration policy, in which it was purported that Vice President Dick Cheney and Secretary of Defense Donald H. Rumsfeld had severely restricted U.S. chief negotiator Christopher Hill's freedom to negotiate, Rep. Jim Leach (R-IA), the chairman of the House International Relations subcommittee on Asia and the Pacific, accused the White House of giving U.S. negotiators "constrained options" and urged a more creative approach. These would include direct talks with Pyongyang, in recognition that the six-party approach appears "moribund." As Representative Leach put it: "It's time for the United States to lead . . . [rather than] . . . indebting us to the diplomacy of countries that may have different interests." Leach furthermore suggested that the United States and North Korea should establish "liaison offices" in each other's capitals.[37]

By March 23 a major strategic breakthrough for the burgeoning Sino-Russian "Eurasian" alliance took place following the visit of Russian president Putin to Beijing. Russia and China signed twenty-two cooperation agreements, which included significant exchanges in energy cooperation to supply China's burgeoning demand, plus deals involving defense technology and military coordination, in addition to the expansion of the Shanghai Cooperation Organization to include more states, possibly Pakistan, Mongolia, and Iran. The end of March 2006 then saw a return to saber rattling as North Korea warned that "The US should know that a pre-emptive strike is not its monopoly" during U.S.-South Korean military exercises (Reception, Staging, Onward Movement, and Integration). The annual U.S.-South Korean war games in 2006 involved the nuclear-powered aircraft carrier USS *Abraham Lincoln* (as pointed out by the North Korean press); the 2005 exercises had likewise involved the participation of the nuclear powered USS *Kitty Hawk.*

As the six-party talks continued to stall, the United States refused to engage in a more "front-door" approach to multilateralism and toward the formation of a Northeast Asian "regional security community" (that is, until February 2007). The "packaged approach" of attempting to lump together the issues of nuclear weapons, human rights, kidnapping, and illicit black market activities appeared moribund.[38] What was needed, however, was a U.S.-North Korean dialogue that focused on the question of nuclear weapons and security guarantees and then took up the other issues once more-direct U.S.-North Korean ties were established. The proposal of Representative Leach to establish U.S.-North Korean "liaison offices" thus represented a commonsense starting point to breaking the dangerous U.S.-North Korean impasse and to bring North Korea into a "regional security community."

The "hermit kingdom" of North Korea has made some strides to open itself up to what it considers a hostile outside world. Yet, one of the key problems in dealing with the nuclear question is that it is unrealistic to expect North Korea to abandon its entire "peaceful" nuclear program. (This latter appeared particularly true given a looming crisis in terms of rising oil prices following the 2003 Iraq War and given that tensions with Iran could result in yet another steep rise in world oil prices.) At the same time, it is not unreasonable to expect North Korea to accept full international inspections if the United States ultimately will accept the North Korean nuclear program for "peaceful" purposes. (Yet as is the case for for Iran, the problem will be how to wean North Korea away from nuclear power once alternative energy sources become more available. See Chapter 4.)

It has largely been the United States and Japan that have opposed North Korea's nuclear program, arguing that it would make it easier for North Korea to divert its "peaceful" program at a later date to nuclear weaponry. China, Russia, and South Korea have, however, accepted the argument that North Korea should be able to possess a peaceful nuclear program in principle. Conversely, Washington and Seoul might have reached a common agreement to a "peaceful" nuclear energy program in North Korea at some time in the future, but only after Pyongyang completely dismantles its existing nuclear materials and facilities, rejoins the NPT, and accepts inspectors from the International Atomic Energy Agency. The bone of contention has appeared, however, to be the nuclear reactor at Yŏngbyŏn-kun. It was believed that North Korea would probably argue that this facility should be frozen rather than completely dismantled, if it is to have a right to peaceful nuclear energy in the future.[39]

China, the United States, and North Korea

Of the six states involved in the multilateral talks, which do not at all agree on a broad range of questions, it is the United States and China that represent the two states that possess the most important influence on North Korean behavior and actions and that need to develop a common strategy. Getting the United States and China to see eye to eye, however, is also, at least in part, indirectly dependent on U.S. relations with Taiwan and the question of Taiwanese "independence." China's main concern in supporting North Korea is to prevent its collapse in addition to using the North to boost its own influence in South Korea and throughout the Asian region in general. North Korea provides Beijing with bargaining leverage with respect to Taiwan: China tacitly argues that it will help the United States in regard to North Korean nuclear weapons if the United States strongly opposes Taiwanese "independence" and ultimately accepts the "reunification" of China and Taiwan, however defined. China had consequently been reluctant to apply tougher pressures and had argued that it cannot be more effective as long as the United States itself does not engage in a more flexible approach.[40] Beijing had generally not been keen on doing more than simply mediating the dispute (that is until North Korea tested an atomic device in late 2006).

China has thus far supported the "Ukrainian model" of regional security accords in which the United States and Russia used a mix of pressures and rewards or concessions to convince Ukraine to give up its nuclear weapons capability left over after the Soviet collapse. Once Ukraine agreed to give up some of the military aspects of its nuclear capabilities (but keeping its "peaceful" nuclear and ballistic missile programs), Kiev was then granted multilateral U.S.-UK-French-Russian and Chinese "security guarantees." (See Chapters 2 and 10.) China has argued that this basic approach can be applied to North Korea as well. The United States thus far has disagreed. (It should be noted that the 1994 Ukrainian nuclear deal did not prevent the Orange Revolution and "regime change" a decade later.)

The United States has, by contrast, proposed the Libyan model. In negotiations that began before the essentially unilateral U.S. intervention in Iraq, Libya had agreed in December 2003 to eliminate all materiel and programs resulting in the production of nuclear, or other internationally proscribed weapons, in exchange for a step-by-step process of normalization of relations with the United States. The agreement likewise permitted U.S. companies to explore Libyan oil reserves, but Washington did not initially take Libya off the State Department list of countries that support terrorism.[41]

It is highly ironic that after more than a year of refusing to talk since the September 2005 accords that were cut off just a few days later when the United States imposed "sanctions," U.S.-North Korean relations ostensibly took a sudden turn for the better, despite (or because of) North Korea's nuclear test on October 9, 2006.[42]

Proposals: Going beyond the February 2007 Accords

The subsequent February 2007 accords represent a major step toward confronting the security of Northeast Asia: (1) denuclearization of the Korean Peninsula, (2) normalization of DPRK-U.S. relations, (3) normalization of DPRK-Japan relations, (4) economy and energy cooperation, and (5) Northeast Asia peace and security mechanism. But these accords will need to go much further if war is to be averted in Asia, as the United States likewise needs to address Chinese-Japanese-Taiwanese tensions as they relate to the Korean Peninsula. The dilemma is that the Japanese have been the most reticent to engage fully with North Korea as well as with China—and South Korea. (See Chapter 8.)

To obtain Beijing's support in particular, and to coordinate U.S.-Chinese strategy toward North Korea, the United States will need to implement a detailed multilaterally backed plan of economic, agricultural, high-tech, and energy assistance involving Japan and South Korea and possibly the EU, plus assurances of a guaranteed fuel supply. To achieve full North Korean compliance on the nuclear question and convince it to put its nuclear program under international safeguards, the United States will thus need to engage in confidence-building measures and incentives, as well as *conditional security assurances* that ultimately lead to *stronger security guarantees* for Pyongyang through some form of a "multilateral security and defense agreement" along the lines of the Ukrainian model under a general UN mandate. The United States will consequently need to continue its efforts to engage more openly in the process, through "front-door" multilateralism, with the support of South Korea.

Symbolic measures, such as unilateral U.S. troop reductions in South Korea, are not sufficient; these steps, which have been coupled with an increase in South Korean "burden sharing" and greater military "self reliance" under the "Cooperative Self-Defense Pursuit Plan"[43] can be interpreted as a means to cut U.S. losses in case of a preemptive North Korean attack. These reforms have been taking place at the same time that the United States has been focusing on potential threats outside of the two Koreas and has been strengthening defense cooperation with Japan, in effect forming a joint command by bringing together U.S. Forces Japan and Japan's Self-Defense Force. Moreover, U.S. military strategy no longer relies on large-scale troop commitments following the U.S military-technological innovation, what is called the "Revolution in Military Affairs." Yet, such troop cutbacks raise South Korean fears in symbolical terms that the United States might not commit itself to the defense of South Korea. (The United States has stationed nearly thirty thousand troops in Korea, while South Korea has provided the largest contingent of troops in Iraq after the United Kingdom.)

While the United States transformed its command structure and defense relationship with both Japan and South Korea, in accord with the Revolution in Military Affairs, a North Korean refusal to draw back its forward-deployed forces would remain absolutely unacceptable. Roughly 50 to 70 percent of North Korea's military is deployed within forty miles of the DMZ. Both sides would need to compromise and build confidence by engaging in verifiable conventional force reductions.[44] Here, multilaterally financed provisions would eventually be needed to find employment for North Korean military personnel so as to help reduce the North's excessive military spending.

By working to normalize relations with North Korea and to establish overlapping *security assurances* leading to *security guarantees*, Washington (pressed by the 2004 North Korean Human Rights Act) would, at some point, need to engage in *real dialogue* with Pyongyang concerning its severe violation of human rights (involving an estimated ten political prisons and about twenty reeducation and work camps) as well as its support for drug smuggling and "terrorist" activities. Russia, China, and South Korea, however, have all been adamantly opposed to introducing the human rights issue in general, and the issues concerning the abduction Japanese citizens in particular, into the six-party talks. Moreover, if the United States did bring up the issue of counterfeit currency in the six-party context, then Tokyo, which is under domestic pressure to raise the issue, might likewise want to bring the abduction issue up as well. (In February 2006 Tokyo stated that it was set to negotiate with North Korea about possible diplomatic normalization, financial assistance, and compensation as well as economic cooperation—but only once the abduction and security issues are properly addressed.) Here, however, Tokyo has not yet resolved the issue of Korean "comfort women" or slave labor used in Japanese factories during World War II. North Korea might expect as much as $10 billion in compensation.[45]

Despite the severity of the problem, Washington should prevent the human rights issue, as well as the questions of counterfeiting and abductions, from blocking the full normalization of U.S.-North Korean relations. The question of human rights (which would open a can of worms dating from before World War II and the Korean War, involving both the United States and Japan) should thus be dealt with in separate bilateral talks after nuclear talks or else through the UN. Thus, rather than pressing for "regime change," U.S.-North Korean diplomatic engagement, coupled with North Korean acceptance of political-economic reforms and international assistance, can ultimately work to restore trust in the attempt to gradually wean North Korea away from use of work camps and illicit black market activities and help to upgrade North Korean living conditions, in addition to ultimately eliminating North Korea's nuclear weapons.[46]

The Question of Reunification

Assuming the two sides can finally negotiate their deep differences and overcome distrust, the very manner in which North and South Korea "reunify" is problematic. Neither Beijing (nor Tokyo) wants to see a strong unified Korea. As an estimated three million ethnic Koreans live in northeastern China, including from 200,000 to 300,000 illegal, ill-treated Korean refugees, China fears the possibility that a unified North Korea might press its irredentist claims with respect to the 1909 Gando Convention in which colonial Japan ceded the territory of Gando—a portion of Korea's Chosun Kingdom—to China. This agreement established the current border between China and North Korea.[47]

Moreover, with the assertion of China's "one nation policy," historical ethnological disputes between South Korea and China have erupted over the nature of the ancient Koguryo (Goguryeo) Kingdom (37 BCE–CE 668). The latter had expanded into almost all of Manchuria and into part of Inner Mongolia, likewise taking the Seoul region from the Baekje kingdom and making Goguryeo one of the great powers in East Asia of that era.[48] By consequence, as a means to preclude potential Korean irredentist claims (as well as Chinese opposition to Uighur, Tibetan, Mongolian, Bhutanese, and Nepalese nationalism and Taiwanese demands for "independence"), Beijing might demand the implementation of a demilitarized buffer zone with a "unified" Korea. China would also oppose the deployment of U.S. troops north of the current DMZ—although the deployment of UN peacekeepers might prove acceptable.

Another, more realistic option would consequently be to work toward a reassociated *confederal* solution that would avoid an expensive and provocative "buyout" of the North by the South and that would likewise allay Chinese fears of possible U.S. military expansion north of the Yalu, much as NATO expanded into east Germany once Germany unified. A *confederal* approach could likewise mitigate potential revisionist claims of a unified Korea to the territory of Gando and seek out gradual reforms designed to bring the North and South into greater political-economic cooperation, as a *transition* to a North-South Korean *confederation*.

On the one hand, China's fears of North Korean collapse provide an incentive for Chinese cooperation with the United States, Japan, Russia, and South Korea. Although Chinese relations appear to be growing tighter with North Korea, it appears dubious that China can help stabilize and develop North Korea alone. A socially and economically unstable nuclear North Korea that provokes Japan and possibly South Korea itself into obtaining nuclear weapons and BMD defenses does not serve China's regional interests. The fact that China and South Korea, as well as Japan and Russia, have been involved in the bargaining means that North Korea would alienate its leading suppliers of agricultural, energy and financial assistance—if it continued to press for nuclear weapons development. On the one hand, the multilateral approach helps to keep North Korea honest; on the other, it helps to moderate U.S. policy as well.

At the same time, however, if Washington does *not* move past its "backdoor" strategy and thus continue to engage in direct relations with Pyongyang, Beijing will continue to engage in a "sweet and sour" strategy. Beijing could promise assistance to Pyongyang (and tacitly back its nuclear-weapons program) in exchange for a retraction of U.S. backing for Taipei. From this perspective, U.S. normalization of relations with North Korea can help to stabilize and then work to develop and reform North Korea. While working with China, U.S. recognition of North Korea would also tend to undercut (but not eliminate) Chinese leverage and influence in both North and South Korea. A U.S. opening to North Korea can thus indirectly weaken one of China's primary strategic levers that Beijing could use to pressure U.S. policy in support of Taiwan.

The primary problem, however, will be for the United States and China to work in concert to resolve *both* the North Korean and Taiwanese issues (to which can be added the Iran nuclear question as well).[49] From this perspective, it remains an open question as to whether the "reunification" of both North and South Korea and that of China and Taiwan could take place in terms of a reassociated "confederal" relationship in which the United States and South Korea assist North Korea to reform, along with the other interested powers, and in which the United States (or the UN Security Council) could likewise help negotiate a "confederal" power-sharing relationship between China and Taiwan. The considerable dilemma will consequently be for the United States and China to find a fair and appropriate formula to resolve both crises, without fear that either side is taking advantage of the other.

Averting War

Should the February 2007 six-party-talks ultimately fail and should North Korea opt to develop a sufficient nuclear-weapons deterrent, the first step for the United States might be to strengthen the Proliferation Security Initiative (PSI) and then seek to block North Korean trade in counterfeit dollars, illicit drugs, and military technology, a policy that could have destabilizing effects on the increasingly isolated North, pressing it closer to China. At the same time, it is not clear that China is willing or able to support a failing state in the near to long term. By contrast, Washington could also adopt an ostrich-like "quasi-isolationist" policy in which it looks the other way as Japan and South Korea develop their own nuclear weapons and preemptive strike capabilities.[50] But the latter "strategy" would result in a destabilizing conventional and nuclear arms race that is in no one's interests and that could ultimately drag the region, as well as the United States, into major conflict at a later date. From this perspective, nuclear weapons do not necessarily deter conflict, but they could theoretically change the ways and choice of options in which a war would be fought.

Should Washington permit the rearmament of the region in response to the North Korean program—consequently resulting in "insecurity-security dialectic"—overt military conflict would thus become increasingly probable, particularly if tensions between China and Taiwan rise as well. Here, Chinese-Taiwanese relations have begun to heat up once again following the decision of Taiwan's president Chen Shui-bian to scrap Taiwan's National Unification Council on February 27, 2006. There is a further danger that Chinese hard-liners could conclude that a nuclear North Korea provides a diversion from China's plans to force reunification with Taiwan by use of its own expanding cruise and ballistic missile force, as illustrated by the 1995–1996 Taiwan Missile crisis, which was intended by Beijing to protest Taiwanese steps toward "independence." This issue is furthermore complicated by the fact that the Bush administration has begun to tolerate Indian nuclear weapons (New Delhi is a potential Chinese rival). From this perspective, both North Korea and China appear to be using similar forms of "missile diplomacy" and strategic leverage for differing purposes. A number of possible war scenarios have been envisioned in regard to the Korean Peninsula as well as to the possibility of war between the United States and China.[51]

If tensions continue to mount concerning Taiwan, it is therefore possible that Chinese hard-liners could ultimately decide that a minimal North Korean nuclear weapons capability might actually prove useful in diverting attention away from Chinese missiles pointed toward Taiwan.[52] And should North Korea ultimately collapse in political and economic terms, Chinese military intervention remains an option to preclude U.S.-South Korean steps to take control of the region. The risk then is that even a minimal North Korean nuclear deterrent would continue to cause repercussions in Seoul and Tokyo, most likely resulting in rearmament of the entire region at the same time that South Korean and

Japanese disputes over the Dokdo and Takeshima islands do not auger well for defense cooperation between Seoul and Tokyo. (Here, South Korea and Japan's dispute over the Dokdo and Takeshima islands appears to represent a significant test case for the "democratic peace theory" with regard to the question whether two democratic states can necessarily resolve their differences peacefully. In April–May 2006 Seoul sent twenty gunboats to the region to prevent Tokyo from surveying the islands, which possess rich fishing waters and potential offshore gas and oil reserves.[53])

Already North Korea's ballistic missile capabilities (as well as those of Russia and China) have provoked U.S.-Japanese BMD cooperation, coupled with Chinese counterthreats. Following the North Korean 1998 testing of the Taepodong missile over Honshu Island, a number of Japanese defense officials argued that Tokyo should consider the development of a preemptive strike capability.[54] In July 2006 North Korea broke its previous promise not to test missiles, yet its Taepodong-2 launch failed forty seconds after launch. (The series of missile tests might have represented a protest to the June 26 decision of Tokyo and Washington to deploy Patriot interceptor missiles on U.S. military bases in Japan.) Here Japan accelerated deployment of a sea-based TMD system to be deployed on Aegis destroyers and a land-based Patriot system, both scheduled to be completed by the end of fiscal year 2011. While Japan called for an emergency UN Security Council meeting to respond to the tests, the United States affirmed its commitment to six-party talks, but refused to give into North Korean demands for bilateral negotiations leading to a security accord.[55] Despite the return of IAEA inspectors to North Korean facilities in June 2007, Japan was still cautious, particularly after a series of short-range missile tests in late June 2007. Tokyo continues to insist on making the normalization of relations with North Korea dependent on the settlement of claims over Pyongyang's program of abducting Japanese citizens for its spy program in the 1970s and 1980s.

Furthermore, if Pyongyang remains convinced that Washington intends to engage in "regime change" at some point in the future, and if Washington believes that Pyongyang will continue to engage in the sales of illicit drugs, counterfeit dollars, and ballistic missile technology, if not nuclear know-how, *even if* the United States reaches out toward a rapprochement, then it will be very difficult for the two sides to establish confidence. To make the situation even more complex, the fate of North and South Korea is still, at least partly, tied to the fate of the tempestuous China-Taiwan-Japan relationship in geostrategic terms.

If, however, on the more positive side, the United States and China can reach a common accord on the North Korean question, they could also reach a common accord with respect to Taiwan, in which the United States could attempt to facilitate a cross-straits agreement. U.S. rapprochement with North Korea would ironically provide the United States with greater strategic leverage vis-à-vis China in resolving the Taiwan question diplomatically. It will consequently take a earnest effort on the part of the United States to thoroughly engage with North Korea in an attempt to inspire trust on all sides through "front-door" multilateral diplomacy so as to promote a North Asia "security community" that would guarantee Korean "reunification" in terms of a "confederal" relationship—as the major step toward peace for the entire region.

CHAPTER 8

China and Blue-water Dreams:
Toward a Sino-Russian Alliance?

River Elegy

Before the Chinese government crackdown on Tiananmen Square and throughout the country, a controversial film entitled *River Elegy* was aired that argued that a "benevolent" authoritarianism could ultimately lead China out of its contemporary crisis.[1] Such a "new authority" could do so by transforming China into a sea-trading mercantile nation, with naval and military power equal to its global competitors. The film asserted China's right to engage in a "peaceful rise" to regional and world power status from a democratic-nationalist perspective.

Yet, will China be able to rise without provoking conflict as has the rise of previous major powers in history? The late nineteenth century Sino-Japanese war resulted in defeat of China and Japanese seizure of Taiwan, despite the efforts of China's nineteenth-century self-strengthening movement to rebuild China's economy and military power. Although the status of Taiwan subsequently changed, the People's Republic of China never gave up its demands for unification, following the Maoist victory in the civil war and Chiang Kai-Chek's retreat to the "beautiful island." Or will Beijing gradually integrate itself into the global political economic and security system, perhaps ultimately forging a regional security system in Asia in cooperation with the United States, Japan, and Russia, as well as the two Koreas?

The answer to these questions lies in China's post–Tiananmen Square claims to "peaceful development" and to what extent the United States and the other major powers can *channel* China's rise to power through mutual accommodation. The fact, however, that China has not yet renounced the potential use of force has continued to generate regional, if not global tensions (neither the administrations of Richard Nixon nor of Jimmy Carter pressed Beijing to renounce force as a condition for U.S. diplomatic recognition). Because Asia is much more strategically and economically integrated with Europe and the

United States now than in the nineteenth century, the rise of China not only could upset Chinese relations with Japan, but could negatively affect U.S., Russian, and global relations as well.

The essential thesis argued here is that the Chinese government's Tiananmen Square crackdown represented a two-forked strategy. The Chinese Communist party saw Chinese "democrats" as backed by the confluence of two international forces: The reforms engendered by Mikhail Gorbachev's *glasnost* (opening) and *perestroika* (restructuring) and by U.S.-style "democratic liberalization." In the effort to prevent the feared rise of a Chinese version of the Solidarity movement (as in Communist Poland), and to forestall social movements in support of "bourgeois liberalization" and multiparty democracy, the Chinese Communist party opted for the June 4, 1989, Tiananmen Square crackdown.

In their efforts to sustain single-party predominance, the Communist Party subsequently engaged in a dual-forked "sour and sweet" strategy of repression and co-optation of the Chinese democratic reform movement by means of emphasizing economic restructuring and patriotic nationalism (if not xenophobia), and by suppressing efforts to press for democratic opening, rule of law, and transparency. In essence, the Chinese Communist Party elite has sought to co-opt elements of "democracy" and "liberalism" that suit its own interests.

Promises of Domestic Growth

Rather than taking the risks of engaging in much-needed political, social, legal, and economic domestic reforms (that could potentially overturn Communist Party rule), the Chinese Communist elite thus engaged in a risky mix of repression and co-optation in the post–Tiananmen Square era. On the domestic policy side, this assertive patriotic nationalism under the guise of "Socialist Spiritual Civilization" seeks to divert attention from official corruption and mismanagement, greatly widening economic disparities, horrid working conditions, and real demographic and ecological crises. The latter policy represents a drive for greater individual wealth and expansion of the Gross National Product—resulting in a speculative foraging of the world for *guaranteed* access to oil and gas resources. China's development goal for the next twenty years is to reach a $4 trillion GDP with a per capita income of $3,000 for its *xiokang*, or "middle class," goals.

On the foreign policy side, it means orienting the population toward the external "threat" posed by Taiwanese "secession" among other "threats" to China's stability and territorial integrity, such as demands for Tibetan secession (seen as backed by the United States and India) and Uighur independence (which is now blamed on pan-Islamist groups). China regards the Taiwanese "independence" movement as backed by the United States and Japan; Beijing also fears that its dependence on overseas sources of energy could possibly be interdicted by a forward U.S. naval deployment (or that of Japan or India) in case of conflict— unless it can protect those supplies itself. (China claims it spent about $35 billion on the military in 2006, or 1.5 percent of its Gross Domestic Product, but it is probably closer to 2.7 percent of GDP in 2003—while the United States spends 3.7 percent of GDP with a vastly larger GDP.)[2]

China's 2006 National Defense White Paper stresses that China's military—which is to be capable of winning digitalized warfare by 2050—must be able to guarantee China's economic and energy security and defend China's territorial integrity, which includes unifying with Taiwan and asserting control over disputed regions of the South China and East China seas. While the White Paper tries to allay fears of China's rising power potential, and although it emphasizes the doctrine of no-first-use of nuclear weaponry (unlike the doctrines of both the United States and Russia), it also demands improvement in both the defensive *and* offensive capabilities of the People's Liberation Army (PLA) air force, the range and accuracy of its strategic missile forces, and the ability of its blue-water navy to develop long-range, all-weather capabilities.[3] The PLA is consequently intended to win the high-tech communication and information-based warfare in the mid-twenty-first century by means of President Hu Jintao's post-Maoist dictum, "revolutionary heroism and scientific spirit."[4]

The Chinese elite has attempted to foster the glorified image of "Socialist Spiritual Civilization" (a term developed in the mid-1980s after Deng Xiaoping's attacks on bourgeois liberal "spiritual pollution") in the effort of Communist Party elites to sustain their own social-political *predominance* in manipulating Chinese patriotic nationalism and in pressing China's irredentist claims. Here, the concept of Socialist Spiritual Civilization seeks to blend aspects of China's vast history with the contemporary form of oligarchic Chinese Communist leadership, what can be called "socialist *prebendalism*." The Chinese civilization concept thus preceded Samuel Huntington's "clash of civilizations" but is one manipulated by Chinese elites for their own purposes and thus is not necessarily inherent to the culture itself.

If, however, there is a potential "clash" between China and the United States, it is not based on conflicting "civilizational values" in Huntington's sense but rather on an inhuman economy that has based itself on very cheap labor and long working hours with little-to-no environmental controls. The fact that Chinese workers are generally forced to work fourteen to sixteen hours per day provides unfair competition with the United States and Europe. Indications of growing civil society dissent in China (if official statistics can be trusted) have been shown in the significant rise in the number of "mass incidents" from 8,700 in 1993 to 74,000 in 2004, combined with a significant rise in the number of protestors involved (860,000 in 1993 to 3 million in 2003). There have been a number of violent clashes between police and demonstrators over issues such as mass evictions to make way for new construction, illegal land seizures, relocations from dam areas (such as the massive Three Gorges Dam), environmental pollution, unpaid social entitlements, and administrative corruption, among other concerns. Roughly two hundred protests take place daily, which is four times the amount from ten years ago. At the same time, however, the number of individuals arrested for "counterrevolutionary" crimes seems to have declined.[5]

Prior to hosting the 2008 Olympics, Beijing promised to make its legal system more impartial; yet many advocates of greater "openness"—including lawyers (who call themselves "rights defenders" devoted to helping peasants or other people left behind in the economic boom to fight official corruption, land grabs, polluting industries or unpaid wages), writers, academics, and grass-roots organizers—have faced persecution. The Chinese government has additionally closed down online forums and Web sites and banned terms or subjects that domestic Internet search engines must block. Here, to continue to sustain the Communist Party in power will require that it move from the "reflective repression" of any challenge to the regime's authority to a policy of "strategic repression"—which seeks to repress only those movements that represent the greatest threat to the regime's authority.[6]

In terms of protecting labor rights, the focus of Chinese union organization has been on Multinational Corporations (MNCs), and not indigenous Chinese firms. But this has raised the question as to how union activities would affect the investment policies of MNCs in that local unions are controlled by local governments that have been keener in attracting foreign investment than in protecting workers.[7] (Communist Party leaders have previously opposed the establishment of independent unions, yet the All-China Federation of Trade Unions [ACFTU] set up branches at twenty-two Wal-Mart supercenters in China in 2006, in part because Wal-Mart had refused to accept the state-controlled unions from the outset.)

In terms of an economic "threat" to U.S. and European interests, China continues to use subsidies in a number of public sector industries, most crucially, with respect to its currency. In this regard, Chinese foreign exchange reserves topped that of the United States' $1.2 trillion in March 2007, making China the world's largest holder of reserves. In part because China's excess of exports over imports from the United States reached a record $24.4 billion in October 2006, the post-November 2006 democratic-controlled Congress is likely to be concerned with China's widening trade surplus and the yuan-U.S. dollar exchange rate.[8] If the administration of George W. Bush were to agree that the Chinese exchange rate manipulation constituted a "subsidy," the United States could, in theory, take China to the World Trade Organization for violating trade pacts because of "the effective subsidy that an undervalued currency provides for Chinese firms that focus on exporting rather than producing for the domestic market."[9]

The U.S. Treasury Department, however, softened its tone in its semi-annual report in June 2007 and argued that China's build up of reserves (in part because of its high savings rate) has been flooding the country with liquidity and thus raising risks of a "boom-bust" cycle that might harm the global economy. For its part, the U.S Congress threatened tariffs and sanctions in the effort to open the Chinese economy to U.S. products, while the United States has ironically depended upon Beijing to buy up the monstrous U.S. debt and has also urged China's investment in the U.S. economy with its massive $1.2 trillion foreign exchange reserves.

After the 1997 Asian financial crisis, Beijing, however, fears that too rapid an appreciation of its currency will lead to a surge in cheap food imports that would undercut Chinese farm producers and lead to greater migration from the interior to the coastal regions and thus put China's development further out of kilter. Appreciation could also lead to greater speculation on its currency and shifts in interest rates. The fact that much of China's $1.2 trillion in foreign exchange reserves is invested in U.S. dollar-denominated debt, such as U.S. treasuries and government bonds, has raised not entirely exaggerated fears that China might ultimately dump its dollar holdings, thus undermining the U.S. (and world) political economy. That roughly $4.8 trillion of U.S. debt (out of a more than a $8.3 trillion of debt up from $5.7 trillion in 2000 before the September 11 attacks) is considered public debt raises real risks of economic collapse—if the United States has any major confrontation with China (more likely than with Japan). This is because much of that debt is owed to the public and foreign lenders, primarily Japan and China, which will continue to demand higher risk premiums in the form of higher interest rates as the debt increases, or threaten to buy euros.[10] Although the collapse of the U.S. (and world!) economy would not be in China's better interests, and provides reason for Chinese cooperation in economic matters, the geostrategic dilemma is that U.S. trade disputes with China and rising U.S. indebtedness weakens U.S. bargaining leverage with China over Taiwan, North Korea, human rights and other issues, such as currency subsidies, piracy, and copyright infringement.

The final concern is that the Chinese leadership hopes to catch up with wasteful U.S. and European living standards and lifestyles, with a population of more than 1.3 billion, in which its projected consumer demand has been boosted by the rise in automobile ownership. This fact has contributed to the significant surge in Chinese demand for oil in 2006, resulting in higher prices worldwide—as China seeks alternatives to polluting coal for electricity generation, combined with the fact that the big cities are frequently hit by energy shortages.

To meet its massive energy demand, in addition to scouring the world for oil reserves, China has invested in corn produced ethanol alcohol as an alternative energy source, which has purportedly resulted in 30–40 percent price hikes in corn feed and pork over the past year in 2006, as corn is otherwise used for food and animal feed. China is now the third largest producer of ethanol after Brazil and the United States (see Chapter 9). Moreover, China intends to spend at least $50 billion to build thirty-two nuclear plants by 2020 and could purportedly seek to build an astronomical two hundred to three hundred more plants by 2050.[11]

In 2003, President Hu Jintao (who heads the military as well as the ruling Communist Party) had ordered Chinese firms to seek secure oil supplies abroad, preferably ones that could not be blocked by the United States in case of conflict over Taiwan.[12] China has consequently sought to expand its blue-water naval capabilities to protect its growing oil imports through the Indian Ocean and Strait of Malacca, through which 80 percent of its oil imports transit. In January 2006 Beijing stated that it might build its own aircraft carrier.

Sino-Russian (and EU?) Military Cooperation

China has primarily looked to Russia for arms because of a worldwide embargo during the cold war and one specifically imposed on China after the June 1989 Tiananmen Square crackdown. Although China's military purchases from Russia slowed in recent years (because Beijing is able to domestically produce some of the components initially built by Russia and has made progress in developing its own weapon systems, including supersonic cruise missiles, as well as J-10 fighter jets said to be superior to Russian Su-27s),[13] Russian military sales to China are still above $2 billion a year. China has imported Russian-made S-300 air-defense missile systems, combat and transport aircraft, submarines, torpedo boats, and land-based radars. In March 2006 China and Russia signed twenty-two cooperation agreements, which included significant exchanges in energy cooperation to supply China's burgeoning demand, plus deals involving defense technology and military coordination. In addition, China and Russia considered expanding the Shanghai Cooperation Organization to include more states, including Pakistan, Mongolia, and Iran, and possibly India, which are presently observers. (See also Chapter 6.)

Here, it appears that Russia's inability to check NATO enlargement plus stop "colored revolutions" in Georgia, Ukraine, and Kyrgyztan (combined with the prospects of common interests in central Asia and Mongolia) has led an increasingly autocratic Russia and Communist China to move even closer together—after Bejing opted for the repression of its own form of "colored" revolution at Tiananmen in June 1989. Russia has been training Chinese military officers; in August 2006 Russia and China held their first bilateral joint military exercises involving ten thousand troops near Vladivostok, which included an amphibious landing in eastern China near Taiwan.[14] Sino-Russian military maneuvers have raised the prospect of a real Sino-Russian alliance—in which Russia seeks to deflect China's attention from its thinly populated Far East (and toward potential confrontation with the United States and Japan).

In courting the French, which have engaged in naval cooperation with China, Beijing has also attempted to break the arms embargo with the Europeans. In January 2004 the Eiffel Tower glowed red the evening of Chinese president Hu Jintao's visit to Paris. France has demanded the right to sell selected arms and Airbus passenger planes to China with the argument that greater arms cooperation through a "code of conduct" will somehow moderate Beijing's aims with respect to Taiwan. More likely, however, French arms sales would provide China a European option for arms (in a EU-Chinese "Red Eiffel Tower" alliance), thus cutting into Russian arms sales and influence but not weakening Beijing's drive for unification with Taipei. European arms sales would hence cut into Russian sales, concurrently raising Russian fears of isolation and "encirclement" at a time when Moscow might fear losing its military technological advantage over Beijing.

As China has not renounced the right to use force to unify with Taiwan, Chinese objectives appear to be: (1) to prevent the Taiwanese "independence" movement from instigating new movements of secession within the People's Republic, (2) to eliminate Taiwan's export competition with China, (3) to assert control over the Spratly Islands and other off-shore oil reserves and (4) to eliminate a potential strategic-military threat from the island and to be in a better position to defend China from potential rivals. Chinese threats to control Taiwan militarily (with access to deep water for its submarines) furthermore represent a challenge to sea lines of communication and energy routes to Japan from the Persian Gulf—should the People's Liberation Army move into the country.

Russia-China-Japan-India

While Chinese businesses scour the globe for energy resources and markets, China's state-owned oil firms have begun drilling for gas in the East China Sea, just west of the line that Japan regards as its border, which is seen as "only a prelude of the game between China and Japan in the arena of international energy."[15] The major problem is that Japan has no significant oil and gas resources and is dependent on imported energy, with approximately 85 percent of its oil purchased from the Middle East. Much of the renewed tension between Japan and China (over the Daioyo/Senkaku islands for example) results from a dispute over the boundaries of "exclusive economic zones" (EEZs). China argues the boundaries start on the edge of the submerged continental shelf, while Japan insists an EEZ starts two hundred miles from shore.[16]

In November 2004 China and Japan risked confrontation when a Chinese nuclear-powered submarine moved into Japanese waters off the Okinawa Islands. Japan's December 2004 National Defense Program consequently identified China as a potential security threat for the first time. These tensions subsequently led Tokyo to change the laws governing the Japanese Self-Defense Force (JSDF) so as to give it an expanded role. The JSDF has now engaged in noncombat and logistical support operations, such as providing medical support and provisions to U.S. forces. As the United States has reduced its military presence in the Asian region, Japan has sought to build up its defense and naval capabilities. Despite popular Japanese opposition, the JSDF contributed peacekeepers to Iraq, probably to guarantee U.S. support for Japanese defense and for the deployment of theater missile defenses (TMD). Japan has been seeking to cooperate with NATO while accelerating deployment of a sea-based TMD system to be deployed on Aegis destroyers and a land-based Patriot system; both are scheduled to be completed by the end of fiscal year 2011.[17] The deployment of U.S. BMD systems in both eastern Europe and Asia has raised the specter of closer Sino-Russian defense coordination.

As Japan backed Russia's bid to enter the World Trade Organization, Russian president Vladimir Putin likewise proposed a Russo-Japanese economic partnership to help counterbalance China's growing economic influence at the November 2005 joint Russo-Japanese summit in Tokyo. Russia also looked to Japanese defense spending to compensate for the decline in Chinese orders. In general, however, Moscow has sought to counterbalance Japanese influence with closer economic and military pacts with China, in part because of a failure to resolve the Kurile Islands/Northern Territories question, and because of close U.S.-Japanese defense ties.

In addition to seeking out a new relationship with Moscow (which would lead to China's fears of "encirclement"), Tokyo could possibly link with India as a potential counterpoise to Beijing. In addition to raising concerns in Japan and the United States, China's attempt to secure sea lines of communication (SLOCs) along the Indian Ocean has led to fears in India over China's encroachment into its backyard as part of a wider Chinese policy to encircle India.[18] More than 50 percent of India's trade passes through the Strait of Malacca, while more than 80 percent of Japan's oil imports transit the strait. In addition to investing in energy saving technology and solar energy, Japan has hoped, if possible, to increase the proportion of oil developed and/or imported by domestic Japanese companies from 15 to 40 percent by 2030.[19] But this may prove very difficult due to aggressive Chinese pursuit of energy resources, U.S. efforts to sanction Iranian oil production (which cuts Japan from a major source of energy), uncertainty over access to Russian pipelines, and the Sakhalin-2 project, plus rising oil and energy prices in general.

The rise of China as a significant military, naval, and space exploration power, fear of Russian military backing for a stronger China, possible U.S. disengagement from the Asian-Pacific, China's claims to Taiwan and to the Spratly Islands in the oil-rich South China sea, the Sino-Japanese territorial dispute over the Senkaku/Diaoyu islands and three oil and gas fields, and China's commercial and naval links to Pakistan all represent factors that bring Japan and India closer together. This is particularly true, because India, with the world's fifth-largest navy, can provide a counterweight to that of China and thus protect Japan's SLOCs to the South China Sea. India has consequently set up a Far Eastern Naval Command facility off Port Blair on the Andaman Islands. This appears intended to increase its military presence in the Strait of Malacca, if not monitor Chinese naval activities in the region.

New Delhi moreover appears to be seeking closer ties with Malaysia, Singapore, Thailand, Vietnam, and South Korea to counterbalance China's close ties to Pakistan and Burma/Myanmar. Beijing and New Delhi likewise appear to be competing for control of the Andaman Sea on the west coast of Burma/Myanmar, leading to the choke point at the Strait of Malacca. Indian strategy seeks to develop Myanmar oil reserves and to gain access to the burgeoning markets of southeast Asia to balance the influence of China and "counterterrorist" groups that have been operating in northeast India from Burma/Myanmar.

For its part, much like the United States, Japan has largely attempted to "balance" relations with both India and Pakistan in supporting the efforts of both parties to improve relations since late 2003. India is the leading recipient of Japanese assistance, and it is in desperate need of major investment in its infrastructure; Japan is also the leader in technologies dealing with energy efficiency and conservation.[20] Both Japan and India intend to join the "space race" and expand their blue-water navies. In response to China's antisatellite weapons test in January 2007, India announced that it would establish an aerospace defense command. The fact that India is the world's sixth-largest oil consumer while Japan is the world's third-largest oil consumer and second-largest oil importer means that both should have a common interest as consumer countries in the quest for energy resources in the Middle East, Africa, central Asia, Russia, and Latin America, but also in rivalry with China. (See Chapter 6.)

United States-India-Pakistan

Despite India's position as the world's most populous democracy, U.S.-Indian relations only began to warm since the Bill Clinton administration. (India is expected to overtake China in population by 2050, growing from 1.08 billion to

1.63 billion people, while China is expected to reach 1.44 billion, up from 1.3 billion currently.)

It was then in 2006 that the United States began to accept Indian (and Pakistani) nuclear weapons as a fait accompli. Although still raising Chinese and Pakistani concerns, the United States consequently sought to *manage* India's capacity through the U.S.-India Peaceful Atomic Energy Cooperation Act signed in December 2006. The United States pledged to assist India in emerging as a "world power" with cooperation in the fields of maritime security, information technology, space cooperation, military-to-military relations, growing trade and investment, and common positions on numerous international issues ranging from Islamic extremism to China's rise. Asserting its independence, however, India not only opposed the Iraq War but it has also opposed U.S. policy toward Iran, Myanmar (Burma), and Sudan. It has backed the formation of a "multipolar" world with respect to the principles of sovereignty and nonintervention.[21]

It is interesting to note that while India has largely opposed nuclear proliferation, Pakistan purportedly assisted North Korea (and other states, such as Libya and Iran) with its nuclear program (through the A. Q. Khan network) by providing uranium enrichment technology in exchange for North Korean assistance to Pakistan's ballistic missile program (by providing it with the Nodong/Ghauri ballistic missile). Here, it appears that only Pakistan's geostrategic position in the "war on terrorism"—and fears that its leadership could fall to more militant pan-Islamic movements—has largely saved it from U.S. wrath. The United States appears to be counterbalancing Indian and Pakistani nuclear capabilities but possibly tilting more toward India (which outspends Pakistan on defense by as much as four times) to press Pakistan to act more in the U.S. interest in the "war on terrorism." (See Chapter 6.)

"Great Game of Go" in Central Asia and the Caspian Sea

China has now developed a "Go West" strategy in search of energy and resources in central Asia and in Russia. There is a risk, however, that the "Go West" strategy could turn sour, resulting in increasing rivalry with Russia, the United States, and other regional powers, in what can be called the "Great Game of Go" in which Anglo-Russian rivalry is supplanted by polycentric rivalry between the United States, Russia, China, the European Union, Japan, Turkey, and Iran in the twenty-first century.

Japan has interests in the Baku-Tbilisi-Ceyhan (BTC.) oil pipeline, which came online in June 2006 and could potentially be extended to Kazakhstan's Kashagan oil field. In 2005 Russia had promised pipelines for Japan that would go to Nakhodka instead of going to Daqing in northeastern China (thus cutting out China). Russia's Gazprom then announced in June 2006 that it would build two oil and gas pipelines to China, leaving the Japanese access to Russian oil from the Sakhalin-2 project uncertain. Here, Russia seems to be flip-flopping between seeking stronger political-economic ties with Japan or China.

By December 2005 the Kazakh Atasu-Alashankou oil pipeline to China was opened and appears to have undercut the Russian monopoly and enhanced the strategic leverage of both Kazakhstan and China vis-à-vis Russia. China has also considered participation in the projected Iran-Afghanistan-Pakistan-India pipeline as well as a Turkmenistan-Afghanistan-Pakistan-India pipeline. In addition, China has discussed prospective gas pipelines with Uzbekistan and Turkmenistan and has offered to fund energy exploration in both states. China also intends to import Turkmen gas from Tajikistan by 2009–2010. A Pakistan-China energy connection "would only heighten the existing nexus of energy, security and maritime power projection exemplified by China's support for the construction of a major deep-sea port in Gwadar, Pakistan."[22]

Despite Chinese efforts to link with central Asia through Pakistan, the most important oil producer for China remains Iran. Tehran supplies 15 to 17 percent of annual Chinese oil imports, and closer cooperation might lead to greater Iranian exports. In November 2004 China's second biggest state oil firm signed a $70 billion deal for oil field and natural gas development with Iran, which already supplies 13 per cent of China's gas needs. This has made China reluctant to sanction Iran's nuclear program.

Scouring the Earth in Search of Energy and Markets

Previously a net-oil exporter, China surpassed Japan as the world's second largest consumer of energy in 2004, after the United States. China has appeared to be going out of its way to finalize oil and natural gas agreements with less-competitive suppliers such as Angola, Brazil, Iran, Nigeria, Venezuela, and Sudan in addition to more competitive producers such as Kazakhstan and Russia. By mid-2007, Iraq and China discussed the possibility of developing Iraqi oil fields. As many of these deals do not appear that competitive for the moment, China's drive to secure oil supplies (in part because of its own inefficient use of resources) appeared to be based on longer term fears of either world recession, and declining supplies, or else the possible interdiction of its energy imports by the United States, Russia, Japan, or other powers in the case of accidental cutoff or conflict. China's overseas investments could, however, create domestic economic problems in that an overheated economy (based on a significant internal debt) fuels increased oil prices: "Beijing may end up in an early 1990s Japan situation, where it is forced to sell recently purchased overseas assets for a fraction of what it paid for them."[23]

While China has begun to invest in energy industries throughout Latin America (raising U.S. concerns), China's investments in Russia/central Asia and Middle East/Africa are still much greater. China now receives more than a third of its total oil imports from Africa, and Angola is just behind Saudi Arabia and Iran in supplying China with oil—about a half million barrels a day, while China's oil imports from Latin America are still relatively limited, though growing.[24] At the same time, however, the Chinese-Brazilian trade deal included a joint oil drilling and pipeline program at three times the cost of simply buying oil on the market.[25]

In November 2006, in a demonstration of China's growing influence in the region, Chinese president Hu Jintao met leaders of forty-eight African nations in a historic China-Africa summit, which concluded with a declaration and a plan of action for 2007–2009 that would seek to construct a new type of strategic partnership between China and Africa ostensibly on the basis of political equality, mutual confidence, "win-win" economic relationships, and cultural exchanges. Outcompeting Japan and India for contracts, a total of sixteen commercial agreements were signed between twelve Chinese businesses and ten African countries, for a value of $1.9 billion. Commercial exchange is expected to double between 2006 and 2010 to $100 billion; Chinese credit and loans are expected to reach $5 billion by 2009. (See also Chapter 6 on the Sudan.)

Theater Missile Defenses

In a sign of Japan's growing concern with China as a potential military "threat," the U.S.-Japan "two-plus-two" statement of 2005 identified the "peaceful resolution" of the Taiwan issue as a "common strategic objective," while Japan identified China as a potential security threat in its National Defense Program Outline in 2004. Here the United States and Japan for the first time jointly urged China to solve the Taiwan dispute. The joint statement was issued just before the passage of the Anti-Secessionist Law on March 14, 2005, by the Chinese People's Assembly (which has recently appeared more active so as to provide a semblance of "democracy"). Right after passage of the "Antisecession Law," the United States and Japan then announced an agreement to upgrade their military alliance and to construct a new generation of military equipment as part of theater missile defenses (TMD). Thus far the United States has tried to play a balancing game: on the one hand, it has protected Taiwan with its fleet and supported it through arms sales and its alliance with a militarily strengthening Japan; on the other hand, it has thus far checked Taiwan's political steps to independence.

China, however, has feared that TMD will strengthen the Taiwanese independence movement and augment the political, economic, and military costs of preventing Taiwanese independence. It believes that TMD will strengthen the U.S.-Japanese military alliance with a concurrent failure to define geographic boundaries and encourage Japan's remilitarization under a missile shield. China is also concerned that U.S. national missile defense (NMD) would negate its minimal nuclear deterrent that is presently capable of a second strike in case of a preemptive strike. Yet, the burgeoning capabilities of U.S. antimissile defense systems (linked to satellite surveillance) threaten that limited deterrent. This has led to China to show that it could protect fixed missile sites to ensure China's retaliatory capacity and that it could take out U.S. satellites.[26] These military technological innovations have led China to reassess its nuclear strategy that seeks to strengthen the survivability of its nuclear systems (through developing hardened silos for example) so as to improve its retaliatory capability. Combined with an apparently strengthening Sino-Russian alliance (thus far based more on mutual use and profit than on anti-U.S. solidarity), China has enhanced its efforts to develop a blue-water navy and has sought to deploy more medium-range IRBMs and long-range ICBMs and SLBM systems and to develop countermeasures, such as warheads with multiple independently retargetable vehicles (MIRVs), as well as asymmetrical options designed to break U.S. systems (such as antisatellite weaponry).[27]

In January 2007 Beijing tested a missile capable of destroying satellites in orbit. The latter action, in particular, potentially threatens U.S. military and intelligence satellites used to conduct military reconnaissance, to pinpoint nuclear tests, and to direct guided missiles and other "smart" weaponry. Assuming a treaty effectively banning further tests or use of antisatellite (ASAT) weapons cannot soon implemented, China's antisatellite test (raising Russian and U.S. suspicions) could spark a renewed weapons buildup in both outer space and on the ground, as part of the post-September 11 "insecurity-security dialectic."

Rather than seek to demilitarize outer space, however, the Bush administration has sought to sustain its ostensible *superiority* in space systems. The Bush administration (which has engaged in its own advanced laser tests of antisatellite weaponry) has accordingly asserted U.S. rights to "freedom of action in space" as being as "important to the United States as air power and sea power." The U.S. policy is also determined to "dissuade or deter others from either impeding those rights or developing capabilities intended to do so." The United States would accordingly "deny, if necessary, adversaries the use of space capabilities hostile to U.S. national interests."[28] If so, the latter position, combined with the Chinese threats to obtain regional hegemony, sets the grounds for potential conflict, which in turn, could possibly draw in U.S. ally Japan, as well as Australia and New Zealand because of ANZUS treaty obligations. Here, burgeoning Chinese nuclear capabilities have raised fears of a Finlandization of the Asia-Pacific region if China is not countered by U.S. forward naval deployment and ballistic missile defense.

The Question of Taiwan Arms Sales

Under Secretary of Defense Donald Rumsfeld, the Pentagon sought to strengthen the U.S. Pacific Command. The United States sought to shore up its alliances with South Korea (see Chapter 7), Japan (building TMD), and even with Thailand (as a major non-NATO ally) and the Philippines—in addition to establishing closer ties with Mongolia and even with Vietnam with its fast-growing economy following U.S. diplomatic recognition under President Clinton. The U.S. Army headquarters in Hawaii is to become a war-fighting command; the thirteenth Air Force is also to have a war-fighting headquarters on Hawaii as well. A nuclear aircraft carrier, the USS *George Washington* (CVN 73), is to replace the aging forty-six-year-old USS *Kitty Hawk* in 2008, which has been the historic centerpiece of the largest carrier strike group (CSG) in the U.S. Navy.[29] At the same time, the United States is also strengthening its forward position on Guam (moving the third Marine Expeditionary Force from Japan's politically sensitive Okinawa) as a deterrent bridgehead to East Asia.

In the effort to "strengthen" Taiwan, the Bush administration had proposed $15–18 billion in arms sales to Taipei in April 2001. These systems included eight diesel-electric submarines, four *Kidd*-class guided missile destroyers, and twelve P-3C patrol and antisubmarine aircraft, along with 155 mm howitzers, minesweeping helicopters, torpedoes, Harpoon antiship missiles, and amphibious assault vehicles. As the deal lifted the ban on submarines, it was regarded as particularly provocative from the Chinese point of view and appeared to indicate strengthened U.S. support for Taiwan, against previous U.S. promises to China. The Bush administration then signed into the law the 2003 National Defense Act, which made Taiwan a major non-NATO ally so that it could purchase advanced U.S. weapons systems. The United States subsequently encouraged Taiwan to buy the Patriot PAC-3 antimissile system, advanced ground-based and satellite-based radars, and a C4ISR (command, control, communications, computers, intelligence, surveillance, and reconnaissance) network that would allow Taiwan's armed services to share real-time data.

The proposed arms sales had represented another significant step away from previous U.S. policy and one that is very provocative from the Chinese perspective. This is because the U.S.-PRC Joint Communiqué of August 17, 1982—that had helped establish the basis for a working relationship between Washington and Beijing—had committed Washington to "reduce gradually its sales of arms to Taiwan." But by 1992 the Bush Sr. administration overturned this accord by agreeing to sell Taiwan 150 F-16 fighter aircraft over virulent objections from China. The U.S. government argued that 1979 Taiwan Relations Act, a U.S. domestic law aimed at maintaining peace and stability of the Taiwan Straits, would take precedence.

Despite U.S. pressures, this major arms package proposed by the Bush administration has so far been stalled by the domestic power struggles between the Taiwanese Democratic Progressive Party (which supports the sale) and the Chinese Nationalist Party (KMT) and the People First Party, which oppose it. The latter two parties argue that the referendum held in 2004 (in which less than 50 percent votes) in conjunction with the presidential election has made illegal the government's purchase of three Patriot PAC-3 antimissile batteries from the United States.[30] Interestingly, from a technocratic viewpoint, increased democracy in Taiwan has made it more difficult to push through major defense packages because of deep parliamentary divisions and exposure to the media.

In general, the latter groups that seek eventual reunification with China, see the proposed arms sale as too expensive and provocative. From a military point of view, Taiwanese critics argue that *Kidd*-class guided missile destroyers are outdated; they would prefer up-to-date destroyers equipped with Aegis systems. Still others prefer lighter, faster missile-armed ships that are more in tune with the "Revolution in Military Affairs" and asymmetrical warfare. Critics recognize the risk that U.S. Aegis missile cruisers, destroyers, and nuclear aircraft carriers are themselves increasingly vulnerable and may not be able to enter the Straits. U.S. warships would have to be defended by smaller anti-missile systems against Chinese-built Silkworm missiles and Russian-built Sunburn ship-to-ship or shore-to-ship missiles that can carry five hundred-pound warheads or tactical nuclear weapons. Furthermore, the short distance between Chinese launch points and Taiwan (as well as North Korean launch points and South Korea) tend to stretch out the capability of planned U.S. systems and might overextend the nature of BMD system requirements and architecture.[31]

In January 2007, in an effort to push through the arms deal, Taiwan president Chen Shui-bian (of the Democratic Progressive Party) stated that Beijing had deployed nearly one thousand missiles against Taiwan—up from 160 ballistic missiles in place in 1996. According to Maj. Gen. Wang Cheng-hsiao, "the

Chinese Communists have stockpiled 880 ballistic missiles and more than 100 cruise missiles, placing the whole of Taiwan under their range."[32] On March 4, Taiwanese leader Chen Shui-bian said that the island should pursue independence and change its official title, "the Republic of China." This statement was denounced by Beijing as a "deliberate provocation" and "a dangerous step"; Beijing, in turn, announced a 17.8 percent defense increase (an amount probably underestimated).

In the meantime, the United States has hinted that it might be less obligated to defend Taiwan if the Taipei does not purchase the arms and TMD systems.[33] Ironically, the U.S. Navy, which lobbied for years for nuclear powered subs, has opposed the sale of cheap, silent diesel submarines, which are made in Europe (but could be licensed in the United States), and has thus put stumbling blocks in the way of the sale.[34] Ironically, this is taking place in the context of the arcane cold war strategic debate in which nuclear submarines were seen as the major deterrent versus the Soviet nuclear threat as they were regarded as a mobile, deep water, and undetectable force (thus providing a second-strike capacity) versus the new, more innovative, concept of lighter, faster submarines (and vehicles in general) capable of striking and running, thus emphasizing speed and stealth. The previous dispute appears rooted, in part, by the reluctance or inability of U.S. military culture to transcend older cold war tactics in order to deal with the new forms of asymmetrical warfare.

More crucially, the debate over the whole arms package underscores the very nature of the *insecurity-security dialectic*. The U.S. assumption is that a major weapons buildup, coupled with TMD, will deter the Chinese from attacking, while a weak Taiwanese defense posture will encourage Chinese attack. The Chinese perspective is quite the contrary. In addition to representing a threatening military-technological innovation from the Chinese perspective, the U.S. push for an arms buildup increases the chances that Taiwan will press for full de jure independence, which would, in turn, impel China toward *preemptive* or *preclusive* military intervention.[35]

Radical Shift in the Regional and Global Equilibrium

As Chinese military and economic power rises (despite its sociopolitical instability), questions are being posed in terms of the nature of deterrence and the concept of "Finlandization"—as were once posed with regard to a nuclear Soviet Union during the cold war: Will the Pacific Rim countries regard U.S. deterrent capabilities as sufficient to protect them from the threat of Chinese conventional and nuclear weaponry? Or will the possibility of Chinese nuclear attack on U.S. cities make the Pacific Rim countries doubt the reliability of U.S. guarantees against the possibility of Chinese aggression, even when U.S. forces are present? Would the United States be willing to risk Los Angeles for Taipei?

The United States needs to guarantee permanent access to energy: The U.S. forward presence on the Pacific Rim itself helps to provide reassurance for countries in the region, but that forward deployment must likewise counterbalance China's size, proximity, and growing military and economic power. Yet, to prevent China from "Finlandizing" the Pacific Rim, the United States must counterbalance the leverage that China already possesses in the region and that it is extending globally. In this respect, U.S. bilateral treaties with Japan, the Republic of Korea, and Australia may not be sufficient, thus making the existing bases in the region, in South Korea, Japan, Okinawa, Guam, and Diego Garcia extremely important. The loss of the bases in the Philippines (if not regained ostensibly for use in the "global war on terror") makes the task of counterbalancing a rising China significantly more difficult. (See Chapter 1.)[36]

Most pertinent, tensions over Taiwan and the control of the Taiwan Straits, which have involved access to the supply of oil and to the control of shipping lanes, have continued to militarize U.S.-Japanese-Chinese-Indian relations. The fears of external foreign influence in China have led Chinese authorities to sustain their repression in Tibet and Xinjiang Province (where China has attempted, with reluctant U.S. backing, to brand certain Uighur Muslim movements as "terrorist"). Chinese authorities have also continued to oppose U.S. democratic-liberal influence as undermining Communist controls and have tried their best control the media—and even control the World Wide Web. The question of Taiwan and its geostrategic position guarding sea lines of communication, perhaps indirectly linked to that of North Korea, appears to represent the key dispute that could drag the United States and China into confrontation in the not-so-distant future—unless U.S.-Chinese cooperation over North Korea can be expanded to include cooperation over Taiwan in the formation of a China-Taiwan confederacy (see Chapter 7).

The United States should encourage Russo-Japanese cooperation where possible at the same time that it draws Russia into closer collaboration in the NATO-Russia Council. What will be needed is a real U.S.-EU-Russian-Japanese "diplomatic revolution" intended not to isolate or "contain" China—but to *channel* Beijing's rise to major power status.

CHAPTER 9

Three Dimensions of "Montezuma's Revenge": Hugo Chávez's Bolivarian Vision, "War on Drugs," and "Illegal" Immigration

Revolution in America's Backyard

With the post-September 11, 2001, geostrategic focus primarily on Afghanistan, Iraq, Iran, and North Korea, and given the fact that the Soviet Union/Russia finally withdrew its support from Fidel Castro's Cuba, the United States has largely tended to overlook, if not totally neglect, major transformations taking place within its own backyard in Latin America in addition to ignoring the issue of "illegal" immigration within its own borders. It was seven years into his presidency that George W. Bush finally deigned to visit the region, provoking significant protest somewhat reminiscent of Richard Nixon's tumultuous tour in 1958 or that of Governor Nelson Rockefeller in 1969.

U.S. tensions with the regime of Hugo Chávez, the issues of drug use and the "war on drugs," and the question of "illegal" immigration all represent contentious concerns that have been vehemently debated by the U.S. Congress and the American public. The problem raised here is that American strategy appears to be failing in all three areas. Not only does the Chávez regime appear to be getting stronger, partly as a result of the steep (and hopefully temporary) rise in world oil prices, but also U.S. international economic policies and efforts to press for the Free Trade Area of the Americas pact appear to be further antagonizing much of Latin America in that American products appear heavily subsidized particularly in the domain of agri-industry. A second major concern is that the war on drugs appears to be not only widening but also failing to stop the flow of drugs to the United States and elsewhere. And lastly, as the U.S. Congress and the Bush administration debate immigration law, there is a real risk that American threats to restrict and deport illegal immigrants will result in augmenting unemployment in Mexico and other Central American countries, while cutting off huge remittances that help float these economies. Unless compensated by an adequate temporary work plan, as well as "fair trade" and international aid and assistance, American anti-immigration policies will tend to exacerbate social-political and economic instability, opening the region to greater foreign influence while concurrently augmenting trends toward U.S. hemispheric isolationism at the same time as Washington tries to grapple with the drugs, criminal mafias, and gangs, if not acts of terrorism, plus the Bolivarian challenge led by Hugo Chávez.

George Kennan's Warning

As George Kennan once forewarned, the United States would be at a loss should socialist movements come to power democratically rather than through the use of force. While socialist-oriented regimes, such as that of Jacobo Arbenz in Guatemala in 1954 and Salvatore Allende in Chile, were overthrown by coups d'état in 1954 and 1973, respectively (with significant behind-the-scenes CIA assistance), it appears that the United States will have its hands full in the contemporary situation—in which Venezuelan oil money is ironically helping to fuel a number of populist and left-wing movements, at least in the medium term, in the presumed effort to establish a "Bolivarian confederation" that is largely intended to exclude American political-economic and social influence.

The failure to get Iraqi oil pumping after the U.S. military intervention in 2003 has thus far resulted in skyrocketing prices. (See Chapters 3 and 4.) Oil-producing countries such as Iran, Russia, and Venezuela have consequently been able to use high oil prices as a form of strategic leverage to press their regional and global interests and to oppose U.S. demands for reforms or changes in domestic policy (democratization and human rights in the case of Saudi Arabia, which is also beginning to assert its own policy in the Middle East).

Furthermore, there are significant financial interests at stake. The declining value of the dollar relative to the euro means that the price of oil becomes relatively more expensive, while more and more countries will put their dollar assets in euros or other currencies as a means to hedge their assets. The U.S. dollar's almost 10 percent loss in value in 2006 (against the euro, in particular) directly reduces the purchasing power of oil-producing countries as well. Iran has, since at least 2003, been shifting reserves out of dollars to other currencies—in large part as a response to U.S. efforts isolate Tehran over its nuclear enrichment program.[1] (See Chapter 4.) Other oil producers such as Indonesia, Saudi Arabia, and the other Gulf states likewise plan to place more money into the euro. Russia, however, has stuck to its own currency, the ruble. The Gulf states additionally plan to forge their own currency with the creation of a common currency on the model of the euro by 2010.[2] Interestingly, Saddam Hussein bet on the euro rising before the second Persian Gulf War.

Part of Venezuelan president Hugo Chávez's strategy is thus to direct Venezuela's oil revenues into euros as a response to the deterioration of the dollar, while reducing dollar holdings. Chávez thus called on OPEC to sell oil denominated in euros rather than dollars at a meeting of the group in Caracas on June 1, 2006, supporting a proposal made by Iran.[3] From a domestic American standpoint, the rise of the strong euro puts pressure on the (generally declining) U.S.

dollar to stop U.S. deficit spending. The rise of the euro as a reserve currency consequently harms present and future American efforts to boost defense spending to sustain the U.S. military presence in Iraq and Afghanistan and to engage in the "global war on terror" and thus could ultimately press the United States toward greater ostrich-like "isolation"—particularly if Washington does not want to cut back significantly on domestic entitlements.

The Chávez regime has accordingly obtained a new lease on life following the boost in oil prices in 2004 after U.S. intervention in Iraq. As Venezuela represents the world's fifth-largest crude oil exporter and sells some 60 percent of its output to the United States, thus accounting for 15 percent of American petroleum imports, its policies have significantly affected the U.S. economy. The Venezuelan state also has a major stake in refining and distribution in the United States through its ownership of its subsidiary Citgo, ironically based in Houston, Texas, President Bush's own state. In effect, Chávez cannot be ignored.

Illiberal Democracy

The Chávez government is perhaps best characterized as something close to an increasingly centralized "illiberal democracy." It is not—at least not yet—an entirely repressive authoritarian regime—although there have been significant accusations of government discrimination against the generally middle- and upper middle-class opponents. The opposition asserts that the Chávez government has used computerized controls to compile what is known as the *Maisanta* list of 12.4 million political opponents—which is purportedly used to reject the applications of those on the list for government jobs, a business license, or a passport.

Chávez initially possessed large public (and military) support, although he has tended to alienate the middle and professional classes, particularly following the passage of his land reform bill, plus laws tightening government controls over the oil industry in November 2001. This took place as a set of forty-nine laws by decree that went into effect following passage of an "enabling act" by the Chávez-controlled National Assembly in December 10, 2002.

In April 2002, as opposition to his autocratic rule mounted, he survived a coup attempt (which Chávez blamed on the United States).[4] In late 2003 he waited out a national strike led primarily by white-collar workers and management in which thousands of employees of Petroleos de Venezuela (PDVSA), the state-run oil company, had been dismissed by the Chávez government, to be replaced by political appointees. The strike paralyzed oil production and cut back energy supplies to the United States, helping to raise oil prices to $30 a barrel, and purportedly slowed the U.S. intervention in Iraq, as Washington wanted to fill its petroleum reserves before going into action. (Moreover, with former U.S. president Jimmy Carter and the Organization of American States trying to mediate, Brazil, Russia, and other Latin American countries supplied emergency fuel to keep the industries running, thus internationalizing the situation.)

Defeated by 59 percent of voters, the highly polarized August 2004 referendum attempt sought to recall Chávez, who then sought to obtain even greater control over the communications media by starting his own media empire,

Telesur, which seeks to rival CNN, BBC, and American media coverage in South America, much like *Al-Jazeera* in Qatar in relation to the greater Middle East. Chávez continued to put greater pressure on the opposition media and non-governmental organizations (NGOs). In May 2007, Chávez then shut down the very popular Radio Caracas Television (RCTV) on the pretence that it supported the coup attempt in 2002, as did most private media outlets, and that it promotes consumerism and violence in broadcasting popular soap operas and serials; Chávez then expropriated RCTV infrastructure for the government's own station, which the government claims will be more inclusive and participatory. The dispute was to be appealed in the courts. However, Chávez's opposition to popular media might have cost him significant support among the lower classes.

Despite rising tensions and clashes that raised fears of civil war, the government was able to fund a surge in government spending by means of record oil revenues. Economic growth then reached 9.1 percent in 2005, and Chávez's approval rating thus rose to 68 percent by October 2005.[5] At the same time, however, unemployment only declined from 17 percent in early 2004 to 14 percent in February 2005. Voter turnout in the December 2005 parliamentary elections was also very low, with only about 25 percent of 14.5 million registered voters casting a ballot.[6]

Chávez and the United States

With the use of militant rhetoric, Chávez plays on fears of U.S. intervention in the effort to build his popularity, yet those fears are not entirely unfounded. In August 2005, TV evangelist Pat Robertson made a number of public statements, manipulating the bogeymen that Venezuela was supporting both the Communist and Islamic threats (Cuba and Iran), and appeared to indicate that Chávez should be assassinated.[7] In the process, Robertson, with strong influence in religious right, the Republicans, and the White House, ironically helped build Chávez's legitimacy and media image as a persecuted opponent of the United States. (Robertson, by the way, also made the image of American Protestant fundamentalist ministers look as bad as that of some militant imams!)

Then, rather than merely denouncing Bush administration policies, Chávez promised to assist Americans in need. In late 2005, in an effort to embarrass President Bush and neutralize criticism of his regime, Venezuela decided to send cheap oil to the United States to offset the growing cost of home heating for low-income families. The oil was to be sold to the United States at an estimated 40 percent below market value and shipped to Massachusetts by way of Venezuela's subsidiary, Citgo Petroleum.[8]

Despite the low voter turnout in the December 2005 elections, the Fifth Republic Movement, Chávez's party, won 114 seats (up from 89 seats) in the unicameral National Assembly; allies of the president won the rest of the seats out of 167—after the five conflicting opposition parties boycotted the elections. The boycott was based, in part, on the fear that the polling booths and voting systems did not guarantee individual confidentiality, so that the government could determine who voted for whom with the use of the Maisanta list.

While moving toward autocratic control at home, Chávez maintained his political offensive against the Bush administration. In his UN General Assembly address on September 20, 2006, Chávez stated that the United States is "the greatest threat" to the planet and repeatedly depicted President Bush as "the devil." It seemed, however, that Washington has since been impelled into acquiescence following the December 2006 elections, when President Chávez defeated his opponent, Manuel Rosales, by 63 to 37 percent. (Rosales's campaign sought to revitalize foreign investment and offered to provide state-issued debit cards to give the poor more direct access to oil wealth. Rosales is from the oil-rich Zulia Province, which has secessionist tendencies—much like many wealthier regions in the world.)

Chávez thus obtained another six-year term, forging what he called a "participatory" democracy based on the president's direct relationship with the "people."[9] In January 2007 the National Assembly passed (with little debate) an "enabling law" granting the president far-reaching legislative powers for eighteen months. Step by step, Chávez has put his supporters in power in the attorney general's office, the Supreme Justice Tribunal, the electoral council, and in the army command structure and has furthermore been accused of nepotism.[10]

In January 2007 Chávez announced plans to nationalize companies in the telecommunications and electricity industries. He also stated he would seek another "revolutionary enabling law" from the National Assembly that would allow him to approve bills by decree, in addition to a decree that would strip the Central Bank of its political autonomy. In the effort to become a one-man show, he had announced that he would seek a fusion of the coalition of parties that support him into a single socialist party in December 2006.

Chávez also appeared to signal that he wanted to obtain greater national controls over four multibillion-dollar oil projects in the Orinoco River basin, in which Venezuela already has stakes along with Exxon Mobil, Chevron, British Petroleum, and Conoco Phillips (forcing Exxon Mobil and Conoco Phillips out in mid-2007 at a time of record profits for both firms).[11] At the risk of losing technical expertise and taking advantage of high oil prices in the short run, Chávez hopes to unite all state petroleum and gas companies in the region in one giant complex, Petrosur, which will be able to compete with, and ultimately exclude, the major multinational oil companies. Chávez had already started to renegotiate energy contracts with foreign oil companies. He significantly raised taxes on royalties and has worked on setting up a new Caribbean oil consortium.[12] In his efforts to divert oil revenues to infrastructure and social programs, he has additionally arranged energy pacts with Brazil, China, India, and Russia.

Venezuela now claims that China receives 15 percent of its petroleum and related products and hopes that the percentage of the petroleum will increase to 45 percent by 2012.[13] Chávez has repeatedly called for closer ties with China in the energy sector: "We have been producing and exporting oil for more than 100 years, but they have been years of dependence on the United States. Now we are free and we make our resources available to the great country of China."[14]

Whereas Iran has been playing "high-tension" nuclear enrichment politics, Chávez has also tried to play the nuclear card. In August 2005 he proposed that Venezuela purchase a nuclear power plant from Argentina, which has sold nuclear technology to Egypt, Australia, Algeria, and Peru. Perhaps more ominously from the American perspective, however, Chávez also talked of working with Iran on nuclear power development. With his diplomatic opening to Iran and call for a "multipolar world," Chávez might well have been seeking to provoke Washington, but might also have gone too far. Venezuelan links to China, Russia, India, Belarus, and Iran, plus purported secret links to North Korea, have already raised American fears of foreign influence operating and meddling in the American hemispheric backyard, thus potentially evoking the Monroe Doctrine and its interventionist "Roosevelt corollary." Here, much as the United States opposed historical Spanish, British, German and Soviet influence in Latin America, the entrance of states such as Russia, China, Belarus and Iran into the historic U.S. sphere of influence and security has already begun to cause friction.

Social Development

Chávez has obtained popularity through supporting social service programs (called *misiones*) in the formation of a new form of populist socialism based on participation of all sectors of society in managing local affairs. He seeks to transform Venezuela into a developed state into what he calls a "small major power." This new form of socialism mixes state intervention in the economy with the acceptance of an independent private business sector as well as support for peasant and worker cooperatives through "participatory democracy." His party seeks to engage the different sectors of Venezuelan society in "endogenous development" projects in an effort to develop the heartland. The ideology of his Fifth Republic Movement emphasizes Catholic "liberation theology" with heavy doses of nationalism, supported by his "Bolivarian" militants.[15] Yet his introduction of Cuban doctors, for example, to live among the poor in the *barrios* has not entirely pleased Venezuelan medical professionals.

At the same time, the public sector abounds in corruption, as well as crime, diamond smuggling and drug trafficking. Inflation-driven uncertainty is aggravated by the appearance of some food shortages in stores and markets. In his December 2006 electoral victory speech, Chávez said that the Venezuelan people would have to "redouble the battle against counter-revolution, that is, bureaucracy and corruption; we need new and true Bolivarian morals." In June 2007, Venezuela unexpectedly stated that it would abide by the Kimberley Process, a UN-backed initiative intended to curb the illegal trade in conflict diamonds.

As a means to achieve his "socialist" dream fueled by black gold, Chávez has expropriated "unused" land for distribution to peasants and has started up agricultural and industrial development projects within Venezuela's heartland. Under the November 2001 land decrees, the government can tax or seize "unused" farm sites. This has raised fears of a Zimbabwe-style expropriation among large property owners, in that Venezuelan authorities have identified more than five hundred farms, including fifty-six large estates, as idle. A further forty thousand farms are to be inspected.

The key sociopolitical problem is that the Venezuelan population has moved from 25 percent poverty in the late 1970s to around 50 percent (or more by some estimates) by 2004. From 1978 to 1989, Venezuela's per capita GDP shrank 29 percent (back to the level of 1953). In this period, some five hundred thousand Venezuelans emigrated, many of whom were skilled professionals. But then real GDP suddenly jumped up to over 30 percent in March 2004, when record oil prices raised reserves to $21.3 billion, before leveling back down to about 7–10 percent growth in 2005. Both oil and non-oil sectors grew substantially between 2003 and 2004, following the first Iraq War, but dropped back slightly in 2005.[16]

Subsidies and Ethanol Competition

The key issue now is to what extent Chávez is subsidizing the social aspects of his Bolivarian Revolution and to what extent is he investing in future oil development and exploration. His popularity stems largely from high oil prices, plus heavy, probably unsustainable borrowing—with inflation highest in the hemisphere. If oil prices eventually fall and production of the state-owned oil company, PDVSA, goes down, he will need to cut those social programs that are not self-generating employment and profits.[17] The question thus remains as to whether Venezuela is at full capacity and capable of exploiting present reserves and to what extent Venezuela can realistically expect to expand its markets beyond its present dependency on U.S. demand, looking to Latin America, China, India, and abroad.[18]

The possibility of an eventual decline in world oil prices is likewise a question of producing energy alternatives. (See Chapter 4.) Here, the Bush administration has signed a deal with Brazil to produce ethanol-based fuels in an effort to reduce Latin America's overall dependence on foreign oil and to take some of the pressure off oil prices, concurrently reducing the influence of Hugo Chávez's oil-rich Venezuela. Chávez counterattacked by accusing the United States of trying "to substitute the production of foodstuffs for animals and human beings with the production of foodstuffs for vehicles, to sustain the American way of life."[19]

Not only does Chávez oppose the accord, but U.S. ethanol producers (whose corn-based ethanol industry has been protected by tariffs and government mandates and is far more expensive to produce than ethanol produced by sugarcane) have sought to block the deal with Brazil in that it might result in cheaper ethanol imports. As a result of domestic lobbying, it appears dubious that the Bush administration will offer money or loan guarantees for construction of ethanol plants in other countries, nor will it press for a reduction in American tariffs on foreign ethanol—the United States puts a tariff of 54 cents a gallon on imported ethanol. Here, the U.S. ethanol industry complains that Brazil subsidizes its ethanol production.[20] Concurrently, gas and oil interests argue that it takes significant amounts of fuel to make ethanol in the first place and that cars do not run properly without a mix of fuels. The true cost-benefit ratio of biofuels, which takes into account environmental pollution and affects on food staples, needs to be analyzed. (See also Chapters 6, 8, 9, and 10.)

The U.S.-Brazilian agreement is also aimed at poor sugar cane-producing countries in the Caribbean and Central America, which can produce limited amounts for the U.S. market under current law. And it is hoped that many African countries (including Angola, Mozambique, and South Africa), and countries such as Thailand, can become major producers of ethanol. As Antonio Simões, the director of the energy division of the Foreign Ministry of Brazil, put it in an interview, "The good thing is that a poor country can reduce what it pays for imported oil and earn money exporting this. . . . That way they will have more money to invest in social programs, and the production of energy will be democratized in the world, with 100 countries producing energy instead of just 15 or 20."[21]

At the same time, however, there is real concern that the use of farmland to produce bioenergy alternatives will cut back on land available for food, opening yet another dimension of resource and energy-related conflict.[22]

Bolivarian Vision

Since Chávez won office in Venezuela in 1998, many South American countries have shifted to the "left." Many of these political movements might, at least to a certain extent, share in the Bolivarian vision of an *exclusive* Latin American regional bloc. Former labor union leader Luiz Inácio Lula da Silva has won the elections in Brazil and the pragmatic left-wing politician, Néstor Kirchner, leads Argentina. In Chile, center-left candidate Michelle Bachelet won the presidential election. (Her father, General Alberto Bachelet, had been tortured to death by the Pinochet regime.) Chávez has additionally been regarded as manipulating elections in Bolivia and Honduras and of supporting indigenous movements in Ecuador; he has possibly been funding Colombia's new united left wing, the Democratic Alternative Pole.

Other left-oriented governments gained power in 2006. In Nicaragua, a more moderate Daniel Ortega, once leader of the Sandinista National Liberation Front against the Somoza regime, which the United States sought to overthrow in covert war in support of the Contras (financed in part from revenues earned through the Iran-Contra affair), won back the presidency that he had lost in 1990 by the ballot, not the bullet, in November 2006.[23] (In Mexico opinion polls had initially indicated that Andrés Manuel López Obrador, a left-wing populist, would replace Vicente Fox after the July 2006 elections proved too close to pronounce a winner; the victor, however, proved to be Filipe Calderón of the National Action Party (PAN).

Not all these left-leaning (and nationalist) governments will necessarily agree on all policies. The moderate left-leaning governments of Argentina and Brazil could try to curb the potential "radicalism" of presidents-elect Rafael Correa in Ecuador and Daniel Ortega in Nicaragua, as well as that of Evo Morales in Bolivia. In addition, Raúl Castro (brother of Fidel) has said he is open to talks with Washington now that Castro's health is unstable. The fact that Fidel Castro shifted power to his brother Raúl represents a new milestone in Communist nepotism. Despite the fact that Washington has denounced Cuba as an "outpost of tyranny," could the United States ultimately recognize the Cuban regime? Much increasingly depends on what Washington can offer to counter that offered by Chávez.

As a supporter of a "multipolar" world system, Chávez claims to support Simon Bolivar's vision of a unified South America in the effort to forge a more autonomous power bloc in the world. Bolivian president Evo Morales described Bolivar's vision in this way: "What unites us with Chávez is the concept of the integration of South America. This is the old dream of a great fatherland, a dream that existed even before the Spanish conquest, and Simon Bolivar fought for it later on. We want a South America modeled after the European Union, with a currency like the euro, one that's worth more than the dollar."[24]

As part of the Bolivarian vision, the socialist leaderships of Bolivia and Chile hope to resolve their historic disputes with other countries. Chile, for example, has agreed to talk about sea access for Bolivia over coastal territories that Chile took from Bolivia in the War of the Pacific between Chile, Bolivia, and Peru between 1879 and 1884. Despite their territorial dispute, the interests of Chile and Bolivia have been seen as complementary in that Chile needs Bolivian natural resources and Bolivia needs access to the sea. As Evo Morales put it: "The sea has divided us and the sea must bring us back together again." Here, there is at least an attempt to cooperate among traditionally suspicious states.

Organizing against the U.S.-backed Free Trade Area of the Americas (FTAA)

Chávez has worked to undermine U.S. efforts to create a Western Hemispheric Free Trade Area of the Americas (FTAA)—a key Bush administration foreign policy goal. Left-leaning countries have attempted to forge a stronger front against the United States (with Venezuelan financing)—in thumbing their noses at the neoliberal "Washington Consensus." In accord with his Bolivarian ideology, Chávez has accordingly sought to forge a "People's Trade Treaty" between Venezuela, Bolivia, and Cuba, plus an exclusionary regional Mercusor pact, as an alternative to the U.S.-backed FTAA.

Bolivia and Venezuela have consequently signed eight different accords dealing with two hundred different projects concerning energy, mining, education, sports, and cultural exchanges. Most important, Venezuela has agreed to invest over $1 billion to help industrialize Bolivia's natural gas production, including construction of a petrochemical complex. Venezuela is also providing diesel fuel, which Bolivia does not produce, in exchange for the sale of soybeans. (This pact is designed to counter the U.S.-Colombian trade accord that means that cheap, subsidized U.S. grains will flood Colombia, driving out Bolivian soybeans.)

In an effort to further integrate Latin American energy infrastructure, Chávez has agreed to construct a two-way gas pipeline between Colombia and Venezuela, as part of a larger project that is intended to bring crude oil from Venezuela to the Pacific Ocean, where it will then be transported to China and Asia. Venezuela and Argentina have likewise discussed building a natural gas pipeline connecting the two countries that would be part of a larger project involving Peru, Bolivia (which is South America's second-largest source of natural gas after Venezuela), Chile, and Ecuador. Chávez believes that the massive pipeline project would guarantee energy "to all of South America for the next 200 years."

Brazil, and many other Latin American governments have regarded the FTAA as not being fair to Latin American farmers and of essentially rewarding highly subsidized American agroindustry. It had been estimated that U.S. spending on farm subsidies in 2005 would reach a record total of $22.67 billion. As one example of unfair trade, the WTO ruled in favor of Brazil that U.S. cotton subsidies, which are estimated to be $4 billion a year, broke trade rules and depressed world prices.[25] The issue continues to be the focus of the WTO in that trade disputes over U.S., EU, and Japanese agricultural subsidies and tariffs versus "high" industrial tariffs imposed by developing countries, such as India and Brazil, had largely paralyzed WTO deliberations in Potsdam in June 2007, leading to fears that the Doha Round might break down altogether, possibly resulting in the general rise of protectionism, if the United States, in particular, could not find a compromise.[26]

At the same time, however, efforts of Bolivia to raise resource prices put it in conflict with Brazil and other countries, thus weakening efforts to achieve Latin American unity. Despite his Bolivarian claims, President Morales entered into disputes with Brazilian president Luiz "Lulu" de Silva by doubling gas prices, for example. Both Brazil and Argentina have significant investments in Bolivia's gas fields and import gas at prices well below the world market. Venezuela is also signing a financial accord aimed at bolstering Bolivia's banking and monetary system to reduce pressure from the IMF and international lending institutions.

Yet the political-economic alliance between Venezuela and Bolivia works to ameliorate both Brazilian and Argentinean concerns over Morales's determination to exert greater control over natural gas exports. "Bolivarian solidarity" was revealed when Chávez agreed to buy public debt from Argentina, thus helping Néstor Kirchner resolve Argentina's debt budgetary crisis, and provided energy relief to obtain Argentine support against the American-backed FTAA—at a time when the United States was playing tough on Buenos Aires.

Social Tensions in Bolivia

Despite his optimism, Morales may be heading for sociopolitical conflict and domestic instability—in that opponents of his government refuse institutional reforms that seek to rewrite the constitution, transform the highly inequitable system of land tenure, and place greater economic power in the hands of the state. On the one hand, militants from Morales's own Movement Toward Socialism (MAS), left-leaning civil society movements, and labor unions have been pressing him to live up to his campaign promises. Major issues include the nationalization of the mines, coca cultivation (in which the U.S. "war on drugs" indirectly serves Morales's interests by helping to increase drug prices), land reform, the constituent assembly (CA), and regional autonomy, combined with problems involving oil and gas refining and distribution.

On the other hand, the elite and essentially middle-class opposition (largely located in eastern lowland regions of Bolivia north and east of the Andes) has argued that the land reform bill (that provides for the acquisition and redistribution of unproductive land like those of Chávez intended to benefit of hundreds of thousands highland peasants from the western departments) jeopardizes its export-oriented agrobusinesses that sustain the economy of the eastern departments, along with natural gas exports. Wealthy elites have thus begun to organize strikes throughout the eastern regions, closing roads and building their private security forces. Journalists, television stations, government buildings, civic associations, and NGOs working for landless peasants and indigenous groups have been attacked, raising the threat of civil war.[27]

After fears were raised that the United States might seek to overturn the Morales regime, Hugo Chávez declared on October 11, 2006, that Venezuela would intervene in Bolivia in the event of a coup. That Venezuela also promised to fund new Bolivian military bases near the borders produced concern in Paraguay, Peru and, to a certain extent, Chile.[28] While the Bolivian government has said the bases are to protect natural resources, opposition leaders in the eastern regions believe they could be used for internal repression.

Military Buildup

Chávez has thus begun to engage in a conventional military buildup in the not-to-be excluded possibility that Washington might opt for military intervention. In addition to threats to Bolivia, such fears appeared justified in that Washington accused the Chávez regime of fostering leftist revolutions—in support of the Colombian Revolutionary Armed Forces of Colombia (FARC)—and of links to Cuba's Fidel Castro and Iranian president Mahmoud Ahmadinejad (not to overlook its previous ties with Saddam Hussein). Following initial American threats (and propaganda by neoconservatives) to intervene in various countries throughout the world after its intervention in Iraq, Venezuela (along with Iran) warned the Bush administration that military intervention would result in a cutoff of oil supplies—and skyrocketing prices at the gas pump.

Chávez has consequently organized civilian defense forces (claimed to number as many as two million), which are ostensibly being taught discipline, job skills, and "love of country." While some of Venezuela's weaponry has been diverted to the black market in small arms, the arms buildup could be destined to support the FARC or other Colombian rebels. The small arms could also be handed over to the new civilian militias for the purpose of crushing the political opposition in the oil-rich province of Zulia next to the Colombian border—in which case they represent a danger to the general population. Venezuela additionally possesses maritime and boundary disputes with Colombia and Guyana.

Chávez has accordingly forged agreements with Russia to supply the Venezuelan military with fighter jets, military helicopters, naval vessels, and one hundred thousand AK-103 assault rifles. (He received the last shipment in November 2006.) Chávez may also be considering the purchase of Russian air defense systems, submarines, and infantry fighting vehicles. The Bush administration had banned U.S. arms exports to Venezuela in May and pressured Spain, Sweden, and Brazil not to sell arms; yet Russia refused to go along. Brazil, Argentina, Peru, and Cuba have all sought to defuse tensions. Here, the UN, the Organization of American States (OAS), and Venezuela's neighbors will need to monitor the regional trade in illicit small arms and alert the the UN and OAS if Venezuela's rifles start appearing on the black market.[29] To obtain peace in the region, the United States should consider the formation of a new "Contact Group" involving Brazil, Argentina, Peru, and Cuba, among other interested parties, like the Contadora process led by Costa Rican president Oscar Arias that worked to resolve the "dirty wars" in the 1980s in Central America.

War on Drugs: Toward a Regional War?

The "war on drugs" has been expanding regional scope and merging with the "war on terrorism." It has cost American taxpayers an estimated $40 billion annually in recent years in *overall* spending, although there has been no comprehensive government tally of all its state and federal spending.[30]

Begun in 2000 as a part of the "war on drugs" (initiated by the administration of Richard Nixon), Plan Colombia has spent $4.7 billion in the effort to halve Colombia's coca crop in five years. Here, it is believed that the FARC, along with state-linked paramilitary forces of the United Self Defense Forces of Colombia (AUC), and which has admitted to drug trafficking, produce some 80 percent of the world's cocaine—while the Ejercito de Liberacion National (ELN) is responsible for a large proportion of about three thousand kidnappings every year in Colombia. (The conflict had begun in the 1960s as a civil war in which left-wing rebels accused the ruling elite *latifundistas*, with 3 percent of the population, of controlling some 70 percent of the best land in the country.)

As the irregular forces of the AUC (backed by wealthy landowners and farmers) and Colombia's military and police have grown in power, fueled by drug sales and illicit activities that have helped recruit members, armed groups from the ELN and FARC (which engaged in heavy clashes with Colombian government forces in February 2005) have passed into Venezuela and Ecuador and engaged in drug trafficking and hostage taking. Both the United States and Colombia have accused Venezuela of harboring two large FARC bases inside its territory, while the Colombian government has accused the Venezuelan military itself of violating Colombian sovereignty. The FARC has furthermore been accused of helping to bring back the Maoist Shining Path, which had terrorized Peru during the 1980s. Chávez had ended his cooperation with the Drug Enforcement Agency (DEA) in 2005, with allegations that some members of the DEA were infiltrating Venezuelan government intelligence. In May 2007, Washington accused Venezuela of not doing enough to crack down on drug trafficking; Caracas counterattacked by saying Washington should do more to control its own borders.

Regional tensions, with Colombia as the focal point, thus appear to be widening as Colombia's forty-year civil war has begun to creep into Venezuela and Ecuador—as well as into Brazil and Panama.[31] In what has become one of the worst recent humanitarian crises in the world (after Sudan, Congo and possibly Iraq), roughly two million people have been forcibly displaced from their homes, while a number of native peoples have been forced into near extinction.

As the previous Colombian president, Andrés Pastrana, had largely failed to achieve a negotiated solution to the conflict with the FARC, the new president, Álvaro Uribe, who was elected in May 2002, intensified both the war on drugs and the war on terrorism with U.S. assistance (including use of special forces) under "Plan Colombia."[32] Consequently, in 2002 the Bush administration asked Congress to approve some $250 million more in military aid, including $98 million to train and supply Colombian army brigades to protect the Cano Limón oil pipeline owned by the U.S corporation Occidental against sabotage by both the FARC and its rival, the ELN.[33] In 2007, the Bush administration has proposed an additional $3.9 billion aid package for Colombia despite allegations of the leadership's involvement with death squads and drug traffickers.[34]

The U.S. war on drugs has additionally sought the forced eradication of coca in Chipare, Bolivia, leading to the virtual militarization of the region. Concurrently, Evo Morales, however, has resisted Washington's hard-line efforts to eradicate coca—and has sought to process coca leaves for herbal teas, medicinal products, and cosmetics. Ecuadorian president Rafael Correa has demanded that the U.S. military leave its base in Manta, Ecuador, which could mean losing a strategic position for engaging in the war on drugs. The dispute is in part because relations between Ecuador and Colombia have grown tense as a reaction to fumigation on the Ecuadorian-Colombian border and the presence of Colombian armed forces on Ecuadorian sovereign territory. At the same time, however, these actions might provide an opportunity for the United States to reconsider its policy.

The irony is that, despite the war on drugs, the price, quality, and availability of cocaine on American streets has remained virtually unchanged. This is because coca has been redistributed to smaller and difficult-to-reach plots, which add to the cost and difficulty of the drug war. Efforts to limit the supply actually result in increased prices and revenues for drug mafias (without necessarily lowering consumption).[35] Moreover, Colombian drug smugglers have begun to use poor countries in West Africa for the transshipment of cocaine to growing market for illegal drugs in Europe.

Much as Nobel Prize-winning economist Milton Friedman had pointed out, antidrug laws represent a government "subsidy" for organized crime (permitting the latter to act as a cartel)—and one can add—for "narcoterrorist" groups that have crossed the line to sell drugs. While the war on drugs may be costing more than $40 billion annually in overall spending in recent years, even this figure does not include indirect social costs: The prohibition of drugs also leads to drug war murders, corruption of law authorities, crime, more and more prisoners and prisons, and poorer law enforcement because police cannot keep up with the traffic.[36] In 2002, half of the jail inmates in the United States were held for either an act of violence or drug offence, almost unchanged from 1996; drug offenders, up 37 percent, represented the largest source of jail population growth between 1996 and 2002; more than two-thirds of the growth in inmates held in local jails for drug law violations was due to an increase in persons charged with drug trafficking.[37]

There has been a real mismatch between U.S. global strategy and the political economic consequences of military intervention. The war on drugs has not eliminated drugs on the street and has resulted in the killing of thousands in Colombia, which has been dubbed a "narco-democracy" (along with Mexico). U.S. intervention in Iraq has resulted in higher oil prices; U.S. intervention in Afghanistan (another narco-state) has resulted in greater opium production.[38] In addition to North Korean involvement in drug trafficking, rice farmers in southern Iraq have purportedly started planting opium poppies. Although the U.S. government has argued that there is no demand for such products for medicinal purposes (see Chapter 6), the United States might consider a legal recourse for the use of opium-derived drugs and coca products for medicinal purposes.

As with alcohol during Prohibition, the United States will soon need to accept the legalization of "softer" drugs in the effort to minimize the use of "harder" even more dangerous ones. It has been estimated that "marijuana is the largest cash crop in the United States, more valuable than corn and wheat combined. Using conservative price estimates, domestic marijuana production has a value of $35.8 billion. The domestic marijuana crop consists of 56.4 million marijuana plants cultivated outdoors worth $31.7 billion and 11.7 million plants cultivated indoors worth $4.1 billion."[39] Here, any legalization or depenalization of a variety of "softer" drugs in controlled circumstances with usage in prescribed areas (that would significantly augment government revenues through taxation) would have to be accompanied by a severe crackdown on the dealers of the most malicious "harder" ones, coupled with extensive education efforts intended to reduce the consumption of all drugs, alcohol and cigarettes included. The ultimate, and still difficult to achieve, goal would not only be to transform drug producers, smugglers, and traffickers into legitimate farmers and businessmen in places like Colombia, Bolivia, Mexico, Burma/Myanmar, North Korea, and Afghanistan, but also separate drug mafias from narco-terrorists. (See Chapter 6.)

Chávez Forever?

With the United States focused on Iraq and Iran, it appears dubious that Washington will focus its sights on toppling Chávez, at least in the next few years. Here, the congressionally funded National Endowment for Democracy (NED) and the State Department's United States Agency for International Development (USAID), plus renewed CIA operations, have supported anti-Chávez political movements, yet thus far to no avail. A Pinochet-style coup appears out of the question, because Chávez appears to control the military and has been preparing his forces for small group guerilla warfare similar to that waged in Iraq after 2003, in addition to granting wage hikes. Before the FTAA fiasco, which once again permitted Chávez to denounce American hegemony, Washington had hoped that it could play Brazil diplomatically against Venezuela, but this largely failed despite the differences between the countries. The fact that Washington was forced to admit Chávez's victory in the ballot box could possibly permit an opening in diplomatic relations with the United States, for negotiation and dialogue, over issues of trade, energy, and the struggle against drugs and terrorism. Chávez himself has called for "transparent dialogue, without conditions, that respects our sovereignty." Yet, it remained unclear whether a dialogue could be started.

The key question remains: How long will the oil boom last? What will happen if and when oil revenues collapse because of increased competition from alternative energy sources? Will Chávez both be able to sustain his Bolivarian revolution and invest sufficiently in developing oil reserves to expand production capabilities?[40] Will Chávez, unlike his predecessors, be able to diversify enough to develop a self-sustaining economy that raises the standard of living for Venezuela and Latin America long after the oil boom no longer reaps profits? Or will the United States triumph over Venezuela, much as it has done in the past, in support of the traditional Monroe Doctrine, finally overthrowing the regime through political-economic pressures or else by coup d'*état* or other means? If so, will this necessarily lead to a regime that is easier for the United States to deal with? Or will the Bolivarian Revolution prove to be the thorn of a bloody red rose that finally began to bloom in the American backyard? Could the United States then bite the bullet and begin to cooperate with Chávez to end the "war on drugs" and help develop the region, seeking to stem the tide of "illegal" immigration to the United States?

The Question of Hispanic Immigration

It is not without great irony that the American effort to repress left-wing movements (particularly in the later 1970s and 1980s during the "dirty wars" in Central America and Operation Condor in South America) eventually helped to cause a counterreaction throughout the entire region—a counterreaction that would go largely unperceived by Washington itself because of its peaceful and largely "democratic" nature. Here, the Bush administration's attention had only belatedly been drawn to the region precisely because of the rise of center-left to far left movements that have begun to nationalize, or place higher taxes on, multinational corporations, given increased demand for energy and natural resources.

This is all the more ironic given the "silent," yet problematic rise of "illegal" migration into the United States, in which migrants (as human beings) are beginning to demand permanent residence status, enfranchisement, and status as *political equals* within highly *inequitable* American socioeconomic conditions and circumstances and are thus ostensibly becoming a "threat" to the U.S. job market in the views of observers such as Samuel Huntington, who contends that American and Hispanic values and cultures are "irreconcilable."[41]—despite the large degree of intermarriage between Americans of differing ethnic backgrounds and Hispanics. Moreover, the United States has largely invited these immigrants to stay. The "push-pull" nature of immigration to the United States is largely the result of the lack of political economic development throughout most of Central America, U.S. efforts to protect its agriculture from Latin American competition through heavy subsidies, tariffs and quotas, and the "pulling" influence of higher U.S. wages, social and health benefits, and living standards.

In addition, the "dirty wars" throughout Central and Latin America sent many into exile or in quest for a better life abroad. The extent of "illegal" immigration also helped create the unclear distinction between "economic" and "political" refugees. During the cold war, economic refugees were seen as those who were seeking better working conditions in the United States but without questioning whether U.S. policies might actually be worsening the political economic conditions of the countries in question. Political refugees were primarily regarded as those escaping Communist persecution (from Cuba particularly), but largely ignoring the plight of those who opposed U.S.-backed dictatorships and military intervention throughout the region.

As the immigration issue is increasingly seen as a major problem for the United States, this section of the chapter shall argue that the creation of a high-tech, multibillion-dollar fence along the Mexican border will not resolve the deeper dilemmas. Moreover, the closely intertwined issues involving the war on drugs, the Chávez challenge, and his "Bolivarian" project for Latin American unity, combined with "illegal" immigration (with the not-to-be played down threat of immigrant "terrorists" in the background) will impel the United States to work toward the real development of its backyard in the effort to truly diversify the Latin American economy, involving greater investment and "fair trade." If the United States does not move in the latter direction, then it could shift toward "paranoid" hemispheric isolationism and protectionism that will concurrently seek to check burgeoning Chinese and Russian political-economic influence in the region, augmenting tensions in the world.

President Bush's Belated Tour

Belated recognition of the major problems confronting Latin America led to President Bush's whirlwind tour to Brazil, Uruguay, Colombia, Guatemala, and Mexico in March 2007. The key issues included a U.S.-mandated Trade and Investment Framework Agreement (TIFA) (which opposes individual bilateral deals among its members) versus Latin American objections to U.S. trade tariffs and quotas and demands for a radical change in U.S. immigration laws that would include a guest worker program, thus far opposed by Congress. As shall be argued, such a "guest worker" program represents an inadequate, but practical option that needs to be accompanied by aid and development assistance, plus "fair" trade with Central and Latin America.

President Bush's "We Care" tour led to a countertour by Venezuela president Hugo Chávez (with their planes "almost crossing paths") to Argentina—indicating the extent to which the United States and Venezuela have entered into a political-economic rivalry for influence over the region. Here, Chávez plays down the annual $1.6 billion in direct U.S. assistance to the region (claiming to be pumping in much more while largely ignoring U.S. assistance through multilateral organizations, plus private trade and investment) and seeks a more protectionist regional Mercosur trade alliance with a stronger anti-America political stance in accord with his exclusionary Bolivarian ideology.[42] While Venezuelan aid appears to go without political strings attached, state recipients of U.S. assistance through the U.S. Millennium Challenge Corporation must show a commitment to political and economic "freedom," anticorruption measures, and other reforms.

The questions of "free"—but not "fair"—trade looms in the background, and whether it is possible for the TIFA and for Mercosur (which, for example, failed to reach an accord with the European Union in 2004) to interlink with other blocs and countries in the world. Of concern here is the tariff placed on Brazilian exports of ethanol fuel to the United States as well as the general problem that U.S. agricultural subsidies, tariffs, and quotas tend to antagonize U.S.-Latin American relations, squelching development prospects, coupled with pressures to open up Latin American economies to U.S. manufactured products.

Moreover, the immigration question adds onto the whole series of other major political economic issues for U.S. domestic policy that play into the hands of "isolationism," including the growing gap in salary between chief executive officers (CEOs) and labor; plus inadequate health care, the close to $9 trillion national debt and widening government budget deficits, and the increasing need to more rapidly develop alternative energy technologies.[43]

Dealing with "Illegals"

It is estimated that during the "dirty wars" in Mexico and Central America from 1979 to 1992,[44] roughly sixty-three thousand to seventy-five thousand Salvadorians and over one hundred thousand Guatemalans were killed (plus an estimated forty thousand "disappeared"). Central American immigration resulted in the rise of a moderately influential antiwar movement in the United States, coupled with the pacifist "sanctuary movement" that had been initiated by the Southern Presbyterian Church in Tucson, Arizona, to protect Salvadorians from deportation. In response to such pacifist "sanctuary movements," Congress, before the Democratic victory in November 2006, attempted to pass legislation that would make efforts to protect "illegal" aliens illegal.

At that time, the United States supported the Contras in Nicaragua against the Cuban-backed Sandinista regime (then led by Daniel Ortega, who was, in turn, elected president of Nicaragua in 2006). Central Americans constituted the overwhelming portion (about two-thirds) of asylum seekers to the United States in the 1980s.[45] Although the "dirty wars" had only a limited effect on Mexico, the political-economic instability caused by these conflicts arguably represented one of the major factors resulting in "illegal" emigration to the United States. In addition to political-economic instability, fear of persecution had led some 20–30 percent of all Salvadorian immigrants to flee. Yet the Immigration and Naturalization Service (INS) only granted some 2 percent of Salvadorian refugees political asylum, despite real fears of persecution from right-wing death squads,[46] while it was relatively easier for people from China, Cuba, and Nicaragua under the Sandinistas or refugees from other Communist countries to obtain political asylum.

In 1986 a general U.S. amnesty under the Simpson-Mazzoli law legalized 2.7 million undocumented workers (of which roughly 2 million were Mexican), but it also mandated the expulsion of those who came "illegally" to the United States after 1982 and made it illegal to knowingly employ "illegals." The law also sought to monitor employers and expand border enforcement. The Simpson-Mazzoli "Immigration Reform and Control Act of 1986" (IRCA) largely continues to govern immigration law and has been regarded as a disaster by hard-line Republicans today and as the major cause of the present immigration "crisis."

As of 2006 the penalty for an employer not checking a prospective employee's Social Security Number was as low as $100 as established by the 1986 IRCA; the penalty for knowingly hiring an illegal alien (which has been hard to prove) was between $250 and $2,500. The only punishment then was some bad publicity for employers if they were caught hiring "illegals." While some employers might pay "illegals" under the table and not report their earnings, other employers simply issue paychecks as if they do not know the worker is illegal and then take out federal, state, and Social Security taxes. It is important to underscore that the Social Security Administration holds the contributions of individuals with invalid names or fake Social Security numbers in what is called the "Earnings Suspense File." The Earnings Suspense File held a total of $463 billion in contributions by 2003. This amount represents an important, yet generally unmentioned, issue that raises questions as to whether some of these funds cannot be used to cover the costs of free public services used by illegal immigrants.

Historical Background

Starting in 1985, the American Baptist Churches began a class action lawsuit against the INS to make it apply fairer standards for Salvadorian and Guatemalan political refugees. Then, in 1987 Salvadorian president Napoleon Duarte issued a request to the White House and Senate that Salvadorians who had entered the United States after 1982 not be expelled. President Duarte made his request on economic, and not humanitarian, grounds reasoning that remittances from legal and illegal (and unauthorized) Salvadorians to El Salvador were estimated to be somewhere from $350 million to as high as $1.4 billion—up from merely $10 million in 1980 at the beginnings of the "dirty war."[47]

In April 1987 the State Department began to revise its policy and asked then attorney general Edward Meese to extend voluntary departure for Salvadorians, as had been the case for Polish, Iranians, Vietnamese, and Nicaraguans. The Attorney General's Office, however, stalled. In effect, it argued that extending voluntary departure would encourage even more illegal immigration (El Salvador had sent the second highest number of immigrants after Mexico). The November 1990 Immigration Act (Public Law 101-649) clearly segregated offenses under labels such as "criminal and related grounds" and "security and related grounds," and included a specific grounds for exclusion/deportation for "terrorist activities." That same year, in 1990, the American Baptist churches reached an out of court settlement with the INS. By 1992, at the closing of the "dirty wars," Congress passed temporary protected status for an eighteen-month period.[48]

In 1996, Congress rewrote provisions in the 1952 Immigration and Nationality Act (INA) that pertain to the circumstances under which certain aliens subject to expulsion from the United States might become legal residents following passage of the Illegal Immigrant Reform and Immigrant Responsibility Act (IIRIRA). At the same time, however, the IIRIRA also restricted economic and legal benefits for other illegal immigrants and expanded grounds for deportation and detention of immigrants.[49] This 1996 legislation affected as many as 300,000 Central Americans who constituted the overwhelming portion (about two-thirds) of asylum seekers to the United States in the 1980s. Salvadorian and Nicaraguan asylum applicants totaled over 252,000 and made up half of all aliens who applied for asylum with the INS from FY1981 through part of FY1991. But these numbers largely understated the total number of Central Americans estimated to have fled to the United States in the 1980s.[50]

The INS has subsequently extended temporary protected status several times since 1996. In February 2006, for example, it granted extension of this status to the approximately 225,000 Salvadorians, 75,000 Hondurans, and 4,000 Nicaraguans who are *legally* registered as aliens, following earthquakes that left 1.5 million people without adequate housing.

"Illegal" and "Unauthorized" Aliens

Now, after the 1986 and 1996 "amnesties," it is estimated that there are between 10 and 12 million "unauthorized" and "illegal" migrants in the United States, if not more. What is to be done?

These following questions appear relevant: How much of a problem is immigration (legal or illegal) in general? Which is the larger problem, "legal" or "illegal" immigration? Are the roughly 10 to 12 million "illegal" and "unauthorized" migrants really harmful to the U.S. economy and society? Do they represent a real "threat" of criminality and/or terrorism? Are Hispanics, in particular, really incompatible with the American way of life? Or do they in some ways benefit American society overall? Will both these kinds of immigrants necessarily try to stay for extended periods? Or are there some incentives that can get large numbers to return to their countries of origin? Or must they be forced to return? If so, at what cost? Are there ways and incentives to prevent more from emigrating in the future?

As these questions are examined, those migrants who have come into the United States legally (but overstayed their visas), which is not yet considered a "crime," should be distinguished from those who came into the country illegally without a visa. Although there are different estimations, about 45 percent of all "illegal" migrants (roughly from 4.5 million to 6 million) come into the United States with visas and then overstay their visit (making them "unauthorized"), while the rest (6 million to 7 million) sneak across the border and often in dangerous conditions (making them truly "illegal").[51] Other estimations state that roughly two-thirds cross the Mexican border and one-third overextend their visas. In either case, it would appear that any future legislation should take into consideration these two separate categories rather than attempt to criminalize both "illegal" and "unauthorized" migrants.

Political Action

The migrant issue has been festering since the 1986, and now Congress and the Bush administration have finally begun to demand action. As of June 2006, the U.S. Senate and House had passed separate legislation—which will be very difficult to compromise. The December 2005 House bill passed, with overwhelming Republican support, by a vote of 239 to 182. The Senate version, however, split the Republicans and needed Democratic votes to pass. Only four democrats voted against it, while only twenty-three of fifty-five Republicans voted for it. A real "showdown" between Democrats and Republicans (and between hard-line Republicans and moderate Republicans) has been in the making.

In May 2006 the Senate passed its version of an immigration bill (Senate bill 2611, or the Hagel-Martinez bill) that seeks to strengthen U.S. border controls to prevent immigrants from crossing from Mexico but that also seeks to create a new program permitting illegal immigrants who had resided in the United States for five years or more to "earn" their citizenship. This process would mean paying a fine as well as any back taxes owed; it would require learning English and holding a job for six years. The Senate bill would also permit illegal immigrants who have resided in the United States from two to five years to apply for a guest worker program. In effect, as President Bush has argued, "illegals" would have to stand in line to obtain citizenship and wait until after those who went the legal route.

By contrast, before the Democratic victory in the House in November 2006 midterm elections, the bill passed by the House in December 2005 was much more severe. The Sensenbrenner Bill sought to turn undocumented immigrants into felons; it augmented detentions and deportations, and it made it tougher for immigrants to get driver's licenses, among other provisions. The House then sought to block any immigration bill that will permit an "amnesty." Rep. James Sensenbrenner (R-WI), generally regarded as a moderate on other issues, was then the chairman of the House Judiciary Committee. He had helped to reauthorize the PATRIOT Act, along with Senate Judiciary chair, Sen. Arlen Specter (R-PA). Sensenbrenner strongly opposed any amnesty like that of 1986 and vowed to block the more "liberal" (in the American sense of the term) Senate bill.[52]

In promulgating a philosophy of "compassionate conservatism," President Bush strongly backed the Senate's "comprehensive" approach to immigration reform, thus dividing the hard-line Republicans from the moderates. Many hard-line Republicans, especially those in the House, argued that the Senate's approach represented a form of "amnesty" that will let in even more aliens.[53] Opponents of the Senate bill, and of President Bush's plans, vehemently opposed any legalization or amnesty program before border security has been strengthened. Concurrently, a selective "skills-based" immigration policy in which immigrants would be chosen according to abilities and the needs of the American workforce was discussed.

In an effort to find a compromise with the Democrats and within the president's own party, the Bush administration has been trying to weave a path between "automatic citizenship" and "automatic expulsion." In accord with his conveniently revived philosophy of "compassionate conservatism," President Bush has advocated compassion for those who prefer to work hard for $5–7 per hour in the United States, as opposed to 50 cents in Mexico, and has asserted that "family values do not stop at the Rio Grande." President Bush's effort to reach a compromise has, however, been condemned by hard-line Republicans as an "amnesty" for "illegal" immigrants and that effort undermined the interests of those who had applied legally.

Confronted with a new Democratic-led Congress in both Houses in 2007, the Bush administration proposed a new plan for immigration reform. The May 2007 compromise bill would allow nearly all of the estimated twelve million undocumented immigrants who entered the country before 2007 to apply for a "Z visa" (temporary legal status) after they first left the country and then pay a series of fees (up to $5,000) and renew their visas every two years. The plan would scale back legal immigration based on family reunification. A temporary-worker program that would grant two-year work "Y visas" for two hundred thousand to six hundred thousand people that would be renewable twice (as long as foreign workers leave the country between each period) was to be implemented on a merit-based "point" system. Applicants would need to pass a background check, remain employed, and receive a counterfeit-proof biometric card. The proposal also sought to strengthen enforcement by fining employers who hire illegal immigrants up to $5,000 for a first offense and up to $75,000 for subsequent offences with possible jail time.[54] The plan would also speed up applications for those who have applied legally. Perhaps, most crucially for U.S.-Mexican relations, the plan called for deploying about six thousand additional Border Patrol agents along the southern border, together with two hundred miles of vehicle barriers, 370 miles of fencing and a 300-mile virtual wall of electronic sensors (at an estimated cost between as "low" as $2 billion and to a "high" of between $8 to $30 billion!)[55]

From their perspective, immigrants expressed distrust that they would be allowed back in, while $5,000 was considered an excessive amount beyond the reach of many. From the employer perspective, the proposal that temporary workers stay in the United States for two years, return home for a year, then repeat that process two more times appeared absurd in that employers could not afford to hire and train migrants who would then leave. This would encourage both employers and workers to find new ways to break the rules. Moreover, the "touchback" provision that requires "heads of household" (separating families) to return to their country of origin to apply for permanent resident status would augment the load for an already overworked State Department.[56]

Compassionate Conservatism or Hispanic Vote?

Whether it was really "compassionate conservatism" that is driving Bush's policy can be questioned, or whether it is the real voting power of the fast-growing Hispanic population that now makes up roughly 12.6 percent of the U.S. population at 35.3 million (up 58 percent since 1990), and that generally (but not always) supports the rights of Hispanic immigrants to remain in the country. The "globalist" element of "compassionate conservatism" really applies to the fact that illegal migrants originate primarily from countries in close proximity to the United States or who have constituents who support their interests within the United States itself.

In this respect, in the 1998 race for governor in Texas, George W. Bush courted the Hispanic vote in Texas, obtaining 49 percent of the Latino vote (and 69 percent of the total ballots cast). He openly distanced himself from the hardline Republican stance as illustrated by California's Proposition 187, which had been backed by Republican governor Pete Wilson and which sought to deny public services to "illegal" immigrants. While Bush won the governorship and then the presidency (and counted on the large turnout of Hispanic voters in the second-term elections against John Kerry in 2004), Governor Wilson's support for Proposition 187 is generally believed to have hurt Republicans in California elections in 1998, and might have contributed to Wilson's failed 2000 presidential bid.[57] Both President Bush and Governor Wilson have been supporters of NAFTA and globalization in general; yet, it appears that not all global free traders support the free movement of labor. The wheels of globalization appear to be stuck in the mud along the Rio Grande.

Deportation?

A major issue, as President Bush himself admits, is that it is very difficult and costly to expel those already in the United States without further extending domestic surveillance and violating civil rights. From 1971 to 1980, about 7.5 million immigrants were expelled; from 1981 to 1990, about 10.2 million immigrants were expelled; and from 1991 to 2000, about 14.5 million immigrants were expelled. Among those deported, not simply excluded, the most common administrative reasons given during the 1990s were "attempted entry without proper documents" (35 percent) and "criminal activity" (31 percent).[58] In December 2001 the INS launched a program to round up 314,000 foreigners who had fled from deportation orders, but it had only found 2,200 by 2003.[59] According to Hispanic media, there had been a 78 percent rise in deportation orders between 2000 and 2005, including over 220,000 orders in 2005 alone, indicating that a crackdown had already been taking place.[60]

Historical evidence suggests that forced expulsion has not worked in the past to dissuade illegal immigrants from entering. Rather, controlled legal immigration has been more successful. This observation is based on the 1942–64 "*bracero* program" that permitted the controlled admission of Mexican farm workers who were employed as seasonal contract labor for U.S. growers and farmers. One study of the *bracero* program showed a 95 percent reduction in the flow of illegal immigration into the United States from 1953 to 1959, while the annual number of Mexican farm workers legally admitted more than doubled from 201,380 in 1953 to an average of 437,937 for the years 1956 through 1959, as did the number of those granted green cards. It was only when the *bracero* program ended in 1964 that illegal immigration began to escalate, with apprehension of "illegals" rising a 1000 percent.[61]

Border Patrols?

Immediate measures President Bush has pressed for is to augment the border patrol from nine thousand to eighteen thousand by 2008 and to increase high-tech border surveillance. A major step in border control is U.S. VISIT (U.S. Visitor and Immigrant Status Indication Technology). U.S. VISIT takes the visitor's fingerprints and photograph and then checks the Department of Homeland Security database for matches with known terrorists and lawbreakers. U.S. VISIT also indicates which foreign visitors might have overstayed the terms of their visas. Whether and how "biometrics" methods would be used to track all aliens and immigrants who enter the country has raised controversy, however.

The next step is to try to block those who try to cross along the seven hundred-mile border with Mexico. This is most feasible in certain areas along the border (though expensive). If individuals are captured, it is relatively easy to return them immediately to Mexico. Complications arise, however, when the individuals are not Mexican and must be shipped to countries farther away, or when they have no papers. The U.S. "Wall" that has two to three layered fences has proved to be effective in some areas, but it may be forcing immigrants to take more dangerous routes (which is why coffins have been attached to the walls on the Mexican side.) In addition, border patrols and fencing might possess an unintended consequence: keeping people in the United States who used to return to Mexico.[62]

Other headaches arise as the U.S. federal government must cooperate not only with Mexican authorities but also with the governors of the Mexican border states, plus the governors of Texas, New Mexico, Arizona, and California. (Some hard-line U.S. politicians regard such cooperation with Mexico as a violation of American sovereignty.) Here, while Americans express fears of criminals crossing the borders, and of the destruction of private property, Mexico has expressed fears (based on the history of U.S.-Mexican relations) that the United States could possibly be "militarizing" the border. Mexicans foresee the rise of xenophobic cowboy vigilantes, such as the Minutemen, who attack or harm immigrants. (The Minutemen, however, claim that they merely report "illegals" crossing the border to the local police, but do not attempt to stop them; yet U.S. public authorities see them as untrained civilians who interfere in their operations against potentially dangerous drug smugglers, for example.)

As of mid 2006, there had been no discussion of joint U.S. National Guard-Mexican military activities, but the rules of engagement of the National Guard still need to be clarified. Interestingly enough, with significant numbers of National Guard units committed to Iraq, plus the need to commit guardsmen in the coming years to potential hurricane duty, with the expected increase in hurricane activity in the Gulf of Mexico—there are major logistical problems in building a border patrol.

And finally, as previously pointed out, under the Secure Border Initiative, the wall—really a "virtual fence" with monitors, sensors, unmanned planes, and communications to help border agents catch illegal immigrants crossing the southern border—could come at a very high cost.

Question of Criminality and Terrorism

Between 2004 and 2006, Department of Homeland Security authorities filed charges against 814,073 people in U.S. immigration courts, yet only 12 were actually accused of terrorism and 114 of national-security-related crimes. Of that number, only 41 were removed from the country, four on charges of terrorism. Yet those few accused of terrorism (from differing countries) had all entered the country legally. Statistics furthermore indicate that, despite its statements to the contrary, the Department of Homeland Security has been focusing far more attention on illegal and non-authorized immigration than on national security threats and espionage, potential terrorists or human traffickers or drug smuggling.[63]

It should be emphasized that a tiny minority of those crossing the border come from all corners of the world (and not just from Central America). This has raised not entirely unwarranted fears that international criminals, drug smugglers, and "terrorists" could be in their midst. "Isolationist" politicians and pundits have raised the issue that the United States is presently engaged in fighting terrorism overseas, but it has left its own borders open to infiltration. At the same time, however, more sophisticated terrorist organizations and mafias could find other ways to cross into the United States and into other countries (Hizb'allah's external organization, for example, raises significant funding from Latin America, and has engaged in terrorist acts in Argentina.) Al-Qaida's February 2007 call for attacks against oil producers that supply the United States (including Canada, Venezuela and Mexico) could attract both Islamic and non-Islamic partisan groups opposed to U.S. policy—and could, ironically represent a cause for U.S.-Venezuelan cooperation.

In addition to Mohammed Abed Abel, a member of Jammaa Islamiyya (which claimed attacks on western tourists in Egypt), who was arrested in Bogotá, Colombia and then deported to Ecuador (his country of origin) in 1998, there have subsequently been reports of an al-Qaida member who attempted to meet with members of the notorious Mara Salvatrucha (MS-13) gang. This gang has engaged in the smuggling of aliens, drugs, and weapons across the U.S.-Mexican border.[64] It has an estimated fifty thousand members throughout the United States and possesses connections in Central America and elsewhere, and was initially created to protect Salvadorians who had immigrated to the United States against other street gangs, including its rival, Mara 18. As one commentator put it, "The cycle seems without end: Children of Central America's bloody wars immigrated to the U.S., where they became violent gang members, then deported back to Central America to begin another generation."[65] The concern raised here is that there are an estimated 150,000 gang members controlling the streets of Central America—a major problem (involving the alienation of teenage youth) that needs to be addressed on a regional basis—if these individuals are not to be recruited by drug mafias and terrorist organizations.

Another gang, "Los Zetas," is made up of former Mexican soldiers, police and federal agents, who were originally trained by the United States as an elite force of anti-drug commandos, but who have been working as mercenaries for Mexican narcotics traffickers (the Mexican drug trade may be worth up to $24 billion). This gang has been linked to hundreds of killings and dozens of kidnappings over a wide area from Laredo to Brownsville, Texas to cities throughout Mexico. In order to protect established turf and drug routes into the United States, the Zetas have targeted U.S. Border Patrol agents and state and local police, along with Mexican military and law-enforcement personnel, as well as rival drug traffickers. As purportedly over one hundred thousand Mexican soldiers have deserted over the past six years, many appear to be joining drug mafias in the quest for higher pay and extravagant lifestyles. This appears to explain why groups such as the Zetas appear to growing in size.[66]

The main point is that the issues of illegal immigration, drugs, criminality, and terrorism all need to be separated and then sorted out in terms of priorities. Over all—combining federal and state prisons—6.4 percent of the nation's prisoners were noncitizens in 2005. This is down from 6.8 percent in 2000. Moreover, evidence suggests that immigrants of the 1990s have a lower crime rate than either earlier immigrants or the native-born population, due to nature of "self-selection" of those who chose to emigrate.[67]

In addition, the fact that drug cartels seek to take advantage of official corruption raises questions about the potential effectiveness of any wall along the Mexican border. The extent of the drug crisis, and the failure to stop it—largely due to powerful American and European consumer demand—should lead to alternative domestic policies regarding the drug trade as previously proposed.

Work Permits or Amnesty?

Other methods, such as more effective controls over immigrant hiring, could be implemented and might prove very discouraging to illegal migrants who hope to stay for long periods. As President Bush had additionally proposed, a stronger measure would be to put higher fines on employers who do not check Social Security Numbers or who repeatedly hire "illegals." Another generally controversial proposal is to create a national ID card for every foreign worker, using biometric technology, such as digital fingerprints, so as to show who can work and who cannot.[68]

Yet, when the new homeland security "Basic Pilot" program is combined with the controls imposed by U.S. VISIT, will employers really comply, thus making it nearly impossible for "illegals" to find jobs—and consequently making it harder for employers to hire workers at low wages? Basic Pilot is presently voluntary, but it could become mandatory, as President Bush has proposed, and it represents an online verification system that is now nationwide and permits employers to confirm the eligibility of new hires by checking the employee's information against federal databases. Yet, would most "illegals" or "unauthorized" aliens who are presently in the country decide to engage a three-year work permit process if they believe they would be kicked out later? Or will they need to be promised some form of amnesty?

Socioeconomic Perspectives

Roughly 32 percent of Americans believe "illegals" should be permitted to stay permanently; some 32 percent say they should be able to stay under a temporary work permit, then leave; while 27 percent say they should all leave.[69] According to another poll, 62 percent prefer better screening of immigrants, while 36 percent seek a reduction in overall numbers.[70]

In general, "illegal" immigration has two major opponents. The first group are high-income voters who believe illegal immigration is increasing their tax burden. The second sees immigrants as increasing the risks of crime and prospects of terrorism, coupled with less-educated voters who fear that migrants might take their jobs. Interestingly, well-to-do voters in Texas, which has a weaker social safety net than that of California, are less opposed to immigration. This can, in part, be explained by the fact Texas has no income taxes and uses a regressive sales tax, while California has the highest state income tax in the country.[71]

In general, immigrants help boost the profits of large firms that require manual labor, such as meat packing plants, poultry processing facilities, vineyards, textile factories, and construction firms. (In general, unionization is less strong in agroindustrial firms than in manufacturing sectors, which makes it easier to employ "illegals.") Small businesses, such as restaurants, home services (lawn and garden service, maids, cooks, and house servants), and small farmers, tend to hire cheaper, generally hard-working, migrants.

But in this regard, both legal and "illegal" immigration creates winners and losers—a fact that works to create a political backlash among the social classes most directly affected. Those opposed tend to be very strongly opposed. They tend to see immigrants as a threat to jobs and believe that their presence leads to the deterioration of their neighborhoods and results in increased crime rates, for example. Opponents of immigration also tend to see deterioration in the quality of public services and public schools. Those who support immigration and who regard it as expanding social diversity and as doing jobs that no one else wants to do only tend to give immigrants lukewarm support, thus forcing a "showdown" with less-numerous, but more bellicose, hard-liners.

A Burden on Society?

But are illegal and unauthorized aliens necessarily a burden to the U.S. society and economy? While 42 percent of the public does rate immigration as a very big problem, they still place it behind problems with the health care system (55 percent), terrorism (50 percent), crime (47 percent), and corrupt political leaders (46 percent). But they do place it a bit ahead of environmental pollution and the availability of good-paying jobs.[72]

One of the major issues is that immigrants use local medical services and public education, which are often free to them. According to PEW study of U.S. public opinion, Americans want to permit education of immigrant children but oppose their use of free medical services. Some 67 percent of Americans thus seek to cut social and medical services for "illegals" as compared to 28 percent against. By contrast, some 71 percent believe the children of "illegals" should remain in school as compared to 26 percent against.[73]

This raises a significant human rights and public health question. Despite the expense to the local community in terms of higher taxes, because "illegals" frequently use public services, coupled with the fact that they generally possess larger families and possess lower family incomes, providing them access to certain medical services is generally in the public interest—for example, inoculations against communicable diseases.

Social Security and Earnings Suspense File

The question of expense leads to an important previously mentioned piece of information that is often missing from the debate: The fact that "illegal" immigrants contribute substantially to U.S. Social Security funds, even if they do use free local public services. Although illegal, and although some employers do pay them in cash under the table, many migrants still pay federal and Social Security taxes out of their generally meager salaries—sums that are generally not claimed. As pointed out previously, the Social Security Administration holds the contributions of individuals with invalid names or Social Security Numbers in what is called the Earnings Suspense File. Since IRCA went into effect, the annual inflow of money into the Earnings Suspense File has risen from $7 billion in 1986 to $49 billion in 2000, for a total of $463 billion in contributions by

2003. (Although the file dates from 1937, the vast majority of contributions started to arrive in 1985.)[74]

From this perspective, it would seem such funds (if not claimed after a certain period) could be used to help pay the costs of health and welfare services, public schools, and language lessons (both Spanish and English) that are used by new (and old) immigrants—if they are not used to construct the fence!

Question of Remittances

Another major issue is that migrants help to stabilize the economies of their own countries. Overall, in Latin America migrant remittances have soared from $1.2 billion in 1980 to about $14.1 billion in 1990, to $31 billion in 2003. It was estimated that Latin American and Caribbean workers living abroad sent some $53.6 billion in remittances back to their homelands in 2005, up by around 17 percent from 2005. Salvadorians have been estimated to send some $2 billion back to El Salvador each year. Mexico is the top recipient of remittances in Latin America with migrants sending back around $20 billion in 2005, up from around $16.6 billion in 2004. As a source of foreign revenue, remittances were only exceeded by Mexican oil exports, overshadowing tourism and rivaling Foreign Direct Investment and the *maquila* industry (factories intended for re-export). In several Latin countries, remittances represented more than 10 percent of the gross domestic product.[75]

As the World Bank reported, "In 2005 remittance flows—defined as the sum of workers' remittances, compensation of employees, and migrant transfers in the balance-of-payments statistics . . . are estimated to have exceeded $233 billion worldwide, of which developing countries received $167 billion. Unrecorded flows moving through informal channels push the total far higher, as they are conservatively estimated to amount to at least 50 percent of the recorded flows."[76] Remittances can consequently have a significant effect on reducing poverty in that they are associated with increased household investment in education, entrepreneurship, and health. Remittances likewise tend to be counter-cyclical and thus support economic activity in the face of adverse shocks. Moreover, by generating a steady stream of foreign exchange, remittances can improve a country's creditworthiness and enhance its access to international capital markets.[77]

Given their size, it appears that any significant cut back of these remittances due to efforts to reduce "illegal" immigration in the United States would greatly harm, if not further destabilize Central American economies (and other countries)—if these lost earnings are not ultimately compensated for by an effectively functioning temporary work program, plus regional aid and development assistance.

At the same time, however, remittances surface questions as to whether the money sent back raises a culture of dependence and whether it makes Mexicans, Salvadorians, and others want to stay at home or flock to the United States. Or do remittances prevent Salvadorians and others from fully developing their new-found communities in the United States? Here the Cuban community built a powerful political-economic base in Miami precisely because Cubans could not send money back home. Ironically, Castro appeared to do his exiles a favor.

Development Assistance

One answer to the development question is the need to implement community-to-community investment and development projects. Such investment and development projects could help form links between Mexican and Salvadorian communities within the United States and abroad, so that these groups are no longer seen as sponging off the American taxpayer.

To really get to the heart of the problem, however, greater development assistance will need to be provided to Mexico and Central America while concurrently engaging in "fair trade." Development assistance, by itself, will not stop the inflow of illegal immigrants into the United States. The most important factor is to build up the agricultural sector through "fair trade"—which would involve the reduction of U.S. agricultural subsidies that hurt Mexican corn producers, for example. The issue of fair trade will need to be effectively addressed by forums such as the World Trade Organization (WTO) in coordination with the World Bank, UNCTAD, the IMF, UNDP, regional development banks, the OECD and other agencies through the Aid for Trade initiative[78]—if the issues of "fair trade' and "illegal" immigration are to be dealt with effectively.

In the meantime, despite the congressional "showdown" over "illegal" and "unauthorized" immigration and concern about the effects on employment by foreign immigration in general, the State Department still offers fifty thousand free immigrant visas to individuals from many countries through its Diversity Lottery (DV) Program each year.

Toward Regional Development

It appears that Congress has not been ready to tackle the real international roots of the "illegal" and "unauthorized" immigration problem, given general congressional reluctance to cut back U.S. farm subsidies and because of political opposition to overseas assistance (particularly with Iraq dominating foreign affairs concerns and the overseas funding agenda). On the domestic side, whether the issue of more than $463 billion in illegal alien contributions to U.S. Social Security could play a major role in the debate on domestic costs of "illegal" and "unauthorized" immigration remains to be seen.

While Democrats and Republicans continue to battle it out with contending proposals, as will the Senate and the House, it appears that Republicans are strongly divided. On the one side are the moderate and more pragmatic "globalists," who are willing to engage in free trade accompanied by a relative free movement of labor; on the other side are the hard-liners, who are more protectionist and who seek to cut taxes and overall public expenses where possible.

A populist alliance appears to be developing between wealthy hard-line Republicans and those Americans whose jobs appear to be most threatened by largely uneducated migrants. The question is whether the Bush administration really possesses enough finesse to weave a compromise between "automatic citizenship" (and general "amnesty") and "automatic expulsion." The fundamental dilemma is that it will be nearly impossible to engage in any large-scale expulsion—and even half steps might lead to a de facto amnesty and eventually to citizenship. In the post-September 11 psychological and political environments, there furthermore appears to be a real danger of imposing drastic police methods should xenophobic hard-liners win the upper hand—in particular if they can continue to confound specific issues, such as "illegal" immigration, with real, or exaggerated, threats of drug smuggling, criminality, and terrorism.

The long-term question is to consider whether the deepening concern with the social and economic "costs" of "illegal" immigration and domestic concerns with inequitable salaries, social security and health insurance, combined with a significant shift from essentially European to Hispanic and Asian immigration since 1990, will likewise help shift American foreign policy priorities toward Latin American and Asian affairs (or even toward greater hemispheric isolationism)—and away from foreign policy issues that concern Europe, Russia and the rest of the world. An ostrich-like isolationist position might increasingly become likely if efforts to reduce immigration in the United States cause a general rise of regional unemployment and a major reduction in remittances to Central America in the coming years, indirectly exacerbating social and political instability in the region. This in turn might lead to a self-fulfilling prophecy most feared by anti-immigrant hardliners, that is, increased criminality—if not major acts of terrorism within the American hemisphere and the United States itself, but not necessarily instigated by Islamist groups. On the other hand, the failure of isolationism to deal with terrorism and other domestic and international crises could eventually flip-flop into an interventionist patriotic-national backlash. (See Chapter 10.)

Due the dangerously precarious nature of the crisis, it might actually be in American interests to engage diplomatically with Venezuela and Chávez where appropriate—in that it is not necessarily certain that a more pro-American leadership will arise out of the domestic power struggle should Venezuela itself enter into another period of political-economic instability (whether instigated by U.S. pressures or not). From this perspective, Washington might need to bite the bullet and work with Venezuela and other states to help keep Latin Americans in Latin America by working toward the full scale development of Central and South America. This can be accomplished through the implementation of interlocking regional security communities that seek compromise between Chavez's Bolivarian vision and Washington's predilection for regional blocs permitting subsidized free trade.

CHAPTER 10

American Hypertrophy and Strategic Options: Toward a Geostrategy for Global Peace

In his essay, "The Vicissitudes of Things," written in 1597 toward the end of the Anglo-Spanish wars (1585 to 1604), which were part of the much wider Eighty Years War involving the Dutch secession from Spanish empire (1567/68 to 1648), Sir Francis Bacon observed at least three factors that could cause major power and regional wars:

> Upon the breaking and shivering of a great state and empire, you may be sure to have wars. For great empires, while they stand, do enervate and destroy the forces of the natives which they have subdued, resting upon their own protecting forces; and then when they fail also, all goes to ruin, and they become a prey. . . . The great accessions and unions of kingdoms do likewise stir up wars; for when a state grows to an over-power, it is like a great flood, that will be sure to overflow. . . . When a warlike state grows soft and effeminate, they may be sure of a war. For commonly such states are grown rich in the time of their degenerating; and so the prey inviteth, and their decay in valor, encourageth a war.

In contemporary circumstances, the first potential cause of war (the breaking and shivering of a great empire) could refer to the collapse of the Soviet Union, which having previously subdued the populations around it, is now subject to terrorist attack and the formation of counteralliances. The second potential cause of war is overexpansion, in which the state is seen as overflowing its appropriate bounds and upsetting the global equilibrium, like a giant flood. In contemporary circumstances, this could refer to NATO (and EU) enlargement, coupled with unilateral U.S. intervention in Iraq. The third cause of war is when a rich and powerful state begins to decline and degenerate and no longer desires to fight for its interests (for example, puts an end to military conscription)—which, in turn, invites attack. While the characterization of such policy need not be accepted as "effeminate," nor the moral stigma of the "decay in valor," it is plausible that retreat—as well as a turn toward domestic policy contemplation away from international engagement—could lead a state leadership to ignore external threats, but then become subject to attack at a later date.

The United States is presently somewhere between the two latter positions. Having broken the Soviet empire, opening a wider zone of conflict throughout central Asia, the Caucasus, the Middle East, and, more indirectly, Africa, the United States has now grown to an "over-power" through NATO enlargement and unilateral intervention in Iraq. At the same time, however, as the U.S. Congress discusses the withdrawal of its troops from Iraq, it risks opening the floodgates to states and antistate movements that seek to take advantage of perceived U.S. weakness and "decay in valor" in Iraq and elsewhere—even if the intervention in Iraq was appallingly ill-conceived and ill-executed—and took place for the trumped up reasons.

Unthinking the Now Thinkable

U.S. global strategy appears to be failing on a number of fronts, yet a radical reassessment of that strategy will only take place once the U.S. leadership and general public understand that the dangers of yet another global war involving the major powers are very real and that such a major power war could take place when least expected. Unlike hyper-rational scenarios in which nuclear war was to be fought out by the "superpowers" through calculated strikes as envisioned by a number of superhawkish cold war pundits, however, but also unlike the apocalyptic vision of mutual nuclear destruction as depicted by dovish peace activists and anti-nuclear movements, a number of differing, less rational, and not quite so apocalyptic, global war scenarios appear very plausible in post-September 11 circumstances.

In effect, such a global conflict could come about precisely in the coming transition period and danger zone in which the United States is caught, on the one hand, between the risks of overengagement and sins of commission and the risks of nonengagement and sins of omission, on the other. The danger of war could be aggravated in the transition period as the technologically advanced countries move away from a petroleum-based infrastructure to an economic infrastructure based on alternative energy resources and energy efficient technologies, particularly if a number of major oil producing countries cannot diversify their economies sufficiently to remain competitive while other countries cannot secure sufficient access to necessary resources and more efficient alternative technologies.

The risk is the disaggregation of one continental empire (the ex-Soviet Union), plus the overexpansion of the predominant overseas empire (the United States), coupled with the relative rise of various nationalist or religious movements, as well as numerous antistate partisan groups willing to use extreme violence, might soon set off another cycle of major-power conflict. Just as superhawkish neoconservatives pressured the administrations of both Bill Clinton and the George W. Bush to take military actions against the regime of Saddam Hussein, the rise of influential extremist factions tends to pressure governments of all kinds to take more militant steps even if the parties and leaderships of those extreme groups do not necessarily obtain political power. This is true because those elites that are in power generally seek to prevent extremist parties from coming to power—ironically by adopting some of their hard-line political demands.

The confrontation with Iran, for example, creates a scenario in which the memory of past injustices, combined with contemporary mutual imprecations, could buildup to the point that a relatively minor, yet symbolic, event (e.g., an assassination of a major leader, the taking of hostages, an act of sabotage) results in a "perfect explosion" in Clausewitzian terms. This scenario could become true if the United States attempts but fails to negotiate from a hawkish "position of strength": The failure to find a face-saving way to open the door to diplomacy with Iran (and Syria), as well as with various Iraqi opposition movements, could provoke the United States and Iran into confrontation (possibly sparked by a third actor, such as al-Qaida).

Or, by contrast, should the United States withdraw its forces too precipitously from Iraq without a firm negotiated settlement, differing states and partisan groups could seek to take advantage of new "power vacuums" caused by a significant withdrawal and perceived U.S. weakness by engaging in "preemptive" military actions in the region and throughout the world (ironically following U.S. footsteps in Iraq in 2003)—in taking the risk that the United States, NATO, or EU would not be willing to re-engage military forces or impose strong sanctions. At the same time, however, perceptions that Washington is permanently bogged down in Iraq could also lead states *outside the region* to take risks involving military action in the belief that the United States will not act elsewhere, even if the U.S. military presence in the Persian Gulf region does, at least for the present, appear to deter states such as Iran but not groups such as al-Qaida.

While it is dubious Turkey would intervene as long the United States maintains a strong presence inside Iraq and in Kurdistan in particular, this could change should the U.S. withdraw from Iraq altogether.[1] A precipitous withdrawal of U.S. forces from Iraq could lead to direct Turkish intervention in northern Iraq against the PKK in an effort to secure oil pipelines, for example, which in turn could draw Iran into the country in confrontation (or tacit cooperation) with Turkey, depending on Ankara's goals and upon how long Turkey stays. In effect, Turkey and Iran could forge a condominium over the Kurdish and Shi'a regions, thereby isolating regions controlled by Sunni factions. In addition to Turkey and Iran, other states could likewise engage in preemptive actions: With Lebanon in the midst of a civil war and Syria threatening intervention, Israel could strike the major Iranian nuclear enrichment facilities much as it stuck the Iraqi Osirak plant in 1981 (if the United States itself does not act); Iran might then try to counter-strike U.S. military bases in the Gulf if it cannot reach Israel or other states. China could wait for such a moment of perceived U.S. weakness to seize Taiwan.

Concurrently, al-Qaida (or other partisan movements) would be better positioned to infiltrate poor states such as Egypt, Jordan, Morocco, Bangladesh, Yemen, and Palestine, plus nuclear-capable Pakistan, or could attack oil rich Persian Gulf allies of the United States. In addition to plotting (or really propagandizing in support of) attacks by alienated groups (including non-Muslims) in the United Kingdom and the United States, the major focus of al-Qaida would be Saudi

Arabia, once Saudi fighters currently in Iraq sneak home. An insurrection there would involve the infiltration by al-Qaida into the police, security services, and the Saudi National Guard.[2] One scenario envisions a sophisticated attack (perhaps by commercial jets) on the Saudi oil complex that could take up to 50 percent of Saudi oil production off the market for at least six months, because over half of Saudi Arabia's oil reserves are contained in just eight fields. As only Saudi Arabia presently possesses sufficient reserves to make up for short falls in the global oil market, this act of catastrophic terrorism would likewise drain most of the world's spare capacity, sending world oil prices skyrocketing.[3] Here, the United States would prepare to seize the oil fields, but to what avail?

There is moreover a real danger that differing states and antistate partisan movements (generally with extreme nationalist or religious ideologies) will continue their struggle against U.S. predominance—whether Washington remains bogged down in Iraqi quicksand and engaging in skirmishes with Iran (thus exhibiting impotence) or whether it withdraws too precipitously from Iraq (thus ostensibly exhibiting cowardliness). Without a firmly negotiated political settlement involving conflicting Iraqi factions and their neighbors, the struggle against U.S. predominance would additionally occur even after a *partial* or *phased* withdrawal of U.S. forces from Iraq—and *even if* Washington claims that it will focus more intently on al-Qaida and remain engaged in the defense of the Gulf region and elsewhere. Such a no-win situation could eventually provoke Washington to re-intervene in a Bonapartist or eagle-like patriotic-nationalist backlash. The more U.S. forces find themselves over-committed and sinking deeper into quicksand in Afghanistan and Iraq, the more the option of global strike planning "without resort to large numbers of general purpose forces" may be considered by the Pentagon—in accord with the Stratcom contingency plan (CONPLAN 8022-02) for dealing with "imminent" threats from countries such as North Korea or Iran.[4]

If events consequently spin out of U.S. control, third parties could become directly or indirectly involved. Iran's threat to develop nuclear and ballistic missiles has already begun to fuel a mushrooming "insecurity-security dialectic" between the United States and Russia, involving a renewed arms rivalry with ballistic missiles and ballistic missile defense (BMD). Likewise, a somewhat similar spiraling "insecurity-security dialectic" is also fueling a ballistic missile and BMD rivalry among the United States, South Korea, China, and Japan over the North Korean threat to develop ballistic missiles and nuclear weaponry, combined with Chinese irredentist claims to Taiwan. The potential deployment of BMD systems by the United States in eastern Europe and Asia might furthermore lead Russia and China to engage in even closer defense collaboration—in the effort to develop new technologies so as to circumvent advanced BMD technology.

On the one hand, China appears to be focusing on the United States as its primary threat (with less mention of Russia) and has been developing a strategy of "active defense," which could possibly envision the preemptive use of nuclear weaponry.[5] On the other hand, the Bush administration's Nuclear Posture Review of December 2001 envisioned possible use of nuclear weapons in conflicts with Iran, Syria, North Korea, Russia, and China (particularly over Taiwan). The 2001 Nuclear Posture Review also envisioned the use of nuclear weaponry in case of use of chemical or biological weaponry against U.S. interests; or else in case of "surprising developments," which include "sudden regime change by which an existing nuclear arsenal comes into the hands of a new, hostile leadership group, or an opponent's surprise unveiling of WMD capabilities."[6] This could refer to Pakistan or Saudi Arabia, among other countries.

Major and regional power conflict could also be sparked by disputes over energy pipelines in the Caucasus and Black Sea regions to Europe or over Sea Lines of Communication (SLOCs) involving trade and energy transport from the Persian Gulf and Indian Ocean to the South China Sea—not to overlook forceful efforts to secure access to oil-rich islets, such as the Tunb isles in the Persian Gulf (claimed by the United Arab Emirates but held by Iran), the Spratly Islands in the South China sea, or the Daioyo/Senkaku and the Dokdo/Takeshima islands in the Pacific, among other possibilities, including Russian, Danish, Canadian, and U.S. claims to vast Arctic resources. As was the case in the battle over the Falklands/Malvinas Islands between Argentina and Britain in 1982, other island disputes and efforts to block major choke points and sea lines of communication could spark significant conflicts, particularly as the development of "swarming" techniques using rapid speed boats permits lesser states and antistate actors to attack large naval vessels.

From Moscow's perspective, NATO and EU enlargement is problematic in that disputes with Russian neighbors threaten to become Alliance and European Union dilemmas as opposed to bilateral concerns, thus making such disputes potentially more difficult to resolve. This appears to be the case with Poland and Estonia in their disputes with Russia, as they begin to be mediated by NATO and the EU (see Chapter 2). Efforts to draw Ukraine and Georgia into NATO raise Russian fears of a "Baltic-Black Sea alliance" that seeks to isolate Moscow and its allies—and consequently condemn Russia to a permanently landlocked status. Opposition to a Baltic-Black Sea alliance, in turn, leads Moscow to retrench in the formation of a Belarus-Russia-Kazakhstan-China axis (plus Iran and India?). With tensions between Russia and Georgia heating up, it also leads Moscow to concurrently grip onto the "frozen conflicts" in the Caucasus as bargaining leverage in opposition to independence for Kosovo.[7]

Here, the Russian Federation's fears of disaggregation, coupled with a burgeoning Muslim population, combined with fears that Ukraine, India, or even China might switch out of relative neutrality (thus aligning with the United States against Russia) could exacerbate geostrategic and political economic tensions in the background. Given Russian nationalist claims to the Crimea, the possibility that Ukraine could splinter into conflicting regions could provoke NATO, EU, and Russian military intervention. Fears of shifting alliances turning against Russia's "vital" interests could accordingly give rise to a Russian patriotic-nationalist backlash (in the form of a "two headed eagle") and make the Russian elite (already afraid of losing their power and privileges) even more adamant about deflecting Chinese attention against the United States. As Moscow seeks to secure control over its far eastside, one geostrategic option could be a Russian-Chinese condominium over Mongolia that is designed to check U.S. and Japanese influence.

For its part, the United States will be concerned with Russia's ability to draw some of these same pivot states (Ukraine, India, China, plus Turkey) into closer alliances. Moreover, really beyond Russia's influence is China's growing, yet unsteady, political-economic influence, combined with its Communist Party's own fears of popular insurgence and disaggregation. These fears lead Beijing to counter U.S. regional and global predominance by means of augmenting its naval and nuclear capabilities, and to threaten to seize Taiwan by force. The latter threats raise U.S. and Japanese fears of a Chinese quest for hegemonic expansion throughout the Asia Pacific—while China, in turn, opposes a more expansionist and militant Japan backed by the United States. In addition to Beijing's threat to pull out some $400 billion invested in U.S. Treasury securities, would the United States be willing to risk Los Angeles for Taipei?

While September 11 took place as a "bolt from the blue sky," other scenarios have forewarned of a "bolt from the blue sea," in which a cargo ship or minisub is set to explode with poisonous chemicals or radioactive materials, or even tactical nuclear weapons. Such a James Bond-type scenario should not be entirely ruled out, given the attack on the USS *Cole* by a small harbor boat loaded with explosives.[8] Or more simply, another scenario would involve the sinking of a supertanker to block the Strait of Hormuz (where roughly 40 percent of the global oil supply passes) or the narrow regions of the Strait of Malacca, where roughly 40 percent of the world's total trade and 50 percent of the world's trade in oil and natural gas transit. The United States could also stage a coup in Venezuela to secure oil supplies and to check foreign influence that could engage in terrorist activities in the region and within the United States itself. (See Chapter 9.) It would likewise seek to secure African oil reserves.

In the assumption that the major powers do not seek to obliterate each other with nuclear weaponry but could still threaten the use of nuclear weaponry to gain political concessions (with Moscow deploying short range missiles in Kaliningrad, for example, to pressure the Baltic states and Poland), even wars between major powers might also take on an *asymmetrical* dimension through the use of cyber-sabotage and "special force" operations that target financial, industrial, energy infrastructure (nuclear power plants, chemical manufacturers, and/or oil refinery facilities), and other targets of either material or symbolic importance. The latter scenario would parallel actions between the two nuclear states, India and Pakistan, in which conflict has taken the form of support for "terrorist" organizations coupled with periodic low intensity border clashes and threats to use nuclear weaponry—as took place in the May-July 1999 crisis in Kargil, Kashmir.[9]

States could likewise seek to destroy satellite and communications technology by conventional means; one of the first targets of major-power war might be to strike space-based communication systems so as to "blind" the enemy, as China's antisatellite test signified in January 2007—and as Russia has likewise threatened in order to counter the U.S. military advantage in space communications and network centric warfare. Or, more even more dangerously, nuclear capable states could explode electromagnetic pulse bombs in the atmosphere in an effort to destroy the enemy's telecommunications capacity and its cyber technology.

As more and more states begin to augment their military-technological capabilities, major powers might simultaneously seek to preempt the burgeoning nuclear and missile capabilities of lesser states that are hostile to their interests through the use of "bunker buster" bombs equipped with earth-penetration aids, for example. As the nuclear threshold lowers due to the miniaturization of nuclear warheads and other explosive devices, the use of "tactical" nuclear weaponry might result in "limited" nuclear wars in regions of dispute. The use of "tactical" nuclear weaponry would ironically "vindicate" the early work of Herman Kahn, Henry Kissinger and Thomas Schelling (but not at all in the way they anticipated) because post-cold war concepts of preemption and asymmetrical warfare have been eroding clear distinctions between differing "useable" and "non-useable" weapons systems and between the cultural and legalistic limitations that had been imposed on differing conventions of warfare during the cold war.[10]

Here, developing states might see a relative advantage in the use of tactical nuclear weapons versus the high-tech military superiority of the "revolution in military affairs." If attacked by a "dual use" cruise missile, for example, a less technologically sophisticated state, such as North Korea, might respond with a nuclear counterstrike, having no idea if the warhead fired at it was nuclear or conventional. At the same time, however, as illustrated by cyber attacks on Estonian communications systems in 2007 (see Chapter 2), even more sophisticated warfare against communication systems could take place without the use of nuclear weaponry, such as a "cyber sabotage" attack on the Federal Reserve's electronic network, which handles all federal funds and transactions, effectively destroying the U.S. government's ability to operate. Other cyber-targets could include the Pentagon and the Homeland Security Organization itself.[11]

Options for American Global Strategy

Despite its clear military superiority and global outreach, the power, interests, and political-economic influence of the United States are increasingly being challenged by a number of emerging or reemerging states, as well as antistate actors, which might or might not align with the interests of various states. What options are available as the United States enters an increasingly hostile international environment? As U.S. policymakers battle it out in Washington, which species of foreign policymaker will win out: Hawks, who represent advocates of peace through strength and the potential use of force; Doves, who are advocates of peace through diplomacy without the threat of force; Superhawks and Vultures, which are varieties of neo-conservative unilateralists who advocate preemption or seek to take advantage of failed states through "regime change" by force if necessary; Gulls, who are "selective" interventionists; Ostriches, who are hemispheric isolationists who seek to limit U.S. diplomatic and military engagements throughout the world; Eagles, who are extremely patriotic nationalists who, unlike superhawks and vultures, advocate engaged diplomacy with regimes of all kinds, but who are also willing to use force unilaterally; Owls, who are multilateralists and flexible realists who seek to use force only as a last resort preferably backed by the UN; or else a hybrid alliance of differing species?

During the cold war, a rather clear dichotomy developed between "hawks" and "doves." The hawks-versus-doves dichotomy has, however, largely been replaced by the essentially post–cold war split between neoconservative "super-hawks" and "vultures" versus multilateralist "owls."[12] While owlish multilateralists essentially had the upper hand in the administrations of George H. W. Bush Sr. and Bill Clinton, superhawks and vultures gained the upper hand in the Ronald Reagan administration as well as that of George W. Bush Jr., at least up into the midterm November 2006 congressional elections, when a mix of hawks, owls, and eagles appeared to gain the upper hand.

In post-September 11 circumstances, dovish voices have certainly been side-lined in the name of the "global war on terrorism" in which the possibility of a conciliatory diplomacy, without the threat or use of force, has largely been ruled out. Conversely, more traditional hawks have come back to the forefront follow-ing the appointment of Robert Gates as secretary of defense to replace Donald Rumsfeld after the Democratic victory in the congressional midterm elections in November 2006. Concurrently, with the publication of the *Iraq Study Group Report*, a more flexible "owlish" strategy has gained ground, cutting into the for-mer neoconservative and Christian conservative predominance that characterized the first-term administration of President George W. Bush. At the same time, however, a number of superhawk neoconservative voices have not entirely lost their position with regard to questions related to the Middle East and Iran, in particular. This is true despite the fact that the superhawkish pretense to take the "high moral ground" has, for the most part, been exposed as a genetically modi-fied fake in Iraq. In other words, in their demands for "regime change" by uni-lateral force in Iraq (and elsewhere), neoconservatives have been revealed to be vultures, if not "chickenhawks" (in that a few avoided the draft during the Vietnam War), as opposed to the superhawks that they had originally claimed to be.

The dilemma posed here is that many of the traditional U.S. foreign policy options appear bankrupt. The hawkish "peace through strength" risks confronta-tion with Iran, Russia, and China. The gullish "selective interventionism" approach remains reluctant to engage in multilateral diplomacy and concerted actions.[13] An ostrich-like return to "isolationism" could result in "domestic paral-ysis" characterized by a debilitating and indecisive U.S. foreign policy—and could actually help set off greater tensions and conflicts abroad by denying all forms of intervention, including diplomatic, outside of North and South America. There is an additional danger that a patriotic-nationalist backlash (resulting in unilateral U.S. overreaction in the name of the bald headed eagle) could come about in the not so long term after perceived defeat in Afghanistan, Iraq or elsewhere. Here, for example, calls to intervene against Iranian nuclear facilities unilaterally, or against Al-Qaida in Pakistan (an action that could further destabilize the country if it is not fully supported by Islamabad) could represent the debut of an American patriotic-nationalist backlash.

Following the ill-conceived and ill-executed intervention in Iraq and given popular U.S. demands to focus on critical domestic problems, the most likely foreign policy option once the administration of George W. Bush leaves office is not so much that of a patriotic nationalist backlash, but that of a *partial* or *phased* withdrawal from Iraq (as the Democrats and some key Republicans appear to be demanding), with corresponding domestic pressures toward isolationism and to avoid military engagement (or at least troop deployments) altogether. At the same time, however, although such groups will no longer be predominant, there will still be some significant pressure for unilateral intervention from those superhawks, vultures, and newly hatched eagles who can sustain their credibility. These pressures (which could demand the return of a military draft) could result in extreme policy flip-flops between demands for intervention and demands for ostrich-like isolationism.

The dilemma with the latter isolationist approach, however, is that if the United States does decide to leave the outside world alone for too long—without attempting to work with other major powers and states in a truly concerted fashion in the effort to manage the present crisis—the world will definitely come back to haunt it—and in more ways than one. This is because an "isolationist" United States would cease to play a role as a defensive "counterbalancer" (and as a potential mediator if it can truly play the role of "honest broker") between conflicting states and partisan movements. An isolationist approach would tend to release major and regional powers to assert their own interests, particularly in situations in which the UN and international mediation could not pick up the pieces precisely because of a lack of U.S. or UN Security Council support. Furthermore, even if the new administration in Washington did not adopt a formal policy of isolationism and sought to hedge its position, it could enter into a period of debilitating and indecisive policy mishmash, which would likewise open the door to major and regional power conflicts as states and partisan groups seek to take advantage of the U.S. unwillingness to intervene or engage in some form of UN-backed multilateral sanctions that could possibly involve the use of force.

From this perspective, between the extremes of a superhawk, vulture-like, or even eagle-inspired interventionism and an ostrich-like isolationism, a more flexible multilateral approach to the contemporary foreign policy dilemmas needs to be adopted. The fact that the world has become increasingly interdependent despite the fact that states possess highly uneven political-economic and military vulnerabilities means that the United States cannot escape playing a leading role in "managing" world affairs, but it must also be willing to let other states and the United Nations lead through contact groups and multilateral diplomacy.

The key U.S. policy dilemma of the post-September 11, 2001 world is accordingly how to implement owlish elements of *multilateral dissuasion* and *persuasion* to draw back the global war on terror, to stabilize Iraq, and to attempt to prevent wider regional conflicts, while concurrently seeking to avert the real possibility of a major-power war—possibly sparked by acts of violence and "terrorism." Moreover, in order to avert such destabilizing acts of "terrorism," a more comprehensive approach to preventing the underlying social, political, economic, and geopolitical causes of violent extremism, coupled with sincere Occidental efforts to engage in more positive cultural interaction with the Arab/Islamic worlds in particular, as far as possible, will need to be implemented. (See Chapter 1.)

Although the United States can and must engage in diplomacy intended to prevent conflict wherever possible, the key question now, in post-Iraq War circumstances, is not so much how to *prevent* societal conflict and war between all societies and states altogether, but rather how to *limit* the number and intensity of acts of "terrorism" often associated with societal conflicts and regional wars so as to prevent or contain the most destructive conflicts. This means a continued willingness to threaten, and possibly engage in, force where absolutely necessary, but also a greater willingness to engage in real dialogue and multilateral actions with both friends *and* "enemies" alike. In that it generally takes years to formulate and implement effective foreign policies, U.S. strategy must soon develop a more truly concerted and multilateral conciliatory approach to major and regional power disputes, sooner rather than later.

Here, the forthcoming administration (whether Republican or Democrat) can begin to apply a truly *peace- and security-oriented* "cost-benefit" analysis that more carefully weighs U.S. national and international interests and then chooses policy options in terms of differing, and often conflicting, geostrategic, political economic, military-technological, energy-ecological, sociocultural/ideological interests, as well as moral/ethical issues and considerations. Such a peace- and security-oriented "cost-benefit" analysis is not to be regarded in strictly "economic" terms, but rather seeks to weigh the long-term domestic and international costs and benefits of "unilateralism" versus "isolationism" versus "multilateralism." Such an approach seeks to weigh the real risk of geostrategic and military-technological *hypertrophy* with domestic political-economic trade-offs and opportunity costs, often resulting from limited resources.

Here, for example, rather than resurrecting a military draft that would not really suit the needs of a high-tech military, the United States could provide incentives to create a truly international peacekeeping corps that would involve itself in peace keeping, ecological cleanup operations, disease eradication, and economic development under a UN mandate. Not at all ignoring moral or ethical considerations, such an approach would likewise seek to weigh questions involving moral/ethical/health issues, such as those related to the potential legalization of drugs in the United States as discussed in Chapters 6 and 9 as well as sociocultural ideological interests (such as proclaimed support for democratic values) with tough questions as to how to go about negotiating with "illiberal" regimes and the consequent risks of "appeasement" in the process of seeking "regime reform" as opposed to "regime change." Such an approach would also seek to choose alternative energies and technologies that are less alienating to man and nature. The ultimate purpose would be to establish a stable global order based upon interlocking regional security communities with a modicum of social and economic justice for the citizens of those regions.

In geostrategic terms, this approach would require a diplomatic revolution involving engagement with both "friends" and "enemies" alike. Such a diplomatic revolution would require that the United States and the EU and Japan move toward an entente, if not an alliance, with Russia, thereby going beyond the presently very tense détente in which Russia is beginning to threaten the use of force to assert its interests, ironically as a means to press the United States and NATO into a closer alliance relationship. This diplomatic revolution would be aimed partly in the effort to mitigate Moscow's apparently increasing tendency toward authoritarianism and partly in the effort to channel China's rise to major power status rather than contain it. As China is projected to become a major military and political economic actor in the coming years, Washington, in working closely with Russia, Japan, and the EU, will need to find the appropriate means to channel China's rise so as not to permit it to radically undercut the U.S., Japanese, and European political economies, while at the same time not isolating Beijing altogether. This would likewise mean working with Russia and China in the effort to moderate regimes such as North Korea and Iran and to forge regional security communities with these same states and others.

In political-economic terms, these regional security communities would be based upon ecologically sound and humanistic principles of sustainable development. This would entail international technological cooperation in developing new alternative energies and energy efficient technologies while assisting major oil producers to diversify their economies and helping other countries develop or implement energy and transport technologies involving solar energy, wind power, flex fuels, hydrogen power, geothermal energy, and so on. This would minimize recourse to nuclear power, except perhaps for "fourth generation" nuclear plants, which are said to be less dangerous, more fuel efficient, and proliferation proof. Here, for example, the United States, Japan, China, and India all have a common interest in reducing their dependence upon imported oil by developing ecological and energy efficient options, while Russia, Saudi Arabia, Venezuela, Iran, Nigeria, and other major oil producing states will need to diversify their economies as much as possible to offset the possible deleterious effects of a future decline in oil revenues. Countries such as Brazil and China and others in the Caribbean, Africa, and Asia will need investment assistance to develop bio and flex fuels and other alternatives without cutting into the production of staple crops such as corn and sugar for human consumption. (See Chapters 4, 8, and 9).

Additionally, accomplishing these grand strategic tasks will require the formation of new alliances between differing domestic species in the United States so that owls, gulls, ostriches, and doves can join forces against superhawks and vultures, while drawing in as many eagles and traditional hawks as possible.

Dividing Walls versus Interlocking Regional Security Communities

One way to deter conflict (and postpone dealing with seemingly intractable political disputes) has traditionally been to build walls. While some contemporary walls have crumbled, other walls appear to be going up. On the one hand, Mikhail Gorbachev did bring down the Berlin Wall unilaterally; on the other hand, unless both NATO and the EU can find ways to work with Russia, both have been erecting a microelectronic curtain along the Polish-Belarusian and Russian borders, which could soon be followed by a partition of Ukraine (if not civil war). Placed under international sanctions, South Africa was able to abolish the internal invisible, but real, walls of apartheid. The Indians and Pakistanis have at least begun discussions about modifying the Line of Control and seeking a fair resolution to the Kashmir crisis.

North and South Korea have at least permitted families to reunite across the Demilitarized Zone, even if that line is still overcharged with land mines, troops, and missiles. In 2007, conflict in Northern Ireland that divided Protestants (who sought strong links between northern Ireland and the United Kingdom) and Catholics (who sought a united Ireland) appears, at long last, to have found an end through a power-sharing government reached between the leadership of First Minister Ian Paisley (Democratic Union Party) and Deputy First Minister Martin McGuinness (Sinn Fein)—an agreement that could serve a possible model for other violent and seemingly intractable conflicts.

Conversely, Israel is building a wall between itself and the Palestinians but on portions of territory claimed by Palestinians (who are, in turn, digging trenches between Fatah and Hamas). Saudi Arabia is constructing a high-tech nine hundred-kilometer fence along the Saudi-Iraqi border to check Iraqi refugees and al-Qaida infiltration. The EU has been trying to build walls between itself and illegal immigrants from Africa and Asia. While the United States abolished the not-so-invisible walls of slavery and Jim Crow, Washington is now constructing a real high-tech "fence" along the Rio Grande on territory once seized in the 1846–1848 War with Mexico (in which President James Polk was, at that time, accused of usurping war-making powers by Abraham Lincoln). The Pentagon has also sought to wall off Sunni and Shi'a communities along the Sunni enclave of Adhamiya in Badhdad. While building BMD systems in Europe and Asia and other regional "theater" TMD systems, there is a real risk that the United States could abandon its NATO commitments and attempt to hide behind the wall of national missile defense.

Once again, walls appear symbolic of deeper tensions and disputes that appear intractable but that require patience, determination, and real leadership to address. The problem is that walls might freeze disputes and conflicts temporarily, but they do not necessarily resolve or transform those conflicts, particularly if there are ways to get over, around or beneath those walls—as any number of terrorist groups and illegal immigrants are finding possible. As walls separate, but do not unite without doors and openings, the primary way to prevent conflict is to forge inclusive and interlocking power sharing arrangements between those in dispute: the tighter the cooperation and the trust, the less the possibility that conflict will occur, and the more doors can remain open.

In terms of state relations, major powers in particular move through differing phases of confrontation as well as *détente, entente,* and *alliance.* The problem then is to prevent the alienation or isolation of any one major power (or significant regional power) so that those states and leaderships can participate in the basic decisions that concern their perceived "vital" interests that affect their well-being and security as well. States do not want to be caught by surprise; if states in disputes can agree on a framework to secure their "vital" interests (even if those interests must be redefined), then they can live in peace and are more likely to accept essential reforms. If not, then disputes and tensions will result in *power-based bargaining* and *strategic leveraging* that might attempt to achieve conflict resolution or transformation by the threat of force—but that could still erupt in conflict.

There is an additional danger that, as formerly hostile leaderships move toward an entente or alliance relationship, third parties could seek to undermine whatever accords are reached, or that the accords accepted might fail to satisfy the expectations of one side or the other and are consequently misinterpreted, possibly reigniting conflict. Another possibility is that one side might seek to take advantage of any accord reached, thus generating accusations of betrayal.

Not all states are power hungry; not all states can expand their power indefinitely. (The United States continues to assert itself as the world's "leading power" despite its catastrophic mismanagement of world affairs after its 2003 intervention in Iraq, but it might soon find itself on a steep political-economic decline and hypertrophy if it continues on its present path.) Most states seek "security," not power; state leaderships and partisan organizations likewise seek recognition and legitimization in terms of both domestic and international support. Yet here, not all states need to adopt neo-realist "self-help" forms of security by developing independent nuclear weapons or WMD capacities, for example.[14] Moreover, in a highly interdependent world characterized by mutual (albeit highly uneven) vulnerabilities and highly inequitable power capabilities and distribution of financial and industrial resources, most states cannot survive alone but need security supports or guarantees, as well as political economic cooperation and financial assistance, from generally more powerful and developed third parties; "self help" is not always a truly "realistic" option.

States can join more traditionally exclusive systems of collective defense, such as NATO, without building their own nuclear weaponry, but they can also join more inclusive "regional security communities" in which their security (and political-economic well-being) is guaranteed by other states in combination, in forms of cooperative or collective security. Given the highly uneven vulnerabilities of the interstate systems, coupled with the vagaries of global market and financial forces in the era of "globalization," regional security communities can also help stabilize domestic economies by providing wider access to markets and promises of investments, and by involving "power sharing" between differing parties and states in a "confederal" context.

As there is really no such a thing as true "national independence" since no country is truly a self-sufficient "island," regional security communities and confederations can provide a viable alternative to anarchy and perpetual interstate and intrastate conflict. Regional security communities—whether tightly or loosely coupled or essentially *exclusive* or *inclusive*—are furthermore much more common than generally recognized. The 1842 Webster-Ashburton Treaty, for example, which helped define the U.S.-Canada border (and which also provided for British-U.S. cooperation in the suppression of the slave trade) represented a "regional security community" since its inception, one that has prevented a "wall" of troops from being built between Canada and the United States. By contrast, NATO and the Warsaw Pact represented two essentially exclusive and conflicting regional security communities that built walls of tanks and missiles between them.

While the European Union thus far represents the most tightly coupled and generally inclusive security community, other more loosely coupled communities include the OSCE, ASEAN, the Organization of American States, and the African Union. The Gulf Cooperation Council might represent a nascent security community as well. A regional security community for North African countries and a new Palestine would require Israeli and Turkish cooperation and could be implemented through a U.S.-EU-backed Mediterranean initiative. (See Chapter 5.) A security community forged by the Black Sea states would require NATO, EU, Russian, and Turkish cooperation as well. (See Chapter 2.)

If granted U.S. recognition and security guarantees, North Korea might eventually accept membership in a "regional security community." On paper, the February 2007 six-party accords with regard to North Korea are a step in the right direction toward the development of a Northeast Asia "regional security community," although much work needs to be done to implement those accords. (See Chapter 7.) While time and money is needed, the Korean example shows that the owlish negotiation process involving "front door" multilateralism is more effective in the long term than would be the neoconservative "solution" of attempting preemptive strikes or pressing for destabilizing regime change.[15]

To find ways to make peace between Colombia and Venezuela, the United States should consider the formation of a new "contact group" involving the OAS states of Brazil, Argentina, Peru, Mexico, and Cuba, among other interested parties, while at the same time seeking ways to develop the countries of Central and South America so as to reduce pressure to emigrate to the United States. The concern raised here is that U.S. efforts to expel illegal immigrants and block further migration could result in the general rise in political economic instability, criminality, drug dealing, if not acts of terrorism, in Central and South America. Although regional integration efforts have failed in the past, strong U.S. support for regional integration with contact group supports should work once the United States sees Central American integration in its own national interest. Here, there needs to be compromise between Hugo Chávez's efforts to forge an exclusive and protectionist "Bolivarian" trade zone through Mercusor versus U.S. efforts to forge a Free Trade Area of the Americas, which, in effect, permits U.S. agricultural production to remain heavily subsidized.

An additional yet related concern is that the "war on drugs" appears to be failing in both Latin America and Afghanistan largely because the United States alone cannot check the forces of worldwide market demand for drugs. In Afghanistan, drug revenues have increased and with them the strength of both pro- and anti-government narcotics traffickers, as well as the Taliban and al-Qaida. The "war on drugs" (what is really a civil war) is devastating Colombian society and strengthening the hand of both pro- and anti-government drug lords who are increasingly linked with various "terrorist" groups. Much as Prohibition in the United States helped strengthen the Mafia and generally augmented the demand for hard liquor, making the situation from 1920 to 1933 even worse, today's drug laws make a very bad situation even worse, strengthening drug cartels if not "terrorist" organizations. While working with Latin American states to find ways to wind down the "war on drugs," one option is to make opium and coca derived drugs (from Afghanistan and Colombia/Bolivia respectively) for medicinal purposes so farmers could produce for a legitimate market. Yet the deeper roots of the problem stem from domestic demand in the United States (and Europe) and needs to be resolved in the United States through a de-penalization and legalization of "softer" drugs in strictly controlled circumstances, combined with a extremely tough crackdown on the most malicious kinds of drugs, coupled with intensive education efforts against the use of *all* drugs, alcohol and cigarettes included. Such a controversial policy would be intended to sever links between newly legalized businesses, mafias, and partisan "terrorist" groups and prevent the United States and NATO from sinking even deeper into these regional quagmires. (See Chapters 6 and 9.)

Establishing regional security communities in the African "zone of conflict" (in the Gulf of Guinea, for example, but ultimately in regions such as Darfur, Congo, and the Horn of Africa) will prove very complicated but could prove possible if a portion of the billions in revenues generated from offshore oil can be more appropriately and equitably reinvested onshore. (See Chapter 6.) In general, significant territorial and legal disputes throughout the world over islands, fishing, minerals, natural gas, and oil in general, in which valuable resources are not being developed or not being utilized precisely because development projects are being held up or delayed, could be adjudicated by the UN as an intermediary, perhaps through a strengthened International Seabed Authority. If so, then the revenues obtained by all sides could then be used to help fund a number of reconstruction and development projects and "regional security communities."

Toward a NATO-EU-Russian "Security Community"

At the end of the cold war, both Germany and Ukraine gave up their option of nuclear independence for the acceptance of security guarantees from third parties in joining differing regional security communities.[16] Rather than seeking to develop its own nuclear capability, a unified Germany looked to an enlarged NATO to protect its expanded sphere of influence and security. (Bonn/Berlin likewise looked to nuclear security guarantees from France and the United Kingdom as well.) While a unified Germany adopted the more traditional approach of seeking collective defense from NATO, Ukraine took a collective security approach in 1994, after being dissuaded by Russian threats and pressures, while concurrently being persuaded by U.S. and UN Security Council incentives, to abandon its nuclear weaponry left over from the Soviet stockpile. More recently, however, Russian pressures have led Ukraine to consider joining a more traditional collective defense community through NATO membership. But here, Ukrainian membership in NATO may be seen as provocative from the Russian perspective and could provoke civil conflict, if not worse, given vested Russian interests and pro-Russian regions in Ukraine. (See Chapter 2.)

In effect, despite the general post-September 11, 2001 opening to the Russian Federation, coupled with the formation of the NATO-Russian Council in May 2002, and despite Russian efforts to maintain positive relations with the United States, the European Union, NATO, and Russia have not yet been able to fully cooperate. In many ways, in part in response to the NATO-EU "double enlargement," as well as a result of the political-economic consequences of post-Soviet collapse, Russia seems to be developing a more authoritarian, "Eurasian" system of overlapping alliances and trade agreements and model of political-economic development, with strong governmental intervention in the "commanding heights" of the economy (an essentially Tsarist approach that predated Leninism)—as opposed to adopting a "liberal democratic" approach as supported by the United States.

These U.S.-NATO-EU-Russian-Ukrainian tensions can, however, be ameliorated by enhanced cooperation in a *strengthened* NATO-Russia Council that would seek joint cooperation in ballistic missile defense, particularly if Washington can be convinced that BMD is excessively costly, that it does not represent a panacea against the new asymmetrical threats, and that sharing security with Russia is in the greater national and international interest. Moreover, the United States and Russia need to renegotiate the CFE treaty and reduce conventional and nuclear forces, including tactical nuclear weaponry. Russia would be permitted a veto in NATO only in specific areas of security that affect its "vital" interests (but here NATO and Russia need to begin the sensitive process of defining those "vital" interests). Both Ukrainian and Russian membership in NATO could help widen and strengthen that "regional security community" by finding compromise over territorial and other disputes, thus preventing the formation of rival military blocs and conflict communities as occurred during the cold war. Such a position would also move NATO and Russia toward *cooperative-collective security* in defense against antistate terrorism and against weapons of mass destruction (WMD) threats from regional powers.

Here, a U.S.-Russian-EU-Turkish partnership or entente is absolutely crucial to establishing Black Sea regional security through the creation of a separate regional command. Closer U.S.-EU-Russian cooperation with regard to Iran is also essential to restraining Tehran's drive for a potential nuclear weapons capability and for obtaining regional hegemony. The NATO-Russian Council likewise needs to engage with Turkey, as well as Romania and Bulgaria, in airspace reconnaissance, border controls, and coastal security in the effort to check drug smuggling, organized crime, human trafficking, and "terrorist" activities, for example.

To finally bring peace to the Caucasus and the Balkans, the NATO-Russian Council should consider the option of deploying Partnership for Peace peacekeeping forces under UN or Organization for Security and Cooperation in Europe mandates—possibly alongside Russian forces—in the "frozen conflicts." Here, the failure to negotiate a loose confederal solution for Kosovo could open a can of worms in both the Balkans and the Caucasus as any number of "suppressed" groups in Georgia, Moldova, and elsewhere could press demands for "independence" despite the need for greater political economic cooperation in a highly interdependent world. Here, the option of confederation, as opposed to demands for national "independence," needs to be strongly emphasized in international policy forums.

As Russia would also oppose the return of the Taliban in Afghanistan, greater U.S.-NATO cooperation with the Collective Security Treaty Organization (CSTO) and with the Shanghai Cooperation Organization (SCO) appears crucial to prevent the ongoing conflicts in Central Asia and the Caucasus from intensifying. At the same time, the United States and Russia need to cooperate with states such as Saudi Arabia and Qatar who can try to mediate between Kabul and the Taliban, among other pan-Islamic movements in central and south Asia.

Toward a Euro-Mediterranean Security Community

A regional security community could also be framed for Israel and the Palestinians, for example, that would protect both sides from acts of terrorism and counterterrorism, as well as from other WMD threats from the region (as Iranian missiles aimed at Israel threaten Palestinians as well). Sincere U.S., EU, Russian and the UN efforts through the quartet group to engage in diplomacy to end the Israeli-Palestinian conflict would go a long way in symbolically showing the way to peace—pointing the way to the potential resolution of other conflicts that plague the Islamic world and that militarize highly educated young men and women, helping divide the militant from the less militant Islamist factions. The Quartet, along with the international community, thus needs to pressure Israel to finally engage in the exchange of land for peace in the West Bank and to resolve other outstanding issues of dispute so as to prevent intra-Palestinian strife between Fatah and Hamas from even further radicalizing Arab and pan-Islamist factions.

The dilemma is that efforts to achieve a power sharing arrangement between Hamas and Fatah have thus far failed miserably; power-sharing efforts on a regional basis can ultimately be attempted if political economic linkages can be forged between Fatah and Palestinians on the West Bank and Jordan and Israel, and if Saudi Arabia, Egypt, and Qatar can influence Hamas (in Gaza) to modify its position and to join a Palestinian confederation linked more indirectly to Egypt and Israel. The deployment of NATO Partnership for Peace forces on Palestinian territories, under a general UN mandate, could help solidify the peace with Israel, as long as these peacekeepers are truly seen as "honest brokers."

In the longer term, the region could become part of a larger Mediterranean union intended to help integrate North African and Levant countries into a larger regional security community backed by Turkey and the European Union. Ankara could take a leading role in any future formation of a Mediterranean union but should also obtain limited voting rights in the EU as an associate member in sectors that concern vital Turkish interests, but with limited rights of migration to Europe. In effect, Turkey would represent a land bridge in mediating between Europe and Russia, as well as between Israel, Iran, and the Arab world. If strongly backed by the EU and United States, Ankara could possibly reach accords between the Kurds and Iraq, and between Armenians and Azerbaijanis through efforts to forge confederal arrangements but without necessarily giving up too much sovereignty to a Kurdish confederation, for example. (See Chapters 2 and 6.)

In addition to the Israel-Palestinian question, the dispute over Kashmir continues to engage pan-Islamist militants. Thus far, while negotiations began in 2006, India has appeared that it might accept some territorial modifications along the Line of Control (LoC) but has not gone further to accept possible autonomy for all of Kashmir, let alone the Kashmir valley. Here, New Delhi and Islamabad would need to agree on the parameters of Kashmiri autonomy, to be overseen by Indian, Pakistani, and Kashmiri observers, if not international forces.

Because of the nature of Pakistani strategy, steps to resolve of the Kashmir question would likewise help to wind down conflict in Afghanistan.

U.S. global strategy will thus need to find ways to resolve both the Palestinian crisis and the Kashmiri conflict (while seeking reforms of "good governance" in Saudi Arabia and other Arab/Islamic countries) if it is to ultimately outmaneuver violent pan-Islamist movements in sociopolitical terms. Despite their disputes, the Gulf states could come closer together, primarily in fear of Iran, which, in turn, not-so-ironically seeks GCC membership so as to better influence GCC policies and to counter U.S. influence. But by entering into direct negotiations with Iran, the United States could, however, actually help to forge closer and more positive Iran-GCC ties, which, in turn, could forge a Persian Gulf security community that could interface with a newly founded Mediterranean union, through investment, aid and development assistance to Palestine and North Africa, among other countries.

The Question of Iraq

It will soon prove time to cut U.S. losses with regard to Iraq much as George Kennan had urged in reference to U.S. military intervention against North Vietnam as early as 1966, so that the conflict in Iraq does not continue to obsess U.S. policymakers to the exclusion of other significant global strategic and economic crises, including U.S. overextension. Moreover, the longer American troops visibly remain in the country, the more the differing opposition groups will be able to turn the population against the American "occupation," so that any government seen as being linked too closely to the United States will eventually lose whatever popular legitimacy that it might possess, despite efforts of the United States to provide security.

Although the wars in Iraq and Vietnam are very different, there are some major parallels. Belated U.S. withdrawal from Vietnam in tandem with a U.S. rapprochement with China finally worked to end the Vietnam War in 1975. But the belated nature of the withdrawal also intensified the struggle, raised the body count on both sides, and resulted in the repression of South Vietnam by the North and indirectly in the "killing fields" in Cambodia. The latter represented a democide which would have probably occurred in some form whether the United States withdrew from Vietnam or not. Had the United States not withdrawn from Vietnam after Henry Kissinger's dramatic rapprochement with Mao, the slaughter of innocent Vietnamese and Cambodians by high altitude B-52 bombing would have continued. The ongoing struggle would have probably resulted in Chinese intervention in Vietnam (as China threatened) and stronger Chinese supports for the Khmer Rouge in Cambodia. The end result would have been an even greater disaster contrary to the implications of President Bush's criticism of the U.S. withdrawal from Vietnam in August 2007 as it ostensibly applies to Iraq. In the contemporary situation, a continued U.S. intervention in Iraq may well mean war with Iran.[17]

In addition, after U.S. withdrawal from Vietnam, other Communist and nationalist movements fought to obtain power (the MPLA in Angola, the African National Congress in South Africa, the Sandinistas in Nicaragua, plus the then-rising Euro-Communist movements in Portugal, France, and Italy, to mention a few).

By comparison, it is likewise possible that a precipitous U.S. withdrawal from Iraq (perhaps following the staged withdrawal of British forces from Basra, which will further open the oil-rich region to rival Shi'a militias and Iranian influence), could result in intensified sectarian conflict in Iraq in the short run (assuming the Iraqis cannot reach accords on their own). If the situation gets completely out of hand, this could result in direct intervention by regional states such as Turkey and Iran. This scenario would, to a certain extent, be comparable to Vietnam's intervention in Cambodia against the Khmer Rouge in 1978, which Hanoi tried to justify as a "humanitarian intervention." U.S. withdrawal could also stimulate extremist groups throughout the world to intensify actions against U.S., European, and Russian interests. While Communist movements were generally backed by the Soviet Union or China, in contemporary circumstances, various partisan movements could seek to take advantage of perceived American weakness. In addition, major and regional powers could take the risk of engaging in unilateral interventions in regional "hot spots" in the assumption that the United States or other major states will not seek to counter those interventions.

Cutting U.S. losses in Iraq, however, will prove necessary despite the risky consequences. The challenge is to do it in such a way that the United States does not appear to be running and hiding by attempting to arrange negotiated accords between conflicting groups and regional powers. The first reason to cut back the U.S. troop presence in Iraq is to pressure the Iraq government to act and meet its obligations to stabilize and develop the country for the benefit of all its citizens (see Chapter 3). (If, however, the Iraqi government cannot meet those obligations, then it will continue to lose both domestic and international legitimacy. As was the case with Vietnam, the United States cannot afford to prop up an instable government that cannot sustain the support of its own people indefinitely.) Other rationale to reduce, then ultimately withdraw, forces include the need to minimize the overall damage done to U.S. prestige by the George W. Bush administration's "preemptive" action and use of torture and the need to reduce costs related to "peacekeeping" and "peacemaking" (not to overlook potentially astronomical military spending with regard to the "global war on terrorism" in general). The dilemma is that the longer the United States remains trapped in quicksand in Iraq without any real freedom of maneuver, the more likely the United States will be drawn into war with Iran, and the more the overall global situation will degenerate (as differing states and political movements will seek to take advantage of U.S. debacle whether the United States leaves or not), and the less prepared the United States (and other countries) will be to meet new and resurgent threats.

As a step toward ending the war in Iraq, the United States will thus need to engage with Syria and Iran while acting in cooperation with Saudi Arabia and the Gulf Cooperation Council (Saudi Arabia and the Gulf states will likewise need to engage in significant domestic reforms). While engaging in multilateral sanctions backed by the UN, the United States will need to take further steps toward a *real dialogue with Tehran*, leading ultimately to *regime recognition*—but not ignoring the need for *regime reform*. As some Iranian elites appear to be looking for a face-saving way out of the impasse, there appears to be room for Washington to make a diplomatic breakthrough if both sides are willing to engage in a real dialogue. If given the right incentives, Iran can help counter the Taliban in Afghanistan and work to moderate the actions of both Hamas in Palestine and Hizb'allah in Lebanon (if Israel likewise takes steps toward peace); it can also influence the Maliki government in Iraq.[18] (See Chapter 4 and *postscript.*)

Regional cooperation among all of Iraq's neighbors, plus other Islamic states, is also essential for winding down civil warfare in Iraq by seeking to establish a confederation linking together the three major communities, Kurds (already quasi-independent), Shi'as (divided into severely conflicting factions) and Sunni groups (who are most opposed to confederation as they now form a minority among the three major groupings). An essentially neocommunitarian approach would also attempt to sustain the rights of lesser minorities (Turkomen, Assyrians and Chaldean Christians, Sufi Muslims, Yazidi, and others) where possible. The UN could ultimately assist an essentially tripartite Iraqi confederation, as long as the latter possessed a central government with perceived legitimacy strong enough to collect tax revenues and redistribute oil profits to poorer areas, in helping to create effective regional police and army units backed by international forces in the "buffer regions." If a settlement can eventually be negotiated, then both international and regional police and army units would seek to establish peace and order between the conflicting communities. A negotiated settlement among the conflicting Iraqi factions could consequently permit international peacekeepers to ease U.S. withdrawal and permit Iraq relatively greater independence, while counter-balancing Iranian attempts to achieve regional hegemony.[19]

In summary, Washington appears to stuck with a ominous dilemma: the United States can either continue to prop up a weak and ineffective Iraqi government and continue to be sucked into quicksand or it can begin to negotiate with Tehran in the effort to moderate the latter's influence in Iraq and the region. If it cannot ultimately engage with Tehran, then Washington and the world can face the burgeoning prospects of direct conflict with not just Iran, but also Hizb'allah and al-Qaida, among other partisan movements—if not a number of states as well.

The Case for Truly Engaged Multilateralism

It is increasingly possible that domestic tensions within the United States could magnify over the issues of highly inequitable salaries, limited social and health care benefits, illegal immigration—coupled with demands for the United States to withdraw its forces from not only Iraq but also Afghanistan. These domestic pressures could lead U.S. political elites to focus more on domestic and hemispheric affairs than on international concerns. Washington could then decide against the complexities involved in fully engaging in multilateral diplomacy that requires long-term financial and military commitments. Yet the fact the United States cannot absolutely isolate itself from both external and internal threats arising from political economic instabilities, and from a highly uneven polycentric global system in which militant partisan groups and states are willing to threaten the use of WMD or engage in acts of terrorism to assert their interests, means that such an isolationist strategy would eventually backfire. Realizing that it can not fully protect itself by hiding behind a National Missile Defense shield, for example, the United States might then opt for periodic unilateral interventions followed by sudden retreat. Yet such a flip-flop "policy" could further destabilize the global system: Only an engaged multilateral strategy can guarantee global peace and stability in the long term.

Given numerous threats and pressures that require immediate attention, plus both domestic and international political and economic constraints, such a long-term strategy might appear "unrealistic." However, the global crisis will only intensify in depth if the next American leadership, whether Democrat or Republican, does not put a priority on developing and implementing a very flexible, pragmatic, and truly engaged multilateral diplomacy. Such a conciliatory peace- and security-oriented strategy will require a proactive U.S. engagement with both "democratic-liberal" and "illiberal" regimes (in the process of reforming both) through the formation of interlocking "regional security communities" in order to prevent the real possibility of wider regional conflicts, if not major-power war.

The Obama Administration: Surmounting Nightmarish Scenarios?

The election of Barack Obama represents a victory for decades of civil rights struggles and by itself generally sends a positive message to the world. On the domestic side, President Obama hopes to heal the social and racial divisions that have divided the United States while concurrently seeking to "remake" America. The huge tasks already before him have been magnified by a global financial crisis that has significantly augmented the public debts of the advanced industrial countries relative to their gross domestic products.1 The general crisis has threatened major transnational corporations with bankruptcy, including General Motors (GM)—the American firm of which it was once said, "what is good for GM is good for the country"—while concurrently exacerbating sociopolitical divisions within the United States and throughout the world. It is from this standpoint that Obama's very first act was to proclaim January 20, 2009, a "National Day of Renewal and Reconciliation." The very first bill that President Obama signed into law was intended to support equal pay for equal work—without gender or racial discrimination. At the same time, however, the financial crisis, combined with deeper sociopolitical disputes over health care, unemployment, and the growing gap between the very rich, middle classes, and the poor, could possibly lead to stronger popular pressures for Washington to adopt a more ostrichlike and isolationist approach to foreign policy issues and thus focus more political attention and economic assistance on the United States itself (see introduction and Chapter 10).

Obama's primordial foreign policy concern has been to rebuild American moral standing. While President Bush had emphasized "compassionate conservatism," his strong support for the death penalty (opposed by the European Union) and efforts to legitimize "enhanced interrogation techniques" (a euphemism for torture) did considerable damage to American prestige abroad. President Obama hopes that the United States can reassert its leadership through example and through dialogue—as opposed to engaging in polemics and overt "double standards" that characterized Bush administration discourse and actions. For the most part, the Obama administration will attempt to tackle tough foreign policy and security dilemmas through multilateral and concerted approaches. Nevertheless, the United States will still keep a number of unilateral eaglelike options open—if multilateral efforts fail. (For an ornithology of foreign policy birds, see the original preface and Chapter 10.)

As one of his first official acts, President Obama signed four directives that put an end to the torture facilities at Guantanamo Bay, restoring the right of habeas corpus. Obama demanded that the Central Intelligence Agency (CIA) abolish any secret detention facilities overseas and comply with Article 3 of the General Provisions of the Geneva Convention. The problem, however, is that the Bush administration legacy possesses complex legal and political ramifications: those detainees who were tortured can use that fact as part of their defense. Moreover, third countries, such as Yemen, have been reluctant to take responsibility for their most militant and unrepentant nationals if released from American custody. In December 2009, Obama ordered the creation of the Thomson Correctional Center in Illinois to facilitate the closure of detention facilities at the Guantanamo Bay Naval Base despite opposition by human rights advocates to prolonged detention, on the one hand, and fears that prisoners could escape or engage in plots on American soil, on the other (see Chapter 1)

With respect to the vital issue of environmental security, in March 2009 in Bonn, international mediators began to negotiate the successor to the Kyoto Protocol that lapses in 2012. By December 2009, however, the Climate Change Summit in Copenhagen failed to obtain significant international commitments to reduce pollution emissions so as to keep average global temperatures from rising no more than 2°C. While the United States could eventually sign the Kyoto Protocol (hoping to cut U.S. emissions by 80 percent by 2050), the Obama administration is under congressional pressure to lower Kyoto standards and costs. Obama will accordingly pursue negotiations on two tracks: on one hand, it will engage in discussions in the UN Climate Change forum; on the other, it will hold bilateral or multilateral talks with the fifteen biggest CO_2 emitters—an approach that closely follows that of the Bush administration. (The biggest emitters include China, the United States, the European Union, and India, plus Brazil and Indonesia due to their rainforests.) Obama's ten-year energy plan stresses alternatives such as wind and solar power, advanced biofuels, and clean coal technologies. Obama also supports tripling loan guarantees to expand nuclear power production, despite problems related to the transport and storage of radioactive waste, among other issues. Obama hopes that making homes and businesses more energy efficient and investing in clean energy facilities will help provide new jobs. His plan is intended to save more oil than the United States currently imports from the Middle East and Venezuela combined through American-built hybrid cars, for example. It remains to be seen, however, how a significant reduction of U.S. (and European) energy dependence on foreign suppliers might, if actually carried out, affect the foreign and domestic policies of those countries that are highly dependent on energy exports and that have not significantly diversified their economies (see Chapters 9 and 10).

President Obama appears well aware of the need to engage in truly concerted efforts in order to resolve a number of disputes and conflicts. In seeking to rebuild the transatlantic relationship, it does appear that Obama will listen more closely to his allies than did the Bush administration. The fact that France has reentered North Atlantic Treaty Organization's (NATO's) military command structure (although still remaining outside the nuclear command) should help strengthen the European Union (EU) position inside the alliance—in that Paris will control the Allied Command Transformation thus putting it in a position to significantly reform the alliance itself. The major problem is to find the appropriate balance between U.S. and European policies (and among the Europeans themselves). Given the range of issues (financial crisis, trade disputes, high energy prices and development of energy alternatives, ecological concerns raised by global warming, etc.) presently confronting the world, the formation of a new Euro-Atlantic Security Council could work to better coordinate U.S., NATO, and EU policies. A Euro-Atlantic Security Council could additionally better coordinate U.S. and European policies toward Russia, China, India, and the Arab and Islamic worlds. Yet contrary to advocates of a "global NATO" (or an alliance of democracies), the United States and EU will need to engage in new systems of "power sharing" with Russia in the formation of a new European security architecture and other "regional security communities" (see Chapters 2 and 10).

For their part, the Europeans will need to focus on geopolitical issues closer to their own territories. Now that the EU has finally ratified the Treaty of Lisbon in 2009, it can better coordinate defense spending, as well as foreign and security policy. At the same time, Europe will still need to find ways to better accommodate the populous states on its own borders, Russia, Ukraine, and Turkey while advancing the development of the Mediterranean, Black Sea, and Caucasus regions. Due to the fact that the full membership of Turkey in the EU appears a dubious prospect, Ankara should be encouraged to play a key role in the Palestinian-Israeli-Syrian peace processes, as well as in Central Asia, in Afghanistan, and in the formation of interlocking "regional security communities" in the Black Sea, Mediterranean, and Caucasus. UN efforts to resolve the dispute over Cyprus that blocks a more positive NATO-EU relationship must be given priority. Ultimately, Ankara should be granted a new status going beyond a "privileged partnership" with the EU and toward a proposed category of "associate EU membership" with limited voting rights (with Schengen membership to be reviewed over a period of time). Failure to bring Turkey into a closer relationship with the EU could, however, lead Ankara to pivot closer to Russia or, more likely, strengthen the influence of militant pan-Islamists within Turkey.

Russia has opposed NATO enlargement to both Ukraine and Georgia; it has generally opposed the new EU "Eastern Partnership" with former Soviet bloc states—Armenia, Azerbaijan, Belarus, Moldova, Georgia, and Ukraine—which Moscow sees as a "Baltic-Black Sea alliance" backed by NATO and the EU that is potentially intended to isolate Russia and break up its own alliances with Belarus and Armenia. Yet another possible option is to bring these states *and* Russia into a new status of "associated" EU membership with limited voting rights. Russia, Ukraine, and other states (including the United States) could thus ultimately join the EU in a loose confederation in the establishment of a "European Union and Associate Member States." Russia and Ukraine could also join a reformed (and renamed) NATO as "associate members" in participating in Black Sea and Caucasus "regional security communities" (see Chapters 2 and 10).

Such an approach would help to nudge the countries of these regions toward a greater respect for human rights and democratic values while permitting greater sociopolitical diversity and regional autonomy.

The Obama administration will additionally need to strengthen efforts to work with the UN Security Council, plus Japan and South Korea, in order to find ways to cajole North Korea into giving up its nuclear weapons capability in exchange for overlapping security guarantees (see Chapter 7). This option is not proving easy given North Korean Taepodong's two "Milky Way" missile tests over Japanese territory in April 2009, resulting in Tokyo's deployment of U.S.-built Patriot and Aegis antimissile systems. Pyongyang not only refused to cancel the test (which it sees as a means to counter both U.S. systems and Japan's H-2A missile launches that possess both military and civilian purposes) but it also exploded a ten- to twenty-kiloton nuclear device in May 2009. By risking talks aimed at helping North Korea with food and fuel assistance in return for abandoning its nuclear weapons program, it appears that Pyongyang's hardliners are pressing President Obama for concessions intended to obtain security accords that will guarantee the long-term domestic stability of the regime through direct bilateral U.S.-North Korean talks. North Korea has warned that it would consider a U.S. and UN embargo (backed by Russia and China in June 2009 and enforced by the U.S.-led Proliferation Security Initiative) as "an act of war." South Korea itself joined the Proliferation Security Initiative just after Pyongyang's explosion of a nuclear device in May 2009; Seoul has also sought stronger security guarantees from Washington. North Korea, in response, has threatened to aim missiles at Hawaii or Alaska, if not use nuclear weaponry in the case of a conflict.

While Beijing has at least attempted to moderate North Korean behavior (it fears the sociopolitical instability and refugee crisis caused by a potential collapse of the regime), it has not yet given up claims to unite with Taiwan by force—despite some new diplomatic overtures in March 2009. On the one hand, coupled with closer military ties with Russia, Beijing has built up a significant missile threat against Taiwan while augmenting its deep-water naval capabilities and ability to interdict sea lines of communication against American naval capabilities. On the other hand, Beijing has promised talks leading to a peace agreement on the basis of the "one-China principle." Taipei, however, has stated that it would prefer to negotiate economic deals before political ones. Nevertheless, one possible option would be to negotiate a confederal arrangement in the name of "one China"—but between two cooperating governments that would still possess separate military capabilities and domestic systems of governance. By December 2009, the Obama administration stated that it planned a major arms sale to Taiwan—an option that is likely to put further strains on the U.S.-Chinese relationship, if it passes Congress. China had only resumed military-to-military ties with the United States in February 2009; U.S.-Chinese relations had been frozen after the Bush administration announced a previous U.S. military sale to Taiwan in October 2008. Beijing has asserted that U.S. arms sales to Taiwan strengthen the goals of separatist movements in Tibet, Xinjiang province, as well as Taiwan itself—despite the fact that Ma Ying-jeou, president of Taiwan, has sought closer ties with Beijing unlike his predecessor, Chen Shui-bian (see Chapter 8).

In Iraq, the largely Shi'a majority regions have generally solidified their goals in expulsing non-Shi'a groups after six years of violent civil warfare (but with strong Iranian influence). The minority Sunni regions essentially feel squeezed between the Shi'a and Kurds, who possess greater population and oil wealth. The regional government of oil-rich Iraqi Kurdistan has witnessed strife between Kurds, Arabs, and Turkomans, among other ethnic groups and terrorist organizations, while engaging in disputes with Baghdad over oil claims. The Kurdish region in Iraq has also been subject to both Turkish and Iranian military intervention (in an effort to repress Kurdish independence movements operating in both Turkey and Iran). As the Kurds continue to develop and assert their interests, one future option might be a Kurdish confederation with overlapping linkages to Iraq, Iran, and Turkey.

Prior to Obama's election, the Bush administration itself rushed to withdraw American troops in accord with the Iraqi government in a deal that provided Iraq some oversight over U.S. military activities. Yet, as not all Iraqi parties have been in agreement, acts of terrorism attempted to weaken the now Shi'a-dominated Iraqi government just as the Americans started to leave at the end of June 2009. Given heavy Bush administration investment in the country, Iraq's significant high-quality petroleum reserves, and fears of a return to widespread violence that could possibly draw in regional powers, it appears difficult to see how Obama can pull American assets and military forces out very easily. This is true despite the fact that it has been firms from China, Russia, France, and Turkey—countries that did not support the war—that have been among the first to take the risks of investment, beating out American firms once security conditions appeared to improve in 2008. U.S. forces consequently will remain on alert in the energy-rich region but will be deployed on military bases, for the most part, outside Iraq—although a residual noncombat "advise-and-assist" brigade could remain within Iraq (see Chapters 3 and 10).

President Obama has decided that strategic priority should be given to Afghanistan (and increasingly, Pakistan) over Iraq—in an effort not to over-stretch American force capabilities. By the end of 2009, Obama decided to deploy 30,000 more U.S. troops in Afghanistan, bringing the total to roughly 100,000, combined with roughly 40,000 troops from NATO members and partners (not to overlook private security and Special Forces). By building up the number of U.S. and Afghan military and police forces, and despite difficulties in convincing NATO members to add more troops, the Pentagon hopes to secure areas already under control of the Afghan government while expanding control over the horseshoe-shaped area from Kandahar to Helmand provinces in order to secure the historical invasion route to Kabul. The latter provinces represent key economic and agricultural producers (including poppy production). In addition to attempting to make certain that development assistance is better coordinated among differing American, international, and nongovernmental organizations, and that it actually goes to the people who most need it, Obama furthermore intends to engage in secret talks promising financial aid, technical assistance, jobs, and protection in an effort to separate the essentially Pashtun partisan groups, war lords, and clans that oppose the government of Afghan president Karzai from the Taliban. On the one hand, the U.S. seeks to weaken the Taliban and other hard-core pan-Islamists aligned with al-Qaida in order to further isolate the latter. On the other hand, Afghan president Hamid Karzai has called for direct talks with the Taliban leadership, claiming that they can enter the government. The Taliban, however, have thus far questioned Karzai's sincerity and have refused his overtures on grounds that U.S. and NATO troops are still present in the country.

The United States furthermore needs to work with as many parties as possible in order to achieve a wider regional peace. A contact group approach needs to seek out Afghan-Pakistani security cooperation—an approach that ultimately requires an agreement over the disputed Durand line that divides the Pashtun region between Afghanistan and Pakistan. Ways to cool Indo-Pakistani conflict over Kashmir must also be found: as India and Pakistan both support greater Pashtun political representation in Kabul, and as both require access to energy resources from Central Asia, it is possible that common interests can help lead the two rivals to overcome a number of their geopolitical and economic disputes. Washington likewise needs to obtain diplomatic support from Russia, China, and Uzbekistan to check pan-Islamic insurgency and provide security and economic assistance to Kabul. But Washington also needs to work with states, such as Saudi Arabia and Qatar, as intermediaries between Islamabad and Kabul, so as to rapidly protect and feed displaced populations and to stabilize the Afghan-Pakistani region through intensive development assistance, enhanced trade relationships, and overseas employment opportunities. A major issue in Pakistan and Afghanistan (among other Islamic countries) is the "youth bulge": there is a continuing danger that large numbers of idle youth can fall prey to pan-Islamic ideology due to lack of job opportunities and promises of social advancement.

Both Afghan president Hamid Karzai and Pakistani president Asif Ali Zardari have appealed to President Obama to put an end to U.S. and NATO air strikes and U.S. predator missile attacks that have resulted in civilian deaths (or so-called collateral damage) and popular demands for revenge. Without a more concerted political and diplomatic approach to the crisis, there is a significant risk that eaglelike unilateral U.S. military actions (which Obama, as presidential candidate, had urged President George Bush, Jr., to undertake), coupled with U.S. support for Pakistani military efforts against Taliban and al-Qaida militants in the Swat valley and in northwest Pakistan, could destabilize Pakistan—in that these military actions have largely been responsible for the not necessarily temporary displacement of millions of internal refugees. As Islamabad has been urged by Washington to crack down on the anti-Afghan but pro-Pakistani Taliban (such as the Haqqani network in Waziristan that attacked the Indian embassy in Kabul in 2008), the potential destabilization of Pakistan raises the prospects of a pan-Islamist military coup in a country with nuclear weaponry.

Al-Qaida has appeared to be acting as a coordinator and mediator between differing Taliban groups inside both Afghanistan and Pakistan and has increasingly focused its attention on Pakistan. Al-Qaida and aligned groups have continued to exploit outrage at Israel's 2008 to 2009 war on Hamas in Gaza, while seeking to exploit sociopolitical tensions elsewhere in the Arab and Islamic worlds. The main regions susceptible to al-Qaida and pan-Islamic doctrine include western Pakistan and the Afghan-Pakistani border region; southern and western Afghanistan; regions of Central Asia and Xinjiang province of China near Afghanistan; the north Caucasus (around Chechnya); the Arabian Peninsula (Saudi Arabia and Yemen); the Horn of Africa, including Somalia and extending southwest into Kenya; Southeast Asia, from southern Thailand to the southern Philippines to Indonesia; West Africa, including northern Nigeria and Mali—not to overlook European and American cities with expatriate or converted Muslim communities. Most recently, al-Qaida has been fueling a Sunni-Shi'a conflict in Yemen, perhaps to deflect American attention away from its efforts to destabilize Pakistan. The United States and Saudi Arabia have backed the dysfunctional Yemeni government in its efforts to repress both a secessionist movement in the south and the essentially Shi'a Houthi movement, purportedly backed by Iran, in the north—raising dangerous tensions in the vital oil transit Bab-el-Mandeb choke point between the Red Sea and Gulf of Aden. In addition, groups such as the Islamic Movement of Uzbekistan have emerged as a more serious threat in several Central Asian countries—a factor that could help bring NATO, Russia, and the Collective Security Treaty Organization (CSTO), and the Shanghai Cooperation Organization (SCO), into closer cooperation (see Chapters 1, 6, and 10).

As witnessed by Obama's March 2009 address on the Iranian holiday Nowruz, his tone and approach have been different than that of the Bush administration, but the goal is similar: to convince the Iranian leadership not to develop a nuclear capability. Obama's speech helped split Iranian elites between those willing to open discussions with Washington versus those who thrive on opposition to American policy. Here, the United States must ultimately show Tehran that a regional arms race involving the United States, the Arab states, and Israel is not in the Iranian interest *itself*. Washington will, however, need to assess the outcome of the chaotic June 2009 elections before it can implement a coherent strategy. President Mahmoud Ahmadinejad's declaration of victory over former presidential candidate Mir Hossein Mousavi, a leader of the opposition Green Movement—despite accusation of massive electoral fraud on the part of Ahmadinejad's supporters—has begun to fuel a dangerous, domestic sociopolitical instability. By late 2009, President Obama threatened a shift from a policy of engagement with Iran to one of sanctions, with the support of France and other European states, but in a situation in which Washington itself has not fully enforced the 1996 Iran Sanctions Act and has actually awarded contract payments, grants, and other benefits to both foreign and American multinationals with subsidiaries who have been operating businesses in Iran over the past ten years. In order to make sanctions effective, and to better coordinate actions vis-à-vis Iran, the United States would need to restrain both American and European multinationals, while simultaneously seeking to obtain support from a reluctant Germany, Japan, Russia and an even more reluctant China. (Moscow generally supports Iran as a counterbalance to Saudi Arabia, which represents a rival energy exporter; Moscow also opposes perceived Saudi influence in Chechnya and throughout Central Asia. Beijing is highly dependent on energy imports from Iran and has additionally supported Iran to counter Russian—and American—influence.)

If they are at all possible to implement, the dilemma is that such sanctions must be aimed at splitting Iranian elites (most particularly, the Revolutionary Guards) and must not hurt the general population; otherwise, such actions could prove counterproductive. (By contrast, sanctions that presently harm the general population and that strengthen the ability of the Revolutionary Guards to benefit from black market activities could be lifted.) Thus far, Russia has appeared more willing to take steps against Iran, while China could at least adopt a position of neutrality, but these positions cannot be taken for certain in the future. Failure to find ways to accommodate *legitimate* Russian interests in Eastern Europe and the Caucasus, as well as China in the Taiwan straits, could exacerbate the crisis, making Russia or China even more reluctant to coordinate foreign policy with the United States and Europeans.

A major missile and high-tech arms race, involving the deployment of ballistic missile defense (BMD) systems throughout the so-called Greater Middle East and in Europe, is clearly in the making. Ultimately, the United States, UN Security Council, and Iran (along with countries such as Turkey who are attempting to mediate) will need to reach agreement over the question of uranium enrichment, among many other issues, so as to bring Iran out of its combative isolation. In the meantime, Tehran will use sanctions measures in a propaganda offensive to deflect attention from Iran's own domestic power struggles and attempt to strengthen its hold over the population. At the same time, Israel (with or without U.S. backing) could attempt to preempt Iranian nuclear sites during a period of social unrest. Al-Qaida, or dissident Iranian groups, could additionally attempt to spark a war between the United States and Iran through provocative terrorist attacks. If the Ahmadinejad government cannot ultimately If the Ahmadinejad government cannot ultimately moderate its position, then another possibility—short of war that would enflame much of the Arab and Islamic worlds—would be a popular insurrection or coup d'état that overturns the present leadership (see Chapter 4).

President Obama's June 2009 address in Cairo was intended to explain that the United States was at war not with the Islamic faith but with violent extremists who manipulate the name of Islam for political purposes (see Chapter 1). Yet in order to further divide more "moderate" factions from more radical pan-Islamist views, Obama will additionally need to significantly boost efforts to resolve the Israeli-Palestinian conflict, which symbolically enflames tensions throughout the Arab and Islamic worlds. Following the brutal December 2008 to January 2009 Israeli intervention in Gaza in response to Hamas's rocket attacks (which followed the November–December 2008 breakdown of a truce between Hamas and Israel), this is evidently not an easy task. Israeli Prime Minister Benjamin Netanyahu's June 14, 2009, speech, while recognizing the possibility of a Palestinian state (with significant conditions), did not go far enough to achieve peace in that it demanded Palestinian recognition of the Jewish state without setting the boundaries of that state and without calling for the dismantling of Israeli settlements in the occupied territories. Since becoming president, Obama has thus far pressed Israel to stop, if not dismantle, its West Bank settlements. The Obama administration likewise denied that the Bush administration had provided Israel with secret permission to continue expanding those settlements in accord with "natural growth." Netanyahu's June 14 speech also insisted on the demilitarization of the proposed Palestinian state, a condition that was regarded by Palestinian spokespersons as an affront to traditional notions of sovereignty.

Following Netanyahu's June 14 speech, the United States and the Quartet Group will need to find ways to reconcile the opposing Palestinian factions, Fatah and Hamas, in the formation of a secular government (in accord with the wishes of the majority of Palestinians). The Quartet Group will need to encourage peace talks with Israel with the assistance of the states most concerned (Saudi Arabia, Egypt, Turkey, and Qatar) and likewise revive the Saudi-backed 2002 Arab League peace initiative, which promised to normalize relations between Israel and the Arab League in exchange for Israel's return to something approximating its 1967 borders. The Quartet must also find a way for Israel and a new Palestine to establish a joint administration in Jerusalem and to compromise over the right of Palestinian refugees to return to Israel itself (both proposals thus far opposed by Netanyahu).

Given greater U.S. and international pressure on Israel, and given the need for Israel to reach out for an entente with Arab countries (as recognized by Netanyahu himself as a means to counterbalance Iran), the result could be a decentralized Palestinian confederation with political-economic linkages to Jordan, Egypt, and Israel. These linkages could be achieved by pursuing joint international industrial and water development projects with multinational investors, such as the Peace Valley project, taking into account significant ecological concerns. Peace between the Israelis and the Palestinians can help further generate peace throughout the region in the establishment of a greater Mediterranean Union linked to the EU. Moreover, in order to prevent Hamas rocket attacks from leading to another Gaza-like conflict and thus to protect both sides from future military intervention, the transition to Palestinian sovereignty could be overseen by the deployment of international peacekeepers. Such peacekeepers (trained by NATO's Partnership for Peace) could link both Israeli and Palestinian security forces to international troops acceptable to both Israel and the new Palestine. The length of the peacekeeping deployment under a general UN mandate would depend on satisfaction of the terms of the Road Map to Peace (see Chapter 5). Failure to reach a peace settlement, however, could result in a radicalization of not just Gaza but the West Bank as well—with Fatah splintering and Hamas forming alliances with even more radical pan-Islamist groups.

President Obama will need to take a fresh look at the African continent. As the Europeans have generally withdrawn from the region (despite French reticence to do so), the United States, China, India, along with Arab states, not to overlook pan-Islamic movements, have begun a new "scramble for Africa" to obtain political-economic influence. The United States and EU will consequently need to better coordinate security and development assistance to North Africa in the formation of a Mediterranean Union, so as to check al-Qaida efforts to forge alliances with pan-Islamic groups operating in North Africa. As conflict on the Horn of Africa is opening the door to both piracy and terrorism that feeds on failed states, ways must be found to redevelop and stabilize that region, particularly given the burgeoning conflict between Saudi Arabia and Iran over Yemen, as previously mentioned. The threat of piracy with more sophisticated weaponry and technologies could more positively lead to greater naval and security cooperation among the United States, the EU, Russia, China, and India. In oil- and mineral-rich West and Central Africa, ways must be found to repatriate profits and engage in power-sharing formulas for conflicting ethnic groups in order to achieve more equitable development for the peoples of the region—so as to prevent future wars of ethnic cleansing and genocide that have already devastated Rwanda and the Democratic Republic of the Congo, for example (see Chapter 6).

In an effort to strengthen its image with regard to human rights, the United States could possibly join the International Criminal Court (ICC). The fact that the UN Security Council oversees ICC decisions means that the U.S. possesses control over ICC decisions in theory; however, in practice, UN Security Council oversight has proven difficult to sustain in the case of Sudan. Obama has stated that he would examine the track record of the ICC before deciding whether the United States should join. He also stated that he would continue to support the ICC in its investigations into Sudanese actions in Darfur. In July 2008, the ICC issued an arrest warrant for President Omar al-Bashir for alleged crimes against humanity. The Sudanese government then expelled thirteen nongovernmental organizations (NGOs) that were at the core of the UN effort to provide food, shelter, and medicine to the people of the war-torn region. In effect, the ICC has been seeking *justice*—as opposed to *peace through negotiation*—but risking the lives of the two million displaced people living in camps in Darfur in the process. In late 2008, the Arab League pressed for a peace settlement during negotiations held in Qatar between the Sudanese government and rebel factions—but the bloodshed has thus far continued unabated. Both African Union and Arab states have generally opposed the ICC's steps to indict Sudanese President al-Bashir, thus placing these states, in addition to China, in general opposition to U.S. and European policy approaches.

Given the war on drugs in Mexico and Russian political-military support for Venezuela, the Obama administration will need to grant extra attention to Latin America, whose governments have become more populist after years of Bush administration neglect, while Brazil, in particular, is becoming a major world actor. U.S. backing for subsidized "free" trade as opposed to "fair" trade, particularly in agriculture, has generally augmented anti-U.S. sentiment. Venezuela has been flexing its oil muscles against the United States in seeking out new international energy markets while concurrently threatening conflict with Colombia. Obama will additionally need to address issues that are more directly affecting Americans themselves, including Hispanic immigration (not stopped by the wall along the U.S.-Mexican border, but slowed by economic downturn) and U.S. drug demand, which is really the root cause of the war on drugs. Roughly six thousand Mexicans were killed in clashes between rival Mexican drug gangs and Mexican police in 2008; some 6,500 were killed in 2009. This dangerous situation has begun to spill across the U.S. border and could lead to a significant reconsideration of U.S. drug policy. (In the United States, the California legislature has been considering the potential legalization of marijuana, primarily as a means to raise taxes in a depressed economy.) The United States announced the creation of a new bilateral implementation office in Mexico for both governments to work against the drug cartels. The Obama administration has stressed the concept of "shared responsibility"—a significant break from past American policy that blamed Mexico alone (see Chapter 9).

Due to the fact that the U.S. isolation of Cuba has not succeeded in "regime change"—and in an effort to check increasing Russian and Chinese influence in

Cuba and the region as a whole—Obama could possibly seek to normalize relations with Havana, but this remains a low priority. (Chinese leader Hu Jin Tao visited Havana in mid-November 2008, bringing millions of dollars in aid after hurricanes struck Cuba, plus promises of closer trade relations. Russian president Dmitry Medvedev also visited in late-November 2008 when Russian-Venezuelan military maneuvers took place.) A U.S. rapprochement with Cuba appears somewhat more plausible due to the fact that anti-Communist Cuban Americans now possess less political influence as the older anti-Castro generation has begun to fade away and as the balance of Hispanic politics has started to change within the United States itself. At the same time, however, if Obama does open the Cuban dossier—along with everything else he has on his plate, from health care, to the Afghan-Pakistani war, to financial crisis—not only will the U.S. prison camps in Guantanamo represent a political issue but so too will U.S. control of that territory, which is claimed by Cuba.

The August 2008 Georgia-Russia conflict was purportedly provoked accidentally on purpose by Georgia itself—in an apparent effort to strengthen U.S., European, and NATO support for Georgian security. (Georgia asserts that Russian forces advanced first; whatever the case, the conflict was certainly an "accident waiting to happen.") The war sent shudders down the spines of those states bordering Russia that continue to fear Russian military and political economic and energy pressures. These fears were magnified once Moscow supported the independence of South Ossetia and Abkhazia in an ostensible tit-for-tat reaction to U.S. recognition of Kosovo's independence. Rather than supporting general goals of peaceful steps toward confederation or autonomy, these actions in support of national independence movements could open a Pandora's Box of secessionist claims throughout eastern Europe and Eurasia; ironically, they could also work against Russian (and Shanghai Cooperation Organization) interests. Moreover, Russian-Ukrainian disputes in the winter of 2008–2009 over energy payments and debts led to a cutoff of gas supplies for European consumers—raising provocative calls for NATO to consider Article V military preparations in case of future energy cutoffs (as if military action could actually do something to stop the breakdown of energy supplies).

Given Russian opposition to U.S. and NATO encroachment into its "near abroad," it is not entirely surprising that in his first State of the Nation address on November 6, 2008, Russian President Medvedev greeted President-elect Obama with warnings that Moscow would deploy nuclear-capable missiles and radar jamming systems in Kaliningrad as a means to counter U.S. National Missile Defense (NMD) systems to be deployed in Poland and the Czech Republic if the United States did not give Russian interests priority. The threat not only represented an effort to halt U.S. plans to deploy NMD systems but also stopped the prospects of NATO enlargement to Georgia and Ukraine, while currently solidifying Moscow's controls over Kaliningrad. In March 2009, in citing U.S. and NATO military expansion up to its borders, President Medvedev announced that Russia must quickly enact a "large-scale rearmament." While Russia did engage in provocative military maneuvers that threatened the use of tactical nuclear weaponry near the Polish border in September 2009, Russia's relatively limited financial means (although world energy prices might again be on the rise after the steep drop in 2008), combined with its inexperienced military capabilities (as witnessed in its conflict with Georgia), appear to make such a military buildup more of a bluff for domestic political consumption.

Medvedev's threats were, however, also accompanied by an offer to negotiate all outstanding issues with the United States on the basis of parity in the formation of a new "pan-European security pact." Medvedev also promised radical reductions in nuclear weapons going beyond the Strategic Arms Reduction Talks (START) agreements but linked to compromises over BMD systems. While President Obama did decide to withdraw BMD systems from Poland and the Czech Republic, his administration still needs to find ways to engage in closer U.S., NATO, EU, and Russian coordination against potential missile threats from third countries, possibly by deploying BMD systems on Russian territory—in defending Europe and Russia as a whole. The United States furthermore needs to significantly reduce all forms of nuclear weaponry, including tactical nuclear arms, through mutual and verifiable agreements with Russia—and other states where possible. Steps to eliminate nuclear weaponry can help to delegitimize the efforts of states such as Iran and North Korea (and others) to acquire such weaponry.

A major question confronting Obama is whether the United States should continue to press for NATO membership for Georgia and Ukraine. Another possible option is to forge a *separate* center for NATO-EU-Russian-Ukrainian Black Sea security coordination, whose headquarters could be based in Sebastopol. (An internationalization of Black Sea defense and security structures would be intended to head off a potential clash between Ukrainian demands that Russia withdraw its fleet from the Crimea by 2017 and Moscow's apparent refusal to comply with Kiev's demands.) Such an approach would also require strong U.S., EU, and Russian backing for NATO-member Turkey's proposals for the "Caucasian Stability and Cooperation Platform" with the deployment of international forces (involving a mix of NATO Partnership for Peace and Russian-backed Collective Security Treaty Organization (CSTO) peacekeepers) in key regions of dispute (the so-called frozen conflicts) in Nagorno-Karabakh, Abkhazia, South Ossetia, and Transnistria, among other areas. Such an approach would necessitate a strengthening of the Black Sea Economic Cooperation organization to make it a more effective "regional security community" under a general Organization for Security and Cooperation in Europe (OSCE) mandate (see Chapters 2 and 10).

These political-security arrangements need to be accompanied by radical reductions in conventional weaponry (as well as tactical nuclear capabilities) through implementation of the adapted Conventional Force in Europe treaty. In order to prevent misperceptions and accidents that could lead to potential conflict, a first step in building confidence would be to better coordinate military activities and oversight. This step could be accompanied by joint NATO-Russian and CSTO flights over areas bordering the Baltic states and Poland. In the near future, a joint U.S., NATO, EU, and Russian headquarters for security and defense coordination could be built in Kaliningrad in order to administer BMD cooperation, joint peacekeeping and antiterrorism measures, and other confidence- and security-building measures, plus cooperation against drug and human trafficking. Partnership for Peace troops could be deployed in the Baltic States (and elsewhere in Eastern Europe) under the auspices of the NATO-Russia Council and the OSCE in order to provide symbolic deterrence and reassurance and to prevent conflict among east European States and Russia (see Chapters 2 and 10).

The Obama administration will need to revamp the U.S. military and make it more mobile, more capable of dealing with counterinsurgency and counterterrorism and more cost effective. The U.S. experience in "peacekeeping" (which has really involved "peacemaking") in Afghanistan, Iraq, and now Pakistan has indicated that the Pentagon and NATO badly need to build deeper expertise in languages, civil affairs, and cultural awareness for reconstruction and society building. The Pentagon and NATO furthermore need to find ways to work more closely with the UN, the EU, and other international governmental organizations (IGOs) and NGOs. U.S. and NATO forces have furthermore been badly overstretched in fighting "asymmetrical" warfare. On the one hand, the Pentagon needs to be prepared for differing contingencies and conflict scenarios; on the other, the U.S. and NATO cannot remain in a cold war mind-set in demanding the procurement of expensive, high-tech weaponry unsuited for contemporary forms of conflict.

The situation will require greater military-to-military cooperation among the United States, Europe, and Russia, along with other countries in moving from an uneasy détente at present to an entente—if not an alliance—so as to overcome fears that Moscow seeks to split NATO and the EU. Moreover, a closer NATO, EU, and Russian entente could help prevent the formation of a tighter Sino-Russian alliance while seeking to better equilibrate the rise of China into the global system. As it is not at all clear how even eaglelike unilateral actions can resolve disputes and conflicts *in the long term*, Washington must find ways to use engaged diplomacy to work with both friends and former "rivals" alike through multilateral and concerted actions wherever possible in the formation of interlocking "regional security communities" with international assistance and backing. Let us hope President Obama can show real foresight and truly effective leadership in the effort to surmount the very dangerous challenges and nightmarish scenarios that presently confront the United States and the world.

Notes

Introduction

1. Literature in the 1980s with themes of nuclear war was nearly double the number of that of the period from 1950 to 1959. See Paul Brians, "Nuclear Holocausts: Atomic War in Fiction," (Pullman, Washington: Washington State University, 2003; 2007) http://www.wsu.edu/~brians/nukepop/chart.html and http://www.wsu.edu/~brians/ntc/NTC8.pdf.
2. J. L. Gaddis, "The Cold War, the Long Peace, and the Future," in *The End of the Cold War: Its Meaning and Implications,* ed. Michael J. Hogan (Cambridge: Cambridge University Press, 1992); John Lewis Gaddis, *The Long Peace* (New York: Oxford, 1987).
3. Cold war battle deaths have been reported at twenty to twenty-five million. One estimate, which includes both "democide" and "genocide," is as high as seventy-six million from 1945–1987. R.J. Rummel, "20th Century Democide" (May, 1998) http://www.hawaii.edu/powerkills/POSTWWII.HTM.
4. On what to do about landmines leftover from the cold war, see the International Campaign to Ban Landmines (ICBL) Web site, http://nobelprize.org/nobel_prizes/peace/articles/williams/index.html.
5. For development of the concept of "security community," see Karl Deutsch, *Political Community: North-Atlantic Area* (New York: Greenwood Press, 1957). See also Emmanuel Adler and Michael Barnett (eds.), *Security Communities* (Cambridge: Cambridge University Press, 1998); Alex J. Bellamy, *Security Communities and their Neighbors* (New York: Palgrave, 2004). See also Chapter 10 this book.
6. Charles Krauthammer, "The Unipolar Moment," *Foreign Affairs America and the World 1990/91*; "The Unipolar Moment Revisited," *The National Interest* (Winter 2002/2003). http://bcsia.ksg.harvard.edu/BCSIA_content/documents/Krauthammer.pdf.
7. Dan Balz and Bob Woodward, "America's Chaotic Road to War," *Washington Post* (January 27, 2002). After consultation with President Bush, vice-president Dick Cheney gave the orders to shoot down the hijacked airliner. Did it crash or was it shot down?
8. Senator Jim Webb (D-VA) mentioned in his response to President Bush's 2007 State of the Union Address the growing gap in CEO pay: "When I graduated from college, the average corporate CEO made 20 times what the average worker did; today, it's nearly 400 times. In other words, it takes the average worker more than a year to make the money that his or her boss makes in one day." http://www.jameswebb.com/articles/wallstjrnl/classstruggle.htm.

9. Samuel Huntington, "The Hispanic Challenge," *Foreign Policy* (March/April 2004). See critique of Huntington's position: Philippa Strum and Andrew Selee, *The Hispanic Challenge? What We Know about Latino Immigration*, Washington, D.C.: Woodrow Wilson International Center for Scholars (March 29, 2004) http://www .wilsoncenter.org/topics/pubs/HispChall.pdf.

Chapter 1

1. See discussion of four forms of terrorism, Hall Gardner, *American Global Strategy and the "War on Terrorism"* (Burlington, VT: Ashgate, 2005; 2007), chapter 3.
2. The National Intelligence Council's 2020 report argues that civilizational movements—that is, religious adherents that include Muslim militants, Christian evangelicals, Hindu nationalists, and Jewish fundamentalists, among others—will generally rise in numbers in the period from 2002 to 2025. National Intelligence Council (NIC), "Mapping the Global Future," Washington, DC: CIA, 2004. http://www.dni.gov/nic/NIC_globaltrend2020.html. This fact, along with increasing rivalry over natural gas, oil, and others sources of energy, opens a "danger zone" of both antistate and interstate conflict in that more individuals are becoming "activists" who tend to see the world in Manichaean "good vs. evil" terms and "connect local conflicts to a larger struggle."
3. Human Security Report 2005/ 2006. http://www.humansecurityreport.info/.
4. See Federal Office for the Protection of the Constitution: http://www.verfassungsschutz .de/en/en_publications/annual_reports/vsbericht2005_engl/.
5. Paul Wilkinson, "Why Modern Terrorism?" in *The New Global Terrorism*, ed. Charles W. Kegley, 120 (Upper Saddle River, NJ: Prentice Hall, 2003). On UK and European efforts to handle terrorism, see Paul Wilkinson, *Terrorism versus Democracy: The Liberal State Response* (London: Routledge, 2006). Xenophobic Russian nationalists are concerned with Russia's rapidly growing Islamic population, which now numbers roughly 25 million out of 143 million and which could represent one-fifth of the Russian population by 2020 in part because of declining fertility rates among ethnic Russians.
6. http://www.csmonitor.com/2007/0206/p06s01-woeu.html?s=itm.
7. http://www.csmonitor.com/2006/0831/dailyUpdate.html?s=mesdu; http://www .cnn.com/2006/POLITICS/08/10/washington.terror.plot/index.html.
8. Human Security Report 2005/ 2006, http://www.humansecurityreport.info/.
9. On spiraling arms races, see Robert Jervis, *Perception and Misperception in International Politics* (Princeton, NJ: Princeton University Press, 1976).
10. For discussion of the security-insecurity "dilemma," see Anthony D. Lott, *Creating Insecurity* (Aldershot, UK: Ashgate: 2004). The concept of "security dilemma" was articulated by John H. Herz, "Idealist Internationalism and the Security Dilemma," *World Politics* 2 (January 1950), but the issue appears more of a dialectical interrelationship and interaction of perceived insecurity countered by a quest for perceived security as opposed to a "dilemma."
11. "Letter May Detail Iraqi Insurgency's Concerns," CNN (February 10, 2004.) This is assuming the letter is authentic.
12. "Denmark's Muslims Welcome Cemetery Plan" *Agence France Presse* (April 8, 2006). In April 2006, the Danish government finally permitted the first Muslim cemetery after seven years of demands. The dead were either returned to their country of origin for burial or interred in the Muslim sections. Danes marrying

non-Europeans can only marry at twenty-four years of age, in part to prevent arranged marriages.

13. Amitai Etzioni, "Leveraging Islam," *The National Interest* 83 (Spring 2006).

14. Spero News. http://www.speroforum.com/site/article.asp?id=6361. Archeologist Muazzez Ilmiye Cig was acquitted by a Turkish court for "inciting religious hatred" in regard to her theory as to the origin of the veil, which might have first been worn by priestesses in ancient Sumer who were initiating young people into sex rites but without being prostitutes.

15. James P. Piscatori, *Islam in a World of Nation-States* (Cambridge: Cambridge University Press, 1986). Piscatori makes distinctions between "conformist" groups that accept the divisions of the global territorial state system and those "noncomformist" groups that seek to overturn the present state system in favor of a pan-Islamic Ummah. But even these categories can be further subdivided.

16. Sayyid Qutb's theories on Islamic values have been regarded promulgating views that are the polar opposite of neoconservative idol Leo Strauss. See Anne Norton, *Leo Strauss and the Politics of American Empire* (New Haven, CT: Yale University, 2005). Yet Strauss was an admirer of Andalusia in the fifteenth century when Muslims, Christians, and Jews lived in creative harmony before the Reconquista in 1492.

17. Dafna Linzer and Thomas E. Ricks, "Anbar Picture Grows Clearer, and Bleaker," *Washington Post*, November 28, 2006.

18. Arthur Bright, "Is Chechen Conflict 'Over'? Death of Basayev Seen as an Opening for Russian-Chechen Relations," csmonitor.com (July 12, 2006).

19. On neocommunitarianism, see Amitai Etzioni, "A Neo-Communitarian Approach to International Relations," *Human Rights Review* 7, no. 1 (July–September 2006). On the potential for a deeper and wider conflict in the Philippines, see Simon Roughneen, "Philippine Escalation May Spark Wider War" ISN Security Watch (August 8, 2007).

20. Robert S. Leiken and Steven Brooke, "The Moderate Muslim Brotherhood" *Foreign Affairs* vol. 86, no. 2 (2007).

21. For a critical analysis of the results of Bush administration efforts to "democratize" authoritarian Middle Eastern regimes, see Chris Toensing, "Regional Implications of the Iraq War" *Foreign Policy in Focus*. http://www.fpif.org.

22. Terrorist Group Profiles, http://library.nps.navy.mil/home/tgp/qjbr.htm.

23. Bright, "Is Chechen Conflict 'Over'?"

24. Juan Cole, Informed Comment (March 26, 2006), http://www.juancole.com/2006/03/at-least-35-killed-lebanon-shiite.html.

25. On a tactical level, the Iranians might have wanted to trade members of the MEK for al-Qaida cadres that were in Iraq. Although it was also on the U.S. list of terrorist organizations, the MEK might have proved useful if Washington was going to engage in "regime change." On a strategic level, the Iranians might have wanted a larger cooperation agreement. Council of Foreign Relations "Leverett: Bush Administration 'Not Serious' about Dealing with Iran" (March 31, 2006), http://www.cfr.org/publication/10326/.

26. In the February 2005 elections, members of the banned Muslim Brotherhood, Egypt's largest and best-organized political force, won 88 seats (running as independents) despite efforts of the Mubarak government to repress the movement.

27. Before the May 2007 elections, Turkish president Ahmet Necdet Sezer stated that the country's secular system of government faced its gravest danger since the founding of the republic in 1923; yet Prime Minister Tayyip Erdoğan of the Islamic AKP party has continued to deny any hidden Islamist agenda. http://www.turkishdailynews.com.tr/article.php?enewsid=70698. In July 2007, the AKP did win the election, along with twenty-seven independent Kurdish candidates, former Islamist Abdullah

Gull then won the presidency in August. See Ben Judah, "Erdogan's AKP wins new mandate" *ISN Security Watch* (July 23, 2007), http://www.isn.ethz.ch/news/sw/details.cfm?id=17893.

28. http://www.fas.org/irp/world/para/milf.htm.

29. Lydia Khalil, "Iraqi President Claims Secret Talks with Insurgents," http://www.isn.ethz.ch/news/sw/details.cfm?id=15788. As of August 2007, the Iraqi government had still failed to meet the demands of even moderate Sunni cabinet members. See Chapter 3.

30. See, for example, Fred Weir, "Russia's Hamas Gambit" *Christian Science Monitor* (February 21, 2006).

31. Tariq Ali, "Who Really Killed Daniel Pearl?" *The Guardian*, April 5, 2002. As Tariq Ali pointed out, "The group which claimed to have kidnapped and killed Pearl—The National Youth Movement for the Sovereignty of Pakistan—is a confection. One of its demands was unique: the resumption of F-16 sales to Pakistan. A terrorist, jihadi group which supposedly regards the current regime as treacherous, is putting forward a 20-year-old demand of the military and state bureaucracy." Yet if it is true that the third al-Qaida leader, Khalid Sheikh Mohammed (as he purportedly confessed under torture) ordered the beheading of Daniel Pearl, then it implies a link between al-Qaida and Pakistan over the question of F-16s! French philosopher B. H. Levy believes Pearl was killed for investigating links between al-Qaida, the Pakistani ISI, and the Pakistani nuclear scientists. See B. H. Levy, *Who Killed Daniel Pearl?* (Hoboken, NJ: Melville House, 2003). In September 2007, the highly acclaimed Doha Debate in Qatar raised the question: "Is It Time to Talk to Al-Qaida?"

32. See Mahan Abedin "The Essence of Al-Qaida: An Interview with Saad Al-Faqih," *Jamestown Foundation* 2, no. 2 (February 5, 2004), http://www.jamestown.org/publications_details.php?volume_id=397&&issue_id=2907.

33. Ibid.

34. *New York Times*, April 24, 2006. By April 2006, bin Laden renewed his propaganda offensive by critiquing American and European policy with regard to the isolation of Hamas; the proposed Western-led peacekeeping force in Sudan; and the Danish cartoons that mocked the Prophet Mohammed. In 2007, al-Qaida warned Hamas not to compromise with Israel by joining the unity government. http://www.nytimes.com/2006/04/24/world/middleeast/24binladen.html?n=Top%2fReference%2fTimes%20Topics%2fOrganizations%2fH%2f Hamas%20.

35. Robert P. Hartwig, "The Cost of Terrorism: How Much Can We Afford?" National Association of Business Economics 46th Annual Meeting, October 4, 2004, Insurance Information Institute: http://www.iii.org/media/hottopics/insurance/sept11/ http://server.iii.org/yy_obj_data/binary/736854_1_0/tria.pdf (Accessed April 15, 2006). Interestingly, bureaucratic infighting between the Environmental Protection Agency and the Bureau of Homeland Security over estimates of potential damage of attacks to chemical facilities makes insurance valuation very difficult.

36. "All Indonesian Communities Vow to Fight Together Terrorism," http://www.world-tourism.org/newsroom/Releases/ 2005/october/bali_tourism.htm.

37. It has been argued that this figure leaves out the costs of American and Saudi backed training of mujaheddin and infrastructure assistance in Afghanistan during the war against the Soviet Union, but it is unclear that this training was totally relevant to the September 11 attacks. See http://www.meforum.org/article/572.

38. Hartwig, "The Cost of Terrorism."

39. Donald Rumseld "Memo: Global War on Terrorism," http://www.globalsecurity.org/military/library/policy/dod/rumsfeld-d20031016sdmemo.htm. While not all

debt is caused by defense spending and the global war on terrorism, the U.S. national debt was $5.6 trillion (57.4 percent of gross domestic product [GDP]) when George Bush Jr. came to office in January 2001; as of April 2007, it stood at roughly $8.9 trillion (roughly 65.5 percent of GDP). By September 2007, the debt will probably reach the $9 trillion limit that Congress had set in March 2006, potentially causing a government shutdown or crisis. The Bush administration has transformed previous U.S. government surpluses into major deficits.

40. See Tony Blankley, "An Islamist Threat Like the Nazis," *The Washington Times*, September 12, 2005. http://www.washingtontimes.com/national/20050912-122024 -9420r.htm.

41. http://www.washingtonpost.com/wp-dyn/content/article/2007/05/14/ AR2007051402265.html.

42. Secretary Rumsfeld, "Working Group Report on Detainee Interrogation in the Global War on Terrorism," *Wall Street Journal On Line*, http://online.wsj.com/public/ resources/documents/military_0604.pdf.

43. The United States has been accused of killing Al-Jazeera journalists critical of U.S. actions in Afghanistan and Iraq. George Bush Jr. considered bombing Al-Jazeera in discussions with Tony Blair in April 2004 after the first siege of Fallujah. See "The War on Al- Jazeera," *The Nation*, December 19, 2005.

44. *International Journal of Human-Computer Studies*, 65, no. 1 (January 2007): 71–84.

45. Lawrence Wright, *The Looming Tower* (New York: Knopf, 2007), 52.

46. For a critique of neoconservatives as a hybrid between Plato's "Timocrats" and Kant's "moralizing politicians," see Hall Gardner, *American Global Strategy and the "War on Terrorism."* For a critique of Bush administration attempts to impose neoconservative "ideals" in Iraq and Afghanistan, see Amitai Etzioni, *Security First* (New Haven: Yale University Press, 2007). On efforts of neoconservatives to distance themselves from the Bush administration's handling of the Iraq intervention, see David Rose, "Neo Culpa," *Vanity Fair* (November 3, 2006). Given the fact that Iraq had no militarily significant weapons of mass destruction (a fact probably known to the Pentagon), intervention there can be seen as preclusive, if not predatory, thus more characteristic of vultures than superhawks. (See Chapter 3.)

47. Sen. John McCain, "Torture's Terrible Toll," *Newsweek* (November 21, 2005), http://www.msnbc.msn.com/id/10019179/site/newsweek/.

48. Military Commissions Act of 2006, http://www.law.georgetown.edu/faculty/ nkk/ documents/MilitaryCommissions.pdf#search='Military%20Commissions%20Act'.

49. Alfred W. McCoy, "Why the McCain Torture Ban Won't Work: The Bush Legacy of Legalized Torture," http://www.tomdispatch.com/index.mhtml?pid=57336.

50. Commission on Human Rights, Economic, Social, and Cultural Rights Civil and Political Rights Situation of detainees at Guantánamo Bay Report of the Chairperson of the Working Group on Arbitrary Detention, Leila Zerrougui. United Nations, February 15, 2006. The United States "considers itself bound by the prohibition of cruel, inhuman and degrading treatment only to the extent that it means the cruel, unusual and inhumane treatment or punishment prohibited by the Fifth, Eighth and/or Fourteenth Amendments to the Constitution of the United States." p. 22, http://www.ohchr.org/english/bodies/ chr/ docs/62chr/E.CN.4.2006.120 _.ppf.

51. Thom Shanker and David E. Sanger, "New to Job, Gates Argued for Closing Guantánamo," *New York Times*, March 23, 2007. Robert Gates is best described as a traditional American "realist"; yet he has generally been more "hawkish" than former Secretary of State James Baker. When Baker had advocated working with Mikhail Gorbachev, Gates, as deputy National Security Council adviser, had been opposed.

(Gates backed the tougher line of then secretary of defense Dick Cheney.) In 1990 President George H.W. Bush Sr. sent him as an envoy to head off a potential Indian-Pakistani nuclear confrontation. In 1991 Gates was appointed head of the CIA even though he was accused of distorting intelligence on the Soviet Union to match more hard-line views and despite being accused of knowing more about the Iran-Contra scandal than he had admitted. In 1994 Gates advocated a military strike against North Korea. In 2004 he and Zbigniew Brzezinski chaired a Council on Foreign Relations study, "Iran: Time for a New Approach" (July 2004), which proposed a selective U.S. engagement with Tehran, but not a "grand bargain."

52. In a September 12, 2006, letter signed by Senators John Warner (R-VA) and Carl Levin (D-MI), both retired military officials, denounced potential changes to the Geneva Convention in the Military Commissions Act of 2006: "As the U.S. has greater exposure militarily than any other nation, we have long emphasized the reciprocal nature of the Geneva Conventions. That is why we believe—and the U.S. has always asserted—that a broad interpretation of Common Article 3 is vital to the safety of U.S. personnel. But the Administration's bill would put us on the opposite side of that argument." http://www.globalsecurity.org/military/library/news/2006/09/mil-060912-sasc01.htm.

53. In April 2006 the UN replaced the Commission on Human Rights, a subsidiary organ of the General Assembly, and established the Human Rights Council, now based in Geneva. http://www.ohchr.org/english/bodies/hrcouncil/docs/A.RES.60.251_En.pdf.

54. Cal Thomas, "Donald Rumsfeld w/ Cal Thomas: Transcript," (December 11, 2006), http://www.townhall.com/Columnists/CalThomas/2006/12/11/donald_rumfeld_w_cal_thomas_transcript.

55. The term "global struggle against violent extremism" (G-SAVE) was to be put into usage in May 2005. http://www.nytimes.com/2005/07/26/politics/26strategy.html?ex=1280030400&en=22b94b0298c1ca6a&ei=5090&partner=rssuserland&emc=rss.

56. See Marcel Van Herpen, "Six Dimensions of the Growing Transatlantic Divide," in *NATO and the European Union: New World, New Europe, New Threats*, ed. Hall Gardner (Aldershot, UK: Ashgate, 2004).

57. Thomas, "Donald Rumsfeld w/ Cal Thomas."

Chapter 2

1. George Kennan, "NATO Expansion Would Be a Fateful Blunder," *International Herald Tribune*, February 6, 1997.

2. President Clinton said he would not submit the adapted CFE agreement to the U.S. Senate for advice or consent to ratification until Russian forces in the North Caucasus "have in fact been reduced to the flank levels set forth in the adapted treaty." http://www.fas.org/nuke/control/cfe/news/991119-cfe-usia1.htm.

3. See Hall Gardner, *Dangerous Crossroads* (Westport, CT: Praeger, 1997), 135.

4. http://news.bbc.co.uk/1/hi/world/europe/2958381.stm.

5. Dario Cristiani, "Russia's New Initiatives in the Persian Gulf," *Power and Interest News Report* (PIRN), March 1, 2007, http://www.pinr.com.

6. See Hall Gardner, "The Genesis of NATO Enlargement and the War 'over' Kosovo," in *Central and Southeastern Europe in Transition*, ed. Hall Gardner (Westport, CT: Praeger, 2000).

7. Andrei S. Grachev, "La Russie à la recherche d'une politique étrangère," *Relations internationales: les Etudes de la Documentation Francaise La Russie 1995–1996* (Paris: la Documentation Francaise, 1996); Andrei S. Grachev, *Histoire Vraie de la Fin de l'URSS* (Paris: Editions du Rocher, 1992), 88–9 2. See also Susan Eisenhower in Ted Galen Carpenter and Barbara Conry, eds., *NATO Enlargement: Illusions and Reality* (Washington, DC.: Cato Institute, 1998).

8. Cited in Stephen Blank, "The NATO-Russia Partnership: A Marriage of Convenience Or a Troubled Partnership?," *Strategic Studies Institute*, 2005, http://www.strategicstudiesinstitute.army.mil/pdffiles/PUB73 4.pdf.

9. Russian Foreign Ministry spokesman Mikhail Kamynin warned the United States against basing BMD systems in Poland. "This could have a negative impact on strategic stability, regional security and the relations between states. . . . Such a new situation objectively requires corresponding measures from us." The Polish defense minister has tried to assure Moscow that the system would not be directed against Russia. Russia had announced earlier in 2006 that it was supplying Belarus with its S-300 antiaircraft defense system. *Agence France Press*, October 3, 2006.

10. *RFE/RL Newsline*, Vol. 11, No. 33, Part I, February 21, 2007.

11. Ibid. Polish deputy prime minister Alexander Vondra stated, "if we turn our back on this [U.S.] request, there is a threat that the [United States] will back away from Europe. If the Poles and the Czechs reject the [request], the Americans will [respond] accordingly."

12. On March 24, 2004, forty-nine retired generals and admirals called for missile defense postponement. See http://www.mapw.org.au/missiledefence/USMilitary -letter-Bush_March2004.html.

13. See comments by Robert Ranquet, cited in Brooks Tigner, "Rethinking NATO's role in Missile Defense," ISN Security Watch, March 20, 2007. See comments by Norman Ray, president for Europe of Raytheon, and NATO's former assistant secretary general for defense support, cited in Brooks Tigner, ibid.

14. *RFE/RL Newsline*, Vol. 11, No. 45, Part I, March 9, 2007.

15. See *RFE/RL Newsline*, February 12, 22, and 23, 2007.

16. Thom Shanker, "U.S. Tries to Ease Concerns in Russia on Antimissile Plan," *New York Times*, February 22, 2007.

17. Richard Weitz, "Revitalizing US-Russian Security Cooperation," *RFE/RL Newsline* 11:33, Part I, February 21, 2007.

18. Jennifer Loven, "Bush Wins Polish Nod for Missile Defense," *The Guardian* (June 8, 2007) http://www.guardian.co.uk/worldlatest/story/0,,-6695301,00.html; http:// www.rferl.org/featuresarticle/2007/06/9e494269-29d1-4e66-b950 -ac846e7e9c2a.html; "Intelligence Brief: Russia-Western Dialogue on B.M.D. Remains Difficult," *PINR*, http://www.pinr.com.

19. Paul T. Mitchell, "Network Centric Warfare: Coalition Operations in the Age of U.S. Military Primacy," *Adelphi Paper No. 385* (London: International Institute for Strategic Studies, 2006).

20. Richard Weitz, *Revitalizing US-Russian Security Cooperation* (London: Adelphi Papers, 2005).

21. *RFE/RL Newsline*, February 20, 2007, http://www.rferl.org/featuresarticle/2007/ 02/3A7C3F97-DBBF-44B7-B568-FEEC11414F37.html. See also Simon Saradzhyan, *Radar Diplomacy*, ISN Security Watch (June 13, 2007).

22. *RFE/RL Newsline*, Vol. 11, No. 33, Part I, February 21, 2007.

23. Ibid.

24. Blank, The NATO-Russia Partnership, http://www.strategicstudiesinstitute.army .mil/pdffiles/PUB734.pdf.

25. Blank, The NATO-Russian Partnership.
26. James A. Lewis, Center for Strategic and International Studies (June 15, 2007) http://www.csis.org/component/option,com_csis_progj/task,view/id,968/; http://news.bbc.co.uk/1/hi/world/europe/6665195.stm.
27. The Nuclear Information Project, http://www.nukestrat.com/nukestatus.htm.
28. *RFE/RL Newsline*, Vol. 11, No. 42, Part I, March 6, 2007.
29. Daryl G. Kimball, "START Over," *Arms Control Today*, June 2007.
30. See Gardner, *Dangerous Crossroads*, chapter 5.
31. See Chapter 6. GUUAM lost Uzbekistan in May 2005 as a member in part because of U.S. criticism of the Uzbek human rights record and consequent U.S. refusal to provide significant development assistance.
32. For analysis, see Jeronim Perovic and Robert Orttung, "Russia's Energy Policy: Should Europe Worry?," *Russian Analytical Digest* 18 (April 3, 2007).
33. See James Sherr, "Ukraine: The Pursuit of Defence Reform in an Unfavourable Context," *Conflict Studies Research Centre Central & Eastern Europe Series 04/08* (June 2004). On the domestic crisis in Ukraine, see James Sherr, "Ukraine: Prospects and Risks," *Conflict Studies Research Centre Central & Eastern Europe Series Research Centre 06/52* (October 2006).
34. NATO, http://www.nato.int/docu/speech/2006/s060914b.htm.
35. Dick Cheney, "Vice President's Remarks at the 2006 Vilnius Conference Reval Hotel Lietuva," Vilnius, Lithuania, http://www.whitehouse.gov/news/releases/2006/05/ images/20060504-1_v050406db-0157jpg-515h.html.
36. Kurt Volker, principal deputy assistant secretary of state for European and Eurasian Affairs, "The Road to NATO's Riga Summit," Testimony before the House International Relations Committee Subcommittee on Europe, Washington, DC., May 3, 2006, http://www.state.gov/p/eur/rls/rm/65874.htm.
37. See Jacques Rupnick, "In Search of East-Central Europe," in *Central and Southeastern Europe in Transition*, ed. Hall Gardner (Westport, CT: Praeger, 2000).
38. See Gardner, *Dangerous Crossroads*, chapter 3.
39. Vladimir Socor, "Russia Cancels Border Treaty, Assails Estonia," http://www.jamestown.org/edm/article.php?volume_id=407&issue_id=3386&article_id=2369959.
40. For background, see Alexey Ignatiev and Petr Shopin, "Kaliningrad in the Context of EU-Russia Relations," *Russian Analytic Digest* 15 (February 20, 2007).
41. "Swedish Security," *The Economist* (February 22, 2007). http://www.economist.com/world/europe/displaystory.cfm?story_id=8744532.
42. http://thomas.loc.gov/home/gpoxmlc109/h5948_ih.xml; http://www.csce.gov/index.cfm?Fuseaction=ContentRecords.ViewDetail&ContentRecord_id=312&ContentType=S&ContentRecordType=S&CFID=25753608&CFTOKEN=51551172.
43. http://www.iht.com/articles/2007/01/11/news/belarus.php.
44. "While Washington perceives Moscow as an opponent, if not a rival in the key issues of Black Sea democratization and reformation agenda, Berlin and Paris share the understanding of Russia's legitimate right to keep its own sphere of influence around its borders in order to balance the extension of the Atlantic Alliance to the east. Based on that presumption, the major European capitals maintain cautious attitude towards the Georgian efforts to transform its positions from a Russian satellite to a Western ally, from a backward dominion of Moscow, to a reformed partner of the West." Ognyan Minchev, "Major Interests and Strategies for the Black Sea Region," *Framework Analytical Review* (September 2006).

45. See Roman Kupchinsky, "Analysis: The Recurring Fear Of Russian Gas Dependency," *RFE/RL*, Prague, May 11, 2006.
46. Blank, The NATO-Russian Partnership.
47. Cornelius Ochmann, "Polish-Russian Relations in the Context of the EU's New Eastern Policy," *Russian Analytical Digest* 15 (February 20, 2007). http://se2.isn.ch/serviceengine/FileContent?serviceID=PublishingHouse&fileid=C68F7FA1-F640-A2CF-DA36-42E321D7EF5A&lng=en.
48. Ibid.
49. Minchev, "Major Interests and Strategies for the Black Sea Region."
50. In July 2006, Romania brought a case to the Hague against Ukraine concerning the maritime boundary between the two states on the Black Sea.
51. "Intelligence Brief: U.S. Military Bases in the Black Sea Region," *PINR*, November 19, 2005. http://www.pinr.com/report.php?ac=view_report&report_id=401. Romanian bases could function as useful NATO assets should the situation in Transnister deteriorate and require more substantial Western intervention.
52. In June 2006, the American Hungarian Federation wrote President Bush and Hungarian prime minister Ferenc Gyurcsány expressing its concern for greater "protection from discrimination and intolerance, as well as positive rights, cultural, territorial and/or personal autonomy" for Hungarian minorities in southern Slovakia, Transylvania, Romania, and Vojvodina, Serbia, http://www.americanhungarian federation.org /docs/Koszorus_Trianon_2006_06-04.pdf.
53. "Economic fundamentals across eastern Europe . . . are increasingly shaky. Romania and Latvia . . . post trade and service deficits of more than 4% of GDP—a size that is tough for all but countries at the top of the credit-quality totem, like the US, to sustain. Slovakia and Croatia have big budget deficits that are getting worse. Several nations—notable Turkey and Hungary—have foreign-currency debt coming due that exceed their reserves of hard currency. Poland, the largest of the new EU members, is fast piling up foreign debt." Joellen Perry, "Troubling Signs in Hungary Woes," *Wall Street Journal*, September 21, 2006.
54. Ronald D. Asmus and Bruce P. Jackson, "The Black Sea and the Frontiers of Freedom," *Policy Review* 125 (June–July 2004).
55. EU members will not be able to reduce their dependence on Russia significantly any time soon. Alternatives are not easy to implement now that Russia's major energy companies (especially Gazprom) are moving to increase their control of Algeria's and Turkmenistan's resources (two of the possible alternative suppliers). "Intelligence Brief: Poland Fumes over Russian-German Projects; Meeting in Lithuania to Counter Russian Influence in F.S.U.," *PINR*, May 2, 2006, http://www.pinr .com/report.php?ac=view_report&report_id=483& language_id=1.
56. The Rioni, Kodori, Inguri Chorokh, Kyzyl-Irmak, Eshil-Irmak, Sakarya, Southern Bug, Dnister, the Danube, Dnieper, and the Don via the Sea of Azov are the main rivers that flow into the Black Sea. With ice-free ports, the Black Sea is the chief shipping outlet of the Ukraine and Russia; Odessa and Sevastopol in Ukraine and Novorossiysk in Russia are major ports. Others include Constanta, Romania; Varna and Burgas in Bulgaria; and Trabzon, Samsun, and Zonguldak in Turkey.
57. Dimitrios Triantaphyllou, "The Black Sea Region and Its Growing Influence," Athens, BSEC Day (July 18, 2006).
58. Marcel de Haas, "Current Geostrategy in the South Caucasus," PINR, December 15, 2006, http://www.pinr.com/report.php?ac=view_report&report_id=595&language_id=1.
59. In terms of potential NATO overstretch, the 2004 addition of Slovenia, Slovakia, Lithuania, Estonia, Latvia, Romania, and Bulgaria doubles "NATO's militarily 'free

riders' under a U.S. security umbrella (given the minimal role of Iceland, Luxembourg, Denmark, Portugal, Greece, Hungary, and Czech republic). NATO must distribute military capabilities through specialized, modern, multilateral force planning, while consolidating links with the EU on counterterrorism, [European Security and Defense Policy (ESDP)], and peacemaking. A 26+ Alliance must also revise voting rules to improve decision-making, limiting consensus to Article V collective defense and new enlargements." See Marco Rimanelli, in Hall Gardner, ed., *NATO and the EU; New World, New Europe, New Threats* (Ashgate 2003).

60. See CFE Treaty: http://www.osce.org/docs/english/1990-1999/cfe/cfefin act99e .htm; http://www.fas.org/nuke/control/cfe/chron.htm; http://www.fas.org/nuke/control/cfe/text/final_act_of_cfe.htm.

61. For background to the frozen conflicts, see Charles King in *Grasping the Nettle*, eds. Crocker, Hampson, and Aall (Washington, DC: United States Institute of Peace Press, 2005).

62. The recognition of Montenegro's independence, discussions about Kosovo's final status, and President Putin's statements about the need to determine universal principles for self-determination have all increased Abkhaz optimism about their own prospects for recognition. For most of the 1990s, Abkhaz elites were willing to discuss "common state" options and federal arrangements with Georgia. Meanwhile Abkhaz and Russian observers charge that the United States, Turkey, and several European countries are arming and training Georgia for an offensive. Minchev, "Major Interests and Strategies for the Black Sea Region."

63. In January 2005, Belgian foreign minister, and chairman in office of the Organization for Security and Co-operation in Europe Karel de Gucht pledged to resolve the "frozen conflicts." He has stated he would not a adopt a tougher stance vis-à-vis Russia while criticizing Moldovan authorities for asking for a unitary state. Russian foreign minister Sergei Lavrov insisted that Russian troops must remain in Transnister after a negotiated settlement to prevent munitions from falling into the wrong hands.

64. Liz Fuller, "Georgia: Is Tbilisi Moving toward NATO Membership?" *RFE/RL*, Prague, June 2, 2006. In 2004 Georgia increased the size of the reserve force, "represent[ing] an increase of 25–30 percent on the figures enshrined in the original IPAP and "rais[ing] questions of affordability." Georgia asserts that it is committed to a peaceful resolution of the conflict, yet its military budget rose in 2005 at a rate higher than any other country in the world. For Georgia the unresolved conflict is an affront to its state-building project, impeding the consolidation of national security, democratic institutions, economic development, and regional integration. Crisis Group http://www.crisisgroup.org/library/documents/europe/moldova/175 _moldova_s_uncertain_future.pdf.

65. Mikhail Vignansky, "Caucasus Reels from Moscow-Tbilisi Fight," *IWPR*, September 6, 2006, http://www.isn.ethz.ch/news/sw/details.cfm?id=16760.

66. Federico Bordonaro, "Georgia: NATO by way of BMD" ISN Security Watch (29 May 2007) http://www.isn.ethz.ch/news/sw/details.cfm?id=17669.

67. Eugene B. Rumer and Jeffrey Simon, "Toward a Euro-Atlantic Strategy for the Black Sea Region," *Institute for National Strategic Studies Occasional Paper* 3, Washington, DC.: National Defense University Press, April 2006, http://www.ndu.edu/inss/Occassional_Papers/OCP3.pdf.

68. The Black Sea Naval Task Force, or BlackSeaFor, was set up in 2001; the group comprises all six riparian states. Operation Active Endeavor (OAE) was created in late 2001 following the September 11 attacks. Turkey launched Black Sea Harmony in 2004 to patrol the southern segment of the Black Sea. Ankara extended an invitation

to other littoral countries to join its security initiative. Igor Torbakov, "Turkey Sides with Moscow against Washington on Black Sea Force," *Eurasia Daily Monitor* 3, no. 43 (March 3, 2006).

69. See Minchev, "Major Interests and Strategies for the Black Sea Region." The Blue stream is said to be a consequence of Romanian and Bulgarian refusal to deal with the Gazprom monopoly. Gazprom is seen as playing a role in restoring central government control over Russia and of representing a major instrument of Russia's foreign policy.

70. Asmus and Jackson, "The Black Sea and the Frontiers of Freedom."

71. Jeffrey Simon, *Black Sea Regional Security Cooperation: Building Bridges and Barriers* (Cambridge, MA: Harvard University, 2006).

72. Rumer and Simon, "The Black Sea and the Frontiers of Freedom."

73. Igor Torbakov, "Kremlin Wary of Emerging Kyiv-Tbilisi Axis," *Eurasia Daily Monitor* No. 72, no. 16 (January 24, 2005), JRL 9032—JRL Home Jamestown Foundation, http://www.jamestown.org.

74. PINR, "Current Geostrategy in the South Caucasus," December 15, 2006.

75. http://www.turkishdailynews.com.tr/article.php?enewsid=69246. In response to the French law, the Turkish parliament threatened to pass a bill labeling the colonial killings of Algerians by French authorities as genocide and making it illegal to deny France's culpability!

76. Nicholas Wood, "EU to Reduce Force in Bosnia," *International Herald Tribune*, February 28, 2007, http://www.iht.com/articles/2007/03/01/europe/web.0301bosnia.php.

77. http://www.unmikonline.org/news.htm#0202.

78. *RFE/RL Newsline*, Vol. 11, No. 45, Part II, March 9, 2007.

79. Thomas Friedman, *International Herald Tribune*, February 15, 2007.

80. See Gardner, *Dangerous Crossroads*.

81. See "An Open Letter to the Heads of State and Government Of the European Union and NATO," September 28, 2004. http://www.newamericancentury.org/russia-20040928.htm. The letter, signed by many neoconservatives, strongly criticizes Putin's steps toward an "authoritarian regime." A counterletter argues for concern, but against exaggeration; See "A Response to the Open Letter to Heads of State and Government of the European Union and NATO of Sept. 28, 2004," http://washingtontimes.com/upi-breaking/20041013-055300-4000r.htm; www.npetro.net/openletter.html.

82. In May 2005, Russian oligarch Mikhail Khodorkovsky, then the richest man in Russia, was sentenced to nine years for fraud, tax evasion, attempted murder, embezzlement, and money laundering. Putin's actions against a number of Russian "oligarchs" have frightened Russian and foreign businessmen. As Marshall Goldman put it: "What is tragic in all this is that now, this has given an excuse for the people around Putin to go after these oligarchs, and in the process, put themselves in a position where they can take over these assets and make themselves just as rich." http://www.cfr.org/publication/8155/goldman.html.

83. http://www.guardian.co.uk/russia/article/0,,2056321,00.html.

84. The Kremlin has been accused of killing journalists critical of Russian actions in Chechnya including Anna Politkovskaya and former KGB agent Alexander V. Litvinenko (a friend of Boris Berezovsky). In regard to the latter (using Polonium 210 as poison in London in November 2006!), London has demanded the extradition of the alleged assassin, Andrei Lugovoi. Moscow has refused arguing that Russian law will not permit its citizens to be put on trial abroad, severely straining Anglo-Russian relations. In turn, Russia seeks the extradition from the United Kingdom of Boris Berezovsky (see ft. 86) who is also accused of plotting to overthrow the government by

force, and Akhmed Zakayev, a Chechen separatist, who Russia sees as a terrorist. The United Kingdom has refused to extradite either. In the case of Berezovsky, London has been backed by the EU and United States, in effect, widening the dispute with dangerous ramifications. *Wall Street Journal Europe* (July 19, 2007).

85. Candidates include associates of Putin: Dmitri Medvedev (seen as pro-Western, pro-business); Sergei Ivanov (former member of the Federal Security Bureau, seen as tough on NATO enlargement); Vladimir Yakunin (also former member of the Federal Security Bureau, seen as benefiting from nomenklatura privatization); and Valentina Matvienko (governor of St. Petersberg, seen as ineffective). http://www.foreign policy.com/story/cms.php?story_id=3694.

86. A possible, if not the most likely, successor to Putin, Sergei Ivanov, has stated that U.S. acceptance of Russia's BMD proposals "will quantitatively change Russian-U.S. relations. A new space for mutual trust will emerge. We may establish a real strategic partnership." Cited in Edward Lozansky, "Is George Bush Boosting the Russian Military-Industrial Complex?" The *Washington Times* (July 10, 2007).

87. Blank, The NATO-Russia Partnership.

88. Ukraine and Russia have declared their intention to join Blackseafor. Multilateralizing Black Sea Harmony not only could become a model for Blackseafor, but also might be subordinated to it after it completes its transformation. NATO's new allies, Bulgaria and Romania, though, remain unenthusiastic about these efforts, seeing them as forms of Turkish domination. Hence, Turkey's preferred approach appears to be to maintain its dominance by preventing NATO from extending Operation Active Endeavor into the Black Sea. Simon, "Black Sea Regional Security Cooperation."

89. Rumer and Simon, "Toward a Euro-Atlantic Strategy for the Black Sea Region."

90. Ochmann, "Polish-Russian Relations in the Context of the EU's New Eastern Policy."

91. Abrahm Lustgarten, "How Shell Lost Control of Sakhalin," *Fortune*, CNN (February 5, 2007), http://money.cnn.com/magazines/fortune/fortune_archive/2007/02/05/ 8399125/index.htm.

Chapter 3

1. January 17, 2007, CBS poll: "Looking back, do you think the United States did the right thing in taking military action against Iraq, or should the U.S. have stayed out?" 39% Right thing; 56% Stayed out. Los Angeles Times Bloomberg Poll, released January 17, 2007, conducted January 13–16, 2007: "All in all, do you think the situation in Iraq was worth going to war over, or not?" 34% Worth It; 62% Not Worth It; Pew Research Center NPR poll, released January 16, 2007; conducted January 10–15, 2007. "Do you think the U.S. made the right decision or the wrong decision in using military force against Iraq?" 40% Right decision; 51% Wrong decision.

2. On the goals of "preemption," see Hall Gardner, *American Global Strategy and the "War on Terrorism"* (Aldershot: Ashgate, 2007). See also Chapter 1, endnote 46.

3. Peter Grier "Iraq's oil production falls short of goals," *Christian Science Monitor* (May 7, 2007). According to the U.S. Government Accountability Office (GAO), Iraq will still need to spend $27 billion more for its electrical system and $20 billion to $30 billion for oil infrastructure. "Iraq Far from U.S. Goals for Energy," *Washington Post* (September 2, 2007). Prior to U.S. intervention, Washington threatened to cut countries that did support the war effort out of the Iraqi oil market. Although burgeoning Chinese influence in Iraq and throughout the world has

been a major concern for U.S. policymakers (see Chapter 8), in mid-June 2007, Iraqi president Jalal Talabani went to Beijing to obtain a significant reduction in Iraq's $8 billion debt to China (out of about $60 billion foreign debt in total) and to expand Iraq-China economic cooperation, including renegotiating Saddam Hussein's 1997 deal for China's National Petroleum Corporation to develop the al-Ahdab oil field. The deal, which was the first for foreign oil investors, could go through if Iraq's parliament passes its controversial new oil law. Jamil Anderlini and Steve Negus, "Iraq revives Saddam deal with China," *Financial Times* (June 22 2007) http://www.ft.com/cms/s/c6c6f958-2108-11dc-8d50-000b5df10621.html. Largely due to the extent of its energy dependency, China appears to be the first willing to take the risk of legal uncertainty and chaos in Iraq. Other oil deals appear to be in the making.

4. See Juan Cole, "Informed Comment," June 22, 2005, 12:00. http://www.juancole .com/2005/06/kos-discussion-of-un-option-many.html.

5. Among the lowest opinion polls were Harry Truman during the Korean War; Richard Nixon before the latter's resignation after the Watergate scandal and during the Vietnam War; Jimmy Carter, ironically during the Iran-hostage crisis, a major issue that weakened Jimmy Carter and helped thrust Ronald Reagan into power. (Bush's approval rating run hit between 27 and 35 percent, with those opposed around 64–65 percent according to ABC).

6. Democrats took a 233 to 202 advantage in the House of Representatives, and a 51 to 49 advantage in the Senate. The Senate figure includes two candidates who ran as independent candidates: Senator Joe Lieberman, for example, won as an "independent Democrat" after he lost the Democratic Party nomination in that he was generally regarded as a "cheerleader" for President Bush's foreign policy, but he then defeated Ned Lamont, an anti-Iraq War Democrat.

7. Edison Media Research and Mitofsky International conducted the polling for The Associated Press.

8. John J. Mearsheimer and Stephen Walt, "The Israeli Lobby and U.S. Foreign Policy," *Working Paper Number RWP06-011* (2006), http://ksgnotes1.harvard.edu/ Research/wpaper.nsf/rwp/RWP06-011. This paper by two major neorealist theorists helped to open debate as to the nature of Israeli "influence peddling" in Congress. The question remains as to what extent U.S. policy would change even without such a powerful lobby. See Mitchell Plitnick and Chris Toensing, "'The Israeli Lobby' in Perspective" *Middle East Report* 243 (Summer 2007).

9. *Wall Street Journal*, January 26, 2007.

10. http://irannuclearwatch.blogspot.com/2006/08/words-not-war-military-leaders -speak.html.

11. Robin Wright and Peter Baker, "White House, Joint Chiefs At Odds on Adding Troops," *Washington Post*, December 19, 2006.

12. "The issue before us is not simply whether the United States should end the regime of Saddam Hussein, but whether we as a nation are prepared to physically occupy territory in the Middle East for the next 30 to 50 years. Those who are pushing for a unilateral war in Iraq know full well that there is no exit strategy if we invade and stay." James Webb, "Heading for Trouble," *Washington Post*, September 4, 2002, http://www.jameswebb.com/articles/washpost/headingfortrouble.htm. Even more important for the Democrats in regard to Middle East policy is the fact that Senator Webb is a former Republican who turned Democrat—largely in opposition to the Bush administration's decision to intervene in Iraq. With a son in Iraq, he is also a Vietnam era war hero and a former secretary of the navy under Ronald Reagan.

Webb is thus symbolic of the former "Reaganites" who have been abandoning the Republican Party largely because of George Bush's policies.

13. Jim Webb, http://www.jameswebb.com/articles/wallstjrnl/ classstruggle.htm. See Chuck Collins, *The Economic Context: Growing Disparities of Income and Wealth*, http://www.mccormack.umb.edu/nejpp/articles/20_1/TheEconomic Context.pdf; Center on Budget and Policy Priorities, "New IRS Data Show Income Inequality is Again on the Rise," October 17, 2005, http://www.cbpp.org/10-17-05inc.htm.

14. "This is the seventh time the president has mentioned energy independence in his State of the Union message, but for the first time, this exchange is taking place in a Congress led by the Democratic Party. We are looking for affirmative solutions that will strengthen our nation by freeing us from our dependence on foreign oil, and spurring a wave of entrepreneurial growth in the form of alternate energy programs." Democratic response to President Bush's State of the Union address, as delivered by Sen. Jim Webb (D-VA), http://www.cnn.com/2007/POLITICS/01/23/sotu.webb .transcript/index.html.

15. A unitary presidency is a "theory under which, once war is declared, the president, as commander-in-chief, can ignore constitutional checks and balances, disregard the bill of rights, suspend accountability, and concentrate dictatorial power in his own hands." Former Sen. Gary Hart, "A Surge of Constitutionalism," HuffingtonPost .com, January 9, 2007. This characterization would appear true except that the role of the vice president, Dick Cheney, makes for a kind of imperial diarchy. On Cheney's overpowering influence on President Bush, see Jack Lechelt, "The Loyal Foot Soldier" in Patrick Hayden, Tom Lansford, Robert P. Watson, (eds.), *America's War on Terror* (Aldershot: Ashgate, 2003).

16. The president's "troop surge" appears to be based, at least in part, on the report by Frederick Kagan and Gen. Jack Keane (Ret.), "Choosing Victory: A Plan for Success in Iraq," American Enterprise Institute (AEI) 2006., http://turcopolier.typepad .com/sic_semper_tyrannis/files/200612141_choosingvictory6.pdf.

17. James A. Baker, III and Lee H. Hamilton, *Iraq Study Group Report*, http:// www.usip.org/isg/. See also "Statement by Co-Chairs of the Iraq Study Group before the Committee on Foreign Relations United States Senate," January 30, 2007.

18. Congressman Lee Hamilton: "The Congress is a co-equal branch of government. I frankly am not that impressed with what the Congress has been able to do. I think the Congress has been extraordinarily timid in its exercise of its Constitutional responsibilities on the question of war-making and conducting war. Now the answers here are not easy, but in a word, I think, very robust oversight is necessary. I think it has been lacking," ibid.

19. This position stems, in part, from James Baker, who has argued that creative diplomacy could woo Damascus away from its strategic alliance with Iran. "If you can flip the Syrians, you will cure Israel's Hizb'allah problem." Baker also indicated that Syria could persuade Hamas' militant external wing to accept Olmert's conditions for direct engagement with the Palestinians. http://www.nytimes.com/2006/ 12/08/world/middleeast/08diplo.html?ex=1323234000&en=a0514a2fefc3b7e4&ei =5088&partner=rssnyt&emc=rss.

20. Further signs of congressional opposition to President Bush were indicated by Sen. Bill Nelson's meeting with Syrian president Bashar al-Assad on December 13, 2006. The White House called Nelson's meeting with the Syrian president "inappropriate" and "undermining democracy in the region." Three other senators, including Republican senator Arlen Specter, likewise visited Damascus in defiance of President Bush, who has resisted talks with Syria, largely in opposition to Syrian actions in both Iraq and Lebanon. See Web site of Sen. Arlen Specter: http://specter.senate.gov.

21. The term comes from the early nineteenth-century Spanish and Portuguese pirates, "filibusteros," who held ships hostage for ransom. It also means an irregular military adventurer; specifically an American engaged in fomenting insurrections in Latin America in the mid-nineteenth century.

22. On January 17, 2007, chairman of the Senate Foreign Relations Committee Joseph R. Biden, Jr. (D-DE), Sen. Chuck Hagel (R-NE), and chairman of the Senate Armed Services Committee Carl Levin (D-MI) introduced a bipartisan, yet nonbinding, Senate resolution expressing their opposition to the deepening U.S. military commitment in Iraq. This is significant in that Chuck Hagel became the first Republican to publicly break with President Bush.

23. For "surge estimates in May 2007, see Paul Rogers, "U.S., Iran: The Fire Next Time" http://www.isn.ethz.ch/news/sw/details.cfm?id=17665 For Congressional Budget Office estimates of costs of troop surge, see http://www.cbo.gov/ftpdocs/77xx/doc7778/TroopIncrease.pdf.

24. Republican senator Mark Warner's (R-VA) proposal was a compromise between his own former proposal and that of Democratic senator Biden's. The new and revised Warner-Levin resolution expressed the Senate's opposition to the surge but promised to sustain funding for the troops. The resolution did not include the language stating the Bush plan is against the national interest (as did the Democratic statement), but it also dropped an earlier provision by Warner suggesting that Senate support the deployment of additional troops, if necessary.

25. Carl Hulse and Jeff Zeleny, "G.O.P. Senators Block Debate on Iraq Policy," *New York Times*, February 6, 2007.

26. "Any resolution that could be construed by American forces that Congress has lost faith in their ability to be successful in Iraq should be rejected because it rings of defeatism at a time when we should be focused on Victory. . . . I believe General Petraeus's new strategy of sending more troops and more economic aid, and improving the political climate in Iraq is our best chance for success, and I support his new effort. To my colleagues who believe Iraq is a lost cause, I urge you to have the courage of your convictions and vote to stop sending more troops into Iraq by cutting off funding. . . . A resolution declaring the new strategy a failure before it is implemented is the worst of all worlds. It is a vote of no confidence in General Petraeus, will empower our enemies, and be demoralizing to our own troops." *Washington Post*, Jan. 31, 2007.

27. Ibid.

28. "The President addressed a range of issues, but none is more important than the struggle against Islamic extremism. This is the central issue of our time. And the primary front in this struggle is Iraq. I understand that the American people are frustrated with the lack of progress in the war, and the many mistakes that have been made. However, there is now a new plan in place with a new commander. While there is no guarantee of success, it is guaranteed that it would be disastrous to our national security if we fail in Iraq. That is why Congress should not impede this new effort to defend the struggling democracy in Iraq."

29. Sen. Susan Colins (R-ME), who is an opponent of Bush's escalation plan, has stated that she has been "getting a lot of pressure" to go along with Bush from her conservative Republican colleagues. She stated that she was "really offended when people say that those of us who are in favor of the resolution are somehow betraying the troops. . . . I don't believe that at all. . . . I think all Americans support our troops." (Interview MSNBC). Other Republicans who opposed President Bush's policies include Maine's Olympia Snowe and Oregon's Gordon Smith.

30. http://www.clw.org/policy/iraq/resources/clippings/new_warner_resolution
_vs_old_warner_resolution/(CNN on Jan. 17).

31. William Branigin, "House OKs Timetable for Troops in Iraq," March 23, 2007,
http://www.washingtonpost.com/wp-dyn/content/article/2007/03/23/
AR2007032300531.html?sub=new.

32. In late January 2007, Congressman Kucinich declared: "The degree to which this
President continues to take steps to go to war against Iran without consulting with
the full Congress is the degree to which he is increasingly putting himself in jeop-
ardy of an impeachment proceeding."

33. http://www.house.gov/apps/list/press/ny15_rangel/CBRStatementDraft05262005
.html. Presidential campaign links between the pro-Iraq war Fox News and the
Congressional Black Caucus may be seen as ways to divide the democratic opposition, in part to support the war effort in Iraq. On July 3, 2002, President Bush proclaimed that all immigrants (which can include illegals) who have served honorably
on active duty in the armed forces after September 11, 2001, shall be eligible to
apply for expedited U.S. citizenship. On the need for immigrant skills, such as trans-
lators, in the war on terrorism, see Margaret D. Stock, *Immigration Policy in Focus*,
Vol. 5, No. 9, November 2006. http://www.ailf.org/ipc/infocus/infocus_11206.pdf

34. http://www.sigir.mil/reports/quarterlyreports/Jan07.aspx.

35. As Senator Levin put it: The president's most recent plan, like previous ones,
includes no mechanism to hold the Iraqis to their commitments. Deepening our
involvement in Iraq would be a mistake. Deepening our involvement in Iraq on the
assumption that the Iraqis will meet future benchmarks and commitments given
their track record would compound the mistake. Opening Statement of Sen. Carl
Levin at the Senate Armed Services Committee Hearing on Iraq. http://www
.senate.gov/~levin/newsroom/release.cfm?id=267518.

36. Tom Lasseter, "Mahdi Army Gains Strength through Unwitting Aid of U.S.,"
McClatchy Newspapers, February 1, 2007.

37. International Office of Migration, "Bleak Prognosis on Iraqi Displacement in
2007," http://www.iom.int/jahia/Jahia/pbnAF/cache/offonce?entryId=13117.

38. Daniel L. Byman and Kenneth M. Pollack, "Things Fall Apart. What Do We Do If
Iraq Implodes?" *Washington Post*, August 20, 2006.

39. http://www.turkishdailynews.com.tr/.

40. http://www.senate.gov/~levin/newsroom/release.cfm?id=267518.

41. *New York Times*, July 20, 2007. By August 2007, Senator Levin urged the Iraqi parliament to vote the government of Prime Minister al-Maliki out of office. This, of
course, should be an Iraqi decision. *New York Times*, August 21, 2007. Senator
Hillary Clinton also called for al-Maliki to step down, as did French Foreign
Minister Bernard Kouchner, who previously stated that he had come to Iraq to "listen," not advise, and to reestablish French relations with Iraq in order to strengthen
the UN role. Former prime minister Ayad Allawi stated that his alliance "had lost
faith" in the present Iraqi government and that Iraq was not closer to reconciliation
and was capable of developing policies that would check Iranian influence. *New York
Times*, August 27, 2007. On the withrawal of al-Sadr's six cabinet members, plus
those of the Sunni Accordance Front and the Iraqiya bloc led by Ayad Allawi from
the Iraqi cabinet, see the *New York Times*, April 16, 2007; August 1, 2007; August
27, 2007.

42. Congressman Murtha, "Testimony before Senate Foreign Affairs Committee,"
(January 23, 2007) http://www.house.gov/list/press/pa12_murtha/PRtestimony
.html.

43. On the debate over defense transformation, see Ronald O'Rourke, "Defense Transformation: Background and Oversight Issues for Congress," Washington, D.C: CRS Reports, November 9, 2006.
44. http://www.nytimes.com/2007/03/10/world/middleeast/10cnd-mtext.html ?pagewanted=2; http://graphics.nytimes.com/packages/pdf/world/Text_of_joint _statement.pdf.
45. As in the Michael Jackson "moonwalk": it was argued that the Pentagon was engaging in a strategy of moving forward while actually sliding backward. Thomas E. Ricks, "Pentagon May Suggest Short-Term Buildup Leading to Iraq Exit," *Washington Post* (November 20, 2006). For a critical perspective, see Juan Cole, http://fairuse.100webcustomers.com/fairenough/salon059.html.
46. http://www.defenselink.mil/transcripts/transcript.aspx?transcriptid=3974 http:// www.nytimes.com/2007/06/03/washington/03assess.html?_r=1&th=&adxnnl=1&oref =slogin&emc=th&adxnnlx=1180888214-N/7COwxrWTTpKTobH/Z0/w. Considerable spending on the U.S. embassy in Baghdad and bases (including Al Asad in Anbar Province, Balad Air Base about fifty miles north of Baghdad, and Tallil Air Base in the south) throughout the country suggests a long term presence.
47. Ali al-Fadhily, "Iraq: U.S. Losing Ground Through Tribal Allies (IPS) Jun 15, 2007 http://www.ipsnews.net/news.asp?idnews=38190.

Chapter 4

1. *Agence France Press*, January 21, 2007.
2. P. R. Kumaraswamy, "China, Russia on Road to Abandoning Iran," *ISN Security Watch*, January 10, 2007.
3. UN Resolution 1747 focuses on constraining Iranian arms exports, the state-owned Bank Sepah—already under Treasury Department sanctions—and the Revolutionary Guard Corps, which is an elite military organization separate from the nation's conventional armed forces. Thom Schanker, "Security Council Votes to Tighten Iran Sanctions," *New York Times*, March 25, 2007.
4. http://www.airforcetimes.com/news/2007/02/apiran070201/.
5. http://www.webb.senate.gov/newsroom/record.cfm?id=270138.
6. http://www.nytimes.com/2007/04/15/world/middleeast/15sunnis.html?page wanted=3&_r=1&th&emc=th.
7. U.S. Department of Energy, "The Hydrogen Posture Plan," February 2004, http:// www.eere.energy.gov/hydrogenandfuelcells/pdfs/hydrogen_posture_plan.pdf. On multilateral development of "fourth generation" nuclear plants, see U.S. Department of Energy: http://www.ne.doe.gov/genIV/neGenIV4.html.
8. Ariana Eunjung Cha, "China Embraces Nuclear Future," *Washington Post*, May 29, 2007, http://www.washingtonpost.com/wpdyn/content/article/2007/05/28/AR200705 2801051_pf.html; Benjamin K. Sovacool, "Think Again: Nuclear Energy," *Foreign Policy* (September 2005). http://www.foreignpolicy.com/story/cms.php?Story_id = 3250&print=1.
9. "Economic Brief: Fallout from Energy Trends," *PINR*, http://www.pinr.com.
10. Kamal Nazer Yasin, "Iran: The Geostrategy of Oil," *ISN Security Watch* (July 18, 2007).
11. The National Geoscience Database of Iran states on its Web page for geothermal energy: "Installed capacity of power plants which is now 29000MW should be increased into 90000MW in 2020 regarding to population and industrial growth

rate. But since in next few years reducing Iran's reliance on oil and 'petrodollars' must be done seriously so renewable energy productivity will not only help to decrease pollution, but will also help Iran diversify its economy." http://www.njdir .irp?PID=15&index=0.

12. Richard Betts, "The Osirak Fallacy," *The National Interest* (Spring 2006). In a report allegedly leaked to embarrass Germany, revealing major German, U.S., UK, and Chinese firms purportedly involved in Saddam's nuclear program, see *The Guardian* (December 18, 2002).

13. It should be noted that in February 1975, the shah stated that Iran had "no intention of acquiring nuclear weaponry but if small states began building them, then Iran might have to reconsider its policy."

14. Richard Perle, cited by *The New American Century*, http://www.newamericancentury .org/iraq-20030224.htm.

15. Even though the Soviet-era Temelín nuclear power plant (Soviet VVER-1000/320 reactors) in the Czech Republic, for example, has been upgraded and refitted with Westinghouse technology, it is continuing to cause concern.

16. http://en.rian.ru/russia/20070219/60947595.html. "Russia, Iran and the Bottom Line," *New York Times*, March 21, 2007.

17. The fact that six out of twelve nuclear research reactors in Moscow had to be shut down in December 2006 should represent a warning in that Russian ecologists have repeatedly called for the removal of all nuclear research reactors from the city to prevent radiation and health risks. *RFE/RL Newsline*, Vol. 10, No. 233, Part I (December 19, 2006).

18. See, "Iranian President: No 'Nuclear Apartheid,'" *CNN Access* (September 17, 2005), http://www.cnn.com/2005/WORLD/meast/09/17/ahmadinejad/index.html.

19. Ibid.

20. Nazila Fathi, David E. Sanger, and William J. Broad, "Iran Says It Is Making Nuclear Fuel, Defying U.N.," *New York Times*, April 12, 2006.

21. David E. Sanger, William J. Broad, "Iran Expanding Nuclear Effort, Agency Reports," *New York Times*, February 22, 2007.

22. William O. Beeman, "After Ahmadinejad: the Prospects for US-Iranian Relations," in *Iranian Challenges*, ed. Walter Posch, Chaillot paper, 89 (May 2006).

23. Bernard Gwertzman, interview of Ray Takeyh, "Takeyh: Iranian Middle Class Growing Disillusioned with Ahmadinejad," December 19, 2006.

24. Algiers Accord, http://www.parstimes.com/history/algiers_accords.pdf.

25. http://www.parstimes.com/history/albright_speech.html.

26. Bernard Gwertzman, "Leverett: Bush Administration 'Not Serious' about Dealing with Iran," Council on Foreign Relations, March 31, 2006, http://www.cfr.org/ publication/10326; Kamal Nazer Yasin, "Bush Administration's 'Strategic Malpractice' on Iran," interview with Flynt Leverett, http://www.isn.ethz.ch/ news/sw/details.cfm?id=16933. For political background, see Shahram Chubin, "Iran's Nuclear Ambitions." Carnegie Endowment for International Peace, 2006; Shahram Chubin and Robert S. Litwak, "Debating Iran's Nuclear Aspirations," *Washington Quarterly* (Autumn 2003). Supreme Jurisprudent Ali Khamenei has argued that atomic weapons are immoral. Informed Comment, April 12, 2006, http://www.juancole.com/2006/04/iran-can-now-make-glowing-mickeymouse .html.

27. Conn Hallinan, "The Democrats & Iran," (December 9, 2006) *Foreign Policy in Focus*, http://www.fpif.org/fpiftxt/3771.

28. Lisa Bryant, "France Defends Talk with Iran on Nuclear Fuel," *Reuters*, February 4, 2005.

29. See "Implementation of the NPT Safeguards Agreement in the Islamic Republic of Iran. Resolution adopted on 24 September 2005." http://www.iaea.org/Publications/Documents/Board/2005/gov2005-77.pdf. Russia has declared that it does not want Iran to possess nuclear arms, but it argued for greater diplomatic efforts before turning Iran over to the UN Security Council.

30. M. K. Bhadrakumar, "China, Russia Welcome Iran into the Fold," *Asia Times On Line* (April 18, 2006), http://www.atimes.com/atimes/China/HD18Ad02.html; Jephraim P. Gundzik, "The Ties That Bind China, Russia, and Iran," June 4, 2005, http://www.atimes.com/atimes/China/GF04Ad07.html; http://www.atimes.com/atimes/Middle_East/FK06Ak01.html.

31. Hassan M. Fattah, "Arab States, Wary of Iran, Add to Their Arsenals but Still Lean on the U.S.," *New York Times*, February 23, 2007.

32. Meghan Clyne, "Congress Outbids Bush on Iran Democracy Aid," *New York Sun*, March 3, 2006.

33. Amitai Etzioni, "Iran: A Faustian Bargain Communitarian," Letter #10, http://hermes.circ.gwu.edu/cgi-bin/wa?A3=ind0604&L=comnet&P=25208&E=1&B=254161802c984fb9&T=text/html.

34. Seymour M. Hersh, "The Iran Plans: Would President Bush Go to War to Stop Tehran from Getting the Bomb?" *New Yorker*, April 17, 2006 (Posted April 8, 2006).

35. "Iraq's neighbors influence, and are influenced by, events within Iraq, but the involvement of these outside actors is not likely to be a major driver of violence or the prospects for stability because of the self-sustaining character of Iraq's internal sectarian dynamics. Nonetheless, Iranian lethal support for select groups of Iraqi Shia militants clearly intensifies the conflict in Iraq. Syria continues to provide safe haven for expatriate Iraqi Bathists and to take less than adequate measures to stop the flow of foreign jihadists into Iraq." National Intelligence Estimate, http://dni.gov/press_releases/20070202_release.pdf.

36. Mark Mazzetti and Michael R. Gordon, "Fissures Emerge on Iran's Role in Iraq Attacks," *International Herald Tribune*, February 14, 2007.

37. AFP, Jan 21, 2007.

38. Heather Stewart, "Iran Crisis 'Could Drive Oil over $90,'" *The Guardian*, January 29, 2006, http://www.guardian.co.uk/oil/story/0,,1697137,00.html.

39. Gareth Porter, "Israeli Realism on Iran Belies Threat Rhetoric," January 30, 2007, http://ipsnews.net/news.asp?idnews=36369.

40. Jacques Chirac, January 20, 2006, http://www.ambafrance-us.org/news/standpoint/stand157.asp.

41. Porter "Israeli Realism on Iran Belies Threat Rhetoric."

42. AIPAC Memo "Proceed with Caution If Engaging Iran and Syria" Dec. 6, 2006 http://www.aipac.org/PDFDocs/AIPAC%20Memo%20-%20ProceedWith Caution.pdf.

43. "Hillary Clinton Calls Iran a Threat to U.S., Israel," *International Herald Tribune*, February 1, 2007.

44. ISN Security Watch staff, "OpEd: The Iran Endgame," January 31, 2007.

45 Ibid.

46. "President Ahmadinejad: The transcript," http://www.msnbc.msn.com/id/14912050/.

47. "President Ahmadinejad Should Visit the US Holocaust Museum if He Speaks to the UN," http://www.ushmm.org/wlc/en/index.php?lang=en&ModuleId=10005143.

48. David Albright, "South Africa and the Affordable Bomb," *Bulletin of Atomic Scientists* (July/August 1994), http://www.thebulletin.org/article.php?art_ofn=ja94albright.

49. See my argument, Gardner, *American Global Strategy and the "War on Terrorism,"* p. 103.

50. Hassan M. Fattah, "Arab States, Wary of Iran, Add to Their Arsenals but Still Lean on the U.S.," *New York Times*, February 23, 2007.

51. Mohammed Abdullah Al Roken, "Dimensions of the UAE-Iran Dispute over Three Islands," http://www.uaeinteract.com/uaeint_misc/pdf/perspectives/09.pdf. The islands might have some value in disrupting shipping at the beginning of a conflict, but following the U.S. "revolution in military affairs," any defenses would be instantly wiped out in the case of an outbreak of serious hostilities.

52. http://www.nato-qatar.com/security/speech2.html.

53. http://bakerinstitute.org/Pubs/BakerHamiltonTestimony070130.pdf.

54. http://www.atimes.com/atimes/Middle_East/HD26Ak02.html. The Iranian Revolutionary Guards might have stuffed the ballots for Ahmadinejad, even though the ruling Ayatollahs control the Supreme National Security Council, the Guardians Council, the foundations, the army, and the media.

55. Informed Comment, April 12, 2006, http://www.juancole.com/2006/04/ iran-can -now-make-glowing-mickey-mouse.html.

56. Hassan Rowhani, *Time Magazine*, May 11, 2006, cited at Global Security.org http://www.globalsecurity.org/wmd/library/news/iran/2006/iran-060511-irna01.htm; http://www.parstimes.com/history/un_598.html; http://www2.irna.ir/ en/news/ view/line-17/0704106338191059.htm.

57. See Ray Takeyh, "A Nuclear Iran: Challenges and Responses Author: Senior Fellow for Middle Eastern Studies," March 2, 2006, http://www.cfr.org/publication/ 10008/nuclear_iran.html?breadcrumb=default.

58. "Director General Briefs Press on Iran's Nuclear Programme" IAEA (14 June 2007) http://www.iaea.org/NewsCenter/News/2007/pressbrief140707.html. IAEA Director General Dr. El-Baradei told reporters that the Board had not adopted the IAEA's 2 percent budget increase for 2008–2009. He said that there was a "gradual erosion" of the IAEA's ability to perform critical functions that directly relate to decisions on war and peace. Without sufficient resources, he cautioned, "I will not be able to certify that we are able to do the critical functions we are expected to perform." Washington toned down its strong opposition to El-Baradei's bid for a third term as Director General, but stated that he needed to get tougher on Iran. *Washington Post* (June 8, 2005) http://www.washingtonpost.com/wp-dyn/content/article/2005/06/ 07/AR2005060701542.html.

59. Here, it should be pointed out that one of the key differences between Iran and North Korea is that Iran has a highly active civil society that does not always support government policy. It is not necessarily certain that nuclear power can continue to serve as a rallying point for the Iranian leadership.

60. Helene Cooper and David E. Sanger, "Iran Strategy Stirs Debate at White House," *Washington Post*, June 16, 2007. In addition, General Wesley Clark rebuked Senator Lieberman's public call to pursue Iranian forces across Iraq's border: "What we need now is full-fledged engagement with Iran. . . . All options are on the table, but we should be striving to bridge the gulf of almost 30 years of hostility before, and only when all else fails should there be any consideration of other options. . . . Only someone who never wore the uniform or thought seriously about national security would make threats at this point . . . What our soldiers need is responsible strategy, not a further escalation of tensions in the region." Gen. Wesley Clark Slams Senator Lieberman on Iran Newsmax (June 13, 2007) http://www.newsmax.com/archives/ ic/2007/6/13/203112.shtml?s=ic.

61. Sam Gardiner, a retired air force colonel and strategy teacher at the National War College, the Naval War College, and the Air Force War College, says President Bush

"talks about the Middle East in messianic terms, and is said to have told those close to him that he has got to attack Iran because even if a Republican succeeds him . . . he will not have the same freedom of action that Bush enjoys." According to Seymour Hersh, Cheney said that the November 7, 2007, midterm congressional elections "would not stop the administration from pursuing a military option with Iran." Hallinan, "The Democrats & Iran."

62. Despite their conflict with Iran, a number of Bush administration officials had experience dealing with Iranian hardliners during the Iran-Contra affair. These include Elliott Abrams, who is deputy assistant to President Bush and deputy national security adviser for global democracy strategy in the second-term Bush administration; David Addington, Vice President Cheney's chief of staff in the second term; John Bolton, the former UN ambassador; Vice President Richard Cheney, who played a prominent part as a member of the joint congressional Iran-Contra inquiry of 1986; Robert M. Gates, successor to Secretary of Defense Donald Rumsfeld, who was accused of knowing more than he admitted once the Iran-Contra scandal broke. See "The Iran-Contra Affair 20 Years On," The National Security Archive, http://www.gwu.edu/~nsarchiv/NSAEBB/NSAEBB210/index.htm. Saudi Prince Bandar was also involved in funding Iran-Contra. For a differing perspective, Seymour M. Hersh, "The Redirection," *New Yorker*, February 25, 2007. Hersh argues correctly that fear of Iran is bringing Saudis, the United States, and Israel closer together; but, like the Iran-Contra affairs, U.S.-Saudi activities in Iraq and Iran possess no accountability. But his perspective does not entirely take into account opening of discussions between Saudi Arabia with Iraq, Syria, and Iran.

Chapter 5

1. On September 10, 2006, Riah Abu El-Assal, bishop of the Episcopal Church of Jerusalem and the Middle East, was one of six invited to meet with Prime Minister Tony Blair at the British consulate in Jerusalem. "Riah Abu El-Assal's Latest Report from the Middle East, Friday, 22 September 2006," http://www.morayrossandcaithness .co.uk/artman/publish/article_111.shtml.

2. U.S. State Department, "A Performance-Based Roadmap to a Permanent Two-State Solution to the Israeli-Palestinian Conflict," http://www.state.gov/r/pa/prs/ps/ 2003/20062.htm.

3. http://www.mfa.gov.il/MFA/MFAArchive/2000_2009/2001/1/Israeli-Palestinian %20Joint%20Statement%20-%2027-Jan-2001.

4. http://www.boston.com/news/world/middleeast/articles/2007/03/27/arab_summit _considers_military_plan/.

5. "The Geneva Accord," Haaretz.com, http://www.haaretz.com/hasen/pages/ ShArt .jhtml? Item No=351461. Annex X, unpublished, was to propose multinational peacekeeping.

6. Amitai Etzioni, "On Giving Your Cake—and Enjoying It Too, Update #69," A Communitarian Letter, http://www.gwu.edu/~ccps/.

7. Reuven Paz, "Hamas and Islamic Jihad," cited in Council of Foreign Relations, http://cfrterrorism.org/groups/hamas.html.

8. Yossi Melman, "Egypt Recommends Hamas Put an End to Terror," April 5, 2006, http://www.haaretz.com/hasen/spages/702512.html.

9. Marwan Bishara, "The Risk of a Third Intifada," *The Guardian*, August 18, 2005, http://www.guardian.co.uk/israel/Story/0,2763,1551402,00.html.

10. Here, the wall around the major Israeli settlement in Ma'ale Adumim reaches from the 1949 cease-fire line into the West Bank for up to 25 kilometers and effectively blocks access from north to south for Palestinian residents of East Jerusalem, Bethlehem, and Ramallah. Israeli hard-liners see construction as a way to cement Jewish control over East Jerusalem and prevent expanding Palestinian villages from encroaching on the nearly five-kilometer-long finger of land linking Ma'ale Adumim to Jewish neighborhoods in East Jerusalem. "Israel Begins Building in West Bank Zone," *ISN Security Watch*, August 25, 2005.

11. BBC Monitoring Middle East, "Hamas PM-designate Comments on Israeli Poll Results, Readiness for Talks," March 29, 2006.

12. In the spring of 1994, apparently accepting the green line, Sheikh Yassin had offered a cease-fire if Israeli forces withdrew from occupied territories, settlements were dismantled and prisoners were released. See, Ami Isseroff, "A History of the Hamas Movement," http://www.mideastweb.org/hamashistory.htm. For citations of Hamas legislators in regard to recognition of Israeli boundaries, see http://www.memri.org/bin/opener_latest.cgi?ID= SD107906.

13. The Palestinian Authority's annual operating budget is roughly US$1.6 billion. roughly two-thirds of which comes from Europe, international donor agencies, the United States, and Asian governments. The US$1.3 billion in foreign aid in 2006 accounted for 32 percent of Palestinian gross domestic product, making Palestinians the biggest recipients of foreign per capita aid in the world.

14. In the 2000–2004 period, the Intifada cost the Israeli economy about $12 billion, or approximately 10 percent of Israel's $121 billion GDP. Israel's potential growth per capita over this period was reduced by 11 percent, with a 30 percent fall in stock prices. Per capita income in Israel would likely have been $18,500 (up from its present $16,700) without the conflict. On the other side, the costs to the Palestinian economy has been $4.5 billion in the same period, or nearly 300 percent of the West Bank's GDP of $1.7 billion. Economic growth was -22 percent, with a loss of GDP per capita of $1,200. (Up to $700 million in the past decade or so has been stolen.) "Journal: Costs of the Intifada," November 19, 2004, http://globalguerrillas.typepad .com/globalguerrillas/2004/11/journal_the_cos.html. See also "Deep Palestinian Poverty in the Midst of Economic Crisis," World Bank, October 2004, http://lnweb18.worldbank.org/mna/mena.nsf/Attachments/Poverty+Report/$File/Poverty+Eng+final.pdf.

15. "Israel Breaks Off Direct Contacts with Palestinian Government," *New York Times*, April 10, 2006, http://www.nytimes.com/2006/04/10/world/middleeast/10mideast .html?th&emc=th.

16. Mitch Potter, "Jimmy Carter's Secret Mission," *The Toronto Star*, January 27, 2006.

17. Dominic Moran, ISN Security Watch, September 16, 2006.

18. Hamas won seventy-six seats; Fatah won forty-three seats; the Popular Front for the Liberation of Palestine (PFLP) won three seats; The Third Way block won two seats; Badil won two seats; and Independent Palestine won two seats and a list of other independents won the remaining four seats. Hamas: Change and Reform (434,817 votes, 43 percent of the total vote, seventy-six seats); Fatah Movement (403,458 votes, 39.9 percent of the total vote, forty-three seats); Martyr Abu Ali Mustafa (41,671 votes, 4.1 percent of the total vote, three seats); The Third Way (23,513 votes, 2.3 percent of the total vote, two seats); The Alternative (28,779 votes, 2.8 percent of the total vote, two seats). Others (53,200 votes, 5.3 percent of the total vote, four seats). Yet, secular parties won 57 percent of the popular vote altogether.

19. Sharmila Devi, "World Bank May Sever Contacts with the PA," *Financial Times*, April 13, 2006.

20. Dina Kraft and Christine Hauser, "Suicide Attack Kills at Least 8 in Tel Aviv," *New York Times*, April 17, 2006.

21. BBC Monitoring Middle East, "Hamas PM-designate Comments on Israeli Poll Results, Readiness for Talks." March 29, 2006.

22. Under the Mecca agreement, Hamas was to hold nine ministries in the cabinet, including the prime minister's post. Fatah was to hold six, and other factions were to hold four positions. Fatah was expected to name independents as foreign minister and two state ministers without portfolio. For its part, Hamas would name independents as interior minister and planning minister and would appoint a state minister without portfolio.

23. Steven Erlanger, "Hamas and Fatah Agree on Unity Government," *New York Times*, March 15, 2007.

24. David Aaron, "Outside View: How to Deal with Hamas," UPI, March 15, 2006.

25. See ibid.

26. Yotam Feldner and Yigal Carmon, "Jordanian Policies on the Palestinian Problem. Part II" *The Middle East Media Research Institute* No. 15 (March 16, 1999).

27. "Terror Leader Admits for First Time That He Ordered 9/11 Attacks," CAIRO, Egypt, CBS News, October 29, 2004.

28. Mark Mackinnon, Reuters; Trish McAlaster, The Globe and Mail, January 17, 2007.

29. Jim Lobe, Inter Press Service, http://www.ynetnews.com/articles/0,7340,L-3340750,00.html.

30. Patrick Seale, "Who Killed Rafik Hariri?" *The Guardian*, February 23, 2005. Unlike others in Lebanon, al-Hariri was not an avowed "enemy" of Syria; although he was forced to resign from his post as prime minister by Syrian military intelligence, he was also thought to be negotiating for Syrian withdrawal as an intermediary between Damascus and the opposition at the time of the assassination. Not all Lebanese have taken an anti-Syrian stance: Michael Aoun, who opposed Syrian intervention in 1989 as Prime Minister, and who is now leader of the Free Patriot Movement, has forged a tactical alliance with Sh'ite parties Hizb'allah and Amal- against Prime Minister Siniora's government, in effect dividing the Christian Maronites. Failure to forge a national unity government could provoke renewed civil war.

31. http://www.cfr.org/publication/13391/fatah_alislam.html.

32. Yoav Stern, "Assad: Peace Talks with Israel Could Be Completed in 6 Months," *Haaretz* (The Associated Press), February 10, 2006.

33. Jerome M. Segal, "Final Status in a New Era," *Haaretz*, February 17, 2007.

34. Robert E. Hunter and Seth G. Jones, Building a Successful Palestinian State (Santa Monica, CA: Rand: 2006); Thomas L. Friedman, "Go Slow-Mo, NATO," *New York Times*, December 12, 2002; "The Hard Truth," New York Times, April 3, 2002. I publicly proposed a NATO-Partnership for Peace approach to Middle East peacekeeping in October 2001 at the Atlantic Council conference in Slovenia.

35. Israeli Raid on Palestinian Prison Ignites Crisis in Occupied Territories. See interview with Naseer Aruri, "Dishonest Broker: America's Role in Israel and Palestine," *Democracy Now*, March 16, 2006, http://www.democracynow.org/article.pl?sid =06/03/16/158202.

Chapter 6

1. Gal Luft and Anne Korin, "Terror's Next Target," *Journal of International Security Affairs* (December 2003).

2. Mark Duffield, *Global Governance and the New Wars* (London: Zed, 2001), chapter 7.

3. "Current Geostrategy in the South Caucasus," Power and Interest Research Group (PINR), December 15, 2006).

4. As Moscow makes a near 150 percent profit on gas it buys from Kazakhstan and then distributes to Europe, the EU hoped to cut Russia out of the equation so as to reduce its dependency. Melissa Hahn, "Moscow Achieves Success with Kazakh Oil Deal," PINR (May 29, 2007). "Current Geostrategy in the South Caucasus," PINR (December 15, 2006). http://www.pinr.com.

5. See Igor Tomberg, "Geopolitics of Pipeline Communication Systems in Eurasia," *World Affairs* Vol 10, No 1 (2006).

6. Paul Rogers "US, Iran: The fire next time" (May 29, 2007) http://www.isn.ethz.ch/news/sw/details.cfm?id=17665.

7. On naval strategy and the war on terrorism (seen as a two front war, with psychological and physical fronts), see Randall G. Bowdish, "Global Terrorism, Strategy, and Naval Forces," chapter 5 in Sam J. Tangredi, ed., *Globalization and Maritime Power*, National Defense University, 2002. http://www.ndu.edu/inss/Books/Books_2002/Globalization_and_Maritime_Power_Dec_02/01_toc.htm.

8. On the roots of U.S. policy toward South Africa, see Chester A. Crocker, "South Africa: Strategy for Change," *Foreign Affairs* (Winter 1980–81).

9. In the words of Zbigniew Brzezinski, the United States "did not push the Soviets to intervene [in Afghanistan], but purposely augmented the chances that they would." See Hall Gardner, *American Global Strategy and the "War on Terrorism."*

10. Edward Jay Epstein, "Who Killed Zia?" *Vanity Fair* (September 1989). http://edwardjayepstein.com/archived/zia.htm.

11. Ivo H. Daalder and James M. Lindsay, *America Unbound: The Bush Revolution in Foreign Policy* (Washington, DC: Brookings Institution Press, 2003).

12. In 2006, Afghan opium exports were estimated at $3.1 billion, one-third of Afghanistan's GDP. The area under poppy cultivation has risen from 8,000 hectares in 2001 to 165,000 hectares in 2006. Despite U.S. and NATO efforts, in 2006, 60 percent more cultivable land was planted with opium compared to 2005; the poppy harvest reached 6,100 tons. Roughly 12 percent of the Afghan population is involved in drug production at some level. Anuj Chopra, ISN Security Watch "Addicted in Afghanistan" (July 17 2007).

13. Michael Weinstein, "Uzbekistan and the Great Powers: Courting Instability," PINR (January 3, 2005). http://www.pinr.com/report.php?ac=view_report&report_id=251&language_id=1; Erich Marquardt and Yevgeny Bendersky, "Uzbekistan's New Foreign Policy Strategy," PINR, November 23, 2005 http://www.pinr.com/report.php?ac=view_report&report_id=404&language_id=1.

14. Amin Tarzi, "Pakistan Hails North Waziristan Peace Deal," *RFE/RL*, October 24, 2006. See Crisis Group critique of "appeasement" in "Pakistan's Tribal Areas." http://www.crisisgroup.org/library/documents/asia/south_asia/125_pakistans_tribal_areas___appeasing _the_milit ants.pdf. Yet, is democratization necessarily the salvation?

15. Ashley J. Tellis, C. Christine Fair, and Jamison Jo Medby, *Limited Conflicts Under the Nuclear Umbrella: Indian and Pakistani Lessons from the Kargil Crisis* (Santa Monica, RAND: 2002). http://www.rand.org/pubs/monograph_reports/MR1450/. For background on Kashmir, see Howard B. Schaffer and Teresita C. Schaffer in *Grasping the Nettle*, eds. Crocker, Hampson, and Aall (Washington, DC: United States Institute of Peace Press, 2005).

16. Robert O. Freedman, "Russia—A Partner for the US in the Post-Saddam era?" *Strategic Insights* 3, no. 4 (April 5, 2004).

17. At the CIS summit in September 2004, Kyrgyz president Askar Akaev stated, "I am a decisive supporter of a strategy of preemptive strikes." Uzbek president Karimov suggested the creation of a CIS-wide list of terrorist organizations and individuals.

18. *Washington Post*, July 30, 2005.

19. Weinstein, "Uzbekistan and the Great Powers: Courting Instability"; Erich Marquardt and Yevgeny Bendersky, "Uzbekistan's New Foreign Policy Strategy."

20. Peter Zeihan, "Post-Turkmenbashi: Gaming the Five 'Stans," *Geopolitical Intelligence Report* (December 26, 2006).

21. On the social and domestic side, notable are the importance of Black American lobbying groups such as TransAfrica, among others, which helped lead the domestic U.S. opposition to apartheid in South Africa and that seeks to link Africa with Black Americans. Congressman Rangel (see Chapter 3) sought to include in the Internal Revenue Code denial of tax credits for taxes paid to South Africa as an antiapartheid measure. http://www.house.gov/rangel/bio.shtml.

22. United Nations Office of the Special Adviser on Africa (OSAA), "Human Security in Africa," December 2005. http://www.sarpn.org.za/documents/d0001972/Human-security_OSAA_Dec2005.pdf.

23. http://www.defensenews.com/story.php?F=2071764&C=mideast.

24. *Boston Globe*, December 21, 2006. http://www.boston.com/news/world/articles/2006/12/21/pentagon_plans_new_command_to_cover_africa/.

25. http://www.globalsecurity.org/military/agency/dod/acri.htm.

26. PINR www.pinr.com/report.php?ac=view_printable&report_id=617&language_id=1.

27. Douglas A. Yates, "Chinese Oil Interests in Africa," in *China in Africa*, p. 224, ed. Garth le Pere (Midrand, South Africa: Institute for Global Dialogue, 2007).

28. John Prendergast, "So How Come We Haven't Stopped It?" *Washington Post*, November 19, 2006. "The deepening intelligence-sharing relationship between Washington and Khartoum blunted any U.S. response to the state-sponsored violence that exploded in Darfur in 2003 and 2004. . . . And since 2001, the administration had been pursuing a peace deal between southern Sudanese rebels and the regime in Khartoum—a deal aimed at placating U.S. Christian groups that had long demanded action on behalf of Christian minorities in southern Sudan. The administration didn't want to undermine that process by hammering Khartoum over Darfur." For background on Sudan, see J. Stephen Morrison and Alex de Waal in *Grasping the Nettle*, eds. Crocker, Hampson, and Aall (Washington, DC: United States Institute of Peace Press, 2005).

29. South Africa ranks third of states with a high degree of criminal violence after Brazil (first), then Russia (second); Canada ranks fourth; France, fifth; the United States sixth. The Human Security Report 2005.

30. http://www.crs.org/get_involved/advocacy/policy_and_strategic_issues/oil_report_full.pdf.

31. Eboe Hutchful and Kwesi Aning, in *West Africa's Security Challenges*, ed. Adekeye Adebajo and Ismail Rashid, p. 211 (Boulder, CO: Rienner, 2004).

32. *Wall Street Journal Europe*, April 11, 2007.

33. Jean-Christophe Servant, "Africa: External Interest and Internal Insecurity: The New Gulf Oil States," http://mondediplo.com/2003/01/08oil.

34. National Intelligence Council (NIC) Project 2020. http://www.dni.gov/nic/NIC_2020_project.html.

35. John Page, "Are the Millennium Development Goals Bad for Growth?" World Economic Forum on Africa 2006 (January 6, 2006).

36. NIC Project 2020.

37. Page, "Are the Millennium Development Goals Bad for Growth?"

38. Michael Deibert, "Following Oil Boom, Biofuel Eyed In Africa" (IPS) July 13 2007

39. UN Press Conference, Jean Marie Guéhenno. http://www.un.org/Depts/dpko/dpko/articles/pr_JMG.pdf.

40. NIC Project 2020. See also the Report on the Panel of UN Peacekeeping. http://www.un.org/peace/reports/peace_operations/.

41. "National Strategy for Combating Terrorism," September 2006. http://www.whitehouse.gov/nsc/nsct/2006/nsct2006.pdf.

42. Adekeye Adebajo, in Adekeye Adebajo and Ismail Rashid, *West Africa's Security Challenges*, chapter 13 (Boulder, CO: Rienner, 2004).

43. Manuel Correia de Barros, "Can the Gulf of Guinea Develop a Common Regional Oil Policy?" in *Oil Policy in the Gulf of Guinea*, eds. Rudolf Traub-Merz and Douglas Yates, Publisher; Friedrich-Ebert-Stiftung. http://library.fes.de/pdf-files/iez/ 02115/barros.pdf.

44. Ibid.

Chapter 7

1. Office of the Director of National Intelligence, "Statement by the Office of the Director of National Intelligence on the North Korea Nuclear Test," October 16, 2006, February 27, 2007. http://odni.gov/announcements/announcements.htm.

2. http://www.state.gov/r/pa/prs/ps/2007/february/80479.htm.

3. PINR, "Intelligence Brief: North Korea Deal Welcomed by China," February 21, 2007, http://www.pinr.com.

4. Audra Ang, "North Korean Nuclear Talks Break Down," *Associated Press*, March 23, 2007. The Russians blamed the Americans for not assuring the Chinese banks that it would not be illegal to deal with the bank transfer. The Americans blamed technical problems.

5. David E. Sanger and William J. Broad, "U.S. Concedes Uncertainty on North Korean Uranium Effort," March 1, 2007.

6. David E. Sanger and Norimitsu Onishi, "U.S. to Hold Direct Talks in North Korea on Arms," *New York Times*, June 21, 2007.

7. Ralph C. Hassig and Kongdan Oh, "North Korea: A Rogue State Outside the NPT Fold," *Foreign Policy Agenda*, March 2005. http://usinfo.state.gov/journals/itps/0305/ijpe/kongdan.htm.

8. http://www.state.gov/r/pa/ei/bgn/2792.htm.

9. Nicholas Eberstadt, "North Korea Triumphs Again in Diplomacy," American Enterprise Institute for Public Policy Research, October 2005. http://www.aei.org/publications/pubID.23277/pub_detail.asp.

10. David E. Sanger, "In North Korea and Pakistan: Deep Roots of Nuclear Barter," *New York Times*, November 24, 2002. http://www.fas.org/irp/threat/missile/rumsfeld/pt2_wright.htm.

11. Yoel Sano, "Talks Aside, North Korea Won't Give Up Nukes," *Asian Times On Line*, March 2, 2004. http://www.atimes.com/atimes/Korea/FC02Dg04.html.

12. Scott Snyder, "South Korea's Squeeze Play," *The Washington Quarterly* 28, no. 4 (Autumn 2005).

13. Bruce Klingner, "China Shock for South Korea," *Asian Times On line*, September 11, 2004, http://www.atimes.com/atimes/korea/FI11Dg03.html (accessed on March 30, 2006).

14. John S. Park, "Inside Multilateralism: The Six-Party Talks," *Washington Quarterly* 28, no. 4 (Autumn 2005).

15. Yoshinori Takeda, "Putin's Foreign Policy toward North Korea," *International Relations of the Asia-Pacific* (March 3, 2006): 1411. http://irap.oxfordjournals.org/cgi/content/abstract/lci141v1.

16. Sieff Martin, "Putin's China Visit Shifts Power," March 23, 2006. http://www.america-russia.net/eng/geopolitics/113619502.

17. Alexander Vorontsov, "FOCUS: Economic Engagement with N. Korea Becoming Reality: Expert," *Japan Economic Newswire*, March 14, 2006. http://asia.news.yahoo.com/060314/kyodo/d8gb1p7o0.html.

18. Darryl Howlen, "A Concert of the Willing: A New Means for Denuclearising the Korean Peninsula," in *Nuclear Non-Proliferation: The Transatlantic Debate*, ed. Ettore Greco, Giovanni Gasparni, and Riccardo Alcaro IAI Quaderni (February 2006).

19. Bruce B. Auster and Kevin Whitelaw, "Upping the Ante for Kim Jong Il: Pentagon Plan 5030, a New Blueprint for Facing Down North Korea," *US News and World Report* (July 21, 2003). http://www.usnews.com/usnews/news/articles/030721/21korea.htm.

20. R. James Woolsey and Thomas McInerney in the Wall Street Journal (August 4, 2003). http://www.benadorassociates.com/article/498.

21. John S. Park, "Inside Multilateralism: The Six-Party Talks," *The Washington Quarterly* 28, no. 4 (Autumn 2005).

22. Erich Marquardt, "U.S. Struggles to Place Pressure on North Korea," PINR, March, 23 2005). http://www.pinr.com/report.php?ac=view_report&report_id=281&language_id=1.

23. "U.S. Reveals New Tactics to Pressure N Korea," ISN Security Watch (February 14, 2005). http://www.isn.ethz.ch/news/sw/details.cfm?ID=10763.

24. "Senator Murkowski Addresses World Trade Center Alaska," *US Fed News* (February 23, 2006).

25. Todd Walters, "The Fourth Round of Six-Party Talks." PINR, September 5, 2005.http://www.pinr.com/report.php?ac=view_report&report_id=360&language_id=1.

26. Howlen, "A Concert of the Willing."

27. Moon Ihlwan, "Bridging the Korean Economic Divide," *Business Week* (March 7, 2006). http://www.businessweek.com/globalbiz/\content/mar2006/gb20060307_843108.htm.

28. North Korea's trade with Japan totaled $190 million in 2005, the lowest since 1977. During the same period, China's trade with North Korea totaled $1.58 billion, up 14.8 percent. China remains North Korea's top trade partner, with two-way trade between the two rising by an average 30 percent per year since 2000. Alexander Vorontsov, cited in *Japan Economic Newswire*, "FOCUS: Economic Engagement with N. Korea Becoming Reality: Expert," (March 14, 2006). http://asia.news.yahoo.com/060314/kyodo/d8gb1p7o0.html.

29. Troy Stangarone, PacNet #6 (February 22, 2007).

30. "South Korea has requested duty-free treatment for products produced in the Kaesong Industrial Complex in prior FTA negotiations with other trade partners. The issues are twofold. The first is substantive: North Korea does not meet internationally recognized core labor standards; rights to associate, organize, and bargain collectively are absent entirely. . . . The real problem is that while conditions in Kaesong may be exploitative, they probably are considerably better than those existing elsewhere in North Korea, and there may be no shortage of North Koreans willing to work on these terms. The second issue is procedural: While the FTA will presumably include a labor standards chapter, South Korea has no way to enforce such commitments in Kaesong, where North Korea is sovereign. One possible solution would be to involve

a third party such as the International Labor Organization (ILO) to monitor conditions in the zone . . . but even this solution would require the cooperation of the North Korean government, which is not a member of the ILO, [and which] has a track record of non-cooperation in other spheres of international engagement, and to date has restricted access to the zone by third-party observers." Marcus Noland, "How North Korea Funds Its Regime," *Congressional Quarterly*, Senate Homeland Security and Governmental Affairs Congressional Testimony (April 25, 2006).

31. Choe Sang-Hun, "Roh Warns U.S. over N. Korea: Blunt Speech Shows Rift between allies," *International Herald Tribune*, January 26, 2006.

32. U.S. ambassador to the Republic of Korea, Alexander Vershbow, argued that the United States "did not place 'sanctions' on North Korea, as is commonly misrepresented in the press; we took law enforcement action against a bank in Macau to protect our financial system from abuse. . . . Like South Korea, the United States is ready to return to the talks. It's in everyone's best interest, including North Korea's, to see the commitments contained in the September 19 Joint Statement implemented. Those commitments include not only denuclearization, but negotiation of a permanent peace regime, normalization of diplomatic relations, and economic integration." "U.S. Ambassador Vershbow Delivers Remarks to the Korea Freedom League," as released by the State Department, *Congressional Quarterly* (April 18, 2006). North Korea countered by saying, in general, that U.S. sanctions apply to North Korean trade, science and technology, investment, real estate, insurance, transportation, communication and immigration, and to prevent their exchanges overseas.

33. Cameron Stewart, "Dirty Secrets of the Soprano State," *The Australian*, March 11, 2006. The Sopranos is an American TV show about a mafia family.

34. Selig Harrison, "North Korea: A Nuclear Threat," *Newsweek*. http://www.msnbc.msn .com/id/15175633/site/newsweek/page/2/. See also comments of Selig S. Harrison in Joseph Kahn, "North Korea to Challenge U.S. on Nuclear Fuel," *New York Times*, September 25, 2006; Donald Gregg and Don Oberdorfer, "Wrong Path on North Korea," *Washington Post*, September 6, 2006.

35. Jong-Heon Lee, "Analysis: N. Korea's Reliance on China," UPI. http://www.upi .com/InternationalIntelligence/view.php?StoryID=20060213-062742-1321r.

36. Donald Kirk, "Back from China, Kim Jong Il Eyes Ally's Success—and Largess," *Christian Science Monitor*, January 19, 2006. http://www.csmonitor.com/2006/ 0119/p04s01-woap.html?s=widep.

37. Rep. James A. Leach (R-IA), "Hearing of the Asia and the Pacific Subcommittee of the House International Relations Committee. Subject: East Asia in Transition: Opportunities and Challenges for the United States."

38. "US Expert Pessimistic about Six-Nation Nuclear Talks' Future," *Yonhap News Agency* (April 7, 2006). Interview with Peter Beck, the Northeast Asia project director of the International Crisis Group, April 6, 2007.

39. Walters, "The Fourth Round of Six-Party Talks."

40. "Sandwiched between the intransigence of the two chief negotiators, China would also like to see a more flexible and practical U.S. policy toward North Korea instead of a take-it-or-leave-it proposal. If not, Beijing will not be able to exercise the leadership that Washington hopes will roll back North Korea's nuclear weapons program." Anne Wu, "What China Whispers to North Korea," *The Washington Quarterly* 28, no. 2 (Spring 2005).

41. "Libya Profile," Nuclear Threat Initiative (NTI). http://www.nti.org/e_research/ profiles/Libya/3939.html#fn6.

42. Office of the Director of National Intelligence, "Statement by the Office of the Director of National Intelligence on the North Korea Nuclear Test," October 16, 2006, February 27, 2007. http://odni.gov/announcements/announcements.htm.

43. For details on South Korean military reforms, see B. B. Bell, commander, United Nations Command, "Fiscal 2007 Budget: Department of Defense, Committee on Senate Armed Services," *Congressional Quarterly* (March 7, 2006).

44. Michael E. O'Hanlon, "A 'Master Plan' to Deal with North Korea," *Brookings Policy Brief*, No. 114 (January 2003). http://www.brookings.edu/comm/policybriefs/pb114.htm.

45. http://www.fpif.org/fpiftxt/3997.

46. Rather than put human rights issues before a UN human rights commission or council governed by states, the UN should sponsor an independent advisory counsel made of world-renowned human rights activists who could critique the human rights policies of all states more fairly and objectively. See Chapter 1.

47. Bruce Klingner "China Shock for South Korea," *Asian Times On line*, September 11, 2004. http://www.atimes.com/atimes/korea/FI11Dg03.html.

48. Ibid.

49. See Dingli Shen, "Iran's Nuclear Ambitions Test China's Wisdom," *The Washington Quarterly* 29, no. 2 (Spring 2006). While sharing U.S. concerns about the dangers of the Iranian nuclear program, neither China (nor Japan) can afford higher oil prices as a result of tensions with Iran. Here, it appears that the United States might need to find a way to engage more directly with both Iran and North Korea, with the concerted backing of China, Russia, Japan, and the Europeans.

50. Ted Galen Carpenter, "Options for Dealing with North Korea," *Foreign Policy Briefing* No. 73, January 6, 2006. http://www.cato.org/pubs/fpbriefs/fpb73.pdf.

51. On rising tensions in Asia, see ibid, chapter 6. See also Colin Robinson and Rear Adm. (Ret.) Stephen H. Baker, "Stand-off with North Korea: War Scenarios and Consequences," *Center for Defense Information*, June 26, 2003. For a theoretical discussion of major power war in Asia, see Aaron L. Friedberg, "The Future of U.S.-China Relations; Is Conflict Inevitable?" *International Security* (Fall 2005).

52. Professor Shi Yinhing of Beijing's Renmin University put it this way: "A North Korea alienated from China would allow the U.S. military to ignore the Korean peninsula in any conflict with China over Taiwan. . . . If there is a confrontation with Taiwan and the (U.S. Navy's) 7th Fleet, what value then can North Korea have? Minimal value if it collapses . . . So it is not denuclearization that is China's number one goal. Number one is peace on the Korean peninsula." See Jim Landers, "China in a Delicate Position Regarding Future of Long-Time Ally North Korea," *Dallas Morning News*, January 6, 2006. http://www.miami.com/mld/miamiherald/13555490.htm.

53. "Korea's and Japan's Dokdo/Takeshima Dispute Escalates toward Confrontation," PINR. http://www.pirn.org.

54. In January 2003, then minister of state for defense Shigeru Ishiba, in his testimony before the Japanese House of Representatives Budget Committee, made an unprecedented explicit reference to Tokyo's use of preemptive force: "We will consider the start [of a military attack] if [Pyongyang] expresses an intention to demolish Tokyo and starts fuelling its missiles to realize that." Park, "Inside Multilateralism".

55. "Intelligence Brief: North Korea's Missile Tests," PINR, July 5, 2006. http://www.pinr.com.

Chapter 8

1. The film's coauthor, Su Xiaokang, was forced into exile after the Tiananmen Square crackdown.
2. Howard W. French, "Letter from China: Is the U.S. Plunging into 'Historical Error'?" *International Herald Tribune*, June 1, 2006.
3. Willy Lam, "China Brief," *Jamestown Foundation* 7, no. 1 (January 10, 2007).
4. Willy Lam, "China Brief," *Jamestown Foundation* 7, no. 5 (March 8, 2007).
5. Human Rights Watch, "China: Curbs on Lawyers Could Intensify Social Unrest" (December 12, 2006). http://hrw.org/english/docs/2006/12/12/china14791_txt.htm. In effect, the more China takes the "capitalist road," the more it is confronted with internal dissent, particularly directed at local and provincial authorities. See Andrew Wedeman in Sujian Guo, ed., *China's "Peaceful Rise" in the 21st Century* (Burlington, VT: Ashgate, 2006).
6. Human Rights Watch, op.cit. See also Andrew Wedeman, ibid.
7. Anita Chan, "Made in China: Wal-Mart Union," *Yale Global*, October 12, 2006. On multinational corporate investments in China and related loss of 2.8 to 3 million manufacturing jobs, see Walden Bello, *Dilemmas of Domination* (London: Zed Books, 2005), 93–97.
8. Matt Benjamin and Julianna Goldman, "Paulson Is Attacked for Softer Stance on Yuan Policy," Update1, Bloomberg (December 20, 2006).
9. Ibid. Federal Reserve chairman Ben Bernanke branded China's undervalued currency an "effective subsidy" for its exporters that was distorting patterns of production and trade. Although Bernanke dropped the phrase in a speech in Beijing, using instead the less inflammatory term "distortion," the Fed was standing by the language of the original text.
10. As of January 2007, Japan held $627 billion; China held $400 billion, oil exporters $112 billion, the United Kingdom $103 billion, South Korea $62 billion, Taiwan, $59 billion, and Hong Kong $54 billion. http://www.ustreas.gov/tic/mfh.txt.
11. On ethanol, see Antoaneta Bezlova, "China: Food First, Not Fuel" (IPS) Jun 15, 2007. Toshiba of Japan spent $5.4 billion in 2006 to acquire the U.S. Westinghouse Electric in part in expectation of the huge China nuclear market. Ariana Eunjung Cha, "China Embraces Nuclear Future," *Washington Post*, May 29, 2007. http://www.washingtonpost.com/wp-dyn/content/article/2007/05/28/AR2007052801051_pf.html. On problems in the nuclear industry in southeast Asia, see: http://www.isn.ethz.ch/news/sw/details.cfm?ID=17896.
12. Richard Spencer, "Tension Rises as China Scours the Globe for Energy," November 19, 2004. http://www.independent.org/newsroom/article.asp?id=1892.
13. Lam, "China Brief" 7, no. 1. It is rumored that China was able to reverse engineer cruise missile technology sold to Beijing by bin Laden from an unexploded missile fired by Bill Clinton in August 1998 at al-Qaida camps in Afghanistan, thus providing some additional profit for al-Qaida.
14. http://www.rferl.org/featuresarticle/2005/08/40554110-295C-4760-9635-BCC86A121F45.html.
15. PINR, "The Emerging Cold War on Asia's High Seas." http://www.pinr.com/report.php?ac=view_report&report_id=439&language_id=1.
16. Li Qingsi in Sujian Guo, ed., *China's "Peaceful Rise" in the 21st Century*, p. 149.
17. Hajime Izumi and Katsuhisa Furukawa, "Not Going Nuclear: Japan's Response to North Korea's Nuclear Test," *Arms Control Today* (June 2007).
18. Mohan Malik, "China's Strategy of Containing India," PINR. http://www.pinr.com/report.php?ac=view_report&report_id=434; PINR, "The Modernization of the

Chinese Navy/" http://www.pinr.com/report.php?ac=view_report&report_id=364; PINR, "India's Project Seabird and the Indian Ocean's Balance of Power." http://www.pinr.com/report.php?ac=view_report&report_id=330.

19. http://www.spiegel.de/international/spiegel/0,1518,352465,00.html.

20. Chietigj Bajpaee, "Strategic Interests Pull Japan and India Together," February 16, 2007, http://www.pinr.com.

21. Ibid.

22. Stephen Blank, "China's Energy Crossroads"Perspective (Volume 16, Number 3 May 2006), http://www.bu.edu/iscip/vol16/blank2.html.

23. Spencer, "Tension Rises as China Scours the Globe for Energy." *Daily Telegraph* (November 19, 2004).

24. http://www.jamestown.org/print_friendly.php?volume_id=415&issue_id = 3821&article_id=2371339.

25. Spencer, "Tension Rises as China Scours the Globe for Energy."

26. Joseph Kahn, "China Shows Assertiveness in Weapons Test," *New York Times*, January 20, 2006. See also Xuetang Guo, in Sujian Guo, ed., *China's "Peaceful Rise" in the 21st Century*, p. 161.

27. Xuetang Guo, in ibid, p. 163.

28. Kahn, "China Shows Assertiveness in Weapons Test."

29. http://www.news.navy.mil/search/display.asp?story_id=27642; Xuetang Guo, in Sujian Guo, ed., *China's "Peaceful Rise" in the 21st Century*, p. 174. See also press conference by Robert Gates in support of a strong American military presence in Asia. http://www.defenselink.mil/transcripts/transcript.aspx?transcriptid=3974

30. http://www.taipeitimes.com/News/taiwan/archives/2007 /01/29/200334675.

31. Kurt M. Campbell; Jeremiah Gertler, *The Paths Ahead: Missile Defense in Asia CSIS* (March 2006) http://www.csis.org/media/csis/pubs/0603_pathsahead.pdf.

32. Chen also pledged to continue his drive for a new independent constitution and to join international bodies like the UN and World Health Organization (WHO)—goals that are strongly opposed by Beijing. Yet here, there should be some diplomatic formula (as a form of confederation) to enhance Taiwanese participation in international regimes. Taiwan's nonmembership in WHO, for example, hurt international efforts to stop the spread of Asian bird flu. http://www.taipeitimes.com/News/taiwan/archives/2007/01/29/200334675.

33. Former secretary of defense William S. Cohen, now chairman of the U.S.-Taiwan Council, warned an audience in Taiwan in November 2003 that "You cannot expect the American people to burden ourselves the way we are to carry out responsibilities for other countries if there is no corresponding effort being made for self-defense."

34. David DeVoss, "Deal or No Deal: The Complicated Business of Defending Taiwan," *Weekly Standard*, November 28, 2006.

35. http://www.apcss.org/Publications/APSSS/Roy-TawainArms.pdf. This is a perfect description of differing perceptions of threat that characterizes the insecurity-security dialectic. The underlying American assumption is that balance of power causes peace by deterring China, while an imbalance favoring China would encourage Beijing to opt for a military solution. The prevailing view in China is the opposite: a balance increases the chances of war because it emboldens Taipei to move toward independence, which would eventually leave China no recourse but military action.

36. Douglas E. Streusand, "Geopolitics versus Globalization," in Sam J. Tangredi, ed., *Globalization and Maritime Power*, National Defense University, 2002. http://www.ndu.edu/inss/Books/Books_2002/Globalization_and_Maritime_Power_Dec _02/01_toc.htm.

Chapter 9

1. *Gulf Daily News* (Bahrain), December 19, 2006. http://www.gulfdailynews
.com/Story.asp?Article=164956&Sn=BUSI& IssueID =29274.

2. "Global systemic crisis in 2007—Financial sector: 'Another bubble' Close to
Bursting." http://www.leap2020.eu/Global-systemic-crisis-in-2007-Financial-sector
-Another-bubble-close-to-bursting_a317.html.

3. Agnes Lovasz and Daniel Kruger, "Energy in 2007: A Chaotic Way Out of the
'Dollar Era' Venezuela, Oil Producers Buy Euro as Dollar, Oil Fall," (Update1)
(Bloomberg). "Dec. 18, 2006. Banco Central de Venezuela slashed the percentage of
its $35.9 billion worth of reserves invested in dollars and gold to 80 percent from 95
percent in 2005. The country, the world's fifth-largest oil supplier, has boosted its
euro holdings to 15 percent, from less than 5 percent in the same period."
http://www.bloomberg.com/apps/news?pid=20601103&sid=aCVBzwWdstPk
& refer=news.

4. On April 12, 2002, in an initial State Department statement, the United States
blamed the Chávez government itself for precipitating the coup, stating that "unde-
mocratic actions committed or encouraged by the Chávez administration provoked"
the crisis. But the next day, as the illegal actions of the de facto government continued, the United States voted in favor of the OAS resolution condemning the coup
attempt. In September, amid further coup rumors, the U.S. embassy in Venezuela
issued a declaration unequivocally stating its opposition to any illegal disruption of
constitutional rule in Venezuela. Human Rights Watch. http://hrw.org/wr2k3/
americas10.html.

5. According to a survey of 1,300 people by pollster Datanalisis. The poll, taken
October 18–25, 2005, has a margin of error of 2.71 percent. Bloomberg.com.
http://www.bloomberg.com/apps/news?pid=10000086&sid=abx10oH0HBc0& refer
=latin_america.

6. Opposition leaders are concerned about voter confidentiality because they say the
government has discriminated against Venezuelans who signed a petition in 2004
seeking a recall vote to remove Chavez from office. The list became public information after Luis Tascon, a congressman from Chavez's own Fifth Republic Movement
Party, acquired a copy and disseminated it. http://www.bloomberg.com/apps/news
?pid=10000086&sid=abx10oH0HBc0&refer=latin_america.

7. "[Chávez] has destroyed the Venezuelan economy, and he's going to make that a
launching pad for communist infiltration and Muslim extremism all over the continent. You know, I don't know about this doctrine of assassination, but if he thinks
we're trying to assassinate him, I think that we really ought to go ahead and do it. It's
a whole lot cheaper than starting a war. . . . We have the Monroe Doctrine, we have
other doctrines that we have announced. And without question, this is a dangerous
enemy to our south, controlling a huge pool of oil, that could hurt us very badly. We
have the ability to take him out, and I think the time has come that we exercise that
ability. We don't need another $200 billion war to get rid of one, you know, strong-
arm dictator. It's a whole lot easier to have some of the covert operatives do the job
and then get it over with." Pat Robertson, The 700 Club, August 22, 2005.
http://mediamatters.org/items/200508220006.

8. ISN Security Watch, Wednesday, November 23, 2005: 18:11 CET.

9. With more than a two-thirds majority in parliament, Chávez could possibly remove
the current constitutional limit of two presidential terms in office and thus consolidate his Bolivarian Revolution.

10. Simon Romero, "Chávez Moves to Nationalize Two Industries," *New York Times*, January 9, 2007.

11. Ibid.

12. Dr. Michael A. Weinstein, "Venezuela's Hugo Chavez Makes His Bid for a Bolivarian Revolution.' http://www.pinr.com/report.php?ac=view_report&report_id=285. In October 2004, Chavez raised the royalty tax on companies working in the Orinoco region from 1 percent to 16.6 percent. Under a law passed in 2001, new projects will have a royalty rate of 30 percent, which does not seem to have discouraged investors in the short term. (For example, on March 31, 2004 Chevron-Texaco announced plans to pursue joint development in the Orinoco belt with Venezuelan state company PDVSA.) But this could be changing in 2007.

13. *BBC News Chinese*, May 12, 2006.

14. Quoted in Gal Luft, "In Search of Crude China goes to the Americas," Institute for the Analysis of Global Security: Energy Security, January 18, 2005. http://www.iags.org/n0118041.htm.

15. Ibid.

16. http://www.latin-focus.com/latinfocus/countries/ venezuela/vengdpsector.htm.

17. "Despite a five-fold expansion in oil prices, Venezuela is currently running a fiscal deficit projected at 2.3 percent for 2006. A decline in oil prices, or perhaps even something less dramatic, will make this house of cards come tumbling down. When it does, it will be the Venezuelan poor who will pay the heaviest price." Francisco Rodríguez, "Why Chávez Wins," *Foreign Policy*. http://www.foreignpolicy.com/story/cms.php?story_id=3685.

18. For details, see Weinstein, "Venezuela's Hugo Chavez Makes His Bid for a Bolivarian Revolution."

19. Jim Rutenberg and Larry Rohter, "Bush and Chávez Spar at Distance over Latin Visit," *New York Times*, March 10, 2007.

20. http://www.ethanolrfa.org/media/press/rfa/2006/view.php?id=683.

21. Edmund L. Aandrews and Larry Rohter, "U.S. and Brazil Seek to Promote Ethanol in West," *New York Times*, March 2, 2007.

22. Lester R. Brown, "Plan B 2.0," Earth Policy Institute, 2006. http://www.earth-policy.org/Books/PB2/Contents.htm.

23. Ironically, Oliver North's statements in Nicaragua in late October 2006 just before the election might have taken votes away from the candidate preferred by the Bush administration and thus helped Ortega at the polls. National Security Archive. http://www.gwu.edu/~nsarchiv/NSAEBB/NSAEBB113/.

24. Der Spiegel, August 28, 2006. http://www.spiegel.de/international/spiegel/0,1518,434272,00.html.

25. Adam Wolfe, "Economic Brief: The Doha Round." http://www.pinr.com/report.php?ac=view_report&report_id=409&language_id=1. On Latin American opposition to the the FTAA and WTO Agreement on Agriculture largely due to northern subsidies, see Walden Bello, *Dilemmas of Domination*, chapters 5–7.

26. As Pascal Lamy put it: "Today the Doha Round is at a crossroad: the path towards success or the slow move towards a deep freeze." If the Doha Round is to succeed, progress must soon be made in agriculture subsidies and tariffs on agriculture and industrial tariffs, as elections in the United States will be held in 2008, to be followed by changes in the European Parliament and in the European Commission in 2009. http://www.wto.org/english/news_e/sppl_e/sppl64_e.htm.

27. Civic groups of at least four of the nine eastern regions (Beni, Pando, Santa Cruz, and Tarija) have demonstrated in town meetings (cabildos) in support of greater regional autonomy—an option opposed by the central government, which, it is

feared, might attempt to break the country into 40 smaller regions. International Crisis Group, "Bolivia's Reforms: The Danger of New Conflicts," *Latin America Briefing* 13 (January 8, 2007).

28. *BBC World News*, "Garcia proposes thaw with Chavez" (June 6, 2006) Peruvian president Alan Garcia has opposed Chávez's "militaristic and backwards expansion project he intends to impose over South America" but seeks good relations and does not intend to lead "a continental anti-Chavez movement."

29. http://www.fas.org/blog/ssp/2006/12/venezuelas_military_buildup _wh.php.

30. Juan Forero, "Colombia's Coca Survives U.S. Plan to Uproot It," *New York Times*, August 19, 2006. http://www.iht.com/articles/2006/08/19/america/web.0819coca .php; http://www.cmu.edu/clips/v212.html - link. In 2004 John Walters, the head of the Office of National Drug Control Policy, stated that the $3.3 billion Plan Colombia begun in 2000 had failed to make a significant dent in the amount of cocaine flowing out of that country. Ted Galen Carpenter, "Yet Another Drug War Failure," August 13, 2004. http://www.cato.org/pub_display.php?pub_id=2783. In 2000, U.S. consumers spent an estimated $36.1 billion on cocaine. For background, see Cynthia J. Arnson and Teresa Whitfield in *Grasping the Nettle*, eds. Crocker, Hampson, and Aall (Washington, DC: United States Institute of Peace Press, 2005).

31. Ricardo Palmera, leader of FARC, was captured in Ecuador in 2004. The Brazilian drug lord Fernandinho Beira Mar had been arrested inside Colombia in 2001 after trying to sell drugs to the FARC in exchange for weapons, which might be attempting to establish Brazilian wing.

32. National Security Archive, "War in Colombia Background." http://www.gwu .edu/~nsarchiv/NSAEBB/NSAEBB69/background.html.

33. At the time of September 11, 2001, the majority of "terrorist" attacks did not occur in the Middle East, but in Colombia, according to U.S. State Department figures, which tended to confound acts of "terrorism" with acts of "sabotage" largely directed against the Cano Limón oil pipeline.

34. Ibid.

35. Assuming it is not an "urban legend," genetically modified varieties of marijuana and other drugs have purportedly become available that are less susceptible to pesticides and that need less space to grow, making eradication even more difficult.

36. "Interview with Milton Friedman on the Drug War." http://www.druglibrary .org/schaffer/Misc/friedm1.htm. As Friedman put it, "[Drug use] does harm a great many other people, but primarily because it's prohibited. There are an enormous number of innocent victims now. You've got the people whose purses are stolen, who are bashed over the head by people trying to get enough money for their next fix. You've got the people killed in the random drug wars. You've got the corruption of the legal establishment. You've got the innocent victims who are taxpayers who have to pay for more and more prisons, and more and more prisoners, and more and more police. You've got the rest of us who don't get decent law enforcement because all the law enforcement officials are busy trying to do the impossible. . . . And, last, but not least, you've got the people of Colombia and Peru and so on. What business do we have destroying and leading to the killing of thousands of people in Colombia because we cannot enforce our own laws? If we could enforce our laws against drugs, there would be no market for these drugs. You wouldn't have Colombia in the state it's in." If the United States can not stop drug use altogether, it will need to modify that usage and demand in such a way as to limit damage both domestically and globally.

37. Bureau of Justice Statistics, http://www.ojp.usdoj.gov/bjs/crimoff.htm#jail.

38. Georges Estievenart, "Opium in and from Afghanistan," *World Political Forum*, (October 27, 2006). See "U.S. Fails to Reduce Opium Crop," *International Herald Tribune* (August 26, 2007).

39. Jon Gettman, "Marijuana Production in the United States" (2006). http://www .drugscience.org/Archive/bcr2/exec.html. New studies indicate that marijuana risks inducing schizophrenia in those susceptible. See also the problems facing the commercial hemp industry as a result of its unfortunate association with marijuana: http://www.hort.purdue.edu/newcrop/ncnu 02/v5-284.html.

40. Venezuela had already attempted to nationalize the oil sector under Carlos Andrés Pérez in the 1970s. The economy, however, collapsed after oil prices crashed in the 1980s, leading subsequent administrations to privatize state companies and open the oil industry to foreign investment.

41. Samuel Huntington. "The Hispanic Challenge," *Foreign Policy* (March/April 2004). See also critique of Huntington's position: Philippa Strum and Andrew Selee, "The Hispanic Challenge? What We Know About Latino Immigration" Woodrow Wilson International Center for Scholars (March 29, 2004) http://www.wilsoncenter.org/ topics/pubs/HispChall.pdf.

42. In an editorial headlined "Uncle Scrooge's Paltry Package," the conservative Brazilian daily newspaper O Estado de São Paulo noted that Bush's offering amounted to "the equivalent of five days' cost of the war in Iraq, and a drop of water compared with the ocean of petrodollars in which Chávezism is navigating at full speed, from Argentina to Nicaragua." See Rutenberg and Rohter "Visit by Bush Fires Up Latins' Debate over Socialism," *New York Times*, March 9, 2007. While the United States has promised roughly $7.5 billion in grants and loans through the Inter-American Development Bank and the World Bank, plus $3 billion in direct aid since 2005, Chavez has promised at least $8.8 billion in 2007 alone, plus undisclosed investments, far more than any single country in the region. Natalie Obiko Pearson and Ian James, "Chavez offers Billions in Latin America," *Other News* (August 28, 2007).

43. On growing income disparities in the United States, see Chuck Collins, "The Economic Context: Growing Disparities of Income and Wealth." http://www .mccormack.umb.edu/nejpp/articles/20_1/The EconomicContext.pdf; Center on Budget and Policy Priorities, "New IRS Data Show Income Inequality Is Again on the Rise," October 17, 2005. http://www.cbpp.org/10-17-05inc.htm.

44. On March 10, 1999, President Bill Clinton apologized for the past U.S. support of repressive regimes in Guatemala. "For the United States, it is important that I state clearly that support for military forces and intelligence units which engaged in violence and widespread repression was wrong, and the United States must not repeat that mistake." On the "dirty war" in Mexico, see http://www.gwu.edu/~nsarchiv/ NSAEBB/NSAEBB89/. On Chile, Edward C. Snyder "The Dirty Legal War: Human Rights and the Rule of Law in Chile 1973-1995," *Tulsa Journal of Comparative and International Law*, 1995. http://cyber.law.harvard.edu/evidence99/ pinochet/HistoryGeneralArticle.htm. For details, see Human Rights Watch, "Chile: Government Discloses Torture Was State Policy," November 29, 2004.

45. For an overview of immigration from Nicaragua, El Salvador, and Guatemala during the 1980s, see Ruth Ellen Wasem "Central American Asylum Seekers: Impact of 1996 Immigration Law," Congressional Research Center (Updated November 21, 1997). http://digital.library.unt.edu/govdocs/crs//data/1997/upl-meta-crs-463/97- 810epw_1997Nov21.pdf?PHPSESSID=e6fec1d875a24eed7972ff3cdb30541a.

46. Teresa Castellanos, "Context for Salvadoran Immigration," Immigrant.info.org. http://www.immigrantinfo.org/KIN/elsalvador.htm.

47. "El Salvador, Foreign Relations, Relations with the United States," p. 3. http//www
.country-date.com/cgi-bin/query/r-4295.html.

48. For details, see Wasem "Central American Asylum Seekers: Impact of 1996
Immigration Law."

49. http://www.uscis.gov/lpBin/lpext.dll/inserts/publaw/publaw-11120?f=templates
& fn= document-frame.htm#publaw-pl104208.

50. Ibid.

51. Pew Hispanic Center Fact Sheet, May 22, 2006.

52. Matthew Continetti, *The Weekly Standard*, June 5, 2006.

53. Steven Camarota of The Center for Immigration Studies, argues that amnesty will
let in 14.4 million "illegals," including 7.4 million illegals who would be made legal,
2.6 million legalized fraudulently, using false documentation, plus 4.5 million family members living abroad. Of the 14.4 million illegals and their family members
who will receive amnesty, 13.5 million would eventually become permanent residents. Camarota argues that his figures are based on the 1986 amnesty. See Steven
Camarota, "Amnesty under Hagel-Martinez." http://www.cis.org/articles/2006/
back606.html.

54. For background on Congressional positions (June 14, 2007) see "Key Issues in the
Immigration Reform Debate," http://www.washingtonpost.com/wp-srv/nation/
documents/immigration_ primer_060807.html?hpid=topnews#overview. Darryl
Fears, "Guest-Worker Program Part of Government's Immigration Plan," *Washington
Post* (March 30, 2007, A08).

55. In September 2006, Department of Homeland Security (DHS) awarded initial contracts—worth upwards of $2 billion—for the high-tech surveillance technology
along border region to weapons giant Boeing. Secure Border Strategic Plan of the
DHS estimated the total costs for equipment, logistics, and manpower at $7.6
billion though FY 2011, but still was not certain. See Frida Berrigan, "Militarizing
the Border" Foreign Policy in Focus (April 12, 2007) http://www.fpif.org/
fpiftxt/4146.

56. See comments of the governor of Arizona, Janet Napolitano, "Don't Forget the
Border," *New York Times*, June 1, 2007.

57. For details, see Gordon H. Hanson, "Why Does Immigration Divide America?
Public Finance and Political Opposition to Open Borders," The Center for
Comparative Immigration Studies Working Paper 129, December 2005, pp. 5–6.

58. Kristin F. Butcher Anne Morrison Piehl, "Why are Immigrants' Incarceration Rates
So Low? Evidence on Selective Immigration, Deterrence, and Deportation" Federal
Reserve Bank of Chicago November 2005 http://www.chicagofed.org/publications/
workingpapers/wp2005_19.pdf.

59. Siobhan Gorman, "New Border Security System Raises Cost-Benefit Concerns,"
National Journal (May 30, 2003). http://www.govexec.com/dailyfed/0503/
053003nj1.htm. As Gorman observes: "A recent Justice Department inspector general's report found that the INS was able to kick out just 13 percent of foreigners
who had not been detained after being issued final deportation orders. The INS successfully deported just 6 percent of those undetained foreigners who came from
countries declared to be state sponsors of terrorism."

60. El Diario/La Prensa, March 6, 2006, cited by Saurav Sarkar, "The False Debate over
'Broken Borders,'" FAIR (May/June 2006). http://www.fair.org/index.php?page
=2896.

61. Stuart Anderson, "The Impact of Agricultural Guest Worker Programs on Illegal
Immigration," The National Foundation for American Policy, November 2003.
http://www.nfap.com/researchactivities/studies/Nov_study1.pdf.

62. Ted Robbins, "San Diego Fence Provides Lessons in Border Control," National Public Radio, April 6, 2006. http://www.npr.org/templates/story/story.php?storyId=5323928.

63. Trac Immigration, Immigration Enforcement: The Rhetoric, The Reality http://trac.syr.edu/immigration/reports/178/. For all but one individual charged under the terrorist label, the section under which they were charged suggested that these individuals had all initially entered the United States legally—they were not individuals who had attempted to slip across our borders. They also were from diverse nationalities: three from Jordan, two from Pakistan, one each from Cambodia, Cameroon, Dominica, Dominican Republic, Germany, Haiti and Liberia. (Language referring to "illegal entrants" has undergone numerous changes over the years. In the 1955 INS Annual Report, the term "wetbacks" was used for those illegally crossing the Mexican border. For many years "deportable aliens" was the phrase of choice. Since 9/11 "terrorists" appears in official documents to refer to all "illegal entrants" whatever their purpose—those seeking work, engaging in cross-border smuggling or other forms of criminal behavior, in addition to terrorists per se.) http://trac.syr.edu/immigration/reports/141/.

64. See Jerry Seper, "Al-Qaida Seeks Tie to Local Gangs," *Washington Times*, September 28, 2004. http://www.washtimes.com/national/20040928-123346-3928r.htm.

65. See Mandalit del Barco, "International Reach of the Mara Salvatrucha," National Public Radio, *All Things Considered*, March 17, 2005. http://www.npr.org/templates/story/story.php?storyId=4539688.

66. For congressional testimony by the FBI on Los Zetas drug cartel (November 17, 2005) see: http://www.fbi.gov/congress/congress05/swecker111705.htm.

67. David Leonhardt, "Immigrants and Prison," *New York Times* (May 30, 2007) http://www.nytimes.com/2007/05/30/business/30leonside.html. See also Kristin F. Butcher Anne Morrison Piehl, op.cit.

68. The White House, "Comprehensive Immigration Reform." http://www.whitehouse.gov/infocus/immigration/.

69. PEW Hispanic Center, "America's Immigration Quandry," March 30, 2006, pp. 1–2.

70. Public Agenda, "Immigration: Bills and Proposals," *NBC/Wall Street Journal*, September 2006.

71. For details, see Hanson, "Why Does Immigration Divide America."

72. PEW Hispanic Center, "America's Immigration Quandry."

73. Ibid.

74. For details, see Hanson, "Why Does Immigration Divide America." Inter-American Development Bank "Remittances" (March 13, 2006) http://www.iadb.org/news/articledetail.cfm?artid=2881&arttype=BP&language=En.

75. Inter-American Development Bank "Remittances" (March 13, 2006) http://www.iadb.org/news/articledetail.cfm?artid=2881&arttype=BP&language=En.

76. World Bank, Global Development Finance Report, 2006. http://siteresources.worldbank.org/INTGDF2006/Resources/GDF06_complete.pdf.

77. Ibid.

78. As Pascal Lamy of the WTO argued, "Aid for Trade aims at improving the capacity of developing countries to reap the benefits of more open trade. For some developing members this will mean setting up testing facilities and reliable institutions to help to ensure that exported products meet the technical, sanitary and phytosanitary regulations and standards of export markets. For some others it would mean larger-scale projects such as improving transport infrastructure and trade logistics," http://www.wto.org/english/news_e/sppl_e/sppl64_e.htm.

Chapter 10

1. M. K. Bhadrakumar, "Turkey not done with the Kurds," *Asia Times Online* (June 12, 2007) http://www.atimes.com/atimes/Middle_East/IF12Ak05.html.
2. Richard L. Russell, "Insurgency in Waiting," *Foreign Policy* (November 2005). http://www.foreignpolicy.com/story/cms.php?story_id=3309.
3. Gal Luft and Anne Korin, "Terror's next target," *Journal of International Security Affairs* (December 2003).
4. William Arkin, "Not Just A Last Resort? A Global Strike Plan, With a Nuclear Option," *Washington Post* (May 15, 2005). http://www.washingtonpost.com/wp-dyn/content/article/2005/05/14/AR2005051400071_pf.html.
5. Larry M. Wortzel, "China's Nuclear Forces," *Strategic Studies Institute* (May 2007) http://www.strategicstudiesinstitute.army.mil/pubs/display.cfm?pubID=776.
6. Nuclear Posture Review (Excerpts) Global Security (January 8, 2002) http://www.globalsecurity.org/wmd/library/policy/dod/npr.htm.
7. Federico Bordonaro, "US, Russia, Belarus: Politics of Democracy." http//www.isn.ethz.ch/news/sw/details.cfm?id=15914 - 28k. "Since Washington and its NATO allies appear determined to include Kiev in their security and economic community, the whole area connecting the Baltic regions to the Caucasus—via Belarus, Moldova, Ukraine, and Georgia—is set to remain a contested zone by competing U.S. and Russian influences. NATO's insistence on penetrating the Russian-dominated Eurasian landmass could therefore prove strategically short-sighted as it will likely undermine a better and more useful partnership between Washington and Moscow."
8. Gal Luft and Anne Korin, "Terror's next target." In January 2000 al-Qaida attempted to ram a boat loaded with explosives into the USS The Sullivans in Yemen. In October 2000 al-Qaida succeeded in ramming a boat packed with explosives into the USS Cole. In June 2002 al-Qaida operatives suspected of plotting raids on British and American tankers passing through the Strait of Gibraltar were arrested by the Moroccan government; in October of 2002, al-Qaida hit a French supertanker off the coast of Yemen.
9. Ashley J. Tellis, C. Christine Fair, and Jamison Jo Medby, *Limited Conflicts Under the Nuclear Umbrella: Indian and Pakistani Lessons from the Kargil Crisis* (Santa Monica, RAND: 2002). http://www.rand.org/pubs/monograph_reports/MR1450/; http://www.rand.org/pubs/monograph_reports/MR1450/.
10. Herman Kahn, *Thinking About the Unthinkable* (Horizon Press, 1962); Henry Kissinger, *Nuclear Weapons and Foreign Policy* (New York: Harper, 1957). Thomas C. Schelling, The Strategy of Conflict (Harvard University Press, 1960; 1980).
11. Walter Laqueur, "Postmodern Terrorism," In *The New Global Terrorism*, ed. Charles W. Kegley, p. 158 (Prentice Hall, 2003). On cyber warfare, see also John Arquilla and Don Ronfeldt, In Athena's Camp (Santa Monica, CA: RAND: 1997).
12. One variety of neoconservatives, who had been dubbed "superhawks" during the cold war, called themselves "vulcans." Superhawks, which appear to have metamorphosed into vultures with their eyes awash in visions of black gold in the case of Iraq, have also been dubbed by their critics as "chicken hawks" in that a number managed to escape military service during the Vietnam War or have had no military expertise whatsoever despite their advocacy of the use of unilateral force. On vulcans and chickenhawks, see James Mann, *Rise of the Vulcans* (Viking, 2004). For the development of an owlish strategy during the cold war, see Graham T. Allison, Albert Carnesale, and Joseph S. Nye, Jr., *Hawks, Doves and Owls: An Agenda for Avoiding Nuclear War* (New York: W.W. Norton, 1985). See also Chapter 1, endnote 46 in this book.

13. For "selective intervention," see Robert J. Art, *A Grand Strategy for America* (Ithaca, NY: Cornell University Press, 2003). What Art calls "selective engagement"—in which the United States would dominate "only" Europe, Northeast Asia, and the Persian Gulf—is hardly "selective" and can still draw the United States into numerous quagmires. For a critique, see Earl Ravenal, "'Isolationism' as the Denial of Interventionism," *Cato Institute Foreign Policy Briefing* No. 57, April 27, 2000. http://www.cato.org/pubs/ fpbriefs/fpb57.pdf.

14. For a critique of neo-realist views and nuclear weaponry, see Hall Gardner, *American Global Strategy and the "War on Terrorism,"* Chapter 4.

15. According to neoconservatives Kaplan and Kristol, "One of the virtues of preemptive action . . . is that it is often less costly than the alternative." See Lawrence F. Kaplan and William Kristol, *The War Over Iraq: Saddam's Tyranny and America's Mission* (San Francisco: Encounter Books, 2003). This dogmatic (and ahistorical) perspective has certainly not applied to the case of Iraq and would be very dubious for either Iran or North Korea!

16. Germany and Ukraine could both rapidly develop independent nuclear weapons if they so decided, as could Japan—yet such weapons would prove highly provocative.

17. "President Bush Attends Veterans of Foreign Wars National Convention, Discusses War on Terror" (August 22, 2007), http://www.whitehouse.gov. In criticizing U.S. withdrawal from Vietnam, as permitting the Communist repression of South Vietnam (as if the war itself dating from the United States, backed French intervention did not already cost between one and five million Vietnamese lives) and as ostensibly permitting the Khmer Rouge to come to power in Cambodia, President Bush attempted to justify U.S. intervention in Iraq by reference to U.S. military interventions against Japan, North Korea, and North Vietnam, as a means to promote democracy "to help make America safer" as opposed to helping make the world "safe for democracy" in Wilsonian terms, thus ostensibly attempting to emphasize U.S. national interest as opposed to altruism.

18. Michael Hirsh, "Iran Has a Message. Are We Listening?" *Washington Post* (July 1, 2007), B01.

19. For a neo-communitarian approach to the Iraq crisis involving "high devolution" (which should be tempered by the deployment of limited numbers of international peacekeepers as a buffer between conflicting communities), see Amitai Etzioni, "Plan Z" http://www.gwu.edu/%257Eccps/documents/1035PlanZ.doc. See also Amitai Etzioni, *Security First*. In addition, see National Intelligence Estimate, "Prospects for Iraq's Stability" (August 2007). The latter argues "that the emergence of 'bottom-up' security initiatives, principally among Sunni Arabs and focused on combating al-Qaida in Iraq, represent the best prospect for improved security over the next six to 12 months" but that "these initiatives will only translate into widespread political accommodation and enduring stability if the Iraqi Government accepts and supports them." Such "bottom-up initiatives" if not fully exploited by the Iraqi Government, "could over time also shift greater power to the regions, undermine efforts to impose central authority, and reinvigorate armed opposition to the Baghdad government." The main problem then is to find a way to balance regional and communal interests with those of the national government, while concurrently providing security against extremists, such as al-Qaida in Iraq and Jaysh al-Mahdi, among others. This would require a buildup of Iraqi national capabilities, which may or may not be strengthened as the United States threatens to withdraw. The problem is that the United States will not be able to wait forever as new and resurgent threats, coupled with more traditional geopolitical pressures from Russia, China, and other states, appear on the horizon.

Postscript

1. An International Monetary Fund study suggests that the public debt of the ten leading industrial countries will rise from 78 percent of the gross domestic product in 2007 to 114 percent by 2014. This, in effect, could threaten to instigate general conditions of sociopolitical instability and result in advanced states focusing inward if the economy does not turn around soon enough and begin to generate employment and income. International Monetary fund, A Staff Team from the Fiscal Affairs Department, *Fiscal Implications of the Global Economic and Financial Crisis* (Washington, DC: International Monetary Fund, June 9, 2009), http://www .imf.org/external/pubs/ft/spn/2009/spn0913.pdf.

Bibliography

Books

Adebajo, Adekeye, and Ismail Rashid. *West Africa's Security Challenges*. Boulder, CO: Rienner, 2004.

Adler, Emmanuel, and Michael Barnett, eds. *Security Communities*. Cambridge: Cambridge University Press, 1998.

Alexander, Yonah, and Michel S. Swetnam, *Usama bin Laden's al Qaida: Profile of a Terrorist Network*. Ardsley, NY: Transnational Publishers, 2001.

Allison, Graham T., Albert Carnesale, and Joseph S. Nye, Jr. *Hawks, Doves and Owls: An Agenda for Avoiding Nuclear War*. New York: W.W. Norton, 1985.

Arquilla, John, and Don Ronfeldt. *In Athena's Camp*. Santa Monica, CA: RAND, 1997.

Art, Robert J. *A Grand Strategy for America*. Ithaca, NY: Cornell University Press, 2003.

Bellamy, Alex J. *Security Communities and their Neighbors*. New York: Palgrave, 2004.

Bello, Walden. *Dilemmas of Domination: The Unmaking of the American Empire*. London: ZED Books, 2005.

Blank, Stephen. *The NATO-Russia Partnership: A Marriage of Convenience or a Troubled Partnership?* Carlisle, PA: Strategic Studies Institute, 2005.

Brians, Paul. *Nuclear Holocausts: Atomic War in Fiction*. Pullman, Washington: Washington State University, 2003; 2007.

Bull, Hedley. *The Anarchical Society*. New York: Columbia University Press, 1977.

Carpenter, Ted Galen, and Barbara Conry, eds. *NATO Enlargement: Illusions and Reality*. Washington, DC.: Cato Institute, 1998.

Crocker, Chester A., Fen Osler Hampson, and Pamela Aall. *Taming Intractable Conflicts: Mediation in the Hardest Cases*. Washington, DC: United States Institute of Peace Press, 2004.

————. *Grasping The Nettle*. Washington, DC: United States Institute of Peace Press, 2005.

Daalder, Ivo H., and James M. Lindsay, *America Unbound: The Bush Revolution in Foreign Policy*. Washington, DC: Brookings Institution Press, 2003.

Deutsch, Karl. *Political Community: North-Atlantic Area*. New York: Greenwood Press, 1957.

Duffield, Mark. *Global Governance and the New Wars*. London: Zed Books, 2001.

Etzioni, Amitai. *Security First*. New Haven: Yale University Press, 2007.

Gaddis, John Lewis. *The Long Peace*. New York: Oxford, 1987.

Gardner, Hall. *American Global Strategy and the "War on Terrorism"*. Burlington, VT: Ashgate, 2005; revised 2007.

———. *Dangerous Crossroads*. Westport, CT: Praeger, 1997.

———. *NATO and the EU: New World, New Europe, New Threats*. Aldershot, UK: Ashgate, 2004.

Grachev, Andrei S. *Histoire Vraie de la Fin de l'URSS*. Paris: Editions du Rocher, 1992.

Guo, Sujian, ed. *China's "Peaceful Rise" in the 21st Century*. Burlington, VT: Ashgate, 2006.

Hayden, Patrick, Tom Lansford, and Robert P. Watson, eds. *America's War on Terror*. Aldershot: Ashgate, 2003.

Hoffman, Bruce. *Inside Terrorism*. New York: Columbia University Press, 1998.

Hogan, M. J., ed. *The End of the Cold War: Its Meaning and Implications*. Cambridge: Cambridge University Press, 1992.

Howard, Lawrence, ed. *Terrorism: Roots, Impact, Responses*. Westport, CT: Praeger, 1992.

Howard, Russell D., and Reid L. Sawyer, eds. *Terrorism and Counterterrorism*. Gilford: McGraw Hill, 2003.

Hunter, Robert E., and Seth G. Jones. *Building a Successful Palestinian State*. Santa Monica, CA: Rand, 2006.

Huntington, Samuel. *The Clash of Civilizations and the Remaking of World Order*. New York: Touchstone, 1997.

Jervis, Robert. *Perception and Misperception in International Politics*. Princeton, NJ: Princeton University Press, 1976.

Johnson, Chalmers. *Blowback*. London: Little Brown, 2000.

———. *The Sorrows of Empire*. New York: Henry Holt, 2004.

Kahn, Herman. *Thinking About the Unthinkable*. Kahn: Horizon Press, 1962.

Kegley, Charles W., ed. *The New Global Terrorism*. Upper Saddle River, NJ: Prentice Hall, 2003.

Kissinger, Henry. *Nuclear Weapons and Foreign Policy*. New York: Harper, 1957.

Lott, Anthony. *Creating Insecurity: Realism, Constructivism and US Security Policy*. Aldershot, UK and Burlington, VT: Ashgate, 2004.

Mann, James. *Rise of the Vulcans*. New York: Viking, 2004.

Mitchell, Paul T. *Network Centric Warfare: Coalition Operations in the Age of U.S. Military Primacy*. Adelphi Paper No. 385. London: International Institute for Strategic Studies, 2006.

Norton, Anne. *Leo Strauss and the Politics of American Empire*. New Haven, CT: Yale University, 2005.

Piscatori, James P. *Islam in a World of Nation-States*. Cambridge: Cambridge University Press, 1986.

Schelling, Thomas C. *The Strategy of Conflict*. Cambridge, MA: Harvard University Press, 1960; 1980.

Simon, Jeffrey. *Black Sea Regional Security Cooperation: Building Bridges and Barriers*. Cambridge, MA: Harvard University, Black Sea Security Program Publications, 2006.

Suskind, Ron. *The One Percent Solution: Deep Inside America's Pursuit of Its Enemies Since 9/11*. New York: Simon and Schuster, 2006.

Tangredi, Sam J. *Globalization and Maritime Power*. National Defense University, 2002.

Tellis, Ashley J., C. Christine Fair, and Jamison Jo Medby. *Limited Conflicts Under the Nuclear Umbrella: Indian and Pakistani Lessons from the Kargil Crisis*. Santa Monica: RAND, 2002.

Thompson, William R. *On Global War*. Columbia: University of South Carolina Press, 1988.

Tuathail, Gearóid Ó. *Critical Geopolitics: The Politics of Writing Global Space*. London: Routledge, 1996.

Waltz, Kenneth. *Theory of International Politics*. Reading, MA: Addison-Wesley, 1979.

Weitz, Richard. *Revitalizing US-Russian Security Cooperation* London: Adelphi Papers, 2005.

Wilkinson, Paul. *Terrorism versus Democracy: The Liberal State Response.* London: Routledge, 2006.

Wright, Lawrence. *The Looming Tower.* New York: Knopf, 2007.

Selected Articles

Abedin, Mahan. "The Essence of Al Qaeda: An Interview with Saad al-Faqih." *Jamestown Foundation* 2, no. 2 (February 5, 2004).

Asmus, Ronald D., and Bruce P. Jackson. "The Black Sea and the Frontiers of Freedom." *Policy Review* 125 (June/July 2004).

Betts, Richard. "The Osirak Fallacy." *The National Interest* (Spring 2006).

Blank, Stephen. "The NATO-Russia Partnership: A Marriage of Convenience Or a Troubled Partnership?," Strategic Studies Institute, 2005. http://www.strategicstudiesinstitute .army.mil/pdffiles/PUB73 4.pdf.

Baker, James A. III, and Lee H. Hamilton. *Iraq Study Group Report.* http://www .usip.org/isg/. See also updated "Statement by Co-Chairs of the Iraq Study Group before the Committee on Foreign Relations United States Senate," January 30, 2007.

Bordonaro, Federico. "US, Russia, Belarus: Politics of Democracy." http://www .isn.ethz.ch/news/sw/details.cfm?id=15914—28k.

Carpenter, Ted Galen. "Options for Dealing with North Korea." *Foreign Policy Briefing* 73. January 6, 2006. http://www.cato.org/pubs/fpbriefs/fpb73.pdf.

———."Yet Another Drug War Failure." August 13, 2004. http://www.cato.org/ pub_display.php?pub_id=2783.

Center on Budget and Policy Priorities. "New IRS Data Show Income Inequality is Again on the Rise." October 17, 2005. http://www.cbpp.org/10-17-05inc.htm.

De Haas, Marcel. "Current Geostrategy in the South Caucasus." PINR (December 15, 2006).

Estievenart, Georges. "Opium in and from Afghanistan," World Political Forum, October 27, 2006.

Etzioni, Amitai. "Leveraging Islam." *The National Interest* 83 (Spring 2006).

———. "A Neo-Communitarian Approach to International Relations." *Human Rights Review* 7, no. 1 (July–September 2006).

Freedman, Robert O. "Russia—A Partner for the US in the Post-Saddam era?" *Strategic Insights* 3, no. 4 (April 5, 2004).

Friedberg, Aaron L. "The Future of U.S.-China Relations; Is Conflict Inevitable?" *International Security* (Fall 2005).

"The Geneva Accord." Haaretz.com. http://www.haaretz.com/hasen/pages/ShArt.jhtml? Item No=351461.

Friedman, Milton. "Interview with Milton Friedman on the Drug War." http:// www.druglibrary.org/schaffer/Misc/friedm1.htm.

Grachev, Andrei S. "La Russie à la recherche d'une politique étrangère," *Relations internationales: les Etudes de la Documentation Francaise La Russie 1995–1996* (Paris: la Documentation Francaise, 1996)

Hanson, Gordon H. "Why Does Immigration Divide America? Public Finance and Political Opposition to Open Borders." The Center for Comparative Immigration Studies, Working Paper No. 129 (December 2005).

Hartwig, Robert P. "The Cost of Terrorism: How Much Can We Afford?" http://www .foreignpolicy.com/story/cms.php?story_id =3700 &page=2.

Herz, John H. "Idealist Internationalism and the Security Dilemma." *World Politics* 2 (January 1950).

Huntington, Samuel. "The Hispanic Challenge," *Foreign Policy* (March/April 2004).

Kagan, Frederick, and Gen. Jack Keane (Ret.). "Choosing Victory: A Plan for Success in Iraq." American Enterprise Institute (AEI) 2006. http://turcopolier.typepad.com/sic _semper_tyrannis/files/200612141_choosingvictory6.pdf.

Krauthammer, Charles. "The Unipolar Moment." *Foreign Affairs: America and the World* (1990/91).

———. "The Unipolar Moment Revisited," *The National Interest* (Winter 2002/2003).

Leiken Robert S., and Steven Brooke. "The Moderate Muslim Brotherhood." *Foreign Affairs* 86, no. 2, (2007).

Luft, Gal, and Anne Korin. "Terror's Next Target." *Journal of International Security Affairs* (December 2003).

Mearsheimer, John J., and Stephen Walt. "The Israeli Lobby and US Foreign Policy." Working Paper Number RWP06–011 (2006). http://ksgnotes1.harvard.edu/Research/ wpaper.nsf/rwp/RWP06-011.

Minchev, Ognyan. "Major Interests and Strategies for the Black Sea Region." *Framework Analytical Review* (September 2006).

Mitchell, Paul T. "Network Centric Warfare: Coalition Operations in the Age of U.S. Military Primacy." *Adelphi Paper* No. 385. London: International Institute for Strategic Studies, 2006.

National Intelligence Council (NIC) Project 2020. http://www.dni.gov/nic/NIC _2020_project.html.

Ochmann, Cornelius. "Polish-Russian Relations in the Context of the EU's New Eastern Policy." *Russian Analytical Digest* 15 (February 20, 2007). http://se2.isn.ch/service engine/FileContent?serviceID=PublishingHouse&fileid=C68F7FA1–F640–A2CF -DA36–42E321D7EF5A&lng=en.

O'Hanlon, Michael E. "A 'Master Plan' to Deal with North Korea." Brookings Policy Brief No. 114 (January 2003). http://www.brookings.edu/comm/policybriefs/ pb114.htm.

Page, John. "Are the Millennium Development Goals Bad for Growth?" World Economic Forum on Africa 2006 (January 6, 2006).

Robinson, Colin, and Rear Adm. (Ret.) Stephen H. Baker. "Stand-off with North Korea: War Scenarios and Consequences." Center for Defense Information (June 26, 2003).

Rodríguez, Francisco. "Why Chávez Wins," Foreign Policy. http://www.foreignpolicy.com/ story/cms.php?story_id=3685.

Rummel, R.J. "20th Century Democide" (May, 1998). http://www.hawaii.edu/powerkills/ POSTWWII.HTM.

Rumer, Eugene B., and Jeffrey Simon. "Toward a Euro-Atlantic Strategy for the Black Sea Region." Institute for National Strategic Studies Occasional Paper 3. Washington, DC: National Defense University Press, April 2006. http://www.ndu.edu/inss/Occassional _Papers/OCP3.pdf.

Shen, Dingli. "Iran's Nuclear Ambitions Test China's Wisdom." *The Washington Quarterly* 29, no. 2 (Spring 2006).

Sherr, James. "Ukraine: The Pursuit of Defence Reform in an Unfavourable Context." Conflict Studies Research Centre Central & Eastern Europe Series 04/08 (June 2004).

———. "Ukraine: Prospects and Risks." Conflict Studies Research Centre Central & Eastern Europe Series Research Centre O6/52 (October 2006).

Stock, Margaret D. Immigration Policy in Focus 5, No. 9, November 2006. http:// www.ailf.org/ipc/infocus/infocus_11206.pdf.

Strum, Philippa and Andrew Selee. "The Hispanic Challenge? What We Know About Latino Immigration." Washington, DC: Woodrow Wilson International Center for Scholars (March 29, 2004). http://www.wilsoncenter.org/topics/pubs/HispChall.pdf.

Takeda, Yoshinori. "Putin's Foreign Policy toward North Korea." *International Relations of the Asia-Pacific* (March 3, 2006).
Tomberg, Igor. "Geopolitics of Pipeline Communication Systems in Eurasia." *World Affairs* 10, no. 1 (2006).
Wasem, Ruth Ellen. "Central American Asylum Seekers: Impact of 1996 Immigration Law," Congressional Research Center (Updated November 21, 1997).
Wortzel, Larry M. "China's Nuclear Forces." Strategic Studies Institute (May 2007)
Zeihan, Peter. "Post-Turkmenbashi: Gaming the Five 'Stans,'" Geopolitical Intelligence Report (December 26, 2006).

Web Sites

American Enterprise Institute: http://www.aei.org/.
American-Israel Public Affairs Committee: http://www.aipec.org/.
America-Russia.net. http:/www.americarussia.net/.
Arms Control Today: http://www.armscontrol.org/act/.
Asian Times: http://www.atimes.com/.
Bloomberg: http://www.bloomberg.com/.
Center for Strategic and International Studies: http://www.csis.org/.
CIAO: Colombia International Affairs Online: http://www.ciao.org/.
Cicero Foundation: http://www.cicerofoundation.org/.
Communitarian Network: http://www.gwu.edu/~ccps/index.html.
Congressional Research Service Reports and Issue Briefs: http://fpc.state.gov/c4763.htm.
Connections PfP consortium: http://www.pfpconsortium.org/info-pages/pubs_en.htm.
Council on Foreign Relations: http://www.cfr.org/.
Crisis Group: http://www.crisisgroup.org/.
Democracy Now: http://www.democracynow.org/.
Defense Link: http://www.defenselink.mil/.
Der Spiegel: http://www.spiegel.de/.
Economist: http://www.economist.com/.
Earth Policy Institute: http://www.earth-policy.org/.
European Union Institute for Security Studies: http://www.iss-eu.org/.
Federation of American Scientists: http://www.fas.org/.
Financial Times: http://www.ft.com/.
Foreign Affairs: http://www.foreignaffairs.org/.
Foreign Policy: http://www.foreignpolicy.com/.
Foreign Policy in Focus: http://www.fpif.org/.
Global Security: http://www.globalsecurity.org/.
Guardian: http://www.guardian.co.uk/.
Haaretz: http://www.haaretz.com/.
Heritage Foundation: http://www.heritage.org/.
Human Rights Watch: http://www.hrw.org/.
Human Security Report: http://www.humansecurityreport.info/.
Inter-American Development Bank: http://www.iadb.org/.
International Atomic Energy Agency: http://www.iaea.org/.
International Herald Tribune: http://www.iht.com/.
International Security Network: http://www.isn.ethz.ch/.
Jamestown Foundation: http://www.jamestown.org/.
Juan Cole, Informed Comment: http://www.juancole.com/.
Jubilee Iraq News: http://www.jubileeiraq.org/.

Middle East Research Information Project (MERIP): http://www.merip.org/.
Middle East Media Research Institute: http://www.memri.org/.
MidEastWeb: http://www.mideastweb.org/.
Moscow Times: http://www.moscowtimes.ru/.
National Intelligence Council: http://www.cia.gov/nic/NIC_2020_project.html.
National Interest: http://www.nationalinterest.org/.
Newsmax: http://www.newsmax.com/.
Nthposition Online: http://www.nthposition.com/.
North Atlantic Treaty Organization: http://www.nato.int/.
NATO Parliamentary Assembly: http://www.nato-pa.int/default.asp?TAB=595.
Nuclear Information Project: http://www.nukestrat.com/.
Nuclear Threat Initiative (NTI): http://www.nti.org/.
Other News: http://other-news.info/index.php.
Power and Interest News Report: http://www.pinr.com/.
Project for a New American Century: http://www.newamericancentury.org/.
Radio Free Europe/Radio Liberty (RFE/RL): http://www.rferl.org/.
Sens Public: http://www.sens-public.org/.
Stratfor: http://www.stratfor.com/.
Tomdispatch: http://www.tomdispatch.com/.
Townhall: http://www.townhall.com/.
Turkish Daily: http://www.turkishdailynews.com/.
The National Security Archive: http://www.gwu.edu/~nsarchiv/NSAEBB/NSAEBB82/.
United Nations. http://www.un.org/.
Untimely Thoughts: http://www.untimely-thoughts.com/
U.S. House of Representatives: http://www.house.gov/.
U.S. Senate: http://www.senate.gov/.
U.S. State Department: http://www.state.gov/.
Wall Street Journal On Line: http://online.wsj.com/.
Washington Post: http://www.washingtonpost.com/.
Washington Times: http://www.washingtontimes.com/.
White House: http://www.whitehouse.gov/.
World Bank: http://siteresources.worldbank.org/.
World Trade Organization: http://www.wto.org/.
World Watch Institute: http://www.worldwatch.org/features/security/briefs.

Index

Breinigsville, PA USA
29 March 2010
235134BV00002B/2/P